THE AUTHOR

Stephen McCaffrey teaches International Law at the University of the Pacific, McGeorge School of Law. He was a member of the U.N. International Law Commission (ILC) for ten years (1982-1991), chaired the Commission's Thirty-Ninth Session (1987-1988) and was special rapporteur for the ILC's work on the Law of the Non-Navigational Uses of International Watercourses (1985-1991). He has served as Counselor on International Law in the State Department, was counsel to Slovakia in the *Gabčíkovo-Nagymaros Project* case and regularly advises governments and international organizations.

PREFACE

This book is intended for the newcomer to international law — whether law student, lawyer or judge, layperson or undergraduate — not the specialist. It attempts to explain in plain English what international law is, why it exists, and the basic subjects it covers. In this sense the title of the book is, I hope, appropriate.

The book deals with the law governing the relations between the countries of the world. This body of law has developed over the centuries through the practice of states, as countries are called in the parlance of international law. States treat this law as having binding force. They benefit from it, and expect other states to follow it. This is even true when the benefit of a rule is indirect, or enjoyed by the international community as a whole, as in the case of the rule prohibiting genocide and other rules protecting human rights.

As I tell my students, international law is similar to domestic law in the broad scope of its coverage: there are international-law counterparts to most of the domestic-law subjects studied in law school. It is thus difficult to do the subject justice within the compass of a three-hour course or a volume such as this one. I have attempted to address this issue by focusing in the present volume on how law is made and functions in the international community, and on the basic subjects of international law. An understanding of these matters should equip the reader to delve into other areas of interest in the field.

While emphasizing these basic issues and subjects, the book attempts to at least touch upon topics of current relevance, such as terrorism, international criminal law, the use and applicability of international law in United States courts, and the law governing the use of military force. This coverage is intended as an introduction only; the interested reader is encouraged to pursue sources discussing these issues in greater depth.

The Law of Treaties is given particular attention, chiefly because of the increasing importance of the treaty in international life. The number of treaties has mushroomed since the Second World War and many of these agreements include over one hundred states as parties. Because of their number and the breadth of their coverage, treaties are thus the main form of international legislation. But since they are also contractual in character, and since many multilateral treaties allow states to place conditions on their acceptance of them, the law governing treaties is necessarily more complex than if they were the exact equivalent of national legislation.

I hope the book will prove helpful in understanding international law, and I welcome readers' comments on it.

Stephen C. McCaffrey
September, 2005

ACKNOWLEDGMENTS

I have been helped greatly in preparing this book by many people. First, a number of research assistants, but chiefly Amie McTavish (Pacific McGeorge '05) and Anna Frostic (Pacific McGeorge '06), have worked cheerfully and tirelessly in finding sources, chasing down citations, proofreading text and footnotes, preparing tables and making valuable suggestions for the improvement of the work. Second, the Reference Librarians at Pacific McGeorge's Gordon D. Schaber Law Library, particularly Susan Van Syckel and Paul Howard, have also been of great assistance, especially in locating obscure and hard-to-find sources. Third, my efficient and very capable secretary, R.K. Van Every, has been most helpful regarding many aspects of the book's production. Fourth, the University of the Pacific, McGeorge School of Law has provided summer research grants throughout the duration of the project. And finally, I could never have completed the work without the unstinting support of my wife, Susan and daughter, Amanda, who are a constant source of inspiration. For all of this help, I am deeply grateful.

GLOSSARY

The following are explanations of certain terms that one often encounters in international law. They are offered for the assistance of the reader and are not intended to be precise definitions or translations.

erga omnes — toward all; obligations *erga omnes* are those owed to all.

jus ad bellum — the rules of international law concerning the right to go to war or to use force.

jus cogens — a peremptory norm of general, or customary, international law.

jus in bello — the law applicable during armed conflict.

lex ferenda (or *de lege ferenda*) — law as it ought to be; law in the process of formation.

lex lata — law as it is; positive law.

lex specialis (or generalia specialibus non derogant) — a principle of interpretation according to which a specific law or provision prevails over a general one.

municipal law — national or domestic law.

pacta sunt servanda — treaties are binding on the parties and must be performed in good faith.

pacta tertiis nec nocent nec prosunt or simply *pacta tertiis* — a treaty creates neither rights nor obligations for a third state (i.e., a state that is not a party to the treaty) without its consent.

travaux préparatoires — preparatory work; "legislative history" relating to a treaty.

uti possidetis iuris — the principle that colonial boundaries will not be disturbed after former colonies achieve independence.

TABLE OF TREATIES AND OTHER INTERNATIONAL INSTRUMENTS

Name of Instrument	Section Location
Abolition of Forced Labor Convention	9.02
African Charter on Human and Peoples' Rights	9.03
Agreement Between the United States and the United Nations Regarding the Headquarters of the United Nations	2.03, 4.07[F], 10.01
American Declaration of the Rights and Duties of Man	9.01[A], 9.03
Antarctic Treaty of 1959	4.05[B][2][e]
Charter of Economic Rights and Duties of States	3.03[B][1], 9.01[B]
Charter of the United Nations	1.01, 2.01[A][1], 3.01, 3.03, 3.03[A], 3.03[B][1], 3.03[D], 4.02, 4.05[A], 4.05[C][3], 4.05[C][4][a], 4.05[D], 4.05[E], 4.07[F], 5.02[B][2], 5.02[D], 5.03[B], 5.03[C][1][a][iii], 7.01, 8.01[A], 8.02, 8.03, 8.04, 9.01[A], 9.02, 10.02, 10.04
Comprehensive Nuclear-Test-Ban Treaty	4.05[C][4][a]
Convention Against Torture and Other Cruel, Inhuman, or Degrading Treatment or Punishment	9.01[C], 9.02
Convention Between the Government of the United States of America and the Government of the United Kingdom for the Avoidance of Double Taxation and the Prevention of Fiscal Evasion with Respect to Taxes on Income and on Capital Gains	6.03[C]
Convention Between the United States and Great Britain (for Canada) for the Protection of Migratory Birds	4.07[C][1]

Name of Instrument	Section Location
European Convention for the Prevention of Torture and Inhuman or Degrading Treatment or Punishment	4.05[B][2][d]
European Convention for the Protection of Human Rights and Fundamental Freedoms	4.05[B][2][d], 9.01[A], 9.03
European Convention on State Immunity	6.04[B]
European Union Treaty	4.05[B][2][e]
"Friendship, Commerce and Navigation" (FCN) Treaty Between the United States and Japan	2.05
G.A. Res. 1803, Permanent Sovereignty Over Natural Resources	9.01[B]
General Agreement on Tariffs and Trade	4.02, 4.05[C][3]
Geneva Convention for the Amelioration of the Condition of the Wounded in Armies in the Field (1864)	9.01[C]
Geneva Convention for the Amelioration of the Condition of the Wounded and Sick in Armed Forces in the Field (1949)	9.01[C]
Geneva Convention for the Amelioration of the Condition of the Wounded, Sick and Shipwrecked Members of Armed Forces at Sea (1949)	9.01[C]
Geneva Convention on the Continental Shelf	4.04
Geneva Convention Relative to the Treatment of Civilian Persons in Time of War (1949)	5.03[C][1][b], 9.01[C]
Geneva Convention Relative to the Treatment of Prisoners of War (1949)	5.03[C][1][b], 9.01[C]
Geneva Protocol I Additional to the Geneva Conventions of 12 August 1949, and Relating to the Protection of Victims of International Armed Conflicts (1977)	7.04, 9.01[C]
Geneva Protocol II Additional to the Geneva Conventions of August 12, 1949, and Relating to the Protection	9.01[C]

Name of Instrument	Section Location
of Victims of Non-International Armed Conflicts (1977)	
Hague Convention for the Pacific Settlement of International Disputes (1899)	10.03
Hague Convention (I) for the Pacific Settlement of International Disputes (1907)	4.05[C][5], 10.03
Helsinki Convention on the Protection and Use of Transboundary Watercourses and International Lakes	4.05[B][1][c]
Hull-Lothian Agreement	4.02, 4.03
Hungary-Slovakia Treaty (1977)	4.05[E][2], 5.02[C]
ILA Montreal Draft Convention on State Immunity	6.04[B]
ILC Draft Articles on Responsibility of States for Internationally Wrongful Acts	4.06, 7.01, 7.02[A], 7.02[B], 7.03[A], 7.03[B], 7.04, 7.05, 9.01[B]
International Covenant on Civil and Political Rights	2.05, 5.02[D], 5.03[C][1][a][iii], 9.02, 9.02[A][2]
International Covenant on Economic, Social and Cultural Rights	5.02[D], 5.03[C][1][a][iii], 9.01[B], 9.02, 9.02[A][3]
International Convention for the Unification of Certain Rules relating to the Immunity of State-owned Vessels	6.04[B]
International Convention on the Elimination of All Forms of Racial Discrimination	9.02
International Convention on the Suppression of Acts of Nuclear Terrorism	6.03[E]
Kellogg-Briand Pact	4.02, 8.01[A]
Montevideo Convention	5.02[B][1]
Montreal Protocol on Substances that Deplete the Ozone Layer	7.05
North American Free Trade Agreement (NAFTA)	4.05[B][2][e]

Name of Instrument	Section Location
United Nations Convention on Jurisdictional Immunities of States and Their Property	6.04[B], 6.04[C][2], 6.04[C][3]
United Nations Convention on the Law of the Non-Navigational Uses of International Watercourses	3.03[B][2], 4.05[B][1][c]
United Nations Convention on the Law of the Sea (1982)	4.05[B][2][d], 6.03[C]
United Nations Convention on the Rights of the Child	4.05[B][2][d], 9.02
United Nations Framework Convention on Climate Change	7.05
United Nations Standard Minimum Rules for the Treatment of Prisoners	9.01[D]
Universal Declaration of Human Rights	5.03[C][1][a][iii], 9.01[A], 9.01[B], 9.02[A][1]
Vienna Convention on Consular Relations	1.02[C], 2.01[A][1], 2.05, 6.04[A]
Vienna Convention on Diplomatic Relations	3.03[A], 4.02, 6.03[B][1], 6.04[A], 7.02[A]
Vienna Convention on the Law of Treaties	2.02, 3.03[A], 3.03[B][2], 3.03[C], 3.03[E][1], 4.04, 4.05, 4.06, 4.07[A], 4.07[B], 5.03[B], 8.04[B], 9.03
Vienna Convention on the Law of Treaties Between States and International Organizations or Between International Organizations	4.05
Vienna Convention on Succession of States in Respect of State Property, Archives and Debts	5.02[C]
Vienna Convention on Succession of States in Respect of Treaties	3.03[B][2], 5.02[C]

TABLE OF CONTENTS

Chapter 1
WHAT IS "INTERNATIONAL LAW"?

Synopsis

§ 1.01 INTRODUCTION

To understand international law it is necessary to think carefully and somewhat differently about the concept of "law." Most courses offered in law schools do not ask the student to consider the question, what is "law?" We therefore tend to form our impressions about the nature of law on the basis of our general experience in society and — for law students and lawyers on the domestic law courses we take, particularly those in the first year of law school. But international law is unlike such domestic law subjects as contracts, property and torts; indeed, in many respects, it is unlike our entire domestic legal *system*. While the latter is centralized, international law is a *decentralized* system: it has *no executive* (although the United Nations Security Council may be said to have certain executive powers, and there is a United Nations Secretary General)[1], *no legislature* (although the measures adopted by the U.N. General Assembly[2] and

---

[1] The Secretary General (SG) is often viewed by the public as "representing" the United Nations and, to some extent, the international community. Technically, however, the SG is "the chief administrative officer" of the UN, responsible for the operations of the UN Secretariat. *See* Charter of the United Nations, 26 June 1945, art. 97, 59 Stat. 1031, T.S. No. 993, 3 Bevans 1153, 1976 U.N.Y.B. 1043 (hereafter UN Charter). But his or her (there has not yet been a female occupant of the office) authority under the Charter goes beyond the mere running of the organization and overseeing its staff. For example, under art. 99 the SG "may bring to the attention of the Security Council any matter which in his opinion may threaten the maintenance of international peace and security." *See generally id.*, ch. XV. The U.N. Security Council may be said to have limited executive authority to enforce provisions of the Charter relating to international peace and security, when acting under Chapter VII of the Charter.

[2] *See id.*, ch. IV. Except as to the U.N. budget (*see* art. 17 of the Charter), the General Assembly has no authority to adopt binding decisions. Its resolutions have the status of "recommendations" only (art. 10) although, as discussed in ch. 3, they may have certain authoritative value.

1

Security Council[3] may have certain legal value) and no judiciary with compulsory jurisdiction (although there *is* an International Court of Justice[4] whose compulsory jurisdiction countries may accept in advance).[5] International law depends much more directly than domestic law upon its addressees, or "subjects," for its making and implementation, and for the settlement of disputes.

Not only is the international legal system different from the domestic one we are familiar with, the rules themselves operate somewhat differently than those on the domestic level. Rules of international law are often referred to as "norms," and not without reason. They are, in fact, akin to societal norms governing human behavior — the difference being, of course, that the "society" in question is the international community, and the entities governed are, largely, countries. But it should not be thought that because they are "norms" they have no influence, or only a very weak influence, on those whose conduct they govern. One can probably think of numerous examples of social customs — whether they take the form of "rules" of etiquette, unwritten but well-understood standards of behavior in such contexts as families and law school classes, or such standards operating in society at large. These customs are powerful, often more powerful than actual laws that apply to our everyday behavior (think of stop signs and speed limits). Humans generally seek to avoid the disapproval of those whose opinions they value. The same applies to countries — which are, after all, merely organized groups of people that occupy defined territories.[6] The maxim *ubi societas, ibi ius* (where there is society, there is law) may thus be said to describe the situation on the international level — but of course it applies only to the extent that there is, in fact, an international "society" or community. We will return to this question in § 1.03, below.

Chapter 1 will introduce the field and concept of international law, distinguish it from the related field of private international law and consider briefly the philosophical question of whether international law is in fact "law," as that term is normally understood. While the chapter thus covers points dealt with in introductory chapters of most international law coursebooks, its importance is largely foundational; the subjects treated are not likely to be raised directly in practice[7] or on an exam, but an appreciation of them is necessary to an understanding of the topics dealt with in subsequent chapters.

---

[3] *See id.*, ch. V. The Security Council does have the authority to adopt binding decisions under Chapter VII of the Charter. *See id.*, art. 25 and, in particular, arts. 41 and 42.

[4] *See id.*, ch. XIV.

[5] *See* ch. 10, *infra*. Moreover, there is no doctrine of *stare decisis*, per se, in the international legal system: even when the International Court of Justice does have jurisdiction over a dispute between states, its judgment has no precedential value. *See* Statute of the International Court of Justice, art. 59: "The decision of the Court has no binding force except between the parties and in respect of that particular case."

[6] We will consider the technical definition of the "state" under international law in Chapter 5.

[7] While it did not deal with the question whether international law is law, the *LaGrand* case decided by the International Court of Justice dealt with the interesting issue of whether provisional measures ordered by the Court, which are analogous to a temporary restraining order, are binding. The Court held that they are. La Grand (Germany v. United States),

§ 1.02   GENERAL DEFINITION

[A]   International Law

"International law" may be defined simply as the law governing the relations between nations.[8] While this is the literal definition of the term, it does not afford a complete picture of the field of international law as we know it today. The Restatement 3d of the Foreign Relations Law of the United States, in effect the Restatement of international law, defines international law in § 101 as: "the rules and principles of general application dealing with the conduct of states and of international organizations and with their relations *inter se*, as well as with some of their relations with persons, whether natural or juridical."[9] It is thus immediately apparent that international law deals with more than "states," as countries are referred to in international legal parlance.[10] It may also address international organizations — such as the United Nations — and, to some extent, individuals and legal entities such as corporations. However, while international law confers certain rights and responsibilities directly upon natural and legal persons,[11] it deals with them for the most part through states, to which it is principally addressed. As we will see later, this can give rise to problems when new developments such as multinational corporations and transnational terrorism call for international regulation or response yet do not fit within the traditional order.[12] But for now, let us not lose sight of the fact that in the main, international law deals with states and their relations with each other. The Restatement puts it simply: "International law is the law of the international community of states."[13]

---

order of 3 Mar. 1999; judgment on the merits, 27 June 2001, paras. 98-109, 2001 I.C.J. 466, *available at* http://www.icj-cij.org, 40 ILM 1069 (2001).

[8] "The Law of Nations, or International Law" is defined in Brierly's classic work as "the body of rules and principles of action which are binding upon civilized states in their relations with one another." 1 J. L. BRIERLY, THE LAW OF NATIONS (H. Waldock, 6th ed. 1963). The expression "civilized state" is not generally used today, both because it may be associated with the colonial era and because of the assumption (which may not always be warranted) that all states are "civilized." When it is used, it is taken to refer to a state with a developed legal system.

[9] RESTATEMENT 3d OF THE FOREIGN RELATIONS LAW OF THE UNITED STATES § 101 (1987) [hereinafter RESTATEMENT 3d]. International law has also been characterized as a process. According to the New Haven school of international law, which is based on the writings of Professors Myres S. McDougal, Harold D. Lasswell and W. Michael Reisman, international law is "a comprehensive process of authoritative decision in which rules are continuously made and remade. . . ." Myres S. McDougal, *A Footnote*, 57 AM. J. INT'L L. 383 (1963).

[10] In 1905, it was possible for Oppenheim to declare that "States solely and exclusively are the subjects of International Law." 1 L. OPPENHEIM, INTERNATIONAL LAW, para. 13 (1905). The latest edition of this prestigious work is more moderate: "States are the principal subjects of international law." R. JENNINGS & A. WATTS, eds., 1 OPPENHEIM'S INTERNATIONAL LAW, para. 6 (9th ed. 1992) [hereinafter OPPENHEIM].

[11] *See* chs. 5 and 9. That international law has not generally conferred rights directly upon individuals is criticized in PHILIP C. JESSUP, A MODERN LAW OF NATIONS 8-10 (1948).

[12] Multinational corporations and terrorism are discussed in ch. 5, *infra*.

[13] RESTATEMENT 3d, *supra* note 9, at ch. 1, Introductory Note, p. 16.

While attempting to develop a working definition of international law, we should consider briefly a question that will be examined in Chapter 3, namely, how is international law made — or, to put it another way, what does international law consist of? The answer is that international law is made chiefly by states, through their practice and agreements. State practice fulfilling certain requirements constitutes "customary international law," while agreements, or treaties, bind the states that are parties to them. Thus, it may be said that international law consists primarily of customary international law and treaties. For those wishing to draw analogies to national law, customary international law may be compared loosely with the custom that formed the basis of the early common law, or the early commercial law of Europe and England.[14] Treaties, on the other hand, may be likened in part to contracts and in part to legislation. The law of treaties bears many similarities to contract law, and multilateral agreements, especially those open to all states, have many of the attributes of legislation. The analogy between multilateral agreements and legislation becomes stronger as the subjects that treaties cover expand, which they have done markedly since the Second World War.

If international law is principally concerned with the relations among states, what of the law that governs private transactions and relationships that involve more than one country?

[B] Public vs. Private International Law

To answer this question it is helpful to distinguish between "public international law" and "private international law." The term used to refer to international law in Europe and many other countries outside the United States is "public international law." As we have just seen, this field consists principally of rules governing the conduct of states, but also affects other actors. "Private international law" is an expression used chiefly in Europe and the civil law world to refer to the field known as conflict of laws in the United States. It deals with choice of the applicable law in private disputes involving more than one jurisdiction and, depending on how the term is defined, may include questions of procedure such as personal jurisdiction and the enforcement of judgments.[15] Issues of private international law may thus arise in disputes between natural or legal persons, and are increasingly likely to do so as advances in transportation, communication and technology make the world ever smaller.

Public international law, on the other hand, is less likely to be relevant in private disputes than in controversies between states; it may, however,

---

[14] For a brief but useful introduction, *see* JOHN HENRY MERRYMAN, THE CIVIL LAW TRADITION 14 (1969).

[15] "Private international law has been defined as law directed to resolving controversies between private persons, natural as well as juridical, primarily in domestic litigation, arising out of situations having a significant relationship to more than one state." RESTATEMENT 3d, *supra* note 9, § 101, comment *c*, referring to RESTATEMENT 2D, CONFLICT OF LAWS § 2.

come into play in private civil[16] or even criminal[17] proceedings before domestic courts. More fundamentally, while private international law contains rules concerning the resolution of multi-jurisdictional disputes between private parties,[18] public international law governs and to a large extent determines the conduct of states, whether or not a dispute exists. This book will adopt the nomenclature generally used in the United States and refer to public international law as "international law."

[C] The Blurring of Distinctions

While there is a relatively clear distinction in principle between public and private international law, the line between the two fields has become somewhat blurred as they increasingly penetrate each other. For example, issues of private international law such as service of process and taking evidence abroad, application of U.S. regulatory law — especially antitrust and securities law — and even enforcement of judgments may have important implications in the field of public international law. Perhaps in part for this reason, states have seen fit to harmonize rules and procedures of private international law in treaties, which are a principal means of making public international law. On the other hand, cases involving questions of private international law can entail public international law issues such as treaty interpretation, international human rights law and the effect of foreign sovereign compulsion (e.g., where another country prohibits compliance with U.S. discovery requests). It is therefore important for private lawyers to have at least a basic understanding of public international law.

Writing in 1956, Philip C. Jessup, then of Columbia University and later a judge on the International Court of Justice, recognized the difficulty of finding a term that embraces the law governing all of the complex problems of a world community "which may be described as beginning with the individual and reaching on up to the so-called 'family of nations' or 'society of states.'"[19] Finding no adequate expression, Jessup coined the term "transnational law," which he defined to include "all law which regulates actions or events that transcend national frontiers. Both public and private international law are included, as are other rules which do not wholly fit into such standard categories. . . . Transnational situations . . . may involve individuals, corporations, states, organizations of states, or other groups."[20]

---

[16] The Act of State doctrine and foreign sovereign immunity are two examples of issues of public international law that may arise before domestic courts. These topics are addressed in ch. 6.

[17] A recent example of the use of international law in domestic criminal proceedings is the use of the 1963 Vienna Convention on Consular Relations in death penalty cases such as *Breard* and *LaGrand*. Breard v. Greene, 523 U.S. 371, 118 S.Ct. 1352, 140 L.Ed.2d 529 (1998); LaGrand v. Arizona, 526 U.S. 1001, 119 S.Ct. 1137, 143 L.Ed.2d 206 (1999). These cases are discussed more fully in chapter 2.

[18] *Cf.* the Restatement's definition, *quoted in* note 15, *supra*.

[19] PHILIP C. JESSUP, TRANSNATIONAL LAW 1 (1956).

[20] *Id.* at 2-3.

Granting that this spectrum of situations exists, and that public and private international law overlap, for our purposes it is sufficient to understand the basic differences between the two fields. This book deals chiefly with public international law, although discussion of private international law will occasionally be unavoidable for the reasons given above.

§ 1.03 IS INTERNATIONAL LAW "LAW"?

There has been much discussion in the literature of the question whether international law can properly be called "law."[21] While this topic has been of more interest to scholars than to governments, judges or practitioners, we should consider it at least briefly because, as suggested earlier, an appreciation of the nature of international law is important to an understanding of the international legal system as a whole.

The legal nature of international law has been challenged chiefly on two grounds: first, that there are no central executive, legislative or judicial institutions; and second, that in fact there is no international "society" or "community" whose values and interests are sufficiently shared to allow us to speak of one international legal system. Although these two questions are somewhat interrelated, let us take them up in turn.

First, the decentralized nature of the international legal system has led some observers to characterize international law as being at most a set of principles of morality or etiquette that lack binding force. Thus John Austin, the 19th century philosopher and jurist known for his "command theory" of law, believed that laws "properly so-called" are commands of a sovereign. Since rules of international law were not commands of a sovereign, Austin characterized them as "law improperly so-called."[22] Most international lawyers today would reject this conclusion and the premise on which it is based.[23] It may be said to stem from what Louis Henkin has described as "a narrow conception of law generally."[24] Just as individuals go about their business "with little thought to law and little awareness that there is law that is relevant," so also we tend to think of international law as "consisting of a few prohibitory rules" such as that proscribing the aggressive use of force. We are not generally aware of the existence of an "international 'society,'" nor that "law includes the structure of that society, its institutions, forms, and procedures for daily activity, the assumptions on which the society is founded and the concepts which permeate it, the status, rights, responsibilities, obligations of the nations which comprise that society, the various relations between them, and the effects

---

[21] *See, e.g.*, BRIERLY, *supra* note 8, at 41-42, 68-76; G. Fitzmaurice, *The Foundations of the Authority of International Law and the Problem of Enforcement*, 19 MOD. L. REV. 1 (1956); LOUIS HENKIN, HOW NATIONS BEHAVE 13-27, 121-127 (2d ed. 1979); 1 OPPENHEIM, *supra* note 10, at 8-13; and Jessup, *supra* note 11, at 1-3, 17.

[22] See JOHN AUSTIN, THE PROVINCE OF JURISPRUDENCE DETERMINED, LECTURES I, V and VI (Hart ed. 1954).

[23] *See, e.g.*, DAVID J. HARRIS, CASES AND MATERIALS ON INTERNATIONAL LAW 6 (5th ed. 1998).

[24] HENKIN, *supra* note 21, at 13.

of those relations."[25] The fact that it is a decentralized system does not make international law any less read.

The second principal ground on which the legal nature of international law has been challenged is that there is no truly universal international law because it cannot be said that there is an international community or society.[26] As we will see presently, the modern system of sovereign nation states emerged in Europe from the ashes of the Thirty Years War in the 17th century. It might be argued that the present international system is so Eurocentric in nature that it lacks the shared values and sense of community necessary for the existence of a truly global legal order. Or, that even assuming that "there was in the past a universal international law, there is little hope that we will ever see its existence again. There will be almost certainly an increasing fissipation into regional and political groupings."[27] In the view of another commentator: "It is . . . pure illusion to expect from the mere arrangement of inter-State relations the establishment of a community order; this can find a solid foundation only in the development of the true international spirit in men."[28] Different regional views as to the meaning of human rights[29] as well as the developments following in the wake of the terrorist attacks on the United States on September 11, 2001,[30] may be seen as adding some force to these arguments.

But if there is no international society, no international community, there must be anarchy, or something close to it. Yet it is obvious that this is far from being the case. It is impossible today for a state to exist in isolation. "Interdependence on a global scale demonstrates the presence of the world community."[31] Even a superpower like the United States cannot "go it alone."[32] Countries have found that it is more in their interest to engage in relations with other states than not to, and for those relations to be stable, governed by some kind of normative order. Professor Henkin has written: "Although there is no international 'government,' there is an international

---

[25] *Id.* at 14.

[26] *See generally* BRIERLY, *supra* note 8, at 41-45 (§ 1. The International Society).

[27] Leslie C. Green, *Is There a Universal International Law Today?*, 23 CAN. Y.B. INT'L L.3, at 32 (1985).

[28] CHARLES DE FISSCHER, THEORY AND REALITY IN PUBLIC INTERNATIONAL LAW 89 (Corbett transl., 3d ed. 1960).

[29] E.g., the disputes between the United States and China as to the treatment by the latter of its citizens.

[30] In particular, efforts by Osama bin Laden to portray the conflict as one between the Moslem world and the United States.

[31] Eisuke Suzuki, *The New Haven School of International Law: An Invitation to a Policy-Oriented Jurisprudence*, 1 YALE STUDIES IN WORLD PUBLIC ORDER 1, 21 (1974). Brierly argues that the interdependence of states "is mainly in material things, and though material bonds are necessary, they are not enough without a common social consciousness. . . ." BRIERLY, *supra* note 8, at 42.

[32] This fact was brought home only too forcefully by the United States' need to form inclusive coalitions following the attacks of September 11, 2001. Yet even before those events, the U.S. relied heavily on its relationships with other countries in such fields as trade, energy, investment, and defense.

'society',"[33] whose structure, "institutions, forms and procedures for daily activity,"[34] are governed by law. Even the determination of whether an entity is a state is made according to law,[35] a law accepted by all nations of the world. Those nations share many interests in common, and more often than not are willing to accommodate the interests of others.

Referring to the "New Haven school" of international law,[36] one commentator has explained that "we speak of 'the world community' because the existence of the high frequency of interaction and the intensity of interdependence on a global scale causes the aggregate of people inhabiting this 'shrunken globe' to realize their common stake."[37] It was this kind of realization that led the nations of the world to form global institutions twice in the twentieth century to enable them to achieve closer cooperation and "to learn to work together for common social ends."[38]

A remarkable set of measures taken by those states, acting through the universal organization they established to facilitate cooperation between them, provides further evidence of the existence of an international community. These are the resolutions adopted by the United Nations Security Council and General Assembly in response to the terrorist attacks on the United States on September 11, 2001. The first was a resolution adopted unanimously by the Security Council on the day after the attacks. In that resolution, the Security Council — which acts on behalf of all U.N. member states in matters relating to international peace and security[39] — "[u]*nequivocally condemns* in the strongest terms the horrifying terrorist attacks which took place on 11 September 2001 in New York, Washington, D.C. and Pennsylvania and *regards* such acts, like any act of international terrorism, as a threat to international peace and security;. . . ."[40] The Security Council took this strong position despite efforts of those supporting the attackers to portray those acts as part of a holy war against the United States, and thus to create divisions among states along religious and regional lines.

---

[33] HENKIN, *supra* note 21, at 14.

[34] *Id.* Also covered by law, according to Professor Henkin, are "the assumptions on which the society is founded and the concepts which permeate it, the status, rights, responsibilities, obligations of the nations which comprise that society, the various relations between them, and the effects of those relations." *Id.*

[35] *See generally* ch. 5, *infra.*

[36] For a listing of many of the major works associated with the New Haven school, see Suzuki, *supra* note 31, at 1. Professor McDougal's work has been carried on at Yale by W. Michael Reisman.

[37] Suzuki, *supra* note 31, at 20. According to Brierly, "Some sentiment of shared responsibility for the conduct of a common life is a necessary element in any society, and the necessary force behind any system of law; and the strength of any legal system is proportionate to the strength of such a sentiment." BRIERLY, *supra* note 8, at 42.

[38] BRIERLY, *supra* note 8, at 44-45.

[39] U.N. Charter, *supra* n. 1, art. 24.

[40] U.N. SCOR res. 1368, 12 Sept. 2001, U.N. Doc. S/RES/1368 (2001) (emphasis in original).

In a resolution adopted later that month, the Security Council expressed its deep concern about the increase of "acts of terrorism motivated by intolerance or extremism" and reaffirmed the principle that "every State has the duty to refrain from organizing, instigating, assisting or participating in terrorist acts in another State or acquiescing in organized activities within its territory directed towards the commission of such acts. . . ."[41] Again, this resolution is remarkable because it evinces a consensus among states on a subject that has the potential to be quite divisive.

The General Assembly, for its part, also adopted a resolution concerning the attacks the day after they were committed.[42] In that resolution, the first one adopted in the General Assembly's first plenary meeting of its 56th session, the Assembly stated among other things that it "[s]*trongly condemns* the heinous acts of terrorism" of September 11th, and "[u]*rgently calls* for international cooperation to bring to justice the perpetrators, organizers and sponsors of the outrages of 11 September 2001;. . . ."[43] The resolutions of the Security Council and the General Assembly relating to the September 11 attacks, together with other action by the United Nations,[44] demonstrate that the countries of the world share important values and interests and can adopt common positions, even in cases that have the potential to polarize them and that may pose domestic political problems in some cases.

It may be concluded that the foregoing considerations, many of them founded on readily observable fact, support the existence of an international community. Clearly the members of the community do not agree on everything; indeed, they may disagree on many things. But the degree to which there are shared interests, and a will to work together to further them, is sufficient to permit the conclusion that the existence of international law cannot be challenged on the basis that there is no community or society of nations.

It should be clear by now that the question posed at the outset of this section, "Is international law 'law'?", is both somewhat simplistic and not particularly meaningful. Implicit in the question seems to be the assumption that to qualify as "law", international law would have to have the same characteristics as domestic law. If this is the test, international law obviously fails. But if the question is understood as asking whether the relations between states are governed by a normative order, one that all of them accept, the answer would have to be in the affirmative. Professor Brierly probably summed it up best when he said of international law: "The truth is that it is neither a myth on the one hand, nor a panacea on

---

[41] U.N. SCOR res. 1373, 28 Sept. 2001, U.N. Doc. S/RES/1373 (2001).

[42] U.N. GAOR res. 56/1, 12 Sept. 2001, Condemnation of terrorist attacks in the United States of America, U.N. Doc. A/RES/56/1 (2001).

[43] *Id.*, paras. 1 and 3 (emphasis in original).

[44] For a summary of the action against terrorism under United Nations auspices, including that following the September 11 attacks, *see* the UN website, www.un.org , and the link to "UN action against terrorism."

the other, but just one institution among others which we can use for the building of a better international order."[45]

But if there is a legal system governing the relations between nations, as all states appear to accept, where did it come from? How did it evolve?

§ 1.04 A BIT OF HISTORY

The "modern" system of international law is generally regarded as having emerged in the aftermath of the Thirty Years War, which ended with the Peace of Westphalia in 1648. With the conclusion of this conflict came the end of the Holy Roman Empire (which, it has been said, was neither holy, nor Roman, nor an empire), the recognition of the sovereign independence of its member states, and the consequent rise of the modern secular state.[46]

But with the disappearance of the unifying influence of the Empire, the question arose as to whether anything would take its place; whether, that is, the very sovereignty of states — a doctrine elaborated in Jean Bodin's *Republic* in 1576[47] — meant that there was nothing binding them together, no order governing their relations. It might be thought that the sovereignty of nations is a negation of the notion that they are subject to law. A country's sovereignty, so the argument might go, means that it alone determines what it does or refrains from doing. "Sovereignty," wrote Philip Jessup in 1948, "in its meaning of an absolute, uncontrolled state will, ultimately free to resort to the final arbitrament of war, is the quicksand upon which the foundations of traditional international law are built."[48] If this is the true meaning of sovereignty, there would seem to be little room for international law.

Yet Bodin himself never conceived of sovereignty in this way. As Brierly points out, for Bodin, sovereignty "was an essential principle of internal political order, and he would certainly have been surprised if he could have foreseen that later writers would distort it into a principle of international disorder, and use it to prove that by their very nature states are above the law."[49] Bodin's sovereign, or supreme power, was an essential attribute of statehood. Bodin believed that such a single source of authority, rather than a chaotic mass of independent ones, was the defining characteristic of a state. However, he also held that the sovereign did not have absolute discretion to act in any way he or she wished. Instead, Bodin's

---

[45] Brierly, *supra* note 8, Preface to the Fifth Edition.

[46] The Reformation played an important role in the secularization of the state. For a brief discussion, see BRIERLY, *supra* note 8, at 5.

[47] JEAN BODIN, DE REPUBLICA (1576). For a translation of the pertinent chapters, see Julian H. Franklin, ed. & transl., JEAN BODIN, ON SOVEREIGNTY: FOUR CHAPTERS FROM THE SIX BOOKS OF THE COMMONWEALTH (1992).

[48] JESSUP, *supra* note 11, at 2.

[49] BRIERLY, *supra* note 8, at 10.

sovereign was subject to certain laws: "the divine law, the law of nature or reason, the law that is common to all nations, and . . . the laws of government."[50] The latter are what we would call today constitutional law.[51] Even Bodin's "supreme power," therefore, was subject to the fundamental law of the state, as well as other kinds of law.

Thus, the doctrine of sovereignty, as originally conceived, did not imply absolute, unbridled power, even on the domestic level; and, it was never intended to apply to the relations of states *inter se*, much less to imply that those relations were not governed by a body of law. Unfortunately, however, it has subsequently been invoked as proof that international law is not really binding on states, since they are "sovereign" and may do as they wish. Yet simple observation of the way in which states relate to each other does not support such an anarchic theory. Humans prefer order to chaos, and states, which are merely groups of humans organized to serve certain purposes,[52] do as well. While there is doctrinal debate about the basis, or source, of international legal obligation,[53] there is not significant disagreement about the general tendency of states to observe international law. Jessup refers in this regard to the Director of the Yale Institute of International Studies who observed that those "who make light of treaty commitments in general seem to ignore the fact that the vast majority of such engagements are continuously, honestly, and regularly observed even under adverse conditions and at considerable inconvenience to the parties."[54] Jessup goes on to note that the legal advisers of governments are typically involved in drafting the diplomatic correspondence exchanged in relation to disputes with other countries, and that states regularly support their actions in the international arena by referring to international law. He concludes: "The record proves that there is a 'law habit' in international relations. It is not immaterial to add that the instances in which judgments of international tribunals have been flouted are so rare that the headline-reader may well place them in the man-bites-dog category."[55] The situation is summed up neatly in Professor Henkin's classic statement: "It is probably the case that *almost all nations observe almost all principles of international law and almost all of their obligations almost all of the time.*"[56]

---

[50] *Id.* at 9.

[51] Even countries without written constitutions, such as the United Kingdom, consider their governments as being subject to a "constitutional law." *See, e.g.*, ERIC BARENDT, AN INTRODUCTION TO CONSTITUTIONAL LAW 26 (1998).

[52] We will look more closely at the attributes of statehood in ch. 5.

[53] The two principal theories are those of fundamental rights and positivism. For a general description and critique of each, see BRIERLY, *supra* note 8, at 49-56.

[54] Brodie, ed., THE ABSOLUTE WEAPON: ATOMIC POWER AND WORLD ORDER 8 (1946), *quoted in* JESSUP, *supra* note 11, at 7.

[55] JESSUP, *supra* note 11, at 8.

[56] HENKIN, *supra* note 21, at 47 (italics in original).

It is this tendency to prefer order to chaos, and to prefer an order based on a set of stable and fair principles, that helps to explain why the end of the Holy Roman Empire and the rise of the sovereign, secular state did not mean the beginning of an era of anarchy among nations. Other forces were also at work, of course, including the inevitable increase in contacts between states through commerce and the consequent need to live together peacefully in order to secure the fruits of trade and promote welfare.[57] All of these factors had a centripetal, rather than a centrifugal, effect upon the states of Europe and gave rise to the need for a set of rules to govern their relations.

How, then, did the resulting system of law spread from Europe to the rest of the world? While there had been scattered previous instances of relations between political units that were governed by law,[58] as we have seen, what we think of as modern international law is generally thought to have grown out of the events in Europe described above.[59] But, as David J. Harris points out, "it was for many generations really no more than the Public Law of Europe."[60] This changed over time, beginning in the eighteenth and nineteenth centuries with the independence of former European colonies in North and South America, and culminating in the establishment of the League of Nations in 1920, which was open to "any" state.[61] According to Harris, this, "as much as any other single event, marked the beginning of the present situation in which international law applies automatically to all states whatever their location or character."[62] Today there are 191 states from all regions of the world that are members of the United Nations.[63] All of these states, as well as the few that are not

---

[57] Brierly lists four factors that tended to bring states closer together during this period: "(1) the impetus to commerce and adventure caused by the discovery of America and the new route to the Indies; (2) the common intellectual background fostered by the Renaissance; (3) the sympathy felt by co-religionists in different states for one another, from which arose a loyalty transcending the boundaries of states; and (4) the common feeling of revulsion against war, caused by the savagery with which the wars of religion were waged." BRIERLY, *supra* note 8, at 6.

[58] "[T]he Greeks, in their classical period, developed rules governing relations between the various Greek states, rules that more closely parallel the modern system of international law than those of any other early civilization." LORI FISLER DAMROSCH, LOUIS HENKIN, RICHARD CRAWFORD PUGH, OSCAR SCHACHTER & HANS SMIT, INTERNATIONAL LAW, *Historical Introduction*, at xxviii (4th ed. 2001). Previous regimes may have encompassed different peoples and even nations, but applied within large empires, such as the Roman Empire and the later Holy Roman Empire. They thus had the character of "domestic" law rather than international law.

[59] A classic, book-length work on the history of international law is ARTHUR NUSSBAUM, A CONCISE HISTORY OF THE LAW OF NATIONS (rev. ed. 1954). For a shorter treatment, *see* DAMROSCH, et al., *supra* note 58, at xxvii.

[60] HARRIS, *supra* note 23, at 16.

[61] COVENANT OF THE LEAGUE OF NATIONS, art. 1 (1920). Ironically, although one of the chief proponents of the League of Nations was President Woodrow Wilson, the United States never became a member.

[62] HARRIS, *supra* note 23, at 16.

[63] For a current list of member states with their dates of admission, *see* the United Nations website, http://www.un.org.

U.N. members,[64] accept that their relations and conduct are governed by international law.

The following chapters of this book will take as a point of departure the proposition that there is an international legal system that governs the relations between states, and applies as well to international organizations and the relations between states and individuals.

---

[64] Perhaps the most prominent of these is Switzerland, which has until now refrained from joining the United Nations largely because of its historic position of neutrality.

Chapter 2
HOW DOES INTERNATIONAL LAW RELATE TO NATIONAL ("MUNICIPAL") LAW?

Synopsis

§ 2.01   INTRODUCTION

This chapter examines the relationship between international law and national, or domestic law. In international legal parlance, the latter is sometimes referred to as "municipal" law. But in this context the terms "national," "domestic" and "municipal" are substantively interchangeable; they all refer to the internal law of a state. In the case of the United States, that includes the U.S. and state constitutions, federal and state statutes, case law and common law.

Some of the questions this chapter deals with are: To what extent does international law come into play in the domestic legal order? To the extent that it does, is domestic law superior to international law, or vice versa? And, to what extent does domestic law come into play in the international legal order, and what is its status there? Are the two in fact component parts of one legal system, or are there two separate systems? Whatever the answers to these questions may be, there is an inevitable cross-fertilization between national and international law. Let us first look at some examples of this "interpenetration" before we consider whether national and international law constitute one system or two.

[A]   International Law in National Law

This subsection considers the influence of international law on national legal systems. We will first look at this subject from a conventional perspective, asking to what extent international law may be applicable, as law, in the domestic legal order. We will then note a recent trend in the decisions of the United States Supreme Court involving the use of international and comparative law to inform decisions on U.S. constitutional issues.

[1] The Applicability of International Law in National Law

We tend to think of our national legal system as being self-contained and almost hermetically sealed, free from outside influences. This is far from being the case, however. The law of other countries may well be applicable in cases before domestic courts by virtue of domestic choice-of-law rules or treaties. A treaty may itself supply the rule of decision in a domestic case,[1] as may a rule of customary international law.[2] And the actions of government officials may be constrained or otherwise controlled by international law. An obvious illustration of the latter situation is provided by international human rights law, which requires government officials on all levels to ensure that individuals are accorded certain basic protections.[3]

In addition, there have recently been a number of cases in the United States involving alleged failures of law enforcement officers to provide information required under the 1963 Vienna Convention on Consular Relations[4] to foreign nationals they have arrested. This treaty has been used (in much the same way as the *Miranda* rule)[5] as the basis of appeals in U.S. death penalty cases[6] and even as the basis of suits against the United States in the International Court of Justice (ICJ) by countries whose nationals were not given the information required under the

---

[1] An example of such a treaty is the 1980 United Nations Convention on Contracts for the International Sale of Goods (often referred to as the "Vienna Convention" or the "CISG"), 19 I.L.M. 671 (1980), which is self-executing as a matter of U.S. law and thus requires no implementing legislation.

[2] See, e.g., the well-known cases of The Paquete Habana, 175 U.S. 677, 20 S.Ct. 290, 44 L.Ed. 320 (1900); and Filartiga v. Pena-Irala, 630 F.2d 876 (2d Cir. 1980).

[3] International Human Rights law is the subject of chapter 9.

[4] Vienna Convention on Consular Relations, 24 April 1963, 21 U.S.T. 77, T.I.A.S. No. 6820, 596 U.N.T.S. 261, art. 36(1)(b) and (c).

[5] Miranda v. Arizona, 384 U.S. 436 (1966) (holding that persons in police custody must be warned that they have the right to remain silent and that anything they say may be used against them; and must be informed they have the right to consult with a lawyer and to have the lawyer present during interrogation).

[6] See, e.g., Breard v. Greene, 523 U.S. 371, 118 S.Ct. 1352, 140 L.Ed.2d 529 (1998); LaGrand v. Arizona, 526 U.S. 1001, 119 S.Ct. 1137, 143 L.Ed.2d 206 (1999); Federal Republic of Germany v. United States, 526 U.S. 111, 119 S.Ct. 1016, 143 L.Ed.2d 192 (1999); United States v. Reyes-Platero, 224 F.3d 1112 (9th Cir. 2000); and Gibson v. United States, 2001 U.S. Dist. LEXIS 16756 (S.D.N.Y. 2001). See also Standt v. City of New York, 153 F.Supp.2d 417 (S.D.N.Y. 2001); United States v. Lombera-Camorlinga, 206 F.3d 882 (9th Cir. 2000). See Frederic L. Kirgis, Restitution as a Remedy in U.S. Courts for Violations of International Law, 95 Am. J. Int'l L. 341 (2001).

convention.[7] Especially interesting for our purposes are developments growing out of the ICJ's decision in the *Avena* case.[8]

In *Avena*, Mexico sued the United States in the International Court of Justice alleging that the United States had breached its obligations under the Consular Convention. According to Mexico, the United States had breached the convention by failing to inform 51 Mexican nationals, who were tried and convicted of capital offenses and sentenced to death in the U.S., of their rights under Article 36, paragraph 1 (*b*) of the convention upon their initial arrest. The Court held, *inter alia*, that the United States had indeed breached those obligations.[9] It found that the appropriate remedy — referred to as "reparation" in international law[10] — would be for the United States "to provide, by means of its own choosing, review and reconsideration of the convictions and sentences of the Mexican nationals" involved in the case.[11] Since the United States, like all members of the United Nations, has undertaken to "comply with the decision of the International Court of Justice in any case to which it is a party,"[12] it is bound by the Court's decision and obligated to implement it. A brief digression will help to put subsequent events in the *Avena* case in context.

In the earlier case of *Breard v. Greene*,[13] Angel Francisco Breard, a Paraguayan national on death row in Virginia, and the Republic of Paraguay, had petitioned the U.S. Supreme Court for writs of certiorari contending that Virginia had violated the Vienna Consular Convention by failing to provide the information required under the convention to Breard and the Paraguayan consulate. Paraguay had also instituted proceedings

---

[7] *See* Vienna Convention on Consular Relations (Paraguay v. United States of America), Provisional Measures (9 Apr. 1998), 1998 I.C.J. 258, *available at* http://www.icj-cij.org (in which the Court, in a provisional measures order, called on the United States to "take all measures at its disposal" to prevent the execution of Mr. Angel Francisco Breard, scheduled to occur five days after the order was issued, pending a final decision of the Court; Mr. Breard was, however, executed by the State of Virginia and by order of 10 Nov. 1998 the case was removed from the Court's docket at the request of Paraguay, I.C.J., Press Release 98/36, 11 Nov. 1998, *available at* http://www.icj-cij.org/icjwww/idocket/ipaus/ipausframe.htm); LaGrand Case (Germany v. United States of America), 2001 I.C.J. 466, *available at* http://www.icj-cij.org, 40 I.L.M. 1069 (2001) (in which the Court found that the United States had breached its obligations to Germany and to the LaGrand brothers under the Vienna Convention on Consular Relations); and Avena and other Mexican Nationals (Mexico v. United States of America), 2004 I.C.J.128, *available at* http://www.icj-cij.org/icjwww/idocket/imus/imusframe.htm (in which the Court found that the United States breached its obligations to Mr. Avena and 50 other Mexican nationals and to Mexico under the Vienna Convention on Consular Relations).

[8] Avena and other Mexican Nationals (Mexico v. United States of America), 2004 I.C.J. 128, *available at* http://www.icj-cij.org/icjwww/idocket/imus/imusframe.htm.

[9] *Id.* at 59, para. 153(4).

[10] A state that has breached an international obligation has an obligation to make reparation to the injured state. Reparation, and other remedies, are discussed in chapter 7.

[11] *Avena, supra* note 7, para. 153(9).

[12] Charter of the United Nations, 26 June 1945, art. 94(1), 59 Stat. 1031, T.S. No. 993, 3 Bevans 1153, 1976 U.N.Y.B. 1043.

[13] Breard v. Greene, 523 U.S. 371, 118 S.Ct. 1352, 140 L.Ed.2d 529 (1998).

against the United States before the International Court of Justice, alleging there as well that the U.S. had breached the convention and requesting provisional measures of protection, pending the Court's decision of the case. The ICJ issued an order on April 9, 1998 stating as follows: "The United States should take all measures at its disposal to ensure that Angel Francisco Breard is not executed pending the final decision in these proceedings, and should inform the Court of all the measures which it has taken in implementation of this Order. . . ."[14] Breard was scheduled to be executed on April 14, 1998. On the latter date the Supreme Court denied relief in both cases, in part on grounds of Breard's procedural default,[15] after which Breard was executed.[16]

The approach of the U.S. executive branch in the *Breard* case is interesting, particularly in light of its later position in domestic litigation relating to the *Avena* case. First, the Departments of State and Justice submitted an amicus brief to the Supreme Court arguing that the Court should not grant the relief requested by Breard and Paraguay, *inter alia*, on the ground that:

> "the 'measures at [the Government's] disposal' are a matter of domestic United States law, and our federal system imposes limits on the federal government's ability to interfere with the criminal justice systems of the States. The 'measures at [the United States'] disposal' under our Constitution may in some cases include only persuasion . . . and not legal compulsion through the judicial system. That is the situation here. Accordingly, the ICJ's order does not provide an independent basis for this Court either to grant certiorari or to stay the execution."[17]

The second step taken by the executive branch was that the Secretary of State, Madeleine Albright, wrote a letter to Virginia Governor Jim Gilmore requesting him to grant a stay of execution.[18] The governor declined to do so.[19]

---

[14] Vienna Convention on Consular Relations (Paraguay v. United States of America), Provisional Measures (9 Apr. 1998), 1998 I.C.J. 248, Order, *available at* http://www.icj-cij.org/icjwww/idocket/ipaus/ipausframe.htm; also quoted in part in *Breard*, 523 U.S. at 374.

[15] "It is clear that Breard procedurally defaulted his claim, if any, under the Vienna Convention by failing to raise that claim in the state courts." 523 U.S. at 375.

[16] *See generally* Jonathan I. Charney & W. Michael Reisman, *Agora: Breard, The Facts*, 92 AM. J. INT'L L. 666 (1998).

[17] Brief for the United States as Amicus Curiae, Breard v. Greene, 523 U.S. 371, 118 S.Ct. 1352,140 L.Ed.2d 529 (1998) (Nos. 97-1390, 97-8214). While in the *Breard* case the United States had argued before the Supreme Court that provisional measures orders of the ICJ were not binding and therefore did not have to be implemented by the United States or Virginia, the World Court later held in *LaGrand* — another case involving alleged breaches of the Consular Convention by the United States — that its provisional measures orders were, in fact, binding. LaGrand Case (Germany v. United States of America), 2001 I.C.J. 466, *available at* http://www.icj-cij.org, 40 I.L.M. 1069 (2001).

[18] Letter from Madeleine K. Albright, U.S. Secretary of State, to James S. Gilmore III, Governor of Virginia (Apr. 13, 1998).

[19] Governor Gilmore's statement of 14 Apr. 1998 is quoted in Charney & Reisman, *supra* note 16, at 674.

Returning now to *Avena*, Jose Ernesto Medellin, one of the 51 Mexican nationals on death row involved in that case, had filed a federal habeas corpus petition on Vienna Convention grounds which was pending when the ICJ decided *Avena*.[20] The Supreme Court granted certiorari in the case but before oral argument, President George W. Bush issued a "Memorandum for the Attorney General" on the subject of "Compliance with the Decision of the International Court of Justice in *Avena*."[21] The operative paragraph of the memorandum states as follows:

> "I have determined, pursuant to the authority vested in me as President by the Constitution and laws of the United States of America, that the United States will discharge its international obligations under the decision of the International Court of Justice in the *Case Concerning Avena and Other Mexican Nationals* . . . by having State courts give effect to the decision in accordance with general principles of comity in cases filed by the 51 Mexican nationals addressed in that decision."[22]

The legal basis for the memorandum is set forth in the amicus brief of the United States in the *Medellin* case.[23]

Thus, the president recognized that the United States has an obligation under international law to comply with the decision of the ICJ in the *Avena* case. While the judgment in *Avena* may be distinguished from the provisional measures order in *Breard*, the fact that between those two cases the ICJ ruled that its provisional measures orders are legally binding[24] may make the difference between the two decisions, in terms of their binding authority with regard to the United States, largely academic.

---

[20] For the history of the case, *see* Medellin v. Dretke, 125 S.Ct. 2088 (2005).

[21] George W. Bush, Memorandum for the Attorney General, 28 Feb. 2005, App. 2 to Brief for the United States as *Amicus Curiae* in Medellin v. Dretke, 125 S.Ct. 2088 (2005), at 9a.

[22] *Id.*

[23] Brief for the United States as Amicus Curiae Supporting Respondent, Medellin v. Dretke, U.S. Supreme Court, No. 04-5928, *available at* http://www.LexisNexis.com, 2004 U.S. Briefs 5928. That brief states at one point:

"Because compliance with the ICJ's decision can be achieved through judicial process, and because there is a pressing need for expeditious compliance with that decision, the President determined to exercise his constitutional foreign affairs authority and his authority under Article 94 of the U.N. Charter to establish that binding federal rule without the need for implementing legislation. Cf. *Dames & Moore* v. *Regan*, 453 U.S. 654 (1981); *Sanitary Dist.* v. *United States*, 266 U.S. 405 (1925). The authority of the President to determine the means by which the United States will implement its international legal obligations is especially important in the context of a treaty, like the Vienna Convention, that not only protects foreign nationals in this country, but also protects Americans overseas. Under the Constitution, it is the President alone who — through diplomatic and other means — can protect Americans deprived of liberty abroad." *Id.* at *42-43.

[24] The I.C.J. so ruled in the *LaGrand* case, (Germany v. United States of America), 2001 I.C.J. 466, available at http://www.icj-cij.org, 40 I.L.M. 1069 (2001). On this case, *see* note 17, *supra*.

On the other hand, various factors raise the possibility that the president's memorandum may have been motivated more by strategic than legal considerations. First, the U.S. government's amicus brief, while stating that "the Executive Branch interprets the decision [in *Avena*] to place the United States under an international obligation to choose a means for 51 individuals to receive review and reconsideration of their convictions and sentences . . . ,"[25] also declared that "the President may decide that the United States will not comply with an ICJ decision and direct a United States veto of any proposed Security Council enforcement measure."[26] Since international law is part of U.S. law,[27] this statement is problematic. Morevoer, the President is sworn to "preserve, protect and defend" the Constitution of the United States.[28] The Supremacy Clause of the Constitution (Article VI, clause 2) provides that "Treaties," together with the Constitution and statutes, are the "supreme Law of the Land." The United Nations Charter, a treaty of the United States,[29] provides that: "Each Member of the United Nations undertakes to comply with the decision of the International Court of Justice in any case to which it is a party."[30] The President would therefore seem to be under a constitutional obligation to ensure that the United States complies with decisions of the ICJ in cases to which it is a party, such as *Breard* and *Avena*. At the very least, a presidential decision not to comply with an ICJ judgment would put the United States in violation of its obligations under international law — to wit, Article 94(1) of the U.N. Charter.

Another possible explanation for the president's action, assuming it was not motivated strictly by a determination to follow international law, is that the executive branch may have thought it preferable to order state courts to give effect to the ICJ's decision in this case, "in accordance with general principles of comity," rather than take the chance that the Supreme Court might find that the president, and state courts, were compelled to give effect to the World Court's decision. The president could always make a different decision in another case if the decisive authority in this one were his own order, whereas he would not be free to do so if the Supreme Court came to the same conclusion as a matter of United States law. As to "comity," this term refers to a motive to act voluntarily, out of courtesy and good will, as contrasted with an obligation to act because one is legally compelled to do so. However, since the president had already recognized in his memorandum that the ICJ's decision gave rise to "international obligations" for the United States, the reference to comity is probably superfluous.[31]

---

[25] Brief for the United States as Amicus Curiae, *supra* note 23, at *40.

[26] *Id.* at *40-41.

[27] The Paquete Habana, 175 U.S. 677, 20 S.Ct. 290, 44 L.Ed. 320 (1900).

[28] U.S. Const., Art. II, § 1, cl. 8.

[29] Charter of the United Nations, 26 June 1945, 59 Stat. 1031, T.S. No. 993, 3 Bevans 1153, 1976 U.N.Y.B. 1043.

[30] *Id.*, art. 94(1).

[31] *See generally* Frederic L. Kirgis, *President Bush's determination Regarding Mexican Nationals and Consular Convention Rights*, ASIL Insight, Addendum, March 2005, *available at* http://www.asil.org/insights/2005/03/insights050309.html#_edn4.

These cases well illustrate the interaction of international law and domestic law, even if they are much more highly visible and politically charged than the more common kinds of cases involving foreign and international law.[32] The *Avena* case demonstrates how international law can influence even state criminal proceedings, long after trial, judgment and sentencing. And this effect does not necessarily depend upon action by the president. In *Osbaldo Torres v. State of Oklahoma*,[33] the Oklahoma Court of Criminal Appeals, giving effect to the ICJ's decision in *Avena* before President Bush issued his memorandum, ordered Torres' execution date stayed pending its further order, granted his request for an evidentiary hearing and remanded to the trial court.[34] In a "specially concurring" opinion, one of the judges pointed out that treaties are the supreme law of the land under the Supremacy Clause of the U.S. Constitution (Article VI, clause 2) and that "[a]s this Court is bound by the treaty itself, we are bound to give full faith and credit to the *Avena* decision."[35]

Another oft-cited illustration of the possible interplay between international law and domestic law is the following: Suppose the United States declares a customs enforcement zone that extends farther from the coast than is permitted by international law.[36] Suppose further that the U.S. Coast Guard seizes a foreign vessel beyond the limit recognized by international but within the zone established by the U.S. May the owner of the vessel challenge the legality of the seizure in U.S. court on the ground that it violates international law?[37] Such cases raise the question of whether international law may be asserted in U.S. court, and, if so, whether it prevails over U.S. domestic law. We will take up these issues in § 2.02, below.

---

[32] As indicated earlier, the "garden-variety" cases that probably occur on a daily basis involve the application of foreign nations' laws, and the influence of treaties on such subjects as trade, commerce, service of process, and taking of evidence.

[33] Oklahoma Court of Criminal Appeals, No. PCD-04-442, 13 May 2004.

[34] The Court of Criminal Appeals remanded to the District Court of Oklahoma County for a hearing on the following issues: "(a) whether Torres was prejudiced by the State's violation of his Vienna Convention rights in failing to inform Torres, after he was detained, that he had the right to contact the Mexican consulate; and (b) ineffective assistance of counsel." *Id.*

[35] *Id.* (Chapel, J., concurring).

[36] A similar situation was involved in the Fisheries Jurisdiction Case (U.K. v. Iceland), 1974 I.C.J. 3, where the U.K. challenged Iceland's declaration of a 12-mile exclusive fishing zone, at a time when the territorial sea was three miles.

[37] A case involving similar facts was *The Over the Top*, 5 F.2d 838 (D. Conn. 1925). During prohibition, the crew of a British cargo vessel lying some 19 miles off the U.S. coast sold whiskey to individuals who turned out to be U.S. government agents. The vessel was later seized by the Coast Guard and the captain and crew, who were not U.S. nationals, were placed under arrest. In a proceeding by the government for forfeiture and sale of the ship and cargo, the owners contended that since the sale had occurred on the high seas, beyond the 3-mile territorial jurisdiction of the United States then recognized by international law, there could be no violation of U.S. law. The government's suit was ultimately dismissed, on the ground that the law under which the seizure had been made only extended U.S. jurisdiction 12 miles from the coast, not 19. Thus, the court did not reach the question whether U.S. law prevailed over international law, although it suggested that if the question had been presented it would have been compelled to enforce U.S. law, even if it contravened international law.

[2]   The Use of International and Comparative Law to Inform National Court Decisions[38]

Beyond the applicability of international law as binding authority in national legal systems, it may be drawn upon by domestic courts as persuasive authority to assist them in deciding cases under national law. In the United States there have been several recent instances of the use by the Supreme Court of international and comparative law and practice in determining generally prevailing standards in different fields. For example, international and foreign law have been referred to by the Court in cases prohibiting the juvenile death penalty,[39] supporting affirmative action measures,[40] and upholding personal privacy rights.[41] Although the Court did not rely exclusively upon either international or foreign law in these cases, and these sources of law did not determine the outcome, a majority of the Court has found that international and foreign law "does provide respected and significant confirmation of our own conclusions."[42] The underlying assumption seems to be that there are indeed fundamental values that are widely shared among different countries, and that consideration of international and comparative experience is helpful in deciding difficult constitutional issues.

This approach is not shared by all justices on the Supreme Court, however. Some see a "discussion of these foreign views [as] meaningless dicta. Dangerous dicta, however, since 'this court should not impose foreign moods, fads, or fashions on Americans.'"[43] But the more pragmatic members of the Court, such as Justice Breyer, believe that taking international and foreign law into account may "cast an empirical light on the consequences of different solutions to a common legal problem."[44] While it seems likely that the use of constitutional comparativism[45] will continue,

---

[38] The author would like to express special appreciation to Anna Frostic, Pacific McGeorge 2006, for her excellent assistance with regard to this section.

[39] In Roper v. Simmons, 125 S.Ct. 1183 (2005), Justice Kennedy wrote a majority opinion that referred repeatedly to international and foreign law in striking down the juvenile death penalty in the United States. In determining the "evolving standards of decency" that characterize an 8th amendment analysis, Kennedy wrote that "it is proper that we acknowledge the overwhelming weight of international opinion against the juvenile death penalty." *Id.* at 1200.

[40] In Grutter v. Bollinger, 539 U.S. 306 (2003), the Court upheld the University of Michigan's Law School admissions policy as a valid affirmative action measure under the Equal Protection Clause of the 14th Amendment. Justices Ginsburg and Breyer concurred specifically to note that the majority's holding was in accordance with "the international understanding of the office of affirmative action." *Id.* at 344.

[41] In Lawrence v. Texas, 539 US 558 (2003), Justice Kennedy authored an opinion for the majority that struck down an anti-sodomy law as violative of the Equal Protection Clause of the 14th Amendment. The opinion featured an in-depth discussion of international and foreign law regarding homosexual conduct which supported its conclusion.

[42] Roper, 125 S.Ct. at 1186.

[43] Lawrence v. Texas, 539 US 558, 598 (2003) (Scalia, J., dissenting).

[44] Justice Stephen Breyer, "The Supreme Court and the New International Law," Speech before the American Society of International Law, 2003.

[45] *See* Roger P. Alford, *In Search of a Theory for Constitutional Comparativism,* 52 UCLA L. REV. 639 (2005) (discussing the four classic theories of constitutional interpretation, their

with the arrival of two new members of the Court, Chief Justice Roberts and Justice Alito, it is difficult to predict to what extent a comparative approach will be embraced by a majority of the justices.

[B]   National Law in International Law

Just as international law may come into play in national legal systems, national law may be applicable in cases governed by international law. Perhaps the most obvious example of the applicability of national law in international law is provided by Article 38(1)(c) of the Statute of the International Court of Justice.[46] While we will return to this provision in Chapter 3, we may note for present purposes that subparagraph (c) permits the ICJ to apply "the general principles of law recognized by civilized nations" in disputes that are submitted to it.[47] As we will see, these are indeed "general" principles, and ones that are generally recognized throughout the world, such as the principles of estoppel, good faith and *res judicata*, as well as the principle that one cannot profit from one's own wrong, that the commission of a wrong entails an obligation to provide a remedy, and that one may not be a judge in one's own case. The use of such domestic law principles in disputes between states may be justified on the ground that they are so widely recognized that a state would not object to having them applied in a case to which it was a party. In addition, international law being less well developed than national law, it can benefit by borrowing the most generally recognized principles of the latter. As Brownlie puts it, "international tribunals have employed elements of legal reasoning and private law analogies in order to make the law of nations a viable system for application in a judicial process."[48] This is true not only of the ICJ, but of international arbitral tribunals, as well.[49]

§ 2.02   "MONISM" VS. "DUALISM"

Given the coexistence and interpenetration of national and international law, two questions naturally arise: (1) Are they in fact two separate systems, or two components of one system? (2) If there is a conflict between national law and international law, which one prevails?

---

relation to constitutional comparativism, and the possibility of a separate theory of comparativism); Kenneth Anderson, *Foreign Law and the U.S. Constitution*, POL'Y REV. No. 131 (June–July 2005), *available at* http://www.policyreview.org/jun05/anderson.html (discussing how different philosophies of judging allow for varying degrees of reference to international and foreign law).

[46] The I.C.J.'s "Statute" may be thought of as the Court's constitution.

[47] STATUTE OF THE INTERNATIONAL COURT OF JUSTICE, Art. 38(1)(c). The Statute is an integral part of the Charter of the United Nations, which was signed on 26 June 1945 and came into force on 24 Oct. 1945.

[48] IAN BROWNLIE, PRINCIPLES OF PUBLIC INTERNATIONAL LAW 16 (6th ed. 2003).

[49] See BROWNLIE, *id.*, at 17 for examples of the use by arbitral tribunals of general principles of national law.

Whether national and international law belong to one or two systems is the theoretical battleground for two schools of thought: "monism" and "dualism."[50] As these denominations suggest, monist doctrine holds that national and international law are part of one system, while according to the dualist school each of the two is a separate system unto itself. Monists believe that all law forms part of what may be viewed as a pyramidic structure, with international law at the apex, national law in the central area and local ordinances and the like at the base. All legal authority is thus derived from international law through a process of delegation.[51] It follows that in the event of a conflict between international and national law, international law prevails. It may be said that international law is itself essentially monist in nature, in that it does not permit a state to rely upon its domestic law as an excuse for violating international legal obligations.[52]

Dualists, on the other hand, argue that there cannot be a conflict between the two systems because they are entirely separate, sharing no common field of application. Each is therefore, by definition, "supreme in its own sphere."[53] Thus, it is perfectly possible for a country to act consistently with its own law (e.g., requiring that its United Nations dues be withheld) and yet commit a breach of its obligations under international law (its duty under the U.N. Charter to pay dues).

The United States in many respects follows dualist doctrine,[54] although as we have seen, treaties are the supreme law of the land by virtue of the Supremacy Clause and courts may apply them as well as customary international law. To the extent that the two systems are separate the question arises, which system prevails in the event of a conflict? The short answer is that as a matter of U.S. law, rules of United States and international law are equal in rank; the one that arose later in time will therefore prevail over the earlier one in the event that they are found to be incompatible.[55] However, if the subsequent rule is one of U.S. domestic law, the fact that it overrides the international obligation does not release the United States from that obligation. Let us examine these general propositions in somewhat more detail. There are four important points to bear in mind. They will be discussed in the following two sections.

---

[50] *See generally*, 1 OPPENHEIM'S INTERNATIONAL LAW 53-54 (R. Jennings & A. Watts 9th ed. 1992) (hereinafter OPPENHEIM); BROWNLIE, *supra* note 48, at 31; and RESTATEMENT 3d OF THE FOREIGN RELATIONS LAW OF THE UNITED STATES, ch. 2, Intro. Note, at 40-41 (1987) (hereinafter RESTATEMENT 3d).

[51] OPPENHEIM, *supra* note 50, at 54.

[52] *See, e.g.,* art. 27 of the 1969 Vienna Convention on the Law of Treaties, U.N. Doc. A/CONF.39/27 (1969), which provides in relevant part: "A party may not invoke the provisions of its internal law as justification for its failure to perform a treaty."

[53] OPPENHEIM, *supra* note 50, at 53. For a development of this view, see Sir Gerald Fitzmaurice, *The General Principles of International Law Considered from the Standpoint of the Rule of Law*, 92 REC. DES COURS (1957-II) at 70-80.

[54] The Restatement states flatly (perhaps too flatly): "International law and the domestic law of the United States are two different and discrete bodies of law. . . ." RESTATEMENT 3d, *supra* note 50, ch. 2, Intro. Note, at 40.

[55] *See* RESTATEMENT 3d, *supra* note 50, § 115.

§ 2.03 INTERNATIONAL LAW AS LAW OF THE UNITED STATES

First, as we have already seen in the context of the Consular Convention cases, much of international law is actually part of U.S. law.[56] The historical origins of this are that international law formed part of the law of England and was incorporated into the law of the United States upon independence. In *The Paquete Habana*, the U.S. Supreme Court famously declared, "International law is part of our law, and must be ascertained and administered by the courts of justice of appropriate jurisdiction, as often as questions of right depending upon it are duly presented for their determination."[57] This begins to sound somewhat "monist," in that international law is part of the law of the United States. As we will see presently, however, while monist doctrine holds that international law is supreme, and therefore trumps inconsistent domestic law, this is not necessarily true as a matter of U.S. law.

Second, it follows from the first point that for those rules of international law that are part of U.S. law, conflicts between domestic rules and those "international" rules are resolved in the same way as conflicts between rules of purely domestic law (e.g., two federal statutes). How are such conflicts resolved? Very simply, in principle: If the sources are equal in stature, the rule arising later in time would prevail.[58] We have seen that the Supremacy Clause of the U.S. Constitution provides, *inter alia*, that treaties of the United States are "the supreme Law of the Land. . . ." While customary international law is not expressly mentioned, it is now accepted that it is part of federal law and enjoys supremacy over state law under Article VI.[59] Thus, as a matter of U.S. law, the Constitution would prevail over all other sources of law in the event of a conflict, while federal statutes, international agreements and customary international law enjoy co-equal status and would prevail over state law. The fact that they are equal in rank means that in the event that one of these sources (e.g., a federal statute) conflicts with another (e.g., a treaty[60]), the latter in time would prevail.[61]

---

[56] *See generally* JORDAN J. PAUST, INTERNATIONAL LAW AS LAW OF THE UNITED STATES (2d ed. 2003). It should be borne in mind that much of the body of customary international law and many international agreements "do not have the quality of law for the courts in that they do not regulate activities, relations, or interests in the United States." RESTATEMENT 3d, *supra* note 50, § 111, cmt. c, at 43-44.

[57] 175 U.S. 677, 700, 20 S.Ct. 290, 299, 44 L.Ed. 320 (1900).

[58] As we will see, this "last-in-time" rule rests on the assumption, not always warranted, that the later rule was intended to override the earlier one.

[59] RESTATEMENT 3d, *supra* note 50, ch. 2, Intro. Note, at 42.

[60] Technically, the treaty would have to be "self-executing" for it to be operative as U.S. law and thus for this rule to apply. *See* Whitney v. Robertson, 124 U.S. 190, 8 S.Ct. 456, 31 L.Ed. 386 (1888); and RESTATEMENT 3d, *supra* note 50, § 111(3). Self-executing treaties are dealt with in § 2.05, below.

[61] *See, e.g.*, Head Money Cases, 112 U.S. 580, 5 S.Ct. 247, 28 L.Ed. 798 (1884) (giving effect to a later statute); Whitney v. Robertson, 124 U.S. 190, 8 S.Ct. 456, 31 L.Ed. 386 (1888).

Third — and this is a crucial point — U.S. courts will go to great lengths to avoid interpreting a statute as being in conflict with a rule of international law. We have seen that if a statute is irreconcilable with a pre-existing rule of international law, the courts will give effect to the statute. They do not do this lightly, however, because finding that the statute pre-empts the rule of international law usually means that the international rule will not be observed. The courts have long recognized that Congress should not be presumed to have intended to put the United States in violation of its international legal obligations. In *Murray v. Schooner Charming Betsy*, Chief Justice Marshall laid down what has become the guiding principle: "an Act of Congress ought never to be construed to violate the law of nations if any other possible construction remains. . . ."[62]

The strength of this principle was dramatically illustrated in a case involving the Permanent Observer Mission to the United Nations of the Palestine Liberation Organization (PLO).[63] In 1987, Congress passed a law, the Anti-Terrorism Act (ATA),[64] forbidding the establishment or maintenance of "an office, headquarters, premises, or other facilities or establishments within the jurisdiction of the United States at the behest or direction of, or with funds provided by" the PLO.[65] This law appeared to directly contradict the Headquarters Agreement between the U.S. and the U.N.,[66] a treaty requiring the United States to, *inter alia*, permit permanent observers invited by the United Nations to maintain missions (offices similar to embassies) in New York. The PLO was — and is — such a permanent observer and has maintained a mission to the United Nations since 1974.

The day the ATA took effect, the United States brought suit in the federal court for the Southern District of New York seeking injunctive relief mandating the closure of the PLO Mission. The court denied the requested

---

(enforcing a later statute); and Cook v. United States, 288 U.S. 102, 53 S.Ct. 305, 77 L.Ed. 641 (1933) (giving effect to a later treaty). *See generally* Restatement 3d, *supra* note 50, § 115. *But see* note 56, *supra*. The argument has been made that while a bilateral treaty may have to give way to a subsequent inconsistent statute, a general multilateral treaty should not. This approach would follow the practice of some European countries, but it has not prevailed in the United States. *See* Restatement 3d, *supra* note 50, § 115, Reporters' Note 1. Finally, this last-in-time doctrine may be difficult to apply in the case of customary international law because of the difficulty of proving when a customary norm "crystallized" into an international legal obligation.

[62] 6 U.S. (2 Cranch) 64, 118, 2 L.Ed. 208 (1804). *See also* Weinberger v. Rossi, 456 U.S. 25, 33, 102 S.Ct. 1510, 1516, 71 L.Ed.2d 715 (1982). *See generally* RESTATEMENT 3d, *supra* note 50, § 114.

[63] United States v. The Palestine Liberation Organization, 695 F.Supp. 1456 (S.D.N.Y. 1988).

[64] Title X of the Foreign Relations Authorization Act for Fiscal Years 1988-89, Pub. L. 100-204, §§ 1001-1005, 101 Stat. 1331, 1406-07; 22 U.S.C.A. §§ 5201-5203 (West Supp. 1988).

[65] 22 U.S.C. § 5202(3).

[66] Agreement Between the United States and the United Nations Regarding the Headquarters of the United Nations, G.A. Res. 169 (II), U.N. GAOR, 11 U.N.T.S. 11, No. 147 (1947), 61 Stat. 756, T.I.A.S. No. 1676, authorized by S.J. Res. 144, 80th Cong., 1st Sess., Pub. L. 80-357, set out in 22 U.S.C. § 287 (1982).

relief, holding that the ATA did not require closure of the PLO Mission. The court reasoned that in this case, the ATA and its legislative history, when viewed against the background of the Headquarters Agreement and the well-established position of the PLO Mission, "fail[ed] to disclose any clear legislative intent that Congress was directing the Attorney General, the State Department or this Court to act in contravention of the Headquarters Agreement."[67] While the court acknowledged Congress' power to abrogate prior international obligations of the United States, it declared that "unless this power is clearly and unequivocally exercised, this court is under a duty to interpret statutes in a manner consonant with existing treaty obligations."[68] The court noted that this is a rule of statutory construction "sustained by an unbroken line of authority for over a century and a half."[69] Since Congress had failed to manifest its intent to override the international obligations of the U.S. under the Headquarters Agreement "clearly and unequivocally," the court reconciled the statute and the treaty by "finding the ATA inapplicable to the PLO Observer Mission."[70]

This case leaves no doubt that even where a U.S. statute plainly appears on its face to be inconsistent with a pre-existing obligation under international law, the courts will not find incompatibility in the absence of a clearly expressed congressional intent to override the international obligation. The policy underlying this rule is that Congress should not be deemed to have passed a law that would cause the United States to violate its international obligations unless Congress has made its intent known beyond question.

It is possible, of course, that despite this strong policy a statute could be found to override a pre-existing rule of international law. The effect of such a finding is the subject of the following section.

§ 2.04   THE EFFECT OF ACTIONS OF THE PRESIDENT OR CONGRESS THAT VIOLATE INTERNATIONAL LAW

The fourth and final point to bear in mind in considering the effect of dualist doctrine in America is the following. Let us assume that despite the courts' reluctance to find that a subsequent statute is irreconcilable with, and overrides, an obligation of the United States under international law, a court so finds in a given case. Imagine, for example, that the court in the *PLO Mission* case found that the ATA overrode U.S. obligations under the Headquarters Agreement. What is the effect of such a ruling? There are, in fact, two effects: one on the domestic, and one on the international plane.

---

[67] 695 F.Supp. at 1465.

[68] *Id.*

[69] *Id.*

[70] *Id.*

On the domestic level, the court enforces the statute.[71] In our hypothetical case, the PLO Mission would be closed. The international obligation (to allow the PLO to maintain its mission) would have no legal effect on the domestic level from that moment on.

On the international level, however, the obligations of the United States are unaffected. In most cases, implementation of a decision that a statute overrides international obligations of the United States will place the country in the position of being in breach of those obligations. In the hypothetical case, the U.S. would be in breach of the Headquarters Agreement. It would therefore be under an obligation to provide the remedies to the U.N. that are required under international law.[72]

The same consequences would follow from actions of the President that, while consistent with U.S. law, were in violation of international law. An interesting question is whether the President may constitutionally act in violation of international law, given that (a) international law is part of the law of the United States, and (b) the President has the duty under Article II, Section 3 of the Constitution to "take care that the Laws be faithfully executed." However, the courts have not compelled the President to observe international law, at least when the President is acting within his constitutional authority.[73]

§ 2.05   SELF-EXECUTING TREATIES

The doctrine of self-executing treaties deals with the question of whether a treaty is directly applicable on the domestic level. That is, does the fact that a treaty is in force for a state mean that it has the status of domestic law in that state? The answer to this question depends upon the country concerned and the language of the treaty at issue. This section will focus upon the law of the United States.[74]

As we have seen, treaties are expressly characterized by the Supremacy Clause of the U.S. Constitution as forming part of the "supreme Law of the Land. . . ." We have also seen that the term "supreme" in this context

---

[71] The statute would remain valid whether or not the court found that it was inconsistent with an international obligation. Courts may only find statutes invalid if they are unconstitutional.

[72] Specifically, the United States would have to make "reparation" to the United Nations. What remedies a breaching state is required to provide to an injured state is a question governed by the law of international responsibility, discussed in chapter 7, below.

[73] *See, e.g.,* Garcia-Mir v. Meese, 788 F.2d 1446 (11th Cir. 1986), *cert. denied,* 479 U.S. 889, 107 S.Ct. 289, 93 L.Ed. 2d 263 (1986), upholding the Attorney General's authorization of the detention of aliens even though such detention violated international law. The court found that the President, when acting within his constitutional authority, could act in disregard of international law — but it did not go on to find that the President was acting within that authority in detaining the aliens in question. *See* RESTATEMENT 3d, *supra* note 50, § 115, Reporters' Note 3.

[74] For a survey of the approaches of different countries, see THOMAS BUERGENTHAL, SELF-EXECUTING AND NON-SELF-EXECUTING TREATIES IN NATIONAL AND INTERNATIONAL LAW, 235 RECUEIL DES COURS (1992-IV) 303 (1992).

means that international agreements of the United States are superior to the law of U.S. states, although they give way to the Constitution as a matter of U.S. law. But the question presently at issue is whether treaties are directly applicable in the U.S. legal system or must be implemented through congressional or executive action, i.e., whether treaties are "self-executing."[75] The answer is that it depends on the treaty and the intent of the political branches.

When the United States enters into a treaty with State X, it is bound under international law to comply with the treaty. How it does so is generally up to the United States. Therefore, whether additional action is necessary for the implementation of a treaty is determined by the intention of the United States. Intent may be revealed by the language of the treaty itself or by the action or attitude of the Executive Branch or Congress. In *Foster & Elam v. Neilson*,[76] Chief Justice Marshall stated that a treaty is "to be regarded in courts of justice as equivalent to an act of the legislature, wherever it operates of itself, without the aid of any legislative provision. But when the terms of the stipulation import a contract, when either of the parties engages to perform a particular act, the treaty addresses itself to the political, not the judicial department; and the legislature must execute the contract, before it can become a rule for the court."[77]

This is thus an example of a case in which the courts would have to interpret the provisions of the treaty in question. However, the President may make a statement concerning the need for implementing legislation in transmitting a treaty to the Senate for its advice and consent. Or the Senate, in giving such approval, may condition it upon the passage of implementing legislation or simply declare that the treaty is not to be considered self-executing. For example, and surprisingly, when giving its advice and consent to the most basic human rights treaty, the International Covenant on Civil and Political Rights,[78] the Senate declared its substantive provisions to be non-self-executing.[79] It might be wondered, especially in light of *Foster & Elam*,[80] whether the Senate has the final word on this question or whether it is a matter for the courts.[81]

---

[75] *See generally* BUERGENTHAL, *id.*; and RESTATEMENT 3d, *supra* note 50, § 111, and cmt. h and Reporters' Note 5.

[76] Foster & Elam v. Neilson, 27 U.S. (2 Pet.) 253 (1828).

[77] *Id.* at 314.

[78] International Covenant on Civil and Political Rights, 19 Dec. 1966, G.A. Res. 2200 (XXI), 21 U.N. GAOR, Supp. (No. 16) 52, U.N. Doc A/6316 (1967), *reprinted in* 6 I.L.M. 368 (1967).

[79] "[T]he United States declares that the provisions of articles 1 through 27 of the Covenant are not self-executing." Text available on the U.N. treaty website, http://untreaty.un.org/ENGLISH/bible/englishinternetbible/partI/chapterIV/treaty6.asp. Articles 1-27 are the provisions of the Covenant setting forth human rights; the remaining provisions are of a procedural character.

[80] *See* text at note 76, *supra*.

[81] *See* Malvina Halberstam, Alvarez-Machain II: The Supreme Court's Reliance on the Non-Self-Executing Declaration in the Senate Resolution Giving Advice and Consent to the International Covenant on Civil and Political Rights, 1 J. NAT'L SECURITY L. & POL'Y 89 (2005).

This issue has not been definitively settled, however. In any event, if neither of the political branches takes any action with regard to a treaty's implementation the courts will generally presume that the President and Congress consider the treaty to be self-executing.[82]

A related but analytically separate question is whether a treaty creates private rights that may be asserted directly in court.[83] While many treaties do not create such rights, the Supreme Court has long recognized that it is possible for them to do so. In *Head Money Cases*, the Court stated that a treaty between two countries may include "provisions which confer certain rights upon the citizens or subjects of one of the nations residing in the territorial limits of the other, which partake of the nature of municipal law, and which are capable of enforcement as between private parties in the courts of the country."[84] In *Asakura v. City of Seattle*,[85] the Supreme Court permitted a Japanese national to attack an ordinance of the City of Seattle which would have prevented him from continuing to operate as a pawnbroker on the ground that it violated a treaty between the United States and Japan.[86] In *Sei Fujii v. California*,[87] however, the California Supreme Court held that the provisions of the United Nations Charter relied upon by another Japanese national[88] whose land had been escheated to the state were not self-executing. Whether a treaty has the effect of conferring rights directly upon natural or legal persons that they can assert in court thus ordinarily depends upon judicial interpretation of its provisions. But as we have seen, on occasion the U.S. Senate will make a declaration on this point when giving its advice and consent to a treaty.

The International Court of Justice has recently made statements of present relevance in cases concerning the rights of foreign nationals under the Vienna Convention on Consular Relations.[89] For example, in the case of *Avena and Other Mexican Nationals*,[90] the Court stated as follows in

---

[82] See RESTATEMENT 3d, *supra* note 50, § 111, Reporters' Note 5, stating that "if the Executive Branch has not requested implementing legislation and Congress has not enacted such legislation, there is a strong presumption that the treaty has been considered self-executing by the political branches, and should be considered self-executing by the courts."

[83] See generally RESTATEMENT 3d, *supra* note 50, § 907.

[84] Head Money Cases, 112 U.S. 580, 598-99, 5 S.Ct. 247, 254, 28 L.Ed. 798 (1884).

[85] 265 U.S. 332, 44 S.Ct. 515, 68 L.Ed. 1041 (1924).

[86] 37 Stat. 1504, proclaimed 5 April 1911. This was a typical "Friendship, Commerce and Navigation" (FCN) Treaty, or Treaty of Amity, of which the United States has concluded a large number. The Court did not specifically address the question of an individual's right to assert rights under the treaty, however, contenting itself with declaring that "[i]t operates of itself without the aid of any legislation, state or national," and that it "is binding within the State of Washington" under the supremacy clause, art. VI § 2 of the Constitution. 265 U.S. at 341.

[87] 242 P.2d 617 (Cal. 1952).

[88] The provisions relied upon were those relating to human rights: the preamble, and arts. 1, 55 and 56.

[89] Vienna Convention on Consular Relations, 24 April 1963, 21 U.S.T. 77, T.I.A.S. No. 6820, 596 U.N.T.S. 261, art. 36(1)(b) and (c).

[90] Avena and other Mexican Nationals (Mexico v. United States of America), 2004 ICJ Rep. 128, *available at* http://www.icjcij.org/icjwww/idocket/imus/imusframe.htm.

addressing the United States' argument that Mexico's claim was inadmissible because the individuals in question had failed to exhaust local remedies: "The Court would first observe that the individual rights of Mexican nationals under subparagraph 1 *(b)* of Article 36 of the Vienna Convention are rights which are to be asserted, at any rate in the first place, within the domestic legal system of the United States." It further recalled "that, in the *LaGrand* case, it recognized that 'Article 36, paragraph 1 [of the Vienna Convention], creates individual rights [for the national concerned], which . . . may be invoked in this Court by the national State of the detained person'."[91] Statements of this kind would be of relevance when interpreting a treaty but generally would not be binding, *per se*, upon national courts when determining whether individuals may assert rights under a treaty as a matter of domestic law.

Even if an agreement does confer rights on private persons, however, suit against a state may be precluded by sovereign immunity.[92]

---

[91] *Id.*, para. 40, citing *LaGrand*, 2001 I.C.J. 494, at para. 77.

[92] Suit against a foreign state in the United States is governed by the Foreign Sovereign Immunities Act of 1976, 28 U.S.C. § 1330, while suit against the U.S. government is possible only where Congress has consented through legislation. Foreign Sovereign Immunity is dealt with in ch. 6, below. On the immunity of the U.S. government in suits for violations of international law, see generally RESTATEMENT 3d, *supra* note 50, § 907, Reporters' Note 2.

Chapter 3
THE SOURCES OF INTERNATIONAL LAW

Synopsis

§ 3.01   INTRODUCTION

This chapter addresses the question, where does international law come from? This is another way of asking how international law is made. As suggested in Chapter 1, an understanding of the international law-making process is central to an appreciation of the nature of international law itself.

International law is made chiefly[1] in one of two ways: through *agreements* between states — "treaties" — or through *practice* by states that fulfills certain requirements — "customary international law," sometimes referred to simply as "custom." This chapter will discuss both treaties and custom as sources of international law but will not deal with the *law* of treaties, a subject covered in Chapter 4.

---

[1] The other source of international law, to be discussed in § 3.03[C], below, are general principles of national law.

For one accustomed to lawmaking on the domestic level, the methods of creating law on the international level can seem rather subtle. Taking the United States as an example, on the domestic level there are federal and state constitutions allocating lawmaking authority to the Congress and state legislatures, and certain judicial powers to the courts. Of course, the latter also derive authority to interpret, apply and even make law from the common law system. The situation is entirely different on the international level. There is no global constitution conferring authority upon states to make law.[2] Nor is there a supreme international legislature that has determined that treaties are binding or a court with compulsory jurisdiction.[3] Rather than deriving its force through top-down, or "vertical," processes of this kind, international law is more of a "horizontal" system: it is created directly by the very entities to which it is chiefly addressed, namely, states, which also enforce it. The lack of supranational authorities that make and enforce international law could cause one to wonder why it is binding. The following section deals with this question, focusing upon the two main forms of international law, treaties and custom.

§ 3.02   WHAT GIVES THE "SOURCES" OF INTERNATIONAL LAW LEGAL FORCE?

It may fairly be asked, what is it that gives treaties and custom legal force? Why are they binding upon states, which after all are sovereign, independent and autonomous? It is generally thought today that the answer is found in the acceptance by states, in their practice, of certain law-creating *processes* as legitimate ways of making law. These processes are what we call the "sources" of international law.[4] As Oppenheim explains: "The source of a rule of law is . . . to be found in the process by

---

[2] The closest counterparts are the U.N. Charter and the Statute of the International Court of Justice (ICJ). Charter of the United Nations, 26 June 1945, art. 2(3), 59 Stat. 1031, T.S. No. 993, 3 Bevans 1153, 1976 U.N.Y.B. 1043 (hereinafter U.N. Charter); Statute of the International Court of Justice, 26 June 1945, art. 1, 59 Stat. 1055, T.S. No. 993, 3 Bevans 1153, 1976 U.N.Y.B. 1052 (hereinafter ICJ Statute). The Charter does have some characteristics of a constitution for the international community and gives the Security Council certain powers that could be considered legislative. But the Charter does not address the authoritativeness of the two principal sources of international law, treaties and custom. The Statute of the ICJ, which forms an integral part of the Charter (U.N. Charter, *supra*, Article 92), does deal with this question in its Article 38 (discussed in § 3.03, below). However, that Article is addressed to the Court and not to states generally.

[3] *See* chapter 1, § 1.01. Of course, states may voluntarily accept the compulsory jurisdiction of the International Court of Justice under art. 36(2) of the Court's Statute, as discussed in chapter 10.

[4] Some authorities disfavor the term "sources," preferring the the more neutral and descriptive expression, "law-creating processes." For example, Schwarzenberger views the "metaphor 'source'" as being ambiguous and refers to "the inclination towards self-aggrandisement which this metaphor appears to foster among some of these 'sources' of international law. . . ." 1 GEORG SCHWARZENBERGER, INTERNATIONAL LAW 26 (3d ed. 1957).

which it first becomes identifiable as a rule of conduct with legal force and from which it derives its legal validity."[5]

The theory that the legal force of international law derives from state acceptance of certain law-creating processes is known as positivism.[6] This theory is sometimes more narrowly defined in voluntarist terms as holding that states are bound only by those rules of international law to which they have voluntarily consented. Indeed, both the International Court of Justice and its predecessor have made statements to this effect.[7] The classical statement of a positivist and voluntarist view of international law by an international court is that of the Permanent Court of International Justice in the *Lotus* case: "The rules of law binding upon States . . . emanate from their own free will. . . ."[8] And in the *Nicaragua* case, the International Court of Justice stated that "in international law there are no rules, other than such rules as may be accepted by the states concerned, by treaty or otherwise."[9]

The idea that international law is made by humans through states is to be contrasted with natural law theory, or naturalism. Natural law theory holds that all law, including international law, derives from the law of nature. The overall contribution of this doctrine was summed up well by the great legal historian, Sir Henry Maine, writing in the mid-19th century: "The grandest function of the Law of Nature was discharged in giving birth to modern International Law. . . ."[10] In fact, the deepest roots of international law are

---

[5] 1 OPPENHEIM'S INTERNATIONAL LAW § 8 at 23 (R. Jennings & A. Watts 9th ed. 1992) (hereafter referred to as OPPENHEIM). A distinction is sometimes made between "formal" and "material" sources of international law. A *formal* source is one from which a rule derives its binding force and validity. In U.S. domestic law this would ultimately be the federal or a state constitution. In international law it refers to the processes by which a rule becomes valid and binding, chiefly custom and treaties. A *material* source is one that provides the actual substance of the rule. In the case of customary rules on a particular topic, e.g., the use of international watercourses, the material source is state practice. *See generally id.*; and IAN BROWNLIE, PRINCIPLES OF PUBLIC INTERNATIONAL LAW 3-4 (6th ed. 2003).

[6] There are many definitions of "positivism." It has been called "a label for a whole array of differing approaches to international legal theory." Bruno Simma & Andreas L. Paulus, *The Responsibility of Individuals for Human Rights Abuses in Internal Conflicts: A Positivist View*, 93 AM. J. INT'L L. 302, 303 (1999). More narrowly, positivists have been described as believing that "international law is no more or less than the rules to which states have agreed through treaties, custom, and perhaps other forms of consent." Steven R. Ratner & Anne-Marie Slaughter, *Appraising the Methods of International Law: A Prospectus for Readers*, 93 AM. J. INT'L L. 291, 293 (1999). "Modern positivism" moves beyond the "beauty of traditional [positivist] theory — namely, its clarity and rigidity" but still regards formal sources as "the core of international legal discourse" and rejects relativism or the conflation of "law, political science and politics plain and simple." Simma & Paulus, *supra*, at 307, 308 and 305. *See also* CHRISTIAN TOMUSCHAT, INTERNATIONAL LAW: ENSURING THE SURVIVAL OF MANKIND ON THE EVE OF A NEW CENTURY 28, 29 [1999] RECUEIL DES COURS (2001), likewise defining positivism in more modern terms.

[7] *See* the statements of the PCIJ in the *Lotus* case and the ICJ in the *Nicaragua* case, quoted in the following text, at notes 8 and 9.

[8] S.S. "Lotus" (Fr. v. Turk.), 1927 P.C.I.J. (ser. A) No. 10, at 18.

[9] Military and Paramilitary Activities in and Against Nicaragua (Merits) (Nicar. v. U.S.), 1986 I.C.J. 9, at 135.

[10] HENRY S. MAINE, ANCIENT LAW 92 (3d ed. 1864).

traceable to natural law theorists, principally St. Thomas Aquinas (1225-1274) of Italy, and two Spanish scholars, Francisco de Vitoria (ca. 1486-1546) and Francisco Suárez (1548-1617).[11] These philosophers believed that all human law is based on the law of God, which is superior to human law and is manifested both in Scripture and in the law of nature. For these writers, the law of nature was a body of immutable principles that humans could discover through reason.[12] Since it was part of the law of God, it did not vary with context or circumstances. It was fixed, static.

Later natural law writers, such as Hugo Grotius (1583-1645) of the Netherlands and Samuel Pufendorf (1632-94) of Germany, departed from this theory of the law of nature. They viewed principles of human reason, rather than divine authority, as the basis of natural law. Grotius, who is sometimes described as the founder or father of international law (something of an overstatement, since it does not give due credit to other writers[13]), is best known today for his book *De Jure Belli Ac Pacis* (On the Law of War and Peace), published in 1625, and for having developed the theory of the freedom of the seas in his 1609 work, *Mare Liberum*. Since these and subsequent writers viewed the law of nature as deriving from human reason rather than from the law of God, they were able to free it from its static, immutable quality. What was legal was what was reasonable, and that could vary with the context and circumstances.

While the law of nature was later overtaken by positivism as the dominant theory of international law, as we will see, it has made an enduring contribution to the field and still has a place in the international legal order. Its influence may be seen in such fields as human rights and international criminal law, and in the important role in international law of the doctrines of reasonableness and equity. No legal system, domestic or international, can cover all possible cases that may arise; there must be some body of principles that can be used to fill in the gaps and cover unprovided-for cases. This body of principles has its roots in the law of nature. It is routinely resorted to by states and international tribunals in interpreting and applying international law, and provides the basis for solutions that are reasonable under the circumstances.[14] Christian Tomuschat expresses the point well: "Like a modern constitution, the international legal order comprises not only principles and rules, but also basic values which permeate its entire texture, capable of indicating the right direction when new answers have to be sought for new problems."[15]

---

[11] According to Brierly, a "long and continuous history, extending at least as far back as the political thought of the Greeks, lies behind the conception" of the law of nature. J. L. BRIERLY, THE LAW OF NATIONS 17 (H. Waldock, 6th ed. 1963) (hereinafter BRIERLY) (footnote omitted). *See generally* ARTHUR NUSSBAUM, A CONCISE HISTORY OF THE LAW OF NATIONS 147 et seq. (rev. ed. 1954).

[12] Otherwise, the law of God was revealed directly through Scripture.

[13] To this effect, see, e.g., BRIERLY, *supra* note 11, at 28.

[14] BRIERLY, *id.*, at 23-24, discusses the proposition that to "appeal to reason" in new or unprovided for cases "is merely to appeal to a law of nature." *Id.* at 24.

[15] TOMUSCHAT, *supra* note 6, at 28, 281.

It may be debated whether natural law, as manifested in these ways today, is in fact a "consensual" source — that is, a source of law that depends upon state acceptance, or consent, for its binding quality. Some scholars challenge the positivist notion that all sources of international law are consensual,[16] citing as examples natural law, "general principles of [national] law," and norms having the character of *jus cogens* — that is, overriding rules that states may not contract out of through treaties.[17] But it can also be argued, along voluntarist lines, that it is precisely through state acceptance that natural law has the contemporary influence that it does, and thus it is through that acceptance that both general principles of law and *jus cogens* rules have a binding character.

In any event, natural law was gradually displaced by positivism[18] in international law theory as the nation state grew in strength and importance, especially from the latter part of the 18th century to the early 20th century.[19] As we have seen, in general, positivists may be said to look to state conduct rather than metaphysical principles, finding that international law is binding upon states because they accept, through their conduct, rules created through certain processes.[20] These processes consist chiefly of those that produce treaties and customary international law. Treaty, or "conventional," law is based on express consent, while customary law is formed through what positivists regard as tacit consent, arising when states follow a certain practice they consider obligatory,[21] as we will see below.

---

[16] For classical and modern definitions of positivism see note 6, *supra*.

[17] *See, e.g.*, MARK W. JANIS, AN INTRODUCTION TO INTERNATIONAL LAW 55-67 (4th ed. 2003); MARK W. JANIS & JOHN E. NOYES, INTERNATIONAL LAW 133 (2nd ed. 2001). The seminal article on norms of *jus cogens* is Alfred von Verdross, *Forbidden Treaties in International Law*, 31 AM. J. INT'L L. 571 (1937). On the role of consent in the making of international law *see* Johnathan I. Charney & Gennady M. Danilenko, *Consent and the Creation of International Law*, in BEYOND CONFRONTATION: INTERNATIONAL LAW FOR THE POST-COLD WAR ERA 23 (Lori Fisler Damrosch, Gennady M. Danilenko & Rein Müllerson eds. 1995).

[18] Positivism is discussed earlier in this section. See note 6, *supra*, for classical and modern definitions of positivism. The first exponent of positivism was the English jurist Richard Zouche (1590-1660), who published JURIS ET JUDICII FECIALIS, SIVE JURIS INTER GENTES in 1650. Other early positivists include Cornelius van Bynkershoek (1673-1743) of the Netherlands; J.J. Moser (1701-1785) of Germany; and Emerich de Vattel (1714-1767) of Switzerland. On the positivists, see NUSSBAUM, *supra* note 11, at 164. On positivism generally, see WOLFGANG FRIEDMANN, LEGAL THEORY, ch. 21 (5th ed. 1967). For "a defense of modern positivism," see Bruno Simma & Andreas L. Paulus, *The Responsibility of Individuals for Human Rights Abuses in Internal Conflicts: A Positivist View*, 93 AM. J. INT'L L. 302, at 306-308 (1999). For a survey of criticisms of positivism, see Joseph H.H. Weiler & Andreas L. Paulus, *The Structure of Change in International Law or Is There a Hierarchy of Norms in International Law?*, 8 EUR. J. INT'L L. 545, 549-58 (1997).

[19] For a review of other modern theories, or methods, of international law, see *Symposium on Method in International Law*, 93 AM. J. INT'L L. 291 (1999).

[20] A caveat is in order here: the statement in the text should by no means be taken to imply that whatever some states actually do is the law, or that a state is entirely free to accept or reject rules of international law. As we will see below in the section on custom, a departure from international law is simply a violation of it.

[21] Some scholars have recently challenged the normative nature of customary international law, as we will see in § 3.03 B, below.

Now that we have considered what it is that gives legal force to the sources of international law, we may proceed to examine these law-creating processes themselves, as enumerated in Article 38 of the ICJ's Statute.

§ 3.03 ARTICLE 38 OF THE STATUTE OF THE INTERNATIONAL COURT OF JUSTICE[22]

The Statute of the International Court of Justice[23] (ICJ or World Court) forms an integral part of the United Nations Charter.[24] Based upon the Statute of its predecessor, the Permanent Court of International Justice (PCIJ),[25] it may be thought of as the "constitution" of the ICJ.[26] It thus establishes the manner in which the Court is organized and is to function. In a chapter on the Court's competence,[27] the Statute provides in Article 38 for the law the Court is to apply in resolving disputes that are brought before it. Article 38 does not use the term "sources" and by its terms is directed only to the Court. However, it is generally acknowledged that Article 38 contains an exclusive listing of the sources of international law.[28] The article provides as follows:

Article 38

1. The Court, whose function is to decide in accordance with international law such disputes as are submitted to it, shall apply:

   a. international conventions, whether general or particular, establishing rules expressly recognized by the contesting states;

   b. international custom, as evidence of a general practice accepted as law;

---

[22] *See generally* CLIVE PARRY, THE SOURCES AND EVIDENCES OF INTERNATIONAL LAW (1965).

[23] I.C.J. Statute, *supra* note 2.

[24] U.N. Charter, *supra* note 2, Article 92.

[25] *Id.* The Permanent Court of International Justice (PCIJ) was established as a part of the League of Nations system in 1920. It was replaced by the ICJ, whose Statute is largely identical to that of the PCIJ. Both tribunals, whose seat has always been at The Hague, are commonly referred to as the World Court. The PCIJ Statute was drafted in 1920 by an Advisory Committee of Jurists appointed by the League of Nations. The legislative history is contained in Permanent Court of International Justice, Advisory Committee of Jurists, *Procés verbaux of the Proceedings of the Committee*, June 16-July 24, 1920 (League of Nations Publication, 1920).

[26] The I.C.J. is actually established by Article 7 of the U.N. Charter, *supra* note 2. Obligations of U.N. member states in relation to the Court are provided for in Chapter XIV of the Charter.

[27] I.C.J. Statute, *supra* note 2, ch. II.

[28] *See, e.g.*, SCHWARZENBERGER, *supra* note 4, at 26: "The significance of this enumeration [i.e., that in Article 38(1)] lies in its exclusiveness. It rules out other potential law-creating processes such as natural law, moral postulates or the doctrine of international law." It is, of course, states which, through their practice, determine what the sources of international law actually are. But Article 38 contains a catalogue that states generally accept.

    c. the general principles of law recognized by civilized nations;

    d. subject to the provisions of Article 59, judicial decisions and the teachings of the most highly qualified publicists of the various nations, as subsidiary means for the determination of rules of law.

  2. This provision shall not prejudice the power of the Court to decide a case *ex aequo et bono*, if the parties agree thereto.[29]

The text of Article 38 is substantially identical to that of the same article of the PCIJ Statute.[30]

A threshold question concerning Article 38 is whether the sources it enumerates are listed hierarchically, so that in the event of a conflict between two sources, the one appearing higher on the list would prevail.[31] The answer is generally thought to be in the affirmative. While the Advisory Committee that drafted the original text of the article decided not to so state,[32] it appears that they recognized that as a practical matter the Court would generally consider the sources in the order in which they are listed.[33] Thus, for example, an applicable rule contained in a treaty (source (a)) between the parties to a dispute would generally take precedence over an otherwise applicable rule of customary international law (source (b)),[34] and so on. It must be recognized, however, that there is an inevitable interrelationship between the sources. For example, rules of custom — source (b) — and general principles of national law — source (c) — may be resorted to in interpreting treaty provisions — source (a). For this reason as well as others,[35] Article 38(1) may be regarded as generally

---

[29] ICJ Statute, *supra* note 2, art. 38.

[30] Article 38 of the PCIJ Statute consists of four paragraphs, one for each of the subparagraphs of paragraph 1 of the ICJ Statute. It combines the sentence in paragraph 2 of the ICJ Statute with paragraph 4 of the latter ("Subject to the provisions of Article 59, . . ."). The ICJ Statute adds to its paragraph 1 the words "whose function is to decide in accordance with international law such disputes as are submitted to it."; The PCIJ Statute is available at http://www.worldcourts.com/pcij/eng/laws/law03.htm.

[31] *See generally* Michael Akehurst, *The Hierarchy of the Sources of International Law*, 47 Brit. Y.B. Int'l L. 273 (1974-75); Michel Virally, *The Sources of International Law*, in Manual of Public International Law 116 (Sørensen ed. 1968); and Weiler & Paulus, *supra* note 18.

[32] The drafters decided not to include language stating that the Court should consider the sources in the order in which they are listed. *See* Akehurst, *supra* note 31, at 338.

[33] See the statement by M. Ricci-Busatti, *id* at 337, and the Committee's final decision, *id.* at 338, indicating it was not necessary to state that the sources should be considered in a particular order.

[34] This result may be supported either on the basis that the treaty is the source of the parties' mutual obligations or by virtue of the maxim *lex specialis derogat legi generali*, indicating that a special rule — a *"lex specialis"* — would ordinarily take precedence over a general one. The qualifier "generally" in the text above is necessary because as we will see, a norm of *jus cogens*, whose source is customary international law, would always take precedence over — and indeed would invalidate — an inconsistent treaty. On the *lex specialis* maxim, *see, e.g.*, art. 55 of the International Law Commission's draft articles on State Responsibility, and the commentary thereto, 2001 I.L.C. Rep. 356-59 (2001).

[35] *See, e.g.*, the point made about norms of *jus cogens* in the previous footnote.

reflecting a hierarchy, but one to which there are exceptions and qualifications.

Let us now turn to each of the individual sources, beginning with "international conventions," or treaties.

[A] Treaties

Article 38(1)(a) of the I.C.J.'s Statute designates, as the first of the sources of international law the Court is to apply in cases that are submitted to it, "international conventions, whether general or particular, establishing rules expressly recognized by the contesting states;. . . ." Two preliminary matters should be covered before discussing this source of international law. The first concerns terminology. Article 38(1)(a) speaks of "international *conventions*." The term "convention" is often used in common parlance to refer to a large meeting, usually of a particular group or organization. In the lexicon of international law, however, the term "convention" is reserved for international agreements, or treaties. The meeting at which a multilateral treaty is negotiated may be referred to as a "conference," but never as a "convention." The adjectival form of the term "convention" is also sometimes used. Thus the expression "conventional law" has the same meaning as "treaty law."

The second preliminary matter is that the *law* of treaties, which as we will see is in some respects similar to the domestic law of contracts, is covered in a subsequent chapter (Chapter 4). This section deals only with treaties as a *source* of international law. These are two entirely separate matters, although they are treated together for convenience in some international law casebooks.

Treaties are agreements between two or more states[36] and thus constitute the source of the rights and obligations of the state parties concerning the matters to which they apply. It is in this sense that they are considered a "source" of international "law."[37] By definition, treaties are based on the consent of the parties. Given the fact that states are sovereign, it might be thought that they would be free to change their minds and withdraw their consent — that is, to repudiate any agreement they entered into with another state.[38] This is not the case, however.[39] Treaties are binding by virtue of the principle *pacta sunt servanda*, meaning that

---

[36] The term "treaty" is defined in art. 2(1)(*a*) of the 1969 Vienna Convention on the Law of Treaties, 23 May 1969, 8 I.L.M. 679 (1969), discussed in chapter 4, below.

[37] Sir Gerald Fitzmaurice has stated that "treaties are, formally a source of obligation rather than a source of law. [T]hey are no more a source of law than an ordinary private law contract. . . ." Gerald Fitzmaurice, *Some Problems regarding the Formal Sources of International Law*, [1958] Symbolae Verzijil 153.

[38] See the discussion of sovereignty in § 1.04.

[39] Nor does entering into an agreement constitute an abandonment of sovereignty. In its very first decision, the Permanent Court of International Justice observed that "the right of entering into international engagements is an attribute of State sovereignty." *The Wimbledon*, 1923 P.C.I.J., (Ser. A) No. 1, at 25.

agreements must be observed.[40] Itself a norm of customary international law,[41] *pacta sunt servanda* has been called "perhaps the most important principle of international law."[42]

Since the binding force of treaties springs from a customary norm, it is difficult, technically, to speak of treaties as a "source" of international *law*. But in practice they are treated as such, and no one questions their inclusion in the list of sources in Article 38 of the Court's Statute. Treaties may be viewed as a source of law because they have been accepted by states as a legitimate process for creating binding rights and obligations.

But referring to treaties as a source of "law" requires clarification. If a treaty is a source of law, who is bound by that law? Any state other than the parties to the treaty? The short answer is no. A treaty, whether bilateral or multilateral,[43] may be said to make law only in the sense that a domestic contract does: both create rights and obligations that are binding on the parties, but not on non-parties.[44] In this connection, however, it is useful to distinguish a concept you are likely to encounter, that of "law-making treaties."[45]

This term is something of an oxymoron since, as just indicated, treaties create obligations only for the states that are parties to them; they do not "make law," per se, for non-party states. And yet especially since World War II, the international community has increasingly resorted to the multilateral treaty to fulfill the kinds of functions that are performed by legislation on the domestic level.[46] While there is no international legislature

---

[40] Art. 26 of the 1969 Vienna Convention on the Law of Treaties, *supra* note 36, entitled "*Pacta sunt servanda*," provides simply: "Every treaty in force is binding upon the parties to it and must be performed by them in good faith."

[41] While it is customary in origin, *pacta sunt servanda* is embodied in art. 26 of the Vienna Convention on the Law of Treaties. *See id.*

[42] RESTATEMENT THIRD OF THE FOREIGN RELATIONS LAW OF THE UNITED STATES § 321 cmt. a (1987) (hereinafter RESTATEMENT 3d).

[43] In addition to bilateral (two parties) and multilateral (more than two parties) treaties, the Vienna Convention on the Law of Treaties recognizes a kind of treaty that has been called restricted multilateral or "plurilateral," as will be seen in chapter 4. These are treaties as to which, because of their object and purpose and the limited number of negotiating states, no reservations are permitted.

[44] For treaties, *see* the 1969 Vienna Convention on the Law of Treaties, *supra* note 36, art. 34, reflecting the general rule, which is expressed in the maxim *pacta tertiis nec nocent nec prosunt. See also* RESTATEMENT 3d, *supra* note 42, § 324; and OPPENHEIM, *supra* note 5, at 32. However, the I.C.J. has recognized that in certain exceptional cases a treaty such as the U.N. Charter may in fact create rights and obligations for non-party states. *See Reparation for Injuries Case,* 1949 I.C.J. 185; *Namibia Case,* 1971 I.C.J. 56; and OPPENHEIM, *supra* note 5, at 32-33.

[45] See generally BRIERLY, *supra* note 11, at 58; and OPPENHEIM, *supra* note 5, at 32.

[46] "It must be conceded that the great body of rules of international law are now of treaty origin and that the trend towards a written law is probably irreversible and must become ever more rapid as time goes on. But this does not mean that conventional law is replacing customary law; more often it merely adds to it, custom retaining its binding force. It is otherwise only when a collective treaty abrogates a customary rule or introduces a new rule which contradicts a customary rule." Virally, *supra* note 31, at 128-29.

as such,[47] international agreements that have been negotiated in fora open to all states and accepted by a large number of those states may be thought of as the international community's rough counterpart to national legislation. It is chiefly in this sense that treaties may constitute a means of international "lawmaking," or a form of international "legislation." Of course, the analogy may only be taken so far: while all citizens of a country are bound by its legislation, the only states bound by a treaty are those that are parties to it, as we have seen.[48]

There is, however, a rather subtle but important way in which a state that is not a party to a treaty may be bound, not by the treaty, but by rules expressed in it. This would be the case when the treaty "codifies," or sets down in written form, previously unwritten rules of *customary* international law.[49] It bears emphasis that as to such non-party states, it would not be the *treaty* per se, but rather the *customary rule reflected in the treaty* that would be binding. The treaty would thus serve as evidence of customary rules of law that bind non-party states.[50] Such treaties are often referred to as "codification conventions." They are generally based on preparatory work by the International Law Commission of the United Nations (ILC), whose mission is the codification and progressive development of international law.[51] Treaties of this kind are open to all states and, because they reflect existing customary international law at least to some extent, may also be regarded as belonging to the category of "lawmaking treaties." But again, as treaties, they are technically binding only on the states that are parties to them.

---

[47] *See* chapter 1, § 1.01.

[48] This statement is subject to the caveat relating to the U.N. Charter expressed in note 44, *supra*.

[49] Examples of such treaties are the 1961 Vienna Convention on Diplomatic Relations, 14 April 1961, 500 U.N.T.S. 95; and the 1969 Vienna Convention on the Law of Treaties, *supra* note 36.

It is also possible that a treaty provision, while not originally codifying custom, may attract state practice that ripens into custom and thus eventually reflect a customary rule. The ICJ has recognized that "this process is a perfectly possible one and does from time to time occur." *North Sea Continental Shelf* cases, 1969 I.C.J. 3, at 41, para. 71. In this situation also, therefore, the treaty would reflect a rule that is binding on states that are not parties to it. For discussions by the International Court of Justice of the relationship between treaties and custom *see* the *North Sea Continental Shelf* cases, *id.*; and the *Military and Paramilitary Activities* case, 1986 I.C.J. 14.

[50] For example, in the *Gabčíkovo-Nagymaros* case, 1997 I.C.J. 7, the Court ruled that at least certain of the provisions of the Vienna Convention on the Law of Treaties were declaratory of customary international law and were thus binding on the parties (*id.* at 38, para. 46), even though the Convention itself was not binding since the 1977 treaty at issue in the case was concluded prior to the dates on which the two states became parties to the Convention.

[51] *See generally* UNITED NATIONS, THE WORK OF THE INTERNATIONAL LAW COMMISSION (5th ed. 1996). The ILC's Statute defines "codification" as "the more precise formulation and systematization of rules of international law in fields where there already has been extensive State practice, precedent and doctrine." STATUTE OF THE INTERNATIONAL LAW COMMISSION, art. 15, U.N. Doc. A/CN.4/Rev.2 (1982). Information on the ILC is available at http://www.un.org/law/ilc/.

To summarize the foregoing discussion of "lawmaking treaties," a treaty may be regarded as "lawmaking" if it embodies obligations that are broadly applicable. The obligations may have this character because the treaty has a large number of parties[52] or because it codifies customary international law on a given subject. One other possibility, that was not discussed above, is that the treaty is so universally applicable and important for world order that it may be thought of as laying down law for the international community. This type of treaty is represented chiefly by the United Nations Charter, whose basic principles have been said to be "increasingly regarded as applicable generally in international relations. . . ."[53] Thus, when properly understood, the term "lawmaking treaty" can be useful as a shorthand way of referring to certain multilateral treaties — namely, those that function as the international counterpart of domestic legislation. It is important to bear in mind, however, that to the extent that non-parties are bound by the rules expressed in these agreements, it is not the treaty itself that so binds them but other, external factors such as custom[54] or the will of the international community.[55]

Now that we have distinguished the concept of lawmaking treaties, we may return to treaties as a source of international law, in the sense of Article 38 of the ICJ's Statute. You will note that Article 38(1)(a) instructs the Court to apply, in disputes that are submitted to it, "conventions . . . establishing rules *expressly recognized* by the contesting states." This is the essence of the treaty as a source of law. Insofar as it is applicable to the dispute between the parties, a treaty, whether bilateral or multilateral, supplies the relevant rules because the states concerned have "expressly recognized" them in their agreement. These rules may be different from those of customary international law that would otherwise govern the parties' relationship; or they may simply be more precise than, or even the same as the otherwise applicable customary rules.[56] In any of these cases, the rules contained in the treaty apply;[57] but the rules of customary international law will govern matters not covered by the treaty — they pick up where the treaty rules leave off.

---

[52] E.g., the 1961 Vienna Convention on Diplomatic Relations, Vienna, 14 April 1961, 500 U.N.T.S. 95 (180 parties as of June, 2003); and the United Nations Convention on Biological Diversity, Rio de Janeiro, 5 June 1992, 31 I.L.M. 818 (1992) (178 parties as of June, 2003).

[53] OPPENHEIM, *supra* note 5, at 31. *See also* note 44, *supra*.

[54] *See* note 40, *supra*, and accompanying text.

[55] *See, e.g.,* TOMUSCHAT, *supra* note 6, at 49-50: "The ground rules of the international legal order can be said to represent the constitution of humankind from which no derogation is permitted. . . . Common social interest dictates that they be maintained and preserved without any reservation or exception." Of course, it may also be said that the rights and obligations contained in treaties of this kind have become part of customary international law and are generally binding for that reason. *See also* U.N. Charter, *supra* note 2, art. 2(6).

[56] In the *Military and Paramilitary Activities* case, *supra* note 49, the ICJ stated that "there are no grounds for holding that when customary international law is comprised of rules identical to those of treaty law, the latter 'supervenes' the former, so that the customary international law has no further existence of its own." 1986 I.C.J. at 94.

[57] This is assuming the usual case, i.e., that the agreement does not violate a peremptory, or overriding, norm of international law (*jus cogens*), such as those outlawing the aggressive use of force, genocide, colonialism and *apartheid*. If the agreement does violate one of these norms, it is invalid. *See* the Vienna Convention on the Law of Treaties, *supra* note 36, arts. 53 and 64. For further discussion of the effect of these kinds of norms on treaties, see chapter 4.

To sum up on treaties as a source of international law under Article 38(1)(a), they are, technically speaking, a source of obligation rather than a source of law, per se. But no one questions their inclusion in the list of sources of international law contained in Article 38 of the ICJ's Statute. Moreover, the importance of treaties as a source of the rights and obligations of states continues to grow as states rely upon them to regulate an ever-increasing number and variety of aspects of their international relations.

Having considered treaties as a source of international law, let us now turn to the second source listed in Article 38, custom.

[B] Customary International Law

If treaties contain rules *expressly* recognized by states, customary international law — or custom, for short — may be said to embody norms they tacitly accept, through their conduct. There is no precise counterpart to custom on the domestic level, which makes it somewhat challenging to understand for the newcomer to international law. But there are rough equivalents, such as the concept of custom and usage in commercial law, which may have normative character even though it does not flow from an official source such as statutory or case law;[58] and the common law system itself, which was customary in nature before the courts began to write it down and develop it in their decisions.[59] Custom also plays a significant role in the civil law system that prevails in continental Europe.[60] Indeed the first definition of "law" in Webster's Dictionary is: "a binding custom or practice of a community. . . ."[61] While unofficial, social customs or codes of behavior, including those described in books on etiquette,[62] resemble international customary norms in some respects as well, including the manner in which they develop, the strong pull to compliance they exert, the ways

---

[58] An example is the Uniform Customs and Practices for Documentary Credits (UCP), a set of standards concerning letters of credit published by the International Chamber of Commerce (ICC), a private organization headquartered in Paris. The UCP is so widely used that its 1993 revision, UCP 500, was in effect incorporated in the revised version of Article 5 of the Uniform Commercial Code (UCC) in 1995 — in effect, an official "codification" of existing practice. UCP 500 is available at http://www.jus.uio.no/lm/icc.ucp500.1993/doc.html; the revised art. 5 of the UCC (1995) is available at http://www.law.upenn.edu/bll/ulc/ulc.htm.

[59] "The earliest notion of law was not an enumeration of a principle, but a judgment in a particular case. . . . Afterwards came the notion of a custom which a judgment affirms, or punishes its breach." BLACK'S LAW DICTIONARY 1028 (4th ed. 1968) (quoting HENRY S. MAINE, ANCIENT LAW xv, 5 (3d ed. 1864)). *See also* SIR WILLIAM BLACKSTONE, COMMENTARIES ON THE LAW OF ENGLAND IN FOUR BOOKS 68 (1967); and *Rediscovering the Common Law*, 79 NOTRE DAME L. REV. 755, 758 (2004) (stating "For Blackstone, the common law was the product of what he called 'immemorial usage . . . [of which] judicial decisions are the principal and most authoritative evidence.' (1 William Blackstone, Commentaries *68-69.").

[60] *See, e.g.*, RUDOLF B. SCHLESINGER, COMPARATIVE LAW 229-230, 573-575 (4th ed. 1980); and RUDOLF B. SCHLESINGER ET AL., COMPARATIVE LAW 669-670, 690-694 (6th ed. 1998).

[61] WEBSTER'S THIRD NEW INERNATIONAL DICTIONARY 1279 (1966). *See also* MERRIAM WEBSTER'S COLLEGIATE DICTIONARY 659 (10th ed. 1994).

[62] *See, e.g.*, AMY VANDERBILT'S NEW COMPLETE BOOK OF ETIQUETTE (1963); and JUDITH MARTIN, MISS MANNERS' GUIDE TO EXCRUCIATINGLY CORRECT BEHAVIOR (1982).

in which members of the relevant community sanction non-observance, and the fact that they are unwritten. While no domestic analogy is perfect, it is probably true that, as observed in Oppenheim: "Custom is the oldest and the original source of international law as well as of law in general."[63] Let us, then, consider how customary international law, as a discrete source of law, is formed and changed.

Article 38(1)(b) of the ICJ's Statute refers to "international custom, as evidence of a general practice accepted as law." This formula contains two elements: (1) a *general practice*, that is (2) *accepted as law*. If those two elements are satisfied, a norm of customary international law is established. The manner in which paragraph (1)(b) is formulated may thus appear rather "curious,"[64] since it is a general practice, accepted as law, that is the evidence of a customary norm, not the other way around. But if the term "custom" as used in Article 38 is understood in its factual rather than its legal sense, it may in fact be evidence of a practice accepted as law.[65]

[1] "A General Practice"

Let us now look at the two elements of customary international law. The first is a "general practice." This expression raises two issues: how "general" must the practice be; and what qualifies as "practice." With regard to the first issue, as the term "general" implies, there is no requirement that *all* states follow the practice.[66] But it must at least be followed or accepted by most of what the ICJ has referred to as the "States whose interests are specially affected"[67] (what qualifies as "acceptance" is discussed below).

---

[63] OPPENHEIM, *supra* note 5, at 25 (footnote omitted).

[64] *Id.* at 26, observing that art. 38 refers "somewhat curiously at first sight" to custom as evidence of a general practice accepted as law.

[65] That is, the term "custom," as used in para. 1(b) may be interpreted in its purely factual sense to refer to a habitual practice or usage of states, without implying any judgment as to its legal character, rather than as shorthand for "customary international law." As noted above, it is in this sense that "international custom" may properly be regarded as *evidence* of a practice accepted as law. *Cf. id.*, n. 5.

[66] *See, e.g., North Sea Continental Shelf Cases*, 1969 I.C.J. 3, 218, 229 (Lachs, J., dissenting): "to become binding, a rule or principle of international law need not pass the test of universal acceptance. This is reflected in several statements of the Court, *e.g.*: 'generally . . . adopted in the practice of States' (*Fisheries, Judgment*, I.C.J. Rep. 1951, p. 128). . . . The evidence should be sought in the behaviour of a great number of States, possibly the majority of States, in any case the great majority of the interested States. . . ." And in the *Military and Paramilitary Activities* case, *supra* note 49, the ICJ confirmed that customary rules may be found to exist even if all states do not follow them: "it [is] sufficient that the conduct of states should, in general, be consistent with such rules, and that instances of state conduct inconsistent with a given rule should generally have been treated as breaches of that rule. . . ." 1986 I.C.J. at 98. *See also* RESTATEMENT 3d, *supra* note 42, § 102 comment *b*; BROWNLIE, *supra* note 5, at 6. The concepts of local or regional custom are discussed below.

[67] *North Sea Continental Shelf Cases*, 1969 I.C.J. 3, at 42, 43, paras. 73, 74. That is, most of the states principally affected by or involved in the issue (whether the issue concerns the continental shelf, expropriation, the use of international watercourses, or some other aspect of international practice) should follow or accept the practice. See also the quote from Judge Lachs' dissenting opinion in the *North Sea Continental Shelf Cases* in the previous footnote.

Thus, while "there is no precise formula"[68] for determining what constitutes a "general" practice, it is clear that it is not enough that a majority of states follow it. There is a qualitative element as well as a quantitative one: most states, including those whose interests are specially affected, should follow the practice.

But what about states that do not participate in the practice? Can they exempt themselves from the operation of the rule? The answer is no, unless they have regularly dissented from, or objected to, the rule *during the process of its formation*.[69] A state that has so dissented benefits from the so-called "persistent objector" principle,[70] which allows it, by following this pattern of conduct during the rule's formation, to opt out of a customary rule.[71] Examples of states exempting themselves from a rule through persistent objection during its development are rare, however.[72] Of course, after the rule has been formed, or has "crystallized," objection is fruitless and conduct contrary to the rule is merely a violation of it. However, if the "violations" themselves become the general practice, accepted as law, the old rule is supplanted by a new one defined by what were originally violations.

To summarize, not all states need to participate in the practice that forms the rule of customary international law; of those that do not, the ones that "persistently object" to it during the process of its formation will not be bound by it, provided their objections are effective; and those that do not qualify as persistent objectors will be bound by the rule through a fictional tacit consent, or acquiescence.[73] The result is that there is a presumption of acceptance of a rule if a state fails to oppose it persistently during its formation.[74]

---

[68] RESTATEMENT 3d, *supra* note 42, § 102 cmt. b.

[69] *Id.*, comment *d*. According to the Restatement, this rule "is an accepted application of the traditional principle that international law essentially depends on the consent of states." *Id.*, Reporters' Note 2.

[70] *See generally* Jonathan Charney, *The Persistent Objector Rule and the Development of Customary International Law*, 56 BRIT. Y.B. INT'L L. 1 (1985); Ted Stein, *The Approach of the Different Drummer: The Principle of the Persistent Objector in International Law*, 26 HARV. INT'L L.J. 457 (1986); and David Colson, *How Persistent Must the Persistent Objector Be?*, 61 WASH. L. REV. 957 (1986).

[71] Norway benefitted from this principle in the *Anglo-Norwegian Fisheries Case* by virtue of its having persistently opposed any ten-mile rule for defining "bays." Norway's opposition was held to prevent such a rule, if indeed there was one, from being applied against it. 1951 I.C.J. 116, 131.

[72] RESTATEMENT 3d, *supra* note 42, § 102 cmt. c and Reporters' Note 2. The example of Norway, in respect of bays, is mentioned in the previous note. In addition, Norway and other Scandinavian states succeeded in establishing four-mile territorial seas when three miles was the generally accepted breadth. And Norway was also able to establish its right to use a method of delimiting its territorial sea (straight baselines) that was contrary to the general practice but generally tolerated by foreign states. *Anglo-Norwegian Fisheries Case*, 1959 I.C.J. 116.

[73] On tacit consent and its fictional nature, *see* Virally, *supra* note 31, at 136.

[74] "[W]hen a custom has duly crystallized no state can be allowed to rebut the presumption [of acceptance], or to contend that it does not accept what it has allowed to come into existence without protest." *Id.* at 137.

A final point should be made concerning the requirement that the practice be "general:" this requirement applies only to rules of customary international law of *general application*, also referred to as universal custom. In addition to these rules that are, in principle, applicable to all states, it is also possible that a practice be regional,[75] or even local,[76] and give rise to a corresponding rule binding only on the states that have engaged in the practice.[77] Such "special" or "particular" customary law is exceptional, however, and may be difficult to prove.[78]

Having examined how "general" the practice of states must be to qualify as a "general practice," we may now turn to the second issue raised by that expression, namely, what qualifies as "practice." The practice of states is nothing more than their conduct, or behavior. Conduct may be active, as when a state affirmatively engages in a form of behavior, such as sailing its vessels into certain maritime zones; or it may be passive, as when a state refrains from protesting conduct by another state or from opposing a developing norm.[79] A variety of forms of state conduct may qualify as "practice" for the purpose of developing a norm of customary international law. According to the Restatement, state practice includes: "diplomatic acts and instructions as well as public measures and other governmental acts and official statements of policy, whether they are

---

[75] *See* the *Asylum* case, 1950 I.C.J. 266, in which the Court recognized that art. 38 of the Court's Statute does not exclude the possibility of regional or local custom despite its reference to a "general" practice. In that case, Victor Raul Haya de la Torre unsuccessfully led a military rebellion in Peru in 1948, then sought political asylum in the Colombian embassy in Lima. Colombia claimed a right of "unilateral and definitive qualification" of an offense as a political one, entitling the offender to diplomatic asylum. Colombia relied on an alleged rule of regional custom applicable among Latin American states permitting it, as the state granting diplomatic asylum, to determine unilaterally whether the offense of the individual in question was political or not. Peru objected, insisting that Haya de la Torre be returned to Peru for trial, and denied him safe conduct. The Court held that Colombia had failed to prove any "constant and uniform usage, accepted as law," as to the alleged rule and that Colombia had thus failed to establish that the rule it invoked was one of regional custom.

[76] The practice may be limited to as few as two states. *See* the *Rights of Passage Case*, 1960 I.C.J. 6, 39, where the Court said: "it is objected on behalf of India that no local custom could be established between only two States. It is difficult to see why the number of States between which a local custom may be established on the basis of long practice must necessarily be larger than two. The Court sees no reason why long continued practice between two States accepted by them as regulating their relations should not form the basis of mutual rights and obligations between the two States."

[77] *See generally* OPPENHEIM, *supra* note 5, at 30; and RESTATEMENT 3d, *supra* note 42, §102, comment *e*.

[78] *See* the *Asylum* case, 1950 I.C.J. 266, discussed in note 75, *supra*.

[79] "Inaction may constitute state practice, as when a state acquiesces in acts of another state that affect its legal rights." RESTATEMENT 3d, *supra* note 42, § 102 cmt b. Virally sheds further light on the point: "Inaction no less than action may contribute to the formation of a customary rule, so long as it does not merely reflect an unawareness of the state concerned that it might act rather than abstain from acting, or even mere indifference. So where the state concerned had grounds for adopting a particular course of action and deliberately did not adopt it, as where it grants another a license in a sphere affecting its own interests by allowing the passage of a foreign warship through its territorial sea." Virally, *supra* note 31, at 131.

unilateral or undertaken in cooperation with other states. . . ."[80] Oppenheim adds that the practice of states "in this context embraces not only their external conduct with each other, but is also evidenced by such internal matters as their domestic legislation, judicial decisions, diplomatic despatches, internal government memoranda, and ministerial statements in Parliaments and elsewhere."[81]

Returning to governmental acts "undertaken in cooperation with other states," this form of practice includes conduct of states in the context of international organizations, such as the United Nations. In this connection, it is generally acknowledged that while the U.N. General Assembly has no legislative powers,[82] resolutions it adopts may reflect on contribute to the formation of customary international law.[83] They must be evaluated carefully, but the statements and votes of states in the General Assembly are a form of conduct and may constitute state practice that can serve as evidence of custom.

Statements and votes of governments on certain resolutions were so viewed by the sole arbitrator in the *Texaco/Libya Arbitration*,[84] the late Professor René-Jean Dupuy. Professor Dupuy determined the legal value of the resolutions in question by considering the "circumstances under which they were adopted and by analysis of the principles which they state. . . ."[85] He observed that "those provisions stating the existence of a right on which the generality of the States has expressed agreement . . . do not create a custom but confirm one by formulating it and specifying its scope, thereby making it possible to determine whether or not one is confronted with a legal rule."[86] This is particularly true of resolutions that are entitled "declaration

---

[80] *Id.*

[81] OPPENHEIM, *supra* note 5, at 26. Virally adds: "But, since the distinction between external and internal affairs is far from absolute, many public acts involving domestic policy or domestic law may also constitute precedents, since they indicate the attitide which a state adopts towards a rule of international law." Virally, *supra* note 31, at 130.

[82] See U.N. Charter, *supra* note 2, art. 10, giving the General Assembly only the power of recommendation. However, the General Assembly does have the authority under art. 17 of the Charter to adopt binding decisions on the U.N. budget.

[83] *See* RESTATEMENT 3d, *supra* note 42, § 102 cmt. b and Reporters' Note 2. *See also* Virally, *supra* note 31, at 162.

[84] Award of 19 Jan. 1977, 17 I.L.M. 1 (1978).

[85] *Id.*, para. 86. In particular, the sole arbitrator found that Res. 1803 (XVII) of 14 Dec. 1962 on Permanent Sovereignty over Natural Resources, which had been adopted by a vote of 87 to 2, with 12 abstentions, reflected customary law on the question of the standards governing expropriation of the assets of foreign companies, while resolutions on the Charter of Economic Rights and Duties of States (3171 (XXVII), 3201 (S-VI) and 3281 (XXIX)), did not. He reasoned that the former resolution embodied a compromise that won the support not only of many developing countries but also a number of Western developed countries with market economies, including the United States. On the other hand, while the relevant paragraph of Res. 3171 (XXVII), which disregarded the role of international law in respect of expropriations, had been adopted by a vote of 86 to 11 with 28 abstentions, it "not only was not consented to by the most important Western countries, but caused a number of the developing countries to abstain." *Id.*, para. 85.

[86] *Id.*, para. 87.

of principles" or the like, in part because of the implication that governments intend to set down in the instrument legal principles relating to a particular subject matter.[87]

Again, however, caution must be exercised in attributing legal value to General Assembly resolutions or the statements or votes of governments on them. The Restatement provides the following list of factors to be taken into account in evaluating the contribution of General Assembly resolutions to the lawmaking process: "the subject of the resolution, whether it purports to reflect legal principles, how large a majority it commands and how numerous and important are the dissenting states, whether it is widely supported (including in particular the states principally affected), and whether it is later confirmed by other practice."[88]

Whatever the form of practice, in order to contribute to the formation of a rule of customary international law it must be *consistent.*[89] This requirement is almost self-evident, since a reasonable degree of consistency is inherent in the notion of a "practice." Further, if a practice is not consistent it will be difficult to define it with the specificity necessary to qualify it as a rule of law. Lack of consistency may also bear on whether the practice is "general" within the relevant community (universal, regional or local) as well as on the question of *opinio juris,*[90] discussed below. In holding that Colombia had failed to prove a customary norm in the *Asylum* case, the ICJ said:

> "The facts brought to the knowledge of the Court disclose so much uncertainty and contradiction, so much fluctuation and discrepancy in the exercise of diplomatic asylum and in the official views expressed on various occasions, there has been so much inconsistency in the rapid succession of conventions on asylum, ratified by

---

[87] The U.N. Office of Legal Affairs has stated that a "declaration" "may be considered to impart, on behalf of the organ adopting it, a strong expectation that Members of the international community will abide by it." U.N. Doc. E/CN.4/L. 610. In the *Military and Paramilitary Activities* case, the I.C.J. found that an *opinio juris* (a belief that a practice is obligatory) "may, though with all due caution, be deduced from . . . the attitude of States towards certain General Assembly resolutions, and particularly resolution 2625 (XXV) [of 24 Oct. 1970] entitled 'Declaration on Principles of International Law concerning Friendly Relations and Co-operation Among States in Accordance with the Charter of the United Nations.'; The effect of consent to the text of such resolutions . . . may be understood as an acceptance of the validity of the rule or set of rules declared by the resolution by themselves." 1986 I.C.J. 14, at 99-100, para. 188.

[88] RESTATEMENT 3d, *supra* note 42, § 102, Reporters' Note 2. *See also id.,* § 103 cmt. c, noting that the "declaratory pronouncements" of international organizations "provide some evidence of what the states voting for it regard the law to be."

[89] *See* the Asylum case, 1950 I.C.J. 266, discussed in note 75, *supra,* where the I.C.J. held that Colombia had failed to establish the rule it asserted because it had been unable to show any "constant and uniform usage, accepted as law," as to the alleged rule. *See also* RESTATEMENT 3d, *supra* note 42, § 102 cmt. b; BROWNLIE, *supra* note 5, at 7.

[90] *See* Virally, *supra* note 31, at 135: "The qualities of continuity and generality, requisite in order that an international practice may give rise to a custom, reflect the presence of . . . consent."

some States and rejected by others, and the practice has been so much influenced by considerations of political expediency in the various cases, that it is not possible to discern in all this any constant and uniform usage, accepted as law, with regard to the alleged rule of unilateral and definitive qualification of the offence."[91]

The requirement that a practice must be "constant and uniform" is another way of saying that it must be consistent.

It was traditionally thought that an important element in the formation of a rule of customary international law was that the practice giving rise to the rule be of long *duration*. It could be difficult to determine whether a practice was consistent, for example, if it did not occur over an extended period. A practice that had not stood the test of time might also be challenged on the ground that it was not followed out of a sense of legal obligation. But from roughly the middle of the twentieth century, the time element began to lose much of its relevance, and thus its importance, as it became easier to determine how states were conducting their affairs on the international plane. In its 1969 judgment in the *North Sea Continental Shelf* cases, the International Court of Justice went so far as to say that "the passage of only a short period of time is not necessarily, or of itself, a bar to the formation of a new rule of customary international law."[92] Indeed, the United States is sometimes said to have created "instant custom" when it declared in the 1945 Truman Proclamation[93] that it "regard[ed] the natural resources of the subsoil and sea bed of the continental shelf beneath the high seas but contiguous to the coasts of the United States as appertaining to the United States, subject to its jurisdiction and control."[94] Other coastal states followed suit, the claims were not contested, and the doctrine of the continental shelf was born.[95]

---

[91] 1950 I.C.J. 266, 277. The case is discussed in note 75, *supra*.

[92] 1969 I.C.J. 3, 44.

[93] Proclamation No. 2667, "Policy of the United States With Respect to the Natural Resources of the Subsoil and Sea Bed of the Continental Shelf," 10 Fed. Reg. 12303; 3 C.F.R. 67 (1943-1948), Comp., p. 67, 13 Dept. of State Bull. No. 327, 30 Sept. 1945, p. 485, *reprinted in* 4 M. Whiteman, Digest of International Law 456-57 (1965), and in 40 Am. J. Int'l L., Supp., at 45-46 (1946).

[94] *Id.* The Proclamation made clear that jurisdiction was exercised only over the resources of the continental shelf, not over navigation in the superadjacent waters: "The character as high seas of the waters above the continental shelf and the right to their free and unimpeded navigation are in no way thus affected." *Id.*

[95] "The doctrine of the continental shelf became accepted as customary law on the basis of assertions of exclusive jurisdiction by coastal states and general acquiescence by other states, although for some years actual mining on the continental shelf . . . was not technologically feasible." Restatement 3d, *supra* note 42, § 102, Reporters' Note 2. *See generally* 4 M. Whiteman, *supra* note 93, at 740.

The Soviet Union on October 4, 1957, launched the first artificial satellite, Sputnik 1, which proceeded to orbit Earth, passing through the airspace of a number of states. These states did not protest, causing some to characterize the permissibility of satellites orbiting above states as another instance of "instant custom." *See generally* Bin Cheng, *United Nations Resolutions on Outer Space: "Instant" International Customary Law?*, 5 Ind. J. Int'l L. 23 (1965).

A final question with regard to the notion of practice is whether new states, which did not exist when the practice occurred that gave rise to a customary rule, are bound by the rule.[96] This issue was raised especially by newly independent states that emerged from colonialism, chiefly in the early 1960s. They asked why they should be bound by rules they played no part in creating and, indeed, which were established largely by the very colonial powers from which they had achieved their independence. While there is undeniable logic to this position, these new states did not press it in practice.[97] Indeed, as independent states, they acquired the full panoply of rights and obligations that international law attaches to that status.[98] They could of course elect to challenge the validity of customary rules, but would only be entitled to refuse to observe them as to states that had expressly agreed to waive the rules in question.[99] In addition, the new states participated actively in the international legal system through becoming members of the United Nations and by availing themselves of a variety of benefits under customary law, in fields such as diplomatic law and the law of treaties.[100]

[2] "Accepted as Law"[101]

Now that we have examined issues raised by the first element of customary international law, a "general practice," let us look at the second element: the requirement that the practice be "accepted as law." While the first element is factual or objective, the second has been described as psychological[102] or subjective.[103] This "mental"[104] attitude, that a practice is

---

[96] *See generally* Virally, *supra* note 31, § 3.17, New states and custom.

[97] According to Virally, "[t]here is in fact no instance in modern practice in which reservations as to the application of rules of general international law have been made." *Id.* at 138-39.

[98] *See* OPPENHEIM, *supra* note 5, at 14; Virally, *supra* note 31, at 138. The latter author states that if the new state "has not, before entering into normal international relations, made express and particular reservations, the new state will find itself in exactly the same position as any other in relation to international law." *Id.* It seems doubtful, however, that even a new state could pick and choose among the rules it wished to apply to it (*see, e.g.,* OPPENHEIM, *supra* note 5, at 14), except in respect of particular states that agreed to waive those rules. *See* the following note and accompanying text. The situation is, of course, somewhat different with regard to treaties, as to which the new state is said to begin, for many purposes, with a "clean slate." *See generally* OPPENHEIM, *supra* note 5, at 228-30.

[99] Virally, *supra* note 31, at 138. This author points out that it would not, of course, be possible to waive rules having the character of *jus cogens. Id.*

[100] *See generally* Virally, *supra* note 31; and RESTATEMENT 3d, *supra* note 42, § 102 comment *d* and Reporters' Note 2.

[101] *See generally* BROWNLIE, *supra* note 5, at 8-10; RESTATEMENT 3d, *supra* note 42, § 102 comment *c*; and Virally, *supra* note 31, at 133.

[102] *See, e.g.,* ANTHONY A. D'AMATO, THE CONCEPT OF CUSTOM IN INTERNATIONAL LAW 47 (1971), tracing the idea to GÉNY, MÉTHODE D'INTERPRÉPTATION ET SOURCES EN DROIT PRIVÉ POSTIF § 110 (1899). Gény's reason for making the distinction between the material and psychological elements, according to D'Amato, was to differentiate legal from social usage. D'Amato states that while Gény was concerned with the role of custom in private law, his analysis "passed immediately into international legal thinking. . . ." D'AMATO, *supra,* at 49.

[103] The I.C.J. described as a "subjective element" the "belief that [a] practice is rendered obligatory by the existence of a rule of law requiring it." *North Sea Continental Shelf* cases, 1969 I.C.J. 3, 44.

[104] Virally, *supra* note 31, at 133 (§ 3.15, "The mental element in the formation of custom").

followed out of a sense of legal obligation, is referred to as *opinio juris sive necessitatis*[105] or, simply, *opinio juris*. The requirement immediately raises several questions. The first is, why is it needed? Why not just look at what states actually do, and derive customary rules from that conduct? The answer, of course, is that states do many things regularly, even consistently, that are not legally required. They roll out red carpets for visiting officials, fire salutes, lower flags to half staff, and the like. These are not matters that states would accept as being legally binding. The point that the mere fact of practice is not by itself enough was noted by the ICJ in the *North Sea Continental Shelf* cases:

> "Not only must the acts concerned amount to a settled practice, but they must also be such . . . as to be evidence of a belief that this practice is rendered obligatory by the existence of a rule of law requiring it. The need for such a belief, i.e., the existence of a subjective element, is implicit in the very notion of the *opinio juris sive necessitatis*. The States concerned must therefore feel that they are conforming to what amounts to a legal obligation. The frequency, or even habitual character of the acts is not in itself enough. There are many international acts, e.g., in the field of ceremonial and protocol, which are performed almost invariably, but which are motivated only by considerations of courtesy, convenience or tradition, and not be any sense of legal duty."[106]

The requirement of *opinio juris* thus seems to make sense, to separate the obligatory from the courteous and the convenient, the legal wheat from the habitual but non-binding chaff.

The second question raised by the *opinio juris* requirement has to do with its apparent circularity: how can a rule be formed by a practice that is required by the same rule?[107] It is one thing to say that we must look for a "general practice accepted as law" when attempting to discover an *existing* rule of custom; it is quite another to maintain that the customary rule itself is *formed* by states conducting themselves in a certain way *because they believe they are required to do so*. What is it that supplies that requirement, if the practice has not yet "crystallized" into a customary norm? Perhaps surprisingly, there does not appear to be a clear answer to this question.[108]

---

[105] Literally, "of the opinion that it is a necessary law." This translation does not capture the expression's true meaning in international law, however, which Virally describes as a "conviction on the part of the creators of precedents that they are, in creating them, implementing [a] legal rule." Virally, *supra* note 31, at 133.

[106] 1969 I.C.J. at 44.

[107] *See* the discussion in D'AMATO, *supra* note 102, at 52-53, recounting the International Law Commission's early attempts to deal with the conundrum; and at 66, surveying the theories of writers.

[108] The Restatement offers possible explanations in the Reporters' Notes, including the following: "Perhaps the sense of legal obligation came originally from principles of natural law or common morality, often already reflected in principles of law common to national legal systems . . .; practice built on that sense of obligation then matured into customary law." RESTATEMENT 3d, *supra* note 42, § 102, Reporters' Note 2. *See also* the critical survey of the views of various commentators in D'AMATO, *supra* note 102, at 66-72.

The conundrum has led some commentators and jurists to throw up their hands and simply infer the *opinio juris* from the fact of a constant and uniform practice.[109] Sir Hersch Lauterpacht cut the Gordian knot by shifting the burden of proof: "it would appear that the accurate principle on the subject consists in regarding all uniform conduct of Governments (or, in appropriate cases, abstention therefrom) as evidencing the *opinio necessitatis juris* except when it is shown that the conduct in question was not accompanied by any such intention."[110] This approach was advocated in the dissenting opinion of Judge Ad Hoc Sørensen in the *North Sea Continental Shelf* cases.[111]

Another reason for inferring *opinio juris* from consistent state practice is that it is difficult to prove the state of mind of a state. In the opinion of Judge Sørensen just referred to, for example, that jurist noted that "there may be numerous cases in which it is practically impossible for one government to produce conclusive evidence of the motives which have prompted the action and policy of other governments."[112] But according to Virally, "[t]he truth is that the Court, though it pays lip-service to the concept of the *opinio juris* . . . , is concerned less with analysis of mental states than with the examination and assessment of the facts proved. What it seeks to determine is whether or not they disclose an effective exercise by a state of a right, coupled with a recognition by another state of a corresponding obligation."[113]

That it is difficult to meet even this test is demonstrated by the *North Sea Continental Shelf* cases,[114] in which Denmark and the Netherlands

---

[109] *See* D'AMATO, *supra* note 102, at 53-56, and Virally, *supra* note 31, at 134, discussing the views of several writers. *See also, e.g.*, the dissenting opinion of Judge Tanaka in the *North Sea Continental Shelf* cases, where the judge, after noting the difficulty of proving *opinio juris*, suggests: "There is no other way than to ascertain the existence of *opinio juris* from the fact of the external existence of a certain custom and its necessity felt in the international community, rather than to seek evidence as to the subjective motives for each example of State practice, which is something which is impossible of achievement." 1969 I.C.J. at 176. Kirgis suggests a sliding scale, with a stronger showing of *opinio juris* being necessary as the frequency and consistency of a practice decline. Frederic L. Kirgis, Jr., *Custom on a Sliding Scale*, 81 AM. J. INT'L L. 146 (1987). Roberts characterizes "traditional custom" as emphasizing state practice and "modern custom" as emphasizing *opinio juris*. Anthea Elizabeth Roberts, *Traditional and Modern Approaches to Customary International Law: A Reconciliation*, 95 AM. J. INT'L L. 757, 758 (2001).

[110] SIR HERSCH LAUTERPACHT, THE DEVELOPMENT OF INTERNATIONAL LAW BY THE INTERNATIONAL COURT 380 (1958).

[111] 1969 I.C.J. 3, 246-47 (Sørensen, J., dissenting), quoting the above passage from Judge Lauterpacht's work.

[112] *Id.* at 246. *See also* the dissenting opinion of Judge Tanaka in the *North Sea Continental Shelf* cases, where the judge says: "it is extremely difficult to get evidence of [the] existence [of *opinio juris*] in concrete cases." 1969 I.C.J. at 176.

[113] Virally, *supra* note 31, at 134. This was effectively what the I.C.J. did in the *Anglo-Norwegian Fisheries* case, 1959 I.C.J. 116, where it held that the straight-baseline method established by Norway for delimiting its territorial sea was not contrary to international law given its general toleration by other states and the United Kingdom's "prolonged abstention" from challenging it.

[114] 1969 I.C.J. 3.

were unable to convince the I.C.J. that a provision of the 1958 Convention on the Continental Shelf (which was based on a draft prepared by the International Law Commission) plus corresponding state practice demonstrated the existence of a rule of customary international law.[115] Perhaps precisely because it is so hard to establish *opinio juris* conclusively, the Court itself normally does not attempt to do so in its judgments. Instead it is typically content with determining the legal effect of objective facts or, perhaps more often, with merely declaring that a particular treaty provision reflects customary international law.[116]

But if one did wish to try to establish *opinio juris*, that is, that states followed a particular practice out of a sense of legal obligation, what kinds of evidence would one attempt to marshal? Certainly there must be a factual predicate, i.e., general and consistent practice. As we have seen, one school of thought would allow *opinio juris* to be inferred from such practice, without more.[117] Indeed, the existence of a number of bilateral or possibly multilateral treaties containing similar provisions — so-called treaty practice — may be cited as evidence of the subjective element.[118] Multilateral treaties based on preparatory work by the International Law Commission, or at least provisions thereof, have also been accepted by the ICJ as codifications of custom.[119] Official statements may be cited as well, but caution is necessary because it is not always clear whether a state is actually expressing its view of what the law is. This is true in particular of statements made in connection with the consideration or adoption of resolutions of the U.N. General Assembly or other international meetings, which may reflect a political rather than a legal position.

---

[115] *See, e.g., id.,* para. 76, in which the Court refused to find that a growing practice in the sense of the rule urged by Denmark and the Netherlands was evidence of such a rule: "But from that [practice] no inference could justifiably be drawn that they [i.e., the states engaging in the practice] believed themselves to be applying a mandatory rule of customary international law."

[116] On the latter practice, *see, e.g.,* the *Gabčíkovo/Nagymaros Project* case, 1997 I.C.J. 7, where the Court declared or confirmed that certain provisions of the Vienna Convention on the Law of Treaties (23 May 1969, 1155 UNTS 331) (arts. 60 to 62, *see* paras. 46, 99 and 104 of the judgment) and the 1978 Vienna Convention on Succession of States in respect of Treaties (23 Aug. 1978, 1946 UNTS 3, U.N. Doc. A/CONF. 80/31, 17 I.L.M. 1488 (1978)) (art. 12, *see* para. 123 of the judgment) reflect customary international law. Treaties as to which the Court makes such declarations are usually based upon drafts prepared by the International Law Commission.

[117] This school includes the Restatement, according to which "*opinio juris* may be inferred from acts or omissions." RESTATEMENT 3d, *supra* note 42, § 102 cmt. c.

[118] Of course, it is also possible that the parties concluded an agreement precisely to derogate from a rule of customary international law, or that the reasons for concluding the agreement had nothing to do with an *opinio juris*. *See* OPPENHEIM, *supra* note 5, at 28 n. 15.

[119] But some have not: *see* the *North Sea Continental Shelf* cases, 1969 I.C.J. 3, where the ICJ refused to find that the provision on delimitation in the Convention on the Continental Shelf constituted a codification of custom. On the other hand, in the *Gabčíkovo/Nagymaros Project* case, 1997 I.C.J. 7, the Court bolstered its reasoning by citing the U.N. Convention on the Law of the Non-Navigational Uses of International Watercourses, 36 I.L.M. 700 (1997), just four months after the Convention's adoption. (The Court did not go so far as to hold that the Convention was a codification of custom, however.)

A possible solution to the problem of proving *opinio juris* has been proposed by Anthony D'Amato. Professor D'Amato points to the importance of a "promulgative articulation"[120] of a rule of international law justifying a particular action: "The simplest objective view of *opinio juris* is a requirement that an objective claim of international legality be *articulated* in advance of, or concurrently with, the act which will constitute the quantitative elements of custom."[121] Such a requirement would provide strong evidence that a state believed it was acting out of a sense of legal obligation[122] and would also put other states on notice of the belief, giving them an opportunity to respond by either challenging or accepting the practice.[123] The particular value of this approach to ascertaining an *opinio juris* is that it includes both the material element of custom — an act — and the subjective element — a statement or articulation of the legality of the act. This goes at least some way toward meeting the basic difficulties with establishing custom, namely, that an act may or may not be done out of a sense of legal obligation (here, there is at least a statement that the acting state considers that it is) and that official statements may or may not reflect a government's true position on the law (here, the statement is tied to actual conduct, which makes it reasonable for other states to rely upon it[124]). The law must often infer intent from objective manifestations,[125] and the combination of acts and words characterizing those acts provides a reasonable degree of reliability.

[3]   Recent Challenges to Custom as a Source of Law

Recent scholarship has challenged the idea that customary international law influences national behavior or that it is legitimate or even useful as a form of lawmaking in the modern world.[126] These assaults on the citadel of custom[127] have been launched on a number of fronts. Some writers challenge the generality of the practice and acceptance traditionally considered the basis of custom, arguing that the developing world has largely been left

---

[120] D'AMATO, *supra* note 102, at 75.

[121] *Id.* at 74 (emphasis in original).

[122] Statements of legality that are coupled with acts provide greater assurance of a true *opinio juris* than, e.g., statements to the press, contentions made in disputes, diplomatic notes or the like — even if they may not represent the "true" belief of the state, which would be very difficult, if not impossible, for other states to determine. *See id.* at 39-40.

[123] *Id* at 75.

[124] Again, whether the statement reflects the *true* belief of the state (assuming there is such a thing) is immaterial, since the law must rely on that which can be objectively determined.

[125] An obvious domestic law example is the objective manifestation of consent to be bound that is necessary for the formation of a contract.

[126] *See, e.g.,* N.C.H. Dunbar, *The Myth of Customary International Law,* 1983 AUSTL. Y.B. INT'L L. 1; Jack L. Goldsmith & Eric A. Posner, *A Theory of Customary International Law,* 66 U. CHI. L. REV. 1113 (1999); and J. Patrick Kelly, *The Twilight of Customary International Law,* 40 VA. J. INT'L L. 449 (2000).

[127] With apologies to Justice Cardozo, who declared famously that "the assault upon the citadel of privity is proceeding in these days apace." Ultramares Corp. v. Touche, 174 N.E. 441, 445 (1931).

out of the process.[128] Others maintain that custom emerges not from states following a practice out of a sense of legal obligation, but from their "pursuit of self-interested policies on the international stage."[129] Further, any consistent multilateral practice is said to reflect not customary international law but "coincidences of interest or coercion, [while] regularities that reflect cooperation or coordination arise only in bilateral contexts."[130]

This robust debate is no doubt healthy. By focusing on the weaknesses of the theory of customary international law, it enhances our understanding of the complex process of international lawmaking. It seems clear, however, that most governments, as well as such important institutions as the International Court of Justice and the International Law Commission, accept the existence of customary international law and the manner in which it is formed, as traditionally defined in Article 38, as well as the utility of custom as a normative force. Thus, for the time being, at least, an understanding of the traditional concept of customary international law, as described in this section, remains relevant and important.

We have now considered the two principal sources of international law, treaties and custom. There is, however, one additional source listed in Article 38 that remains to be considered: general principles of law.

[C] General Principles of National Law[131]

Article 38(1)(c) of the ICJ's Statute refers to "the general principles of law recognized by civilized nations." This language refers to general principles of *national* law, rather than of international law.[132] National or domestic law is commonly referred to as "municipal" law in international law parlance. There are three issues to be considered in connection with this source and the way in which it is formulated. First, why should principles of *national* law be regarded as a source of *international* law? Second, what kinds of principles are contemplated? And third, what is meant by "civilized" nations?

The first issue is why principles of national law should be regarded as a source of international law. After all, as principles of domestic law established by legislatures and courts chiefly to govern relations among individuals, by definition they are not created by states to regulate relations among themselves. But, as the Restatement puts it, states may accept a rule of international law "by derivation from general principles common to the major legal systems of the world."[133]

---

[128] Kelly, *supra* note 126.

[129] Goldsmith and Posner, *supra* note 126, at 1115.

[130] *Id.*

[131] *See generally* BIN CHENG, GENERAL PRINCIPLES OF LAW APPLIED BY INTERNATIONAL COURTS AND TRIBUNALS (1953); OPPENHEIM, *supra* note 5, at 36-40.

[132] *See, e.g.,* BROWNLIE, *supra* note 5, at 16; OPPENHEIM, *supra* note 5, at 37. *See also* the *Barcelona Traction* case, 1970 I.C.J. 3, 33-34, 37.

[133] RESTATEMENT 3d, *supra* note 42, § 102(1)(c).

Whether general principles of law are actually a consensual source of international law like treaties and custom, as the notion of acceptance would imply, has been questioned.[134] But in any case, there is broad agreement today that general principles of national law are a source of international law independent of treaties and custom.[135] However, they do not override those two sources, but have been called "secondary" or "supplementary" to them.[136] They are used by international tribunals to fill gaps and generally provide the interstitial material that all legal systems must have but which has not always been furnished by treaties or state practice.[137] Compared to national legal systems, international law is relatively undeveloped. Therefore, as Brownlie explains, "international tribunals have employed elements of legal reasoning and private law analogies in order to make the law of nations a viable system for application in a judicial process."[138] Government legal advisers likewise draw upon general principles of municipal law in formulating advice on international law to officials, as do states themselves in diplomatic exchanges with each other. However, the ICJ itself does not use this source often in its judgments and, when it does, the Court typically refers to it only in general terms rather than justifying its application of a given principle by explicit reference to Article 38(1)(c).[139]

The second issue raised by the formulation of Article 38(1)(c) is, what kinds of principles are contemplated? The principles that have been

---

[134] *See generally* the sources cited in note 17, *supra. Cf. also* the following footnote. The two positions may be summarized as follows: To the effect that they are non-consensual, it can be argued that general principles of law have not been accepted by states as norms of *international* law, in the way that treaties and custom have. The contrary argument is that by accepting the inclusion of general principles of law in Article 38 and the application of those principles by international tribunals, states have in fact accepted general principles of law as a source of international law. The latter position probably reflects the general view. *See* OPPENHEIM, *supra* note 5, at 38-39: Article 38(1)(c) is an "important landmark" because states did "expressly recognize the existence of a third source of international law independent of custom or treaty."

[135] A few well known writers of the past century, including Guggenheim and Tunkin, took the position that general principles of national law can have the status of international law only if states have adopted them in treaties or through custom. *See* the discussion in Humphry Waldock, *General Course on Public International Law*, 106 RECUEIL DES COURS (1962-II) 54.

[136] RESTATEMENT 3d, *supra* note 42, § 102 cmt. l. Oppenheim observes, however, that: "General principles of law . . . do not have just a supplementary role, but may give rise to rules of independent legal force . . . ," noting that they are not included as one of the "subsidiary means" included in Article 38(1)(d). OPPENHEIM, *supra* note 5, at 40.

[137] While the International Court of Justice has made only limited use of this source, arbitral tribunals have often resorted to it. *See* OPPENHEIM, *supra* note 5, at 37-38 (stating that customary and treaty law have generally sufficed in cases before the I.C.J.); and BROWNLIE, *supra* note 5, at 17 (noting that when this source is used by the I.C.J., "it normally appears, without any formal reference or label, as a part of judicial reasoning").

[138] BROWNLIE, *supra* note 5, at 16.

[139] *See, e.g., id.* at 17; and Virally, *supra* note 31, at 148, stating that "neither the International Court nor its predecessor has ever made any express reference to Article 38 (Ic) of the Statute."

recognized as meeting the requirements of Article 38(1)(c) may be grouped into three categories: first, certain principles or postulates that are of a fundamental nature and are said to be universally recognized; second, principles concerning the administration of justice; and third, other principles of municipal law needed to fill gaps in international law.

At least some of the principles in the first category may be said to have a certain moral character and in this sense to be redolent of natural law.[140] Others have to do with fundamental fairness. Examples of principles in this category are good faith,[141] which is said to be significant in "every aspect of international law;"[142] *pacta sunt servanda*, the principle that agreements are binding and are to be performed in good faith;[143] the principle that a wrongdoer must provide redress, or "reparation,"[144] for the breach of an obligation;[145] the principle that one cannot profit from one's own wrong;[146] the principles of estoppel and acquiescence;[147] the principle that one must not abuse one's rights;[148] and probably[149] certain moral principles such as the "elementary considerations of humanity, even more exacting in peace than in war" to which the ICJ referred in the *Corfu Channel* case as a basis of Albania's responsibility for failing to warn ships of mines in its waters.[150]

---

[140] *See* the dissenting opinion of Judge Tanaka in the South West Africa cases (Second Phase), 1966 I.C.J. 6, 294-99. *See also* Sir Gerald Fitzmaurice, *The General Principles of International Law Considered from the Standpoint of the Rule of Law*, 92 RECUEIL DES COURS (1957-II) 1, at 56 n. 1; and OPPENHEIM, *supra* note 5, at 37 n. 1.

[141] *See, e.g.*, the *Border and Transborder Armed Actions* case, 1988 I.C.J. 69, 105. "Good faith" is referred to as a "universally recognized" principle in the Preamble of the Vienna Convention on the Law of Treaties, *supra* note 36. *See generally* ELISABETH ZOLLER, LA BONNE FOI EN DROIT INTERNATIONAL PUBLIC (1977); OPPENHEIM, *supra* note 5, at 38, and sources there cited.

[142] OPPENHEIM, *supra* note 5, at 38, noting that this principle is reflected in Article 2(2) of the U.N. Charter.

[143] *See generally* CHENG, *supra* note 131, at 112-14. And *cf.* art. 26 of the Vienna Convention on the Law of Treaties, *supra* note 36, which provides: "Every treaty in force is binding upon the parties to it and must be performed by them in good faith." The Preamble of the Vienna Convention refers to "the *pacta sunt servanda* rule" as being "universally recognized."

[144] The concept of reparation is discussed in chapter 7. Generally, international law requires a state that has breached an international obligation to make reparation — i.e., to repair the harm or, to the extent that restoration of the *status quo ante* is not possible, to provide compensation and possibly other forms of relief (known as "satisfaction").

[145] *See* the Chorzow Factory case (Merits), P.C.I.J. (ser. A) No. 17, at 29.

[146] *See* the Chorzow Factory case (Indemnity; Jurisdiction), P.C.I.J,. (ser. A) No. 9, at 31, where the court described this principle as one that is "generally accepted in the jurisprudence of international arbitration, as well as by municipal courts."

[147] *See* the Eastern Greenland case, 1933 P.C.I.J. (ser. A/B) No. 53, at. 52, 62, 69; the Arbitral Award of the King of Spain on December 23 1906 case, 1960 I.C.J. 192, 209, 213; and the Temple of Preah Vihear case, 1962 I.C.J. 6, 22, 31, 32. *See* BROWNLIE, *supra* note 5, at 18.

[148] *See* BROWNLIE, *supra* note 5, at 18, referring to the *Free Zones* case, 1930 P.C.I.J. (ser. A) No. 24, at 12 (1930), and 1932 P.C.I.J. (ser. A/B) No. 46, at 167 (1932); and OPPENHEIM, *supra* note 5, n. 5, at 38, and § 124, discussing abuse of right, "including the maxim, *sic utere tuo ut alienum non laedas.*"

[149] *See* OPPENHEIM, *supra* note 5, n. 5, at pp. 38-39.

[150] Corfu Channel case, 1949 I.C.J. 4, 22.

Examples of principles in the second category (principles concerning the administration of justice) are that of *res judicata*,[151] that one may not be a judge in one's own case (*nemo judex in sua causa*), that the passage of time may be raised as a defense to certain claims,[152] and, in general, principles concerning evidence[153] and procedure, including jurisdiction.[154]

The first two categories of principles under Article 38(1)(c) contain those that are best known and most frequently utilized. The third category — principles of municipal law needed to fill gaps in international law — includes certain principles of domestic law that do not fit into the first two categories but which, like the principles in those categories, have been used by international tribunals needed to fill gaps in international law. Examples of principles in this category include the responsibility of a state for acts of its officials,[155] principles concerning interest[156] and the assessment of damages,[157] and principles or municipal law analogies that may be helpful in cases falling outside the ordinary scope of both international and domestic law, such as those involving international organizations and disputes between states and private corporations.[158]

The third and final issue raised by the formulation of Article 38(1)(c) is, what is meant by "civilized" nations? As Waldock has observed, this term has an "antiquated" look today.[159] Its obvious implication is that there are nations that are *un*civilized, something the modern international community is ill-disposed to accept.[160] The expression general principles of law recognized by "civilized nations" is therefore taken today to refer simply to such principles that are recognized by independent states,[161] or that are

---

[151] *See* Effect of Awards of the U.N. Administrative Tribunal case, 1954 I.C.J. 47, 53.

[152] *See* RESTATEMENT 3d, *supra* note 42, § 102 cmt. l. This principle has been applied chiefly with regard to claims by a state on behalf of its citizens.

[153] For example, in the Corfu Channel case, 1949 I.C.J. 4, at 18, the I.C.J. stated that circumstantial evidence is "admitted in all systems of law. . . ."

[154] *See generally* BROWNLIE, *supra* note 5, at 15-18 for a discussion of the use of these principles.

[155] *See* the Fabiani case, 10 UNRIAA 83, discussed in BROWNLIE, *supra* note 5, at 17.

[156] *See* the award of the Permanent Court of Arbitration in the *Russian Indemnity* case, Hague Court Reports, p. 297 (1912).

[157] *See, e.g.*, the Fabiani case, *supra* note 155.

[158] As to relations between international organizations and their employees, *see, e.g.*, the *Administrative Tribunal of ILO* case, 1956 I.C.J. 77, 85-86. There is a multitude of decisions of international arbitral tribunals in cases between states and private business organizations that have recourse to private law analogies. *See generally* OPPENHEIM, *supra* note 5, at 39 and the sources cited in n. 12.

[159] Waldock, *supra* note 135, at 65.

[160] The term may have been felt to be relevant in the colonial era (which substantially ended in the early 1960s), the period during which Article 38 was originally drafted. According to Waldock: "The intention in using it, clearly, was to leave out of account undeveloped legal systems so that a general principle present in the principal legal systems of the world would not be disqualified from application in international law merely by reason of its absence from, for example, the tribal law of a backward people." *Id.*

[161] *Id.*

"common to the major legal systems of the world."[162] It is not necessary to establish that a given principle figures in the law of every country.[163] It is sufficient if it is recognized in the world's principal legal systems.[164] However, owing both to the historical influences of colonialism and to contemporary initiatives to spread Western legal institutions to developing countries as well as those in Central and Eastern Europe, it is probably more likely than not that there will be a commonality of fundamental principles or concepts among the world's chief legal systems and even among most countries. It has not been the practice for tribunals, litigants or states in diplomatic exchanges to engage in "elaborate comparative studies of the legal systems of the world"[165] in order to establish the kinds of principles contemplated under paragraph (1)(c), however. Instead, the tendency — particularly in the case of tribunals — has been simply to refer to these basic legal concepts, sometimes without even qualifying them as being generally recognized or accepted.[166]

This concludes our consideration of the principal features of the source of international law identified in Article 38(1)(c). Before we move on to the "subsidiary means" referred to in subparagraph (1)(d), however, there are two remaining points regarding general principles of national law that merit brief mention. First, it is important not to confuse the kinds of principles referred to in Article 38(1)(c) with general principles of *international* law. Whereas the former are principles of *national*, or domestic law, as we have seen, the latter term is normally taken to refer to principles of international law — i.e., principles accepted by states as governing the relations among them. General principles of international law are ordinarily customary in nature, though they may also be reflected in treaties. The expression is commonly used to refer to principles of a fundamental nature, such as the sovereign equality of states,[167] reciprocity, freedom of the seas and good faith.[168]

The second point to be noted is that some of these general principles of international law have their origin in principles recognized by national legal systems.[169] There is thus the possibility of a relationship between certain general principles of international and the kinds of national law principles contemplated by Article 38(1)(c). Obviously, this can be a source of confusion. The distinction, however, is clear enough: general principles

---

[162] RESTATEMENT 3d, *supra* note 42, § 102(1)(c).

[163] *See* Waldock, *supra* note 135, at 66, stating that "it was never intended under paragraph (c) that proof should be furnished of the manifestation of a principle in every known *legal system* considered to be civilised . . ." (emphasis added).

[164] *See id.*; and RESTATEMENT 3d, *supra* note 42, § 102(1)(c) and cmt. l.

[165] Waldock, *supra* note 135, at 66. *See also* BROWNLIE, *supra* note 5, at 16.

[166] *See* Waldock, *supra* note 135, at 66-67; and BROWNLIE, *supra* note 5, at 16.

[167] This principle is expressed in art. 2(1) of the United Nations Charter.

[168] BROWNLIE, *supra* note 5, at 18, also mentions consent, finality of awards and settlements, the legal validity of agreements and domestic jurisdiction.

[169] *See* RESTATEMENT 3d, *supra* note 42, § 102 cmt. l.

of international law are principles accepted by states, through custom or agreement, as governing their mutual relations, while general principles of national law under paragraph (1)(c) are principles common to national legal systems that tribunals may apply directly to disputes before them. The elemental character of the latter kinds of principles makes it natural that states, through their practice, would accept certain relevant ones as principles of international law.

We have now considered general principles of national law as a source of international law under Article 38(1)(c) of the Court's Statute. Let us turn next to the "subsidiary means" for determining rules of international law identified in Article 38(1)(d).

[D] "Subsidiary Means": Judicial Decisions and Writings

Article 38(1)(d) of the Statute of the International Court of Justice allows the Court to employ in deciding disputes before it "judicial decisions and the teachings of the most highly qualified publicists of the various nations," but only as "*subsidiary* means for the determination of rules of law." The decisions of tribunals and the works of scholars are thus not sources of international law themselves, but supply material that may assist the Court in ascertaining rules of custom which, as we have seen, may be difficult to establish. They are thus often referred to as constituting "evidence" of international law.[170] Decisions and writings may be drawn upon not only by the I.C.J., but also by other tribunals[171] and governments in diplomatic exchanges.

In this section we consider three principal issues. First, as a preliminary matter, we look at the meaning of the opening proviso of subparagraph (d) concerning Article 59 of the Statute. Second, we examine the first category of evidence of international law, "judicial decisions" — which is accepted as including the decisions of both courts and arbitral tribunals. And third, we consider the second category of evidence, "teachings of the most highly qualified publicists of the various nations."

First, then, it is important to understand what is meant by the opening clause of subparagraph (d), "subject to the provisions of Article 59." Article 59 provides, in its entirety: "The decision of the Court has no binding force except between the parties and in respect of that particular case." This provision thus rules out any *stare decisis* or binding precedential effect of decisions of the Court,[172] while codifying the principle of

---

[170] *See, e.g.*, RESTATEMENT 3d, *supra* note 42, § 103, "Evidence of International Law."

[171] These may include international tribunals such as the European Court of Human Rights or ad hoc international arbitral tribunals, or national courts.

[172] *See* the German Interests in Polish Upper Silesia case, 1926 P.C.I.J., (ser. A) No. 7, at 19. BROWNLIE, *supra* note 5, at 20, while noting that Lauterpacht took the position that Article 59 refers to intervention under Article 63 rather than to the *stare decisis* effect of the Court's decisions, points out that this view is refuted by the records of the debate of the Committee of Jurists that drafted the Statute.

res judicata.[173] The rejection of *stare decisis* makes the I.C.J. more akin in this respect to tribunals in the Civil Law system than to those in Common Law countries.

Article 59 reflects the orthodox view that international law does not know the doctrine of *stare decisis.* Nevertheless, prior decisions are in fact quite influential in the practice of the I.C.J. as well as in that of other international tribunals,[174] and the Court refers regularly in its judgments to its own decisions and, less often, to awards of international arbitral tribunals.[175] This is not surprising since the fundamental idea of the rule of law implies a certain consistency, and the Court can achieve this by taking due account of what it has done in earlier, analogous cases.[176] The cross reference to Article 59 in subparagraph (d) may have been regarded as necessary in view of the subparagraph's reference to "judicial decisions," even though its terms make those decisions, along with scholarly writings, relevant only as "subsidiary means for the determination of rules of law."

Having considered the opening proviso of subparagraph (d), we may now turn to the two categories of evidence mentioned in that provision.

[1] Courts and Tribunals[177]

The first category of evidence of international law the I.C.J. is authorized to refer to is "judicial decisions." It makes sense for the Court to refer to previous decisions so it will not have to re-invent the wheel each time a question of law comes before it. Once the I.C.J. has determined that a particular rule of international law exists, it should be able to rely on that determination in subsequent cases. This also promotes the value of consistency, as mentioned above. Other international courts follow the same practice,[178] as do international arbitral tribunals.

But what precisely is intended by "judicial" decisions? Decisions of which courts? Does the term embrace arbitral awards? The answer is that recourse may, in theory, be had to virtually any judicial decision or arbitral award for evidence of international law. However, the stature of the tribunal is an important consideration, and decisions of the Court itself are obviously the most authoritative. Awards of other international courts

---

[173] *See also* art. 94 of the U.N. Charter, *supra* note 2, in which each member state "undertakes to comply with the decision of the [ICJ] in any case to which it is a party."

[174] To this effect, *see* RESTATEMENT 3d, *supra* note 42, § 103, cmt. b. Waldock explains: "It would indeed have been somewhat surprising if States had been prepared in 1920 to give a wholly new and untried tribunal explicit authority to lay down law binding upon all States." Waldock, *supra* note 135, at 91. *See* BROWNLIE, *supra* note 5, at 21-22.

[175] *See* Virally, *supra* note 31, at 150, 151; and LAUTERPACHT, *supra* note 110, at 155.

[176] BROWNLIE, *supra* note 5, at 21, notes that the Court even goes to the extent of distinguishing prior decisions, citing the *Interpretation of Peace Treaties* case, 1950 I.C.J. 65, at e.g., 72.

[177] *See generally* OPPENHEIM, *supra* note 5, at 41-42; BROWNLIE, *supra* note 5, at 19-23; Virally, *supra* note 31, at 149-52; and RESTATEMENT 3d, *supra* note 42, § 103(2) and cmt. b.

[178] E.g., the Court of Justice of the European Communities (ECJ) and the European Court of Human Rights (ECHR).

and of arbitral tribunals also have authoritative value, however, and the latter have been referred to by the Court in its judgments.[179] Even decisions of domestic courts are included in Article 38(1)(d), although the I.C.J. has not relied upon them explicitly. Such municipal court decisions may, however, constitute evidence of custom,[180] or may be useful because of their thorough examination of sources of international law on a given point.[181]

Finally, while Article 38 is directed to the I.C.J., it is probably clear by now that "judicial decisions" — in the wide sense of that expression — are of use not only to the Court, but also to arbitral tribunals and domestic courts seeking evidence of international law. Any of these courts or tribunals may look "up" to decisions of the I.C.J. for evidence of international law, consider their own prior decisions, or look "down" to judgments or awards of tribunals of lower stature.

We now turn to the second kind of evidence of international law Article 38 authorizes the Court to consider.

[2]   Publicists

In addition to "judicial decisions," Article 38(1)(d) identifies "the teachings of the most highly qualified publicists of the various nations" as a "subsidiary means for the determination of rules of law." While the ICJ has not as yet availed itself of this form of evidence in its judgments, references to the writings of scholars in the judges' separate and dissenting opinions suggest that they play an important role in the Court's decision making process.[182] In addition, scholarly works, or doctrine,[183] are also drawn upon by litigants before the I.C.J. and other international tribunals in their pleadings, as well as by arbitral tribunals[184] and national courts.[185]

---

[179] BROWNLIE, *supra* note 5, at 19, states that the I.C.J. and P.C.I.J. have referred to specific arbitral awards only five times, citing the *Polish Postal Service in Danzig* case, 1925 P.C.I.J. (Ser. B) No. 11, at 30; the *Lotus* case, 1927 P.C.I.J. (ser. A) No. 10, at 26; the *Eastern Greenland* case, P.C.I.J. (ser. A/B) No. 53, at 45-46; the *Nottebohm* case, 1953 I.C.J. 119; and the *Gulf of Maine* case, 1984 I.C.J. 302. *See generally* the sources cited in note 174, *supra*.

[180] This may be the case either because judicial decisions may constitute evidence of the practice of particular states (*see* BROWNLIE, *supra* note 5, at 22) or because the "cumulative effect of uniform decisions of national courts . . . afford[s] evidence of international custom. . . ." (OPPENHEIM, *supra* note 5, at 41).

[181] *See, e.g., The Paquete Habana, The Lola*, 175 U.S. 677 (1900); and Filartiga v. Pena-Irala, 630 F.2d 876 (2d Cir. 1980).

[182] *See* BROWNLIE, *supra* note 5, at 24.

[183] The French text of Article 38 uses the term "*la doctrine*" for the English term "teachings."

[184] *See, e.g.,* the *Texaco/Libya* Arbitration Award of 19 Jan. 1977, para. 83, 17 I.L.M. 1 (1978).

[185] For the United States, *see, e.g.,* The Paquete Habana, The Lola, 175 U.S. 677, 20 S.Ct. 290, 44 L.Ed. 320 (1900); Banco Nacional de Cuba v. Sabbatino, 376 U.S. 398, 84 S.Ct. 923, 11 L.Ed.2d 804 (1964); and Filartiga v. Pena-Irala, 630 F.2d 876 (2d Cir. 1980).

What explains the role of scholarly writings in determining rules of international law? Their importance is no doubt due in part to the difficulty of ascertaining rules of customary international law empirically, through the examination and evaluation of evidence of state practice. Scholars will be more likely to have the time and resources to undertake such work than judges, who must decide cases that come before them in a timely fashion. The U.S. Supreme Court explained the role of scholarly writings in *The Paquete Habana* in the following way:

> "where there is no treaty, and no controlling executive or legislative act or judicial decision, resort must be had to the customs and usages of civilized nations; and, as evidence of these, to the works of jurists and commentators, who by years of labor, research and experience, have made themselves peculiarly well acquainted with the subjects of which they treat. Such works are resorted to by judicial tribunals, not for the speculations of their authors concerning what the law ought to be, but for trustworthy evidence of what the law really is."[186]

Clearly, however, the authoritative value of a particular work depends to a great extent upon the stature of the author and the impartiality of the study itself (hence the words "most highly qualified"). The role of scholarly writings on the international level may be compared with that of the work of the American Law Institute (ALI) in the United States or that of "commentaries" by noted authorities in civil law countries.[187] The ALI produces "Restatements" of the law on various topics, such as Contracts, Torts, Property, and the Foreign Relations Law of the United States. U.S. courts regularly refer to Restatements in their judgments, for example, and sometimes even adopt Restatement sections verbatim as rules of decision.[188] Counterparts to the ALI on the international level include learned societies such as the Institute of International Law[189] and the International Law Association,[190] both of which are private organizations that have adopted drafts on various topics of international law.[191]

---

[186] The Paquete Habana, 175 U.S. 677, 700, 20 S.Ct. 290, 299, 44 L.Ed. 320 (1900).

[187] *See, e.g.*, ANTON HEINI, ET AL., KOMMENTAR ZUM BUNDESGESETZ ÜBER DAS INTERNATIONALE PRIVATRECHT (IPRG) VOM 1. JANUAR 1989 (1993); J. VON STAUDINGERS KOMMENTAR ZUM BÜRGERLICHEN GESETZBUCH (13th ed. 1996); and PIERRRE TERCIER, LA PARTIE SPÉCIALE DU CODE DES OBLIGATIONS (1988).

[188] *See, e.g.*, Nedlloyd v. Superior Court, 864 P.2d 1148, 1151, (Cal. 1992) (adopting § 187 of the Restatement 2nd of Conflict of Laws).

[189] Information on the history of the Institute of International Law is available at http://www.nobel.se/peace/laureates/1904/internationallawhistory.html.

[190] *See* the ILA's website, http://www.ila-hq.org/.

[191] *See, e.g.*, INSTITUTE OF INTERNATIONAL LAW, RESOLUTIONS OF THE INSTITUTE OF INTERNATIONAL LAW DEALING WITH THE LAW OF NATIONS: WITH AN HISTORICAL INTRODUCTION AND EXPLANATORY NOTES, COLLECTED AND TRANSLATED UNDER THE SUPERVISION OF AND EDITED BY JAMES BROWN SCOTT (2003).

An official group of experts on international law is the International Law Commission of the United Nations (ILC).[192] The thirty-four members of the ILC are elected by the General Assembly from a list of individuals nominated by governments. The Commission's Statute, or constituent instrument, requires that members be "persons of recognized competence in international law"[205] and provides that "in the Commission as a whole representation of the main forms of civilization and of the principal legal systems of the world should be assured."[206] In practice, this latter requirement has been fulfilled by dividing up seats on the Commission, according to a formula set out in a 1981 General Assembly resolution, on the basis of the five regions used in the United Nations to ensure that committees are composed in a way that is geographically representative: Africa, Asia, Eastern Europe, Latin America, and "Western Europe and Others" (the United States falls in the latter group).[207] This has led to charges that elections to the Commission have become unduly politicized, with insufficient emphasis being placed on the requirement that members possess "recognized competence in international law."[208] In response, it has been pointed out that inclusion on the ILC of some members who are not only international lawyers but also involved in the political domain — typically as ambassadors or ministers — enhances the Commission's chances of producing drafts that will prove to be acceptable by states.[209] But whether they hail from academia or government service, members of the ILC serve in their individual capacities, not as representatives of the countries of which they are nationals. Members are able to continue to hold their full-time positions outside the ILC, since the Commission meets at its seat in Geneva for only twelve weeks each year.[210]

---

[192] *See generally* UNITED NATIONS, THE WORK OF THE INTERNATIONAL LAW COMMISSION (5th ed. 1996); the ILC's website, http://www.un.org/law/ilc/; HERBERT BRIGGS, THE INTERNATIONAL LAW COMMISSION (1965); MOHAMMED EL BARADEI, THOMAS FRANCK & MARC TRACHTENBERG, THE INTERNATIONAL LAW COMMISSION: THE NEED FOR A NEW DIRECTION (1981); and IAN SINCLAIR, THE INTERNATIONAL LAW COMMISSION(1987).

[205] STATUTE OF THE INTERNATIONAL LAW COMMISSION, art.2, U.N. Doc. A/CN.4/4/Rev.2 (1982).

[206] *Id.*, art. 8.

[207] U.N.G.A. res. 36/39 (1981), operative para. 3, assigning seats as follows: Africa — 8 members; Asia — 7 members; Eastern Europe — 3 members; Latin America — 6 members; Western Europe and Other States — 8 members. In addition, one seat rotates as between Africa and Eastern Europe, and one as between Asia and Latin America. The ILC usually includes a member from each of the five states that are permanent members of the UN Security Council (China, France, Russia, the United Kingdom and the United States).

[208] *See, e.g.,* HERBERT BRIGGS, THE INTERNATIONAL LAW COMMISSION 42 (1965); and IAN SINCLAIR, THE INTERNATIONAL LAW COMMISSION 16-18 (1987).

[209] *See* SINCLAIR, *id.* at 16-18; and B.G. RAMCHARAN, THE INTERNATIONAL LAW COMMISSION 34 (1977).

[210] The Commission has of late divided its annual session, held during the months of May to August, into two parts. For details, *see* the reports of the Commission, *e.g.,* ILC, Report on the work of its fifty-fifth session (5 May to 6 June and 7 July to 8 August 2003), *available at* the ILC's website, http://www.un.org/law/ilc/.

The ILC's principal task is the "promotion of the progressive development of international law and its codification."[211] The Commission's Statute defines "codification of international law" as meaning "the more precise formulation and systematization of rules of international law in fields where there already has been extensive State practice, precedent and doctrine."[212] In discharging this function, the ILC has surveyed state practice[213] and prepared draft texts on many of the main subjects of international law, including the Law of the Sea, Diplomatic and Consular Relations, the Law of Treaties, State Succession, Jurisdictional Immunities of States and their Property, State Responsibility, the Law of the Non-Navigational Uses of International Watercourses, and International Criminal Law.[214] The ILC submits these drafts to the U.N. General Assembly, which may decide to convene an international conference open to all U.N. member states for the purpose of negotiating a treaty on the basis of the ILC's text. This has in fact occurred with regard to a number of the Commission's drafts.[215] It seems likely that this process is largely responsible for findings on a number of occasions by the International Court of Justice that particular treaties based on ILC drafts reflect customary international law.[216] Thus, the work of the International Law Commission constitutes a good example of how publicists can be of assistance to the I.C.J. and others in determining the rules of customary international law.

[E] Decisions *ex aequo et bono*

Paragraph 2 of Article 38 provides: "This provision shall not prejudice the power of the Court to decide a case *ex aequo et bono*, if the parties agree thereto." Since this paragraph would allow the Court to ignore the sources of international law enumerated in paragraph 1 of Article 38 it is important that we understand clearly its meaning.

---

[211] STATUTE OF THE INTERNATIONAL LAW COMMISSION, *supra* note 205, art. 1(1).

[212] *Id.*, art. 15, stating that the expression is used in this sense "for convenience." Similarly, "progressive development of international law" is defined for convenience to mean "the preparation of draft conventions on subjects which have not yet been regulated by international law or in regard to which the law has not yet been sufficiently developed in the practice of States." *Id.* For a brief history of efforts to develop and codify international law, *see* THE WORK OF THE INTERNATIONAL LAW COMMISSION, *supra* note 192, at 1-4.

[213] The actual surveys of state practice are usually performed by "special rapporteurs" appointed by the ILC to conduct this work and prepare draft articles for the Commission's consideration. The reports of the special rapporteurs are published in the ILC's Yearbook, in vol. 2, part 1. (Vol. 1 contains summary records of statements made in plenary sessions and vol. 2, part 2 contains the report of the ILC to the General Assembly.) For a detailed description of the ILC's methods of work *see id.*, at 13-21.

[214] The ILC's work on all of these subjects is described in *id.*, which also contains texts of treaties based on ILC drafts.

[215] *Id.*

[216] *See, e.g., Case Concerning the Gabčíkovo-Nagymaros Project* (Hungary/Slovakia), judgment of 25 Sept. 1997, 1997 I.C.J. 7, para. 46, at 38 (rules in the Vienna Convention on the Law of Treaties regarding termination and suspension of treaties).

[1]　The Unutilized Power

It must be noted at the outset that the Court has never used this power. Indeed, the jurisdiction of the Court to decide a case *ex aequo et bono* has apparently been accepted only once.[217] Therefore, it would perhaps be more accurate to say that the power has almost never been conferred upon the Court by states than to describe it as "unutilized."

But what is the meaning of the Latin expression, *"ex aequo et bono?"* The word *"aequo"* sounds very much like "equity," and indeed the Latin term may be translated as "equity" or "fairness."[218] But the Court's power to decide a case *ex aequo et bono* should not be confused with its authority to apply equity: it needs the consent of the parties to do the first, but not the second. As discussed in subsection [2] below, the better view is that the authority of the Court to apply equity derives from Article 38(1)(c) rather than from paragraph 2 of that article.[219] As the ICJ explained in the *Tunisia/Libya Continental Shelf Case*: "Application of equitable principles is to be distinguished from a decision *ex aequo et bono*. The Court can take such a decision only on condition that the Parties agree . . . , and the Court is then freed from the strict application of legal rules in order to bring about an appropriate settlement."[220]

It is generally agreed that, despite the somewhat confusing terminology, a decision *ex aequo et bono* is one that the Court may make without reference to any principles of law at all.[221] Instead, as the Permanent Court said in the *Free Zones* case, to authorize the Court to decide a case in this way would be to give it "power to prescribe a settlement disregarding rights recognized by it and taking into account considerations of pure expediency only. . . ."[222] The power may be viewed more positively, however. As Oppenheim puts it, the Court's decision "will not be based on the application of legal rules but on the basis of such other considerations as the court may in all the circumstances regard as right and proper."[223] For Brownlie, the power "involves elements of compromise and

---

[217] This was by Guatemala, in 1947, in a dispute with the UK over British Honduras. *See* Y.B. I.C.J., 1947-48, p. 155. *See also* OPPENHEIM, *supra* note 5, at 44 n. 7.

[218] The translation of the Latin term depends upon the context in which it is used. It may thus be variously translated as "evenness," "balance," "equality," etc.

[219] *But see* Virally, *supra* note 31, who, in describing the Court's power under Article 38(2), states: "Recourse to a species of equity makes it possible to take full account of the special circumstances in the case, without regard to necessarily general rules." *Id.* at 152. Similarly, OPPENHEIM, *supra* note 5, at 44, states that "equity may be used in the sense of Article 38(2)" of the Court's Statute. Brownlie observes that "the terminology of the subject is not well settled." BROWNLIE, *supra* note 5, at 26.

[220] 1982 I.C.J. 18, 60.

[221] *See, e.g.,* OPPENHEIM, *supra* note 5, at 44; and Virally, *supra* note 31, at 152.

[222] 1930 P.C.I.J. (ser. A) No. 24. *See* BROWNLIE, *supra* note 5, at 26.

[223] OPPENHEIM, *supra* note 5, at 44.

conciliation . . . ."**224** However it is viewed, this power has been given only sparingly by states, and then chiefly to arbitral tribunals.**225**

[2] "Equity" Distinguished

As already indicated, the power of the International Court of Justice to apply principles of equity in deciding a case should be seen as deriving from paragraph 1 of Article 38, not paragraph 2. This is so because in applying equity, the Court is exercising its "function . . . to decide in accordance with international law"**226** the dispute before it. We have just seen that the power that may be conferred upon the Court by states under Article 38(2) involves the opposite — namely, the authority to ignore international law in deciding the dispute before it.

A clear explanation of the authority of the Court to apply principles of equity was given in the Individual Opinion of Judge Manley O. Hudson in the *Diversion of Water from the Meuse* case:**227**

> "What are widely known as principles of equity have long been considered to constitute a part of international law, and as such they have often been applied by international tribunals. . . .
>
> The Court has not been expressly authorized by its Statute to apply equity as distinguished from law. . . . Article 38 of the Statute expressly directs the application of 'general principles of law recognized by civilized nations,' and in more than one nation principles of equity have an established place in the legal system. The Court's recognition of equity as a part of international law is in no way restricted by the special power conferred upon it to decide a case *ex aequo et bono*, if the parties agree thereto."**228**

Judge Hudson thus regarded principles of equity as being "general principles of law recognized by civilized nations" within the meaning of Article 38(1)(c) of the Court's statute. However, equity also plays an important role in certain norms of customary international law, and thus may qualify as a source of law under Article 38(1)(b).

Perhaps the most frequent use of equity by the Court today is in cases involving the delimitation of maritime boundaries.**229** In the *Tunisia/Libya Continental Shelf Case*, the Court examined the concept of equity and its role in international law as well as in the ICJ's jurisprudence. The Court explained:

---

224 BROWNLIE, *supra* note 5, at 26.

225 *See* the examples cited in OPPENHEIM, *supra* note 5, at 44, n. 7.

226 I.C.J. STATUTE, *supra* note 2, art. 38(1).

227 1937 P.C.I.J. (ser. A/B) No. 70, at 76-77.

228 *Id.*

229 The first of these cases were the *North Sea Continental Shelf Cases*, 1969 I.C.J. 3, 46-52.

> Equity as a legal concept is a direct emanation of the idea of justice. The Court whose task is by definition to administer justice is bound to apply it. In the course of the history of legal systems the term 'equity' has been used to define various legal concepts. It was often contrasted with the rigid rules of positive law, the severity of which had to be mitigated in order to do justice. In general, this contrast has no parallel in the development of international law; the legal concept of equity is a general principle directly applicable as law.[230]

In this passage the Court implicitly acknowledges the contrast between law and equity in the historical development of the common law system and emphasizes that there has been no counterpart to this in the evolution of international law. On the contrary, rather than being something separate, equity is part of international law. Yet, as we have already seen,[231] the Court stressed that in applying equitable principles it is not deciding a case *ex aequo et bono*: "The task of the Court in the present case is quite different: it is bound to apply equitable principles as part of international law, and to balance up the various considerations which it regards as relevant in order to produce an equitable result. . . . [T]his is very far from being an exercise of discretion or conciliation; nor is it an operation of distributive justice."[232] Thus, the Court, in applying principles of equity, regards itself as by no means exercising unbridled discretion — as it could in a decision *ex aequo et bono* — but rather as applying principles of law that call for an equitable result or are in other ways informed by equity.

The Court has drawn upon equity in cases involving other kinds of problems, as well.[233] For example, the Court had occasion to invoke a legal rule informed by equity in a case involving international watercourses. In its judgment in the *Gabčíkovo-Nagymaros Project* case, the Court referred to what it termed a state's "basic right to an equitable and reasonable sharing of the resources of an international watercourse."[234] The "right" in question is thus in effect measured in part by considerations of equity. While these are, by definition, flexible, the Court in that case had no difficulty in finding that the "basic right" had been infringed.[235]

---

[230] 1982 I.C.J. 18, 60.

[231] *See* text at note 230, *supra*.

[232] 1982 I.C.J. at 60.

[233] *E.g.*, fishing rights (the *Fisheries Jurisdiction Case* (U.K. v. Iceland), 1974 I.C.J. 3, 30-35); and division of a border-straddling pool (*Burkina Faso/Mali*, 1986 I.C.J. 554, at 631-33, where a Chamber of the Court applied equity *infra legem*, i.e., "that form of equity which constitutes a method of interpretation of the law in force, and is one of its attributes." *Id.* at 567-68.).

[234] *Case Concerning the Gabčíkovo-Nagymaros Project* (Hungary/Slovakia), judgment of 25 Sept. 1997, 1997 I.C.J. 7, para. 78, at 54. *See also id.* at 56.

[235] *Id.* at 56.

Despite the general acceptance of the ICJ's authority to apply equity as part of international law under Article 38(1) of its statute, doubts are sometimes expressed about whether equitable principles are sufficiently precise to be considered rules of international law.[236] One of the most trenchant criticisms came from Judge Gross in his dissenting opinion in the *Gulf of Maine* case, in relation to the use of equity in maritime delimitation cases:

> "[E]quity left, without any objective elements of control, to the wisdom of the judge reminds us that equity was once measured by 'the Chancellor's foot;' I doubt that international justice can long survive an equity measured by the judge's eye. When equity is simply a reflection of the judge's perception, the courts which judge in this way part company from those which apply the law."[237]

Judges doubtless do have a certain degree of freedom in applying equitable principles. However, even the application of rules of law to a given set of facts is hardly a mechanical exercise, as any first-year law student can attest. Application of equitable principles is no different. Moreover, the ICJ now has considerable experience with the application of equity and has developed a body of jurisprudence that will guide it in future cases. This should be of comfort to those who fear that the explicit application of equity introduces into international law an element of subjectivity, "detached from any established rules."[238]

---

[236] The literature contains a wealth of material on this issue. *See, e.g.,* Paul Reuter, *Quelques réflexions sur l'équité en droit international,* Révue Belge de droit International 165 (1980); and Jan Schneider, *The Gulf of Maine Case: The Nature of an Equitable Result,* 79 Am. J. Int'l L. 539 (1985).

[237] 1984 I.C.J. 246, 386.

[238] *Id.* at 388.

Chapter 4
THE LAW OF TREATIES

Synopsis

§ 4.01   INTRODUCTION

"Ever since the days of antiquity, Princes and States have concluded international treaties."[1] Yet because of the increasing interdependence of the members of the international community, the treaty is perhaps more important today than ever. A vital cornerstone of the international system, the treaty has been called an "essential instrument of international relations."[2]

---

[1] PAUL REUTER, INTRODUCTION TO THE LAW OF TREATIES 1 (1989).

[2] *Id.*

In this chapter we first consider several preliminary matters: the nature of treaties, which in some respects are the international community's counterpart to legislation (§ 4.02) but in others more closely resemble contracts (§ 4.03); and the relationship between treaties and customary international law (§ 4.04). We then turn to the main subject of the chapter, the law of treaties (§ 4.05), and consider how this body of law deals with the principal issues, from the making of treaties to their termination, as well as certain related questions. Next we touch upon the relationship between treaties and state responsibility (§ 4.06). Finally, we look at how international agreements are treated in the legal system of the United States (§ 4.07).

§ 4.02　TREATIES AS INTERNATIONAL "LEGISLATION"

Treaties perform a variety of functions in the relations between states and other international actors.[3] They may, for example, proclaim the aspirations of the international community,[4] lay down binding standards to govern aspects of its affairs,[5] or effect transactions between as few as two states.[6] But for our purposes we can view treaties as playing two main roles: they may serve as international legislation, or they may have the character of contracts between members of the international community. The present section touches on their role as legislation, while the following section illustrates how they serve as contracts.

National legislatures, or parliaments, enact legislation laying down rules that are binding within their states. We have seen that there is no international legislature, as such,[7] and that the international community instead relies upon different kinds of lawmaking processes, chiefly treaties and custom.[8] It has increasingly seen fit to use the vehicle of the treaty to "legislate" in fields of particular importance. This is a sign of both the maturation of the international legal system and the need for regulation of particular subjects at a level of specificity and detail that customary international law cannot provide.[9]

---

[3] *See generally id.* at 20-21 (discussing "Contractual treaties and law-making treaties"). For a collection of a variety of treaties covering a broad span of time, *see* Mark W. Janis & John E. Noyes, International Law 29-54 (3rd ed. 2006), reprinting agreements ranging from the Treaty between the Jews and the Romans (ca. 160 B.C.) and the Peace of Westphalia (1648) to the Kellogg-Briand Pact (1928) and the Hull-Lothian Agreement (1940).

[4] The Kellogg-Briand Pact (Renunciation of War as an Instrument of National Policy), 27 Aug. 1928, 2 Bevans 732, 46 Stat. 2343, T.S. 796, 94 L.N.T.S. 57, may be viewed as reflecting the aspirations of the signatories, although Nazi war criminals were charged with violating its provisions at Nuremberg.

[5] *See, e.g.*, the Vienna Convention on Diplomatic Relations, 18 Apr. 1961, 23 U.S.T. 3227, T.I.A.S. No. 7502, 500 U.N.T.S. 95; and the General Agreement on Tariffs and Trade 1994, Marrakesh, 15 April 1994, T.I.A.S.

[6] *See, e.g.*, The Cession of Alaska (U.S.-Russia), 30 Mar. 1867, 11 Bevans 1216, 15 Stat. 539, T.S. 301, in which Russia sold Alaska to the United States for $7,200,000 in gold (art. VI).

[7] *See* chapter 1, § 1.01.

[8] *See* chapter 3, § 3.03.

[9] The development of the treaty is discussed in Reuter, *supra* note 1, at 1-12.

Treaties may thus act as the international community's counterpart of national legislation. The number of treaties alone has increased markedly since World War II,[10] but their scope of coverage has also expanded considerably. International agreements now cover everything from human rights, refugees and disarmament to commodities, the environment and the law of the sea.[11] These are multilateral (as distinguished from bilateral) treaties, most of which are "universal" in character — that is, they are open to all members of the international community. Thus, the subjects they deal with are of global significance and the rules they lay down are designed to be applicable to all states.[12] Many of these agreements may be regarded as "lawmaking" treaties, a concept discussed in Chapter 3.[13]

While one may be tempted to conclude that the growth in the number and importance of treaties will be accompanied by a corresponding decline in the relevance of customary international law, this is true only in a sense. Treaties indeed cover fields formerly governed exclusively by custom, but they cannot occupy them entirely nor can they cover all aspects of international law. Just as the common law remains important in the United States despite the constant growth of statutory law,[14] so also will there always be a role for customary international law in the international legal system.[15] More fundamentally, treaties are binding by virtue of customary law. "In

---

[10] For example, the United Nations Treaty Series (U.N.T.S.), which includes all international agreements registered with the UN Secretariat since 1946, pursuant to art. 102 of the UN Charter, now contains over 50,000 treaties. The agreements are published in more than 2,100 volumes. The United Nations online database provides access to over 40,000 international agreements. *See* http://untreaty.un.org/English/treaty.asp. Among these agreements are major multilateral treaties for which the UN Secretary-General acts as depository. These alone number over 500. They are also available on the website just referred to. For an update on the practice of the Secretary-General as depositary of treaties. *See* Palitha T.B. Kohona, *Some Notable Developments in the Practice of the UN Secretary-General as Depositary of Multilateral Treaties: Reservations and Declarations*, 99 AM. J. INT'L L. 433 (2005).

[11] These categories are drawn from the UN treaty website's discussion of multilateral treaties deposited with the U.N. Secretary-General. *See* http://untreaty.un.org.

[12] While the rules are "designed" to be applicable to all states, they become binding for a state only after it ratifies the treaty and the treaty enters into force, as discussed below.

[13] *See* chapter 3, § 3.03 [A]. OPPENHEIM discusses what the authors refer to as "So-called law-making treaties" in § 583, at 1203-08 (describing them, at 1204, as "treaties concluded for the purpose of laying down general rules of conduct among a considerable number of states"). 2 OPPENHEIM'S INTERNATIONAL LAW § 583, at 1203 (R. Jennings & A. Watts 9th ed. 1992) (hereinafter OPPENHEIM).

[14] The same principle holds true for the civil law system, as well. In an extreme example, Professor Schlesinger notes that the drafters *Preussisches allgemeines Landrecht* (Prussian Code) of 1794 "tried to provide specific rules for every conceivable fact situation, and expressly prohibited the courts from amplifying those rules by 'interpretation'. Although the Prussian Code was a document of excessive length, containing many thousands of sections, it turned out soon after its enactment that there were fact situations which had not been foreseen by the draftsmen and which, consequently, were not covered by the provisions of the Code." RUDOLF B. SCHLESINGER, COMPARATIVE LAW 281-82 (4th ed. 1980).

[15] For evidence of this phenomenon, one need look no further than the ICJ's judgment in the *Gabčíkovo-Nagymaros* case, 1997 I.C.J. 7, discussed below. While the case involved a dispute over a 1977 treaty, customary international law played a significant role in the Court's decision.

that sense, international custom is even more central than the law of treaties since it is the very pillar on which treaties rest."[16] This is true not only of treaties that perform the function of international legislation, but also of treaties that are more akin to contracts between states.

§ 4.03 TREATIES AS INTERNATIONAL "CONTRACTS"

Treaties may also be seen as contracts between two or more states. This is true in at least three senses. First, as with contracts between natural or legal persons, treaties between states[17] are binding agreements which must be performed in good faith and may not be breached or terminated at the will of one of the parties except in accordance with the provisions of the treaty in question. Second, the rules of international law governing the making, performance and termination of treaties are in significant respects reminiscent of the domestic law of contracts,[18] as we will see. And third, as is often true of contracts on the domestic level, many treaties have as their purpose the consummation of a transaction of one kind or another.[19]

As we will see, however, there are two fundamental differences between treaties and private contracts, especially in relation to the second and third points above. First, unlike the treatment of contracts in some municipal legal systems, such as that of the United States, international law does not permit a party to a treaty to elect to breach it — for example, because it would be more efficient for it to do so than to continue performance — and pay damages to the other party. A breach is just that under the law of treaties. It entails the obligation to make reparation to the other party, but does not entitle the breaching party to terminate the treaty — though it may permit the other party to do so, at its election. And second, parties to domestic-law contracts do not have the option of making reservations, that is, of giving their consent to the terms of an agreement subject to specified conditions. This possibility is, however, open to parties to multilateral treaties to the extent permitted by the treaty in question. Indeed the multilateral treaty, especially those that are open to the entire international community, has no real counterpart in domestic legal systems, in terms of either the potential number of parties or the policy of allowing reservations in order to achieve maximum membership. These points will be considered further below. We will next consider the relationship between treaties — chiefly

---

[16] REUTER, *supra* note 1, at 22.

[17] As discussed in § 4.04, below, while treaties were traditionally agreements between states, it is now beyond doubt that international organizations may conclude treaties, as well.

[18] To this effect, *see* RESTATEMENT (THIRD) OF THE FOREIGN RELATIONS LAW OF THE UNITED STATES, Introductory Note to Part III, at 147 (1987) (hereinafter RESTATEMENT 3d), which adds: "The international law of international agreements, indeed, is derived in substantial part from general principles common to the contract laws of state legal systems. . . ."

[19] An apt example is the 1867 treaty by which Russia sold Alaska to the United States, *supra* note 6. *See also* the 1940 Hull-Lothian Agreement, 54 Stat. 2405, 12 Bevans 551.

those that function as international "legislation" but also those that are "contractual" in character — and customary international law.

§ 4.04 TREATIES AND CUSTOMARY INTERNATIONAL LAW

While treaties and custom are often treated separately for analytical purposes, there is in fact a close and complex relationship between these two sources of international law.[20] There are several key points to bear in mind in this connection.

First, as we saw in Chapter 3,[21] treaties are themselves binding by virtue of a norm of customary international law: *pacta sunt servanda*. As discussed below, this norm is in turn reflected in the instrument on which this chapter focuses, the Vienna Convention on the Law of Treaties.[22]

Second, we have also seen that treaties may codify norms of customary international law.[23] These treaties are often based on preparatory work by the International Law Commission of the United Nations (ILC).[24] The Vienna Convention is itself such an agreement.

And third, treaties may in fact generate customary norms. That is, a treaty may attract state practice which, when accompanied by *opinio juris*, eventually crystallizes into a norm of customary international law that binds even states that are not parties to the treaty. In the *locus classicus* on this issue, the *North Sea Continental Shelf* cases, the International Court of Justice recognized that "this process is a perfectly possible one and does from time to time occur."[25] The Court, however, was careful to note that "this result is not lightly to be regarded as having been attained."[26] Specifically, the Court referred to two basic requirements that must be satisfied for a treaty provision to generate a customary norm. First, the provision must "be of a fundamentally norm-creating character".[27] And second, "the other elements usually regarded as necessary before a conventional rule can be considered to have become a general rule of international law" must be satisfied.[28]

---

[20] *See, e.g.*, Richard Baxter, *Treaties and Custom*, 129 RECUEIL DES COURS 25 (1970); ANTHONY D'AMATO, THE CONCEPT OF CUSTOM IN INTERNATIONAL LAW 103-66 (1971); REUTER, *supra* note 1, at 107-09; and IAN SINCLAIR, THE VIENNA CONVENTION ON THE LAW OF TREATIES 252-58 (2nd ed. 1984).

[21] *See* chapter 3, § 3.03[A].

[22] Vienna Convention on the Law of Treaties, 22 May 1969, art. 26, U.N. Doc. A/CONF. 39/27, at 289, 1155 U.N.T.S. 331 (1969), reprinted in 8 I.L.M. 679 (1969) (hereafter Vienna Convention).

[23] *See* chapter 3, § 3.03[A].

[24] *See id.*, especially note 51.

[25] 1969 I.C.J. 3, 41, para. 71. The relationship between treaties and custom is also discussed in the *Military and Paramilitary Activities* case, 1986 I.C.J. 14, e.g., paras. 176.

[26] 1969 I.C.J. at 41.

[27] *Id.*, para. 72.

[28] *Id.*, para. 73.

As to the first requirement, the Court was not satisfied that the provision involved in the case was "of a fundamentally norm-creating character," for three reasons: First, the provision — concerning delimitation of the continental shelf [29] — imposed a primary obligation to effect delimitation by agreement;[30] the Court regarded this as "an unusual preface to what is claimed to be a potential general rule of law" (i.e., delimitation using the "equidistance-special circumstances principle" contained in Article 6(2) of the 1958 Geneva Convention on the Continental Shelf[31]). Second, the role played by "special circumstances" in relation to the asserted rule, as well as the uncertainty as to the meaning and scope of that concept, raised further doubts. And finally, the fact that reservations are permitted to the article "add[ed] considerably to the difficulty" of regarding the equidistance principle as having passed into custom.[32]

Regarding the second requirement, that the "other elements" necessary for a conventional rule to become one of custom be satisfied, the Court focused on the need for either (a) "a very widespread and representative participation in the convention . . ., provided it included that of States whose interests were specially affected," [33] or (b) "State practice, including that of States whose interests are specially affected, [that was] both extensive and virtually uniform in the sense of the provision invoked — and should moreover have occurred in such a way as to show a general recognition that a rule of law or legal obligation is involved."[34] (It is noteworthy that in neither case did the Court require the passage of a considerable period of time, providing the other conditions were met.[35]) In the latter connection, the Court emphasized the importance of establishing that the states involved acted in the way they did out of a sense of legal obligation. The Court explained:

> "The need for such a belief, i.e., the existence of a subjective element, is implicit in the very notion of the *opinio juris sive necessitatis*. The states concerned must therefore feel that they are conforming to what amounts to a legal obligation. The frequency, or even habitual character of the acts is not in itself enough."[36]

---

[29] Geneva Convention on the Continental Shelf, art. 6(2), 499 U.N.T.S. 311 (1958).

[30] *Id.*, art. 6(2), first sentence.

[31] *Id.*, art. 6(2). Article 6(2) provides as follows:

"2. Where the same continental shelf is adjacent to the territories of two adjacent states, the boundary of the continental shelf shall be determined by agreement between them. In the absence of agreement, and unless another boundary line is justified by special circumstances, the boundary shall be determined by application of the principle of equidistance from the nearest points of the baselines from which the breadth of the territorial sea of each state is measured."

[32] 1969 I.C.J. at 41, para. 72.

[33] *Id.*, para. 73.

[34] *Id.*, para. 74.

[35] *Id.*, paras. 73 and 74.

[36] *Id.*, para. 77.

Because the Court found that the foregoing conditions were not met, it concluded that a norm of custom had not been generated by the Geneva Convention.[37]

The foregoing brief discussion has attempted to indicate the basic ways in which treaties and custom are interrelated. This subject and the others we have considered up to this point are, however, only background for the focus of this chapter, which is the law of treaties. Let us therefore now turn to the legal framework for international agreements that is provided by the Vienna Convention on the Law of Treaties.

§ 4.05 THE VIENNA CONVENTION ON THE LAW OF TREATIES

The Vienna Convention on the Law of Treaties[38] — sometimes called the "treaty on treaties"[39] — was concluded on May 23, 1969, at a diplomatic conference held under United Nations auspices at Vienna,Austria. Negotiations at the conference were based on a set of draft articles prepared by the UN International Law Commission.[40] Partly for this reason, a number of the provisions of the Vienna Convention are regarded as codifications of customary international law.[41] For example, in the *Gabčíkovo-Nagymaros* case, the International Court of Justice noted that "it has several times had occasion to hold that some of the rules laid down in [the Vienna] Convention might be considered as a codification of existing customary law."[42]

The scope of the Vienna Convention is defined in Article 1: "The present Convention applies to treaties between States."[43] Two elements of this provision merit brief attention. First, the scope of the Convention is

---

[37] *Id.*, para. 81.

[38] 1155 U.N.T.S. 331, 8 I.L.M. 679 (1969). *See generally* ANTHONY AUST, MODERN TREATY LAW AND PRACTICE (2000); RESTATEMENT 3d., *supra* note 18, §§ 301, 311-313, 321-325; REUTER, *supra* note 1; and SINCLAIR, *supra* note 20.

[39] Richard Kearney & Robert Dalton, *The Treaty on Treaties*, 64 AM. J. INT'L L. 495 (1970).

[40] *See* the Commission's final report on the law of treaties, [1966] 2 Y.B. Int'l. L. Comm'n 10, paras. 9-38, U.N. Doc. A/6309/Rev.1. On the International Law Commission (ILC), *see* chapter 3, § 3.03[D][2].

[41] *See, e.g.*, RESTATEMENT 3d, *supra* note 18, Introductory Note to Part III, International Agreements, at 145 ("This Restatement accepts the Vienna Convention as, in general, constituting a codification of the customary international law governing international agreements. . . .").

[42] *Case Concerning the Gabčíkovo-Nagymaros Project* (Hungary/Slovakia), judgment of 25 Sept. 1997, 1997 I.C.J. 7, para. 46, at 38. The Court continued: "The Court takes the view that in many respects this applies to the provisions of the Vienna Convention concerning the termination and the suspension of the operation of treaties, set forth in Articles 60 to 62 (see *Legal Consequences for States of the Continued Presence of South Africa in Namibia (South West Africa) notwithstanding Security Council Resolution 276 (1970), Advisory Opinion, I.C.J. Reports 1971*, p. 47, and *Fisheries Jurisdiction (United Kingdom v. Iceland), Jurisdiction of the Court, Judgment, I.C.J. Reports 1973*, p. 18; see also *Interpretation of the Agreement of 25 March 1951 between the WHO and Egypt, Advisory Opinion, I.C.J. Reports 1980*, pp. 95-96)" (italics in original).

[43] Vienna Convention, *supra* note 22, art. 1.

limited to "treaties." This term is given a very specific meaning in Article 2 and will be discussed in section [A] below. Second, the Convention only applies to treaties between "States." As discussed in Chapters 1 (§ 1.02) and 5, states are the principal subjects of international law and, historically, were effectively its only addressees. Classically, therefore, treaties were agreements between states. This is reflected in the definition of the term "treaty" in Article 2(1)(a) of the Vienna Convention, as we will see.

However, other actors are becoming increasingly important on the international scene, including international organizations. It is now unquestioned that these organizations may conclude treaties with states, providing they have been given the capacity to do so in the agreements that create them. This development is reflected in the conclusion of the 1986 Vienna Convention on the Law of Treaties between States and International Organizations or between International Organizations.[44] Thus the 1969 Vienna Convention deals with treaties between states, while that of 1986 governs treaties as to which at least one of the parties is an international organization. The two conventions are quite similar, with only those adaptations of the 1969 convention having been made that were necessary to accommodate the different character of international organizations. Since our focus is on treaties between states, let us now turn to the concept of "treaty" as the term is used in the 1969 Convention.

[A] What Is a "Treaty?"

The Vienna Convention defines the term "treaty" in Article 2 as "an international agreement concluded between States in written form and governed by international law, whether embodied in a single instrument or in two or more related instruments and whatever its particular designation;. . . ."[45] Reuter suggests a broader definition: "A treaty is an expression of concurring wills attributable to two or more subjects of international law and intended to have legal effects under the rules of international law."[46] We will focus on the Vienna Convention's definition but will draw upon aspects of Reuter's, as well as others,[47] to enrich our understanding of the concepts involved.

The definition of the term "treaty" in the Vienna Convention, which is consistent with customary international law,[48] contains a number of elements. The first is that a treaty is an "international agreement." Later elements — that the agreement is between "states" and that it is "governed by international law" — assist in understanding what is meant by the

---

[44] 21 March 1986, 25 I.L.M. 543 (1986). This convention was also based on work by the International Law Commission. *See* [1986] 2 Y.B. Int'l L. Comm'n, pt. 2, 9-77

[45] Vienna Convention, *supra* note 22, art. 2(1)(a).

[46] REUTER, *supra* note 1, at 23.

[47] For various definitions of the term "treaty," *see* 14 M. WHITEMAN, DIGEST OF INTERNATIONAL LAW 1-11 (1970) (hereafter WHITEMAN).

[48] To this effect, *see* OPPENHEIM, *supra* note 13, § 582, at 1199.

term "international." The term "agreement" is perhaps best explained by Reuter's concept of "an expression of concurring wills." As with domestic law contracts, disputes may arise as to exactly what it is that was agreed upon, but this would ordinarily be a matter of interpretation of the language of the agreement[49] as opposed to a ground for finding no agreement at all.

The second element of the definition is that the agreement must be concluded "between States." Thus the Vienna Convention does not apply to agreements between states and international organizations, or between two or more international organizations. These are governed by the 1986 Vienna Convention, as we have seen. However, the fact that the Vienna Convention applies only to agreements between states does not mean that agreements between states and other subjects of international law or between those other subjects have no legal effect. Nor does it mean that the rules of international law reflected in the Vienna Convention, but enjoying an independent existence as customary norms, do not apply to international agreements other than those between states.

The third element of the definition is that the international agreement must be "in written form." It is entirely possible for states to conclude a binding agreement that is not in writing,[50] though this would be unusual. Such an agreement would not, however, be governed by the Vienna Convention.

The fourth element is that the agreement must be "governed by international law." The counterpart of this element in Reuter's definition is the phrase "intended to have legal effects under the rules of international law." As Reuter's definition suggests somewhat more clearly, the requirement that the agreement be "governed by international law" has two main implications. First, the states concerned must intend to create binding legal rights and obligations between themselves.[51] Whether such an intent exists depends on the circumstances of each case. The International Court of Justice found an intent to create rights and obligations under international law in *Qatar v. Bahrain*,[52] where minutes of a meeting signed by the foreign ministers of the two states were held to

---

[49] Interpretation of treaties is governed by arts. 31-33 of the Vienna Convention, *supra* note 22.

[50] This possibility is recognized in art. 3 of the Vienna Convention, *supra* note 22. In the *Eastern Greenland* case, the Permanent Court of International Justice held that an oral declaration by the Norwegian Foreign Minister, M. Ihlen, made in the context of negotiations and involving a *quid pro quo*, gave rise to a legal obligation binding upon his country. 1933 P.C.I.J. (ser. A/B) No. 53. Similarly, the ICJ in the *Nuclear Test Cases* held that unilateral public declarations, made orally by French officials, including the president, not in the context of negotiations and not involving a *quid pro quo*, gave rise to a legal obligation binding upon France. 1974 I.C.J. 99, 253, 457.

[51] See the ILC's commentary, art. 2(6), [1966] 2 Y.B. Int'l. L. Comm'n 189.

[52] 1994 I.C.J. 112. *See also* the *Aegean Sea Continental Shelf Case* (Jurisdiction), 1978 I.C.J. 1, 39, in which the Court stated that "it knows of no rule of international law which might preclude a joint communiqué from constituting an international agreement," although it concluded that the communiqué in question did not have that effect.

constitute a treaty. As in that case, registration of the instrument or instruments in question with the United Nations may provide evidence of intent to create a treaty.[53] However, the intent to create a legal relationship is distinct from the intent to create a moral obligation or political commitment. This is exemplified by words of obligation, most commonly "shall," but also "agree," "undertake" and the like. Obviously, references to "rights" and "obligations" are also indicators of intent to create a legal relationship. Terminology such as "should" and "will" do not typically indicate such an intent and are more commonly found in non-treaty MOUs.[54]

The second major implication of the expression "governed by international law" is that the states involved must not have intended the agreement to be subject to domestic law. It is possible that states may decide to conclude agreements subject to municipal law, concerning leases of land[55] or construction projects, for example, "but these will be more in the nature of private law contracts than international treaties."[56]

The fifth element of the definition is that the international agreement may be "embodied in a single instrument or in two or more related instruments." While many treaties are embodied in a single instrument, it is not uncommon for states to conclude an agreement through an "exchange of notes." This is generally accomplished by one state sending a diplomatic note containing the proposed text of an agreement to another state and the other state responding that it accepts the first state's proposal. The "offer," or proposal, and "acceptance" together comprise a treaty consisting of "two . . . related instruments."

The sixth and final element of the definition is that an instrument may be a treaty "whatever its particular designation." That is, the name or title given to an instrument is immaterial so long as the other requirements are satisfied. Indeed, treaties go by many names — e.g., convention, agreement, compact, accord, protocol, act, exchange of notes. It should be noted, however, that the title used for an instrument may be an indication that the parties did not intend to create legal obligations. This can be the case with the title "memorandum of understanding" (MOU), for example. But the critical issue is whether the parties intended to conclude a treaty, not what they called the document. Even an instrument entitled "MOU" may

---

[53] *See, e.g.,* the *Qatar v. Bahrain* case, 2001 I.C.J. 40, where the alleged agreement (signed minutes of a meeting) was registered by one of the parties; the other party (Bahrain) protested the registration. Article 102(1) of the U.N. Charter provides that "Every treaty . . . entered into by any Member of the United Nations . . . shall as soon as possible be registered with the Secretariat and published by it." Para. 2 of that article provides that unregistered treaties may not be invoked before any U.N. organ, including the ICJ.

[54] The expression "non-treaty MOUs" has been used deliberately in recognition of the fact that an instrument that is entitled an "MOU" may in fact be a treaty, as discussed below.

[55] *See* AUST, *supra* note 38, at 25, giving the example of a lease of land for an embassy.

[56] OPPENHEIM, *supra* note 13, at 1200 n. 7.

therefore — and often does in United States practice[57] — constitute a "treaty," in the international law sense of that term.

An important point to note concerns an element that is not included in the Vienna Convention's definition: signature. While treaties are often, perhaps usually, signed by the parties, an instrument does not have to be signed to be a treaty.[58] Again, signature may provide evidence of intent to be bound, for example, but it is not in itself a prerequisite to the conclusion of a treaty.[59]

[B]   The Making of Treaties

[1]   General

How treaties are made seems simple enough on the surface: representatives of the states involved meet with each other, reach agreement on a text through negotiations, and indicate their acceptance of the text in some manner, often by signature. In fact, however, the "conclusion" of treaties is, as Reuter has described it, "a complex process."[60] "Conclusion of Treaties" is dealt within Part II, Section 1 of the Vienna Convention, but the term "conclusion" is not itself defined.

The term may in fact be understood in either a narrow or a broad sense. The narrow meaning of the term refers to the moment in time when the states involved have definitively expressed their intention to be bound.[61] It is at that moment that the states are said to have "concluded" the treaty. In its broad sense the term "conclusion" of treaties refers to a process, a "whole set of procedures involving various instruments, whereby international treaties come into existence."[62] Thus, the section of the Vienna Convention on conclusion of treaties contains 13 articles, on subjects ranging from the capacity of states to conclude treaties and full powers, to adoption and authentication of the text and the means by which consent to be bound may be expressed. We will touch upon several of these subjects here; the reader is encouraged to refer to the Vienna Convention or secondary sources[63] for additional detail.

---

[57] *See* AUST, *supra* note 38, at 31-34. The head of the treaty section of the Legal Adviser's Office in the U.S. Department of State has estimated that MOUs probably constitute ca. 65% of United States treaty practice. Interview of 25 Aug. 2000. Again, the term "treaty" is used here in its international law sense, not in the sense of Article II of the U.S. Constitution, which requires Senate advice and consent as discussed below.

[58] *Cf. also* arts. 12 and 13 of the Vienna Convention, from which it is clear that signature is not necessary.

[59] *See* AUST, *supra* note 38, at 24.

[60] REUTER, *supra* note 1, at 44.

[61] *Id.* at 43.

[62] *Id.*

[63] *See, e.g.,* AUST, *supra* note 38, chs. 4-7.

[a] Overview of the Treaty-Making Process

The following is an overview of the steps involved in the treaty-making process.[64] The process can be quite simple if only two states are involved but grows more complex with the participation of additional states. The main steps, which can be reduced or combined in the case of bilateral treaties, are as follows:

- Ensure all participants have the proper credentials and/or full powers[65] — i.e., that they are authorized to represent their countries in the negotiation and/or conclusion of the treaty.

- Hold negotiations, in small meetings for bilateral treaties and conferences for multilateral treaties.

- Adopt the full text of the treaty.[66] The states participating in the negotiations may have agreed on each individual provision of the treaty, but they must adopt the text as a whole. For bilateral treaties, this is usually accomplished by initialing, but sometimes by signature.[67] Except for a treaty prepared at an "international conference" (a term which the Vienna Convention does not define), "the consent of *all* the States participating in its drawing up" is required. For multilateral treaties adopted at international conferences, a two-thirds majority vote is generally required.[68] But today, adoption by "consensus" is probably the norm at conferences. Voting rules are determined by the rules of procedure adopted by the conference in question; the Vienna Convention's provisions apply in default of such rules.

- Authenticate the text.[69] This establishes that the text is definitive and authentic. It may be done together with adoption, in one step, as is usually the case for treaties negotiated within the United Nations.[70] The participating states may agree on the procedure for authenticating a treaty. Failing such agreed procedure, the Vienna Convention provides for several optional methods.[71]

---

[64] For more detailed discussions, *see id.*; and SINCLAIR, *supra* note 20, ch. 2, at 29-50.

[65] On "Full powers," *see* Vienna Convention, *supra* note 22, art. 7. The term "full powers" is defined in *id.*, art. 2(1)(c).

[66] On "Adoption of the text," *see id.*, art. 9.

[67] *See* AUST, *supra* note 38, at 66-67.

[68] Vienna Convention, *supra* note 22, art. 9(2), requiring such a vote, "unless by the same majority they shall decide to apply a different rule."

[69] On "Authentication of the text," *see id.*, art. 10.

[70] AUST, *supra* note 38, at 73.

[71] Thus, authentication of a treaty's text may be effected by "the signature, signature *ad referendum* or initialling by the representatives of [the participating states] of the text of the treaty or of the Final Act of a conference incorporating the text." Vienna Convention, *supra* note 22, art. 10(b).

- Express consent to be bound.[72] It is not enough for a state to adopt the text of a treaty or to authenticate the text. It must also express its consent to be bound by the treaty. As discussed further in subsection [c] below, this may be accomplished in a variety of ways, including signature, ratification, "or by any other means if so agreed."[73] However, even if a state has consented to be bound it is not necessarily bound by the treaty. For the latter to occur, the treaty must enter into force for that state.

- Take any other steps that are necessary for the treaty to enter into force. In the absence of a provision in the treaty to the contrary, the treaty will enter into force when all "negotiating states"[74] have consented to be bound.[75] This will often make sense for bilateral treaties: unless the domestic law of the states involved requires some further procedure, it is practical for a bilateral treaty to enter into force upon consent to be bound. In the case of multilateral treaties, however, especially those open to a large number of states, it would often be impractical to require that all negotiating states consent to be bound for the treaty to enter into force. Therefore, multilateral treaties normally provide that they will enter into force a certain number of days after the deposit with the treaty's depositary of a specified number of instruments of ratification. Only on that date — i.e., only when the treaty has entered into force — will the states that have expressed their "consent to be bound" actually be bound legally by the treaty. They then become "parties"[76] to the treaty; before entry into force they are not "parties" but may be referred to as "contracting states"[77] — a more general term which also applies to states that have consented to be bound, but for which the treaty has not entered into force.

The foregoing summarizes the basic steps in the treaty-making process. It is important to bear in mind when considering this process that a particular procedural device, such as signature or ratification, may have different legal effects depending upon the context. Thus, signature, for example, may only have the legal effect of authenticating

---

[72] On consent to be bound, *see* Vienna Convention, *supra* note 22, arts. 11-17; and subsection [c] below.

[73] "Means of expressing consent to be bound by a treaty" are set forth in *id.*, art. 11. That article provides that a state may express its consent to be bound by "signature, exchange of instruments constituting a treaty, ratification, acceptance, approval or accession, or by any other means if so agreed."

[74] The term "negotiating state" is defined in art. 2(1)(e) of the Vienna Convention, *id.*, as "a State which took part in the drawing up and adoption of the text of the treaty".

[75] *Id.*, art. 24.

[76] Article 2(1)(g) of the Vienna Convention, *id.*, defines "party" as "a State which has consented to be bound by the treaty and for which the treaty is in force".

[77] Article 2(1)(f) of the Vienna Convention, *id.*, defines "contracting State" as "a State which has consented to be bound by the treaty, whether or not the treaty has entered into force".

the text of a treaty; or it may indicate authentication plus a willingness to continue the procedure (leading to consent to be bound, etc.); or it may result in authentication plus consent to be bound;[78] or, it may indicate only consent to be bound.[79] Signature may also have the effect of bringing the treaty into force.[80] The effect of a particular procedural device in a given case depends upon the context and the provisions of the treaty.

[b]   Obligations Prior to Entry Into Force

We have just seen that signature, one of the procedural devices used in the treaty-making process, can have a number of different legal effects. Yet another legal effect of signing a treaty is provided for in Article 18 of the Vienna Convention, which deals with the rather counterintuitive notion of obligations of states prior to a treaty's entry into force. Article 18 provides, in essence, that if a state takes certain steps in relation to a treaty, such as (a) signing a treaty subject to ratification, or (b) expressing its consent to be bound to a treaty that has not yet entered into force, the state has an obligation "to refrain from acts which would defeat the object and purpose of [the] treaty. . . ."[81] Thus the state is under this fundamental obligation in relation to the treaty even though it is not yet legally bound by it, either as in case (a) above because it has not yet expressed its consent to be bound, or as in case (b) because the treaty has not yet entered into force. As Reuter explains, the rationale for this obligation is that "The negotiating States . . . owe each other a duty of loyalty in their conduct with respect to the proposed treaty. They should not embark on a treaty commitment and at the same time defeat its purpose."[82]

---

[78] On the latter, *see id.*, art. 12, "Consent to be bound by a treaty expressed by signature".

[79] *Id.* On the different possible effects of signature, *see* REUTER, *supra* note 1, at 45.

[80] *See* art. 24 of the Vienna Convention, *supra* note 22, providing in part that a treaty enters into force in accordance with its provisions or in such manner as the negotiating states may agree.

[81] Article 18 provides as follows:

Article 18

Obligation not to defeat the object and purpose of a treaty prior to its entry into force

A State is obliged to refrain from acts which would defeat the object and purpose of a treaty when:

(a)   it has signed the treaty or has exchanged instruments of constituting the treaty subject to ratification, acceptance or approval, until it shall have made its intention clear not to become a party to the treaty; or

(b)   it has expressed its consent to be bound by the treaty, pending the entry into force of the treaty and provided that such entry into force is not unduly delayed.

Vienna Convention, *supra* note 22, art. 18.

[82] REUTER, *supra* note 1, at 52. For the preparatory work on art. 18, *see* THE VIENNA CONVENTION ON THE LAW OF TREATIES: TRAVAUX PRÉPARATOIRES 163-67 (Dr. Ralf Gunter Wetzel ed., Frankfurt am Main, 1978).

According to Aust, "There is virtually no practice in the application of the provision. . . ."[83] Therefore, it is not always a simple matter to determine whether a state has engaged in conduct "which would defeat the object and purpose of a treaty". It is clear that an act that would constitute a breach of the treaty if it were in force is not enough — unless possibly the breach would be so serious as to constitute a "material" breach.[84] That is to say, Article 18 clearly does not mean that a state is *bound* by a treaty that is not in force for it simply because it has taken one of the enumerated steps in relation to the treaty. However, the state clearly should not do anything that would render the treaty pointless and probably should not even engage in conduct that would undermine the treaty or its *raison d'être.*

A recent illustration of practice in relation to Article 18 involved the position of the United States on the 1998 Rome Statute of the International Criminal Court.[85] While the United States signed the Rome Statute, before ratifying the treaty it changed its position to one of opposition to the agreement. Accordingly, the United States Government sent the following communication to the United Nations Secretary-General:

> "This is to inform you, in connection with the Rome Statute of the International Criminal Court adopted on July 17, 1998, that the United States does not intend to become a party to the treaty. Accordingly, the United States has no legal obligations arising from its signature on December 31, 2000. The United States requests that its intention not to become a party, as expressed in this letter, be reflected in the depositary's status lists relating to this treaty."[86]

When read in light of the text of Article 18, it seems clear that the United States' intent in formulating this communication was to (a) "ma[ke] its intention clear not to become a party to the [Rome Statute], under Article 18(a)" and thus (b) to free itself from the obligation "to refrain from acts which would defeat the object and purpose of [that] treaty."

[c] Consent to be Bound

Given the importance of a state's consent to be bound by a treaty, one might think that there would be one method of expressing consent to be

---

[83] AUST, *supra* note 38, at 94. That author does refer, however, to "the apparently only reported decision" involving this rule, in which a Greco-Turkish Mixed Arbitral Tribunal found in 1928 that "a Turkish seizure of Greek property before the entry into force for Turkey of the Treaty of Lausanne was invalid, since if the treaty had then been in force it would have been a material breach." *Id.*, at 95. *See* Megalidis v. Turkey, 8 RECUEIL DES DECISIONS DES TRIBUNAUX MIXTES 386 (Turkish-Greek Mixed Arb. Trib., 26 July 1928), reprinted in 4 I.L.R. 395, 1927/28 ANN. DEG. PUB. INT'L L. 395 (Arnold D. McNair & H. Lauterpacht eds. 1931).

[84] *See* the Greco-Turkish arbitration referred to in the previous footnote. We will consider the concept of "material breach" below in connection with art. 60 of the Convention, which defines that term in its paragraph 3.

[85] July 17, 1998, 37 I.L.M. 1002 (1998).

[86] Communication received by the Secretary-General on 6 May 2002, as quoted on the U.N. treaty website, http://untreaty.un.org.

bound that is applicable to all treaties. This is not the case, however. As with most of the other steps in the treaty-making process, consent to be bound may be expressed in a number of ways.

Article 11 of the Vienna Convention provides that a state's consent to be bound by a treaty "may be expressed by signature, exchange of instruments constituting a treaty, ratification, acceptance, approval or accession, or by any other means if so agreed." Let us take these methods up in turn.

Signature: We have already seen that signature may have a number of different legal effects. Despite common lay usage of the term "signatory" to refer to a state that is bound by a treaty, therefore, caution must be exercised in assessing whether in a particular case signature is indeed an effective method of expressing consent to be bound. (Even if it is, the state will not be bound by the treaty unless and until it is in force for it, as we have seen.) It is not unusual today for signature to have this effect in the case of bilateral treaties, although some states would not agree to such an effect of signature because their own domestic requirements would not allow it.[87] In fact, it is possible that signature of a bilateral treaty may not only indicate consent to be bound but also bring the treaty into force.[88] For multilateral treaties, ratification is ordinarily required by the terms of the agreement. Indeed, most treaties, whether bilateral or multilateral, contain a clear indication of the manner in which they will come into force.[89] Article 12 of the Vienna Convention takes this into account, but also provides for other situations — involving either agreement by the negotiating states or the intention of the state in question — in which signature constitutes an expression of a state's consent to be bound.

Exchange of instruments constituting a treaty: As we saw when discussing the Vienna Convention's definition of the term "treaty," a treaty may take the form of an exchange of notes or other instruments, such as letters. In fact, according to Aust, as many as "one-third of the treaties registered each year with the United Nations are in this form."[90] The exchange of such instruments constitutes consent to be bound if they so provide or if it is otherwise established that the states concerned agreed that the exchange would have that effect.[91]

---

[87] E.g., under Article II, Section 2 of the United States Constitution, the advice and consent of the Senate is necessary before the President may "make," or commit the United States to, a "treaty," as that term is used in the Constitution. This subject is discussed further in § 4.06, below.

[88] *See* AUST, *supra* note 38, at 76, stating that a treaty will be presumed to enter into force upon signature if there is no express or implied indication that ratification is needed.

[89] *See* SINCLAIR, *supra* note 20, at 40. Hans Blix, *The Requirement of Ratification*, 15 BRIT. Y.B. INT'L L. 359-60 (1953), found that the vast majority (1,125 of 1,300) of instruments reproduced in the United Nations Treaty Series from 1946-51 contained clear indications of the way in which they were to enter into force.

[90] AUST, *supra* note 38, at 80.

[91] Vienna Convention, *supra* note 22, art. 13.

Ratification:[92] The term "ratification" is defined in Article 2(1)(b) of the Vienna Convention as follows: "the international act so named whereby a State establishes on the international plane its consent to be bound by a treaty". (As we will see, the same definition applies to "acceptance," "approval" and "accession.") It is important to distinguish this sense of the term "ratification" — i.e., referring to an act on the "international plane" — from use of the term to refer to a process on the domestic plane, such as approval of a treaty by the legislature, which may also be called ratification.[93] The latter may be a prerequisite to the former under the state's domestic law, but since domestic treaty processes are not a concern of international law, the Vienna Convention does not address them.

The circumstances under which a state's consent to be bound is expressed by ratification are listed in Article 14(1) of the Vienna Convention. They are, in essence, that the treaty so provides or it is otherwise established that the negotiating states so agreed, the representative of a state signed the treaty subject to ratification, or the intention of a state "to sign the treaty subject to ratification appears from the full powers of its representative or was expressed during the negotiation."[94] Thus, there should be no surprise that ratification would have this effect.

Multilateral treaties usually state expressly that they are subject to ratification (or to acceptance, approval or accession), often indicating at the same time where the relevant instruments are to be deposited. For example, the 1997 United Nations Convention on the Law of the Non-Navigational Uses of International Watercourses provides in Article 35(1):

> "The present Convention is subject to ratification, acceptance, approval or accession by states and by regional economic integration organizations. The instruments of ratification, acceptance, approval or accession shall be deposited with the Secretary-General of the United Nations."[95]

In the case of multilateral treaties like this one, ratification is accomplished by execution of an instrument of ratification by the organ of government authorized under the law of the state to exercise treaty-making power (usually the head of state or government) and the deposit of the instrument of ratification with depositary designated in the treaty. The process is similar for bilateral treaties, except that instruments of ratification are exchanged between the two states.

---

[92] For an extensive discussion of ratification, *see* OPPENHEIM, *supra* note 13, §§ 602-609, at 1226-35. *See also* AUST, *supra* note 38, at 81-87; and SINCLAIR, *supra* note 20, at 39-41. The ILC's commentary traces the history of ratification, explaining that prior to the 19th century, ratification was an act by which a sovereign confirmed, after the adoption of the text, the full powers of his or her representative to negotiate the treaty. It later came "to be used in the majority of cases as the means of submitting the treaty-making power of the executive to parliamentary control. . . . [I]t came to be the opinion that the general rule is that ratification is necessary to render a treaty binding." [1966] 2 Y.B. Int'l L. Comm'n 197-198.

[93] *See* OPPENHEIM, *supra* note 13, § 602, at 1226.

[94] Vienna Convention, *supra* note 22, art. 14(1)(d).

[95] U.N. Doc. A/RES/51/869, 21 May 1997, 36 I.L.M. 700 (1997).

While there has been a doctrinal debate over the question whether treaties require ratification in the absence of an express provision to that effect, or whether signature is sufficient,[96] this seems now to have been largely overtaken by the Vienna Convention and either prior or subsequent state practice that is consistent with the Convention. Rather than providing any residuary rule to cover cases in which the treaty is silent on the subject of how consent to be bound is to be expressed, the Vienna Convention simply indicates the circumstances in which consent to be bound is expressed by signature, and those in which it is expressed by ratification. "In this respect, it may be said to have respected the principle of the procedural autonomy of the negotiating States," as Sinclair points out.[97] Moreover, the Convention's solution is unlikely to cause significant difficulties in practice, "no such difficulties having arisen before its adoption."[98]

Though it will in most cases be only of academic interest, however, the question does remain whether ratification is required if a treaty is silent on the issue. Since Article 14 of the Convention sets forth the circumstances under which consent to be bound is expressed by ratification, one could well conclude that if none of these conditions is satisfied, ratification is not necessary. Commentators are divided on the issue, however.[99]

Acceptance or approval: The definition of terms "acceptance" and "approval" in Article 2(1)(b) of the Vienna Convention is the same as that for "ratification." These two methods of expressing consent to be bound have developed in state practice largely since the Second World War, chiefly to permit states "to avoid certain internal difficulties which they might experience if they had to go through their constitutional procedures for parliamentary ratification . . . ,"[100] difficulties which are present especially when the parliamentary, or legislative, procedure is itself is referred to as "ratification."[101] These international acts have the same legal effect as ratification.

Accession: This term is also defined in Article 2(1)(b) of the Vienna Convention in the same way as "ratification." A state normally "accedes" to a treaty when it has not signed it or when it did not participate in its negotiation. It is thus an act that would ordinarily be relevant only to multilateral treaties.

---

[96] *See* the discussion in SINCLAIR, *supra* note 20, at 39-40.

[97] *Id.* at 41.

[98] *Id.*

[99] *Contrast* AUST, *supra* note 38, at 82 ("if a treaty is silent on the question of ratification it is presumed that it is not needed"), *with* OPPENHEIM, *supra* note 13, at 1229 (that "treaties regularly require ratification even if this is not expressly stipulated, unless an exception to this general rule is expressed or implied in the treaty . . . represents the better view, although the exceptions, express or implied, are extensive").

[100] OPPENHEIM, *supra* note 13, at 1236. *See also* AUST, *supra* note 38, at 87.

[101] *Id.* There may be other circumstances when one of these procedures is used, however. For example, the United States became a member of the International Labor Organization (ILO) not by ratifying a treaty, but by accepting, pursuant to a joint resolution of Congress, an invitation to become a member. *See* OPPENHEIM, *supra* note 13, at 1236 n. 2.

A state may not have signed a treaty for a variety of reasons. Most simply, the period during which the treaty is open for signature may elapse before the state has signed it. Alternatively, a state may participate in the drawing up of a treaty but decide it does not wish to become a party and therefore not sign it. Or the treaty itself may provide that it may be signed by only certain states.[102]

There is no general right to accede to treaties.[103] Instead, as Article 15 of the Vienna Convention makes clear, a state may only accede to a treaty if the treaty so provides (Article 15(a)), if it is otherwise established that the negotiating states so agreed (Article 15(b)), or if all the parties have subsequently so agreed (Article 15(c)). In practice, most cases will fall within the first of these categories.

Any other agreed means: In what Aust describes as "a good example of the inherent flexibility of the law of treaties,"[104] Article 11 of the Convention provides that consent to be bound may be expressed, in addition to the other means discussed above, "by any other means if so agreed." It is not necessary that the agreement to use other means be express; it may be implied from the treaty or otherwise established.[105]

A striking example of the use of "other means" is the procedure under Article 5 of the 1994 Agreement relating to the Implementation of Part XI of the 1982 U.N. Convention on the Law of the Sea.[106] Because it was important for states that had already ratified the Convention to establish their consent to be bound by the Agreement expeditiously, before the Convention entered into force, Article 5 provided that a state that had ratified the Convention would be considered to have established its consent to be bound by the Agreement if it merely signed the latter instrument, unless it notified the depositary within twelve months that it would not take advantage of this simplified procedure.

[2]   Reservations

The subject of reservations to treaties is believed by some experts to be perhaps "one of the most difficult in the whole of public international law."[107] It

---

[102] *See, e.g.,* the Helsinki Convention on the Protection and Use of Transboundary Watercourses and International Lakes, 17 March 1992, 31 I.L.M. 1312 (1992), which in art. 23 restricts signatories to states members of the U.N. Economic Commission for Europe (ECE), states having consultative status with the ECE and the European Communities.

[103] While there has been debate about whether accession to general multilateral treaties should be open to any state, the idea has not proved acceptable due to what have been described as "weighty theoretical objections". *See* OPPENHEIM, *supra* note 13, at 1237 n. 3.

[104] AUST, *supra* note 38, at 90.

[105] *See id.,* noting that agreement may be established, for example, on the basis of the conduct of the states concerned.

[106] Art. 5(1), 28 July 1994, 33 I.L.M. 1309 (1994). *See* AUST, *supra* note 38, at 90-91 and sources there cited for further discussion of this simplified procedure.

[107] [1995] 2 Y.B. Int'l L. Comm'n 100, pt. 2 (referring to the view of the ILC's special rapporteur on Reservations to Treaties, Professor Alain Pellet, which, according to Prof. Pellet, was shared by his predecessor special rapporteurs on the Law of Treaties).

may be an area in which the Vienna Convention in some respects goes beyond the rules of customary international law on the subject. However, the fact that the Convention is generally regarded, by governments, by the International Court of Justice and by scholars, as an authoritative indication of the law in this field, suggests that to the extent that there are differences between custom and the Convention, these are probably narrowing. Be this as it may, the Vienna Convention's provisions on reservations do leave a number of questions unanswered.[108] In part for this reason, the U.N. International Law Commission has since 1993 been studying the topic of "reservations to treaties" with a view to developing a Guide to Practice regarding reservations for the assistance of states and international organizations.[109]

[a] Multilateral Treaties

It is not uncommon today for states to make reservations to multilateral treaties.[110] For example, the United States entered the following reservations to the 1948 Genocide Convention:[111]

> "(1) That with reference to article IX of the Convention, before any dispute to which the United States is a party may be submitted to the jurisdiction of the International Court of Justice under this article, the specific consent of the United States is required in each case.
>
> (2) That nothing in the Convention requires or authorizes legislation or other action by the United States of America prohibited by the Constitution of the United States as interpreted by the United States."[112]

The first reservation seeks to modify the way in which the dispute resolution provision of the Genocide Convention[113] applies to the United States.

---

[108] Indeed, Prof. Pellet's first report to the ILC identified fifteen main questions that are unresolved and seventeen additional ones. U.N. Doc. A/CN.4/470, paras. 124-5 and 148-9. These are described in general terms in the ILC's report on its 1995 session, [1995] 2 Y.B. Int'l L. Comm'n, pt. 2., 101-102.

[109] *See generally id.* at 100-108. The ILC will thus not be proposing any changes to the Vienna Convention. It does plan to offer model clauses for use by states in treaties they negotiate.

[110] As we will see below, a state may make a reservation to a treaty unless the treaty excludes it or it is otherwise impermissible. *See* Vienna Convention, *supra* note 22, art. 19. Despite this broad scope for entering reservations, however, a 1980 study found that no reservations have been made to 85 percent of all multilateral agreements, and that such reservations as are made rarely concern substantive provisions of agreements. *See* John King Gamble, *Reservations to Multilateral Treaties: A Macroscopic View of State Practice*, 74 Am. J. Int'l L. 372 (1980).

[111] Convention on the Prevention and Punishment of the Crime of Genocide, G.A. Res. 260 A (III), 9 Dec. 1948, 78 U.N.T.S. 277.

[112] *See* Status of Multilateral Treaties Deposited with the Secretary-General, *available at* http://untreaty.un.org.

[113] Article IX of the Genocide Convention provides as follows: "Disputes between the Contracting Parties relating to the interpretation, application or fulfilment of the present Convention, including those relating to the responsibility of a State for genocide or for any of the other acts enumerated in article III, shall be submitted to the International Court of Justice at the request of any of the parties to the dispute." Genocide Convention, *supra* note 111, art. IX.

The second reservation is intended to ensure that the Genocide Convention does not require the United States to do anything that would be contrary to the U.S. Constitution. Both reservations have been the subject of objections by other states parties to the Genocide Convention.[114]

By making its consent to be bound by a treaty subject to a reservation, a state indicates that while it generally accepts and supports the treaty in question, it does not accept, or accepts only on certain conditions, one or more of the treaty's provisions. The possibility of making reservations thus allows states to become parties to treaties they otherwise would not have joined because certain of their provisions were objectionable. Consequently, this device tends to make multilateral treaties more inclusive than they would be if states had to decide whether to accept them on an all-or-nothing basis. Because the possibility of making reservations tends to increase the number of parties to multilateral agreements, it may be seen as contributing to the development of the body of international "legislation" in the form of broadly accepted treaties.

[b] Bilateral Treaties

The situation is different in the case of bilateral treaties, where the rationale for making reservations generally does not apply.[115] If one of the two states involved were unhappy with the treaty it could, in theory, simply continue negotiating the treaty until the problem was resolved. There would thus be no need for reservations. As a practical matter, however, conditions that may be referred to as "reservations" are more likely to be attached during the course of the domestic ratification process, after negotiations have concluded. This is true in particular of treaty practice in the United States, where the Senate sometimes attaches what it terms "reservations" to its advice and consent to bilateral treaties.[116]

But the effect of these so-called reservations is different from that of reservations to multilateral treaties. A reservation to a multilateral treaty is communicated to the other parties (usually upon ratification and through the depositary), which are then free to accept it or object to it. The treaty itself is not re-negotiated. A reservation by the Senate to its approval of a bilateral treaty is in essence a qualification placed by the Senate on its acceptance of the treaty. It amounts to a conditional approval — that is, approval of the treaty subject to the condition that the treaty's text be modified in the way specified in the "reservation." Since the approval of the Senate is necessary under the Constitution in the case of Article II treaties,[117] the President must decide whether to seek to obtain the other state's consent to amend the text of the agreement. The Senate's

---

[114] See Status of Multilateral Treaties Deposited with the Secretary-General, *available at* http://untreaty.un.org.

[115] See generally RESTATEMENT 3d, *supra* note 18, § 313 cmt. f.

[116] AUST, *supra* note 38, at 106, reports that the Senate has done this on more than 100 occasions in the past 200 years.

[117] Senate approval is not necessary where the treaty is entered into solely by the President, for example, as an executive agreement, as discussed below.

"reservation" would thus amount, in essence, to an invitation to the other state to renegotiate at least certain terms of the treaty.[118] Agreed amendments may be formalized through an exchange of notes.[119] Such a process of re-opening negotiations and amending the treaty would not occur in the case of reservations to a multilateral treaty.

[c] "Reservation" Defined

The Vienna Convention defines the term "reservation" in Article 2(1)(d) as:

> "a unilateral statement, however phrased or named, made by a State, when signing, ratifying, accepting, approving or acceding to a treaty, whereby it purports to exclude or modify the legal effect of certain provisions of a treaty in their application to that State."[120]

The first U.S. reservation to the Genocide Convention, set forth above, fits within this definition. It was made unilaterally by the United States when ratifying the Convention and purports to exclude the legal effect of Article IX of the Convention — which provides for compulsory jurisdiction of the International Court of Justice over disputes arising under the Convention[121] — in its application to the United States.

A true reservation should be distinguished from a so-called "interpretative declaration."[122] The latter is a unilateral declaration made by a state, during the negotiation of a treaty or when signing or ratifying it, stating its interpretation of a provision of the treaty. It is not at all uncommon for states to make such declarations, which are often intended to indicate an interpretation that is consistent with the state's domestic law. The United States made interpretative declarations regarding twenty-eight bilateral treaties alone between 1975 and 1995.[123] U.S. interpretative declarations often take the form of "understandings"[124] and are frequently attached by the Senate during the advice-and-consent process. The United States attached both what it referred to as "reservations" and "understandings" to its ratification of the Genocide Convention. The five "understandings" include the following interpretative declarations:

> "(1) That the term 'intent to destroy, in whole or in part, a national, ethnical, racial, or religious group as such' appearing in

---

[118] As the ILC put it in 1966: "A reservation to a bilateral treaty presents no problems, because it amounts to a new proposal reopening the negotiations between the two States concerning the terms of the treaty. If they arrive at an agreement — either adopting or rejecting the reservation — the treaty will be concluded; if not, it will fall to the ground." [1966] Y.B. Int'l L. Comm'n 203, pt. 2.

[119] See AUST, *supra* note 38, at 106, describing the amendment of the 1985 UK-US Supplementary Extradition Treaty in this way after the President informed the UK Government that he could not ratify the treaty unless certain amendments were made.

[120] Vienna Convention, *supra* note 22, art. 2(1)(d).

[121] Article IX of the Genocide Convention is set forth in note 113, *supra*.

[122] On interpretative declarations, *see generally* AUST, *supra* note 38, at 101-05.

[123] *Id.* at 103.

[124] *See generally* WHITEMAN, *supra* note 47, at 164-193.

article II means the specific intent to destroy, in whole or in substantial part, a national, ethnical, racial or religious group as such by the acts specified in article II.

(2) That the term 'mental harm' in article II (b) means permanent impairment of mental faculties through drugs, torture or similar techniques."[125]

Care must be taken, however, to ensure that a statement which is entitled an "understanding" is not in fact a disguised reservation.[126] In the *Belilos* case,[127] Switzerland had made what it styled an interpretative declaration when ratifying the 1950 European Convention for the Protection of Human Rights and Fundamental Freedoms (ECHR),[128] which read as follows:

"The Swiss Federal Council considers that the guarantee of fair trial in Article 6, paragraph 1 (art. 6-1) of the Convention, in the determination of civil rights and obligations or any criminal charge against the person in question is intended solely to ensure ultimate control by the judiciary over the acts or decisions of the public authorities relating to such rights or obligations or the determination of such a charge."[129]

The European Court of Human Rights treated this statement as a reservation and held that it was invalid as a reservation of a general character, which is prohibited by Article 64 of the ECHR.[130]

[d]   Permissibility of Reservations[131]

Reservations to multilateral treaties are generally permitted.[132] Moreover, there is no stigma associated with making a reservation. As Aust puts it, "There is nothing inherently wicked or even undesirable in formulating a reservation to a multilateral treaty."[133] Thus, while it might at first blush seem heartless to make a reservation to a treaty for the protection of children, a number of states have in fact done this in respect of the 1989

---

[125] These statements, as well as the reservations of the U.S. and other parties to the Genocide Convention, may be found on the U.N. treaty website, under Status of Multilateral Treaties Deposited with the Secretary-General, *available at* http://untreaty.un.org.

[126] On disguised reservations, *see* AUST, *supra* note 38, at 104-05.

[127] ECHR Pubs. Series A, vol. 132 (1988), *available at* http://www.menneskeret.dk/menneskeretieuropa/konventionen/baggrund/domme/ref00000019/.

[128] 4 Nov. 1950, Europ. T.S. No. 5.

[129] Quoted from the *Belilos* case, *supra* note 127, para. 29.

[130] *Id.*, paras. 49 and 60.

[131] The term "permissibility" is used here in its general sense. It is not used in the narrow sense of the school of "permissibility" described by the ILC's special rapporteur, discussed below.

[132] *See* Vienna Convention, *supra* note 22, art. 19.

[133] AUST, *supra* note 38, at 108.

Rights of the Child Convention,[134] and few objections have been lodged.[135] Even more surprising, perhaps, would be a reservation to a treaty on the prevention and punishment of the crime of genocide. Yet, as we have seen, these have been made by the United States, among other countries.

There are, however, several cases in which a reservation would not be permitted. These are set forth in Article 19 of the Vienna Convention, which provides that a state may make a reservation unless:

(a) the reservation is prohibited by the treaty;

(b) the treaty provides that only specified reservations, which do not include the reservation in question, may be made; or

(c) in cases not falling under sub-paragraphs (a) and (b), the reservation is incompatible with the object and purpose of the treaty.[136]

These are, then, the exceptions to the general rule permitting reservations. Those stated in paragraphs (a) and (b) are perhaps self-explanatory. Paragraph (a) refers to the cases in which the treaty in question contains an express provision to the effect that no reservations, no reservations of a particular kind, or no reservations to certain articles, are permitted. The 1982 U.N. Convention on the Law of the Sea[137] takes the first of these approaches,[138] as does the 1998 Rome Statute of the International Criminal Court[139] and a number of human rights treaties.[140] The 1950 European Convention on Human Rights[141] prohibits reservations of a general character.[142]

Paragraph (b) of Article 19 contemplates treaties that allow only certain, specified reservations.[143] Any other reservations would not be permitted.

Finally, the exception contained in paragraph (c) of Article 19 refers to reservations that are "incompatible with the object and purpose of the treaty." While this provision makes sense on its face, it is the source of many questions and much debate. First, the obvious: A state should not be

---

[134] U.N. Convention on the Rights of the Child, 12 Dec. 1989, G.A. res. 44/25, annex, 44 U.N. GAOR Supp. (No. 49) at 167, U.N. Doc. A/44/49 (1989), 28 I.L.M. 1448 (1989).

[135] See RESERVATIONS, DECLARATIONS AND OBJECTIONS RELATING TO THE CONCENTION ON THE RIGHTS OF THE CHILD, CRC/c/2/Rev. 8, 7 Dec 1999, listing sixty-nine states which have made declarations and/or reservations to the Convention and thirteen states which have objected to the reservations.

[136] Vienna Convention, *supra* note 22, art. 19.

[137] 10 Dec. 1982, U.N. Doc. A/CONF/62/122, 21 I.L.M. 1261 (1982).

[138] See *id.*, art. 309. No reservations are permitted to conventions of the International Labor Organization (ILO) by virtue of the ILO's constitution. 15 U.N.T.S. 35.

[139] 17 July 1998, Art. 120, U.N. Doc. A/CONF/183/9, 2187 U.N.T.S. 3.

[140] See, e.g., European Convention for the Prevention of Torture and Inhuman or Degrading Treatment or Punishment, 26 Nov. 1987, art. 21, E.T.S. 126, 27 I.L.M. 1152 (1988).

[141] 1950 European Convention for the Protection of Human Rights and Fundamental Freedoms, 213 U.N.T.S. 221 (1953).

[142] *Id.*, art. 64 (as discussed above in connection with the *Belilos* case).

[143] Examples are given in AUST, *supra* note 38, at 109-110.

permitted to join a multilateral treaty and then, through a reservation, exempt itself from what the treaty is trying to accomplish — or worse, undermine the entire purpose of the treaty.[144] This principle is straightforward enough. It is its application that gives rise to problems.

The principle stems — like much of today's law of reservations — from the Advisory Opinion of the International Court of Justice on *Reservations to the Convention on the Prevention and Punishment of the Crime of Genocide* (the *Genocide* case).[145] The United Nations General Assembly had asked the Court for an advisory opinion on certain questions regarding reservations that had been made by a number of states to the Convention on the Prevention and Punishment of the Crime of Genocide of 1948 (the Genocide Convention). The Genocide Convention does not contain a provision on reservations. The first question asked of the Court by the General Assembly was the following: "Can the reserving State be regarded as being a party to the Convention while still maintaining its reservation if the reservation is objected to by one or more of the parties to the Convention but not by others?" In what has been called a "Delphic pronouncement"[146] the Court, by a vote of seven votes to five, stated in response to this question:

> "that a State which has made and maintained a reservation which has been objected to by one or more of the parties to the Convention but not by others, can be regarded as being a party to the Convention if the reservation is compatible with the object and purpose of the Convention; otherwise, that State cannot be regarded as being a party to the Convention."[147]

The Court's proviso has come to be known as the "compatibility test." This test forms the basis of the Vienna Convention's provisions on the permissibility of reservations (Article 19) and on the effect of acceptance of and objection to reservations (Articles 20 and 21). The Court's approach set off a veritable firestorm of criticism, much of which was directed at the compatibility test. The test was, and continues to be, viewed by many as "too subjective and . . . accordingly not suitable for application to multilateral conventions in general,"[148] as "introduc[ing] an element of uncertainty and possible disagreement,"[149] as "radically relativistic,"[150] and as "probably unworkable in practice."[151]

---

[144] Recall here the discussion above of art. 18 of the Vienna Convention concerning the obligation not to defeat the object and purpose of a treaty *prior* to its entry into force. The present discussion principally concerns the period following a treaty's entry into force.

[145] 1951 I.C.J. 15. *See generally, e.g.,* SINCLAIR, *supra* note 20, at 56-58; and RESTATEMENT 3d, *supra* note 18, § 313, Reporters' Note 1.

[146] SINCLAIR, *supra* note 20, at 58.

[147] 1951 I.C.J. at 29-30.

[148] SINCLAIR, *supra* note 20, at 58, describing the view of the International Law Commission in its 1951 study of reservations to multilateral treaties.

[149] RESTATEMENT 3d, *supra* note 18, § 313 cmt. c.

[150] REUTER, *supra* note 1, at 61.

[151] OPPENHEIM, *supra* note 13, at 1245 n. 4.

Why all the fuss? The answer lies in the fact that the Court's compatibility test replaced the traditional rule on the permissibility of reservations. According to that rule, any reservation to a multilateral treaty had to be accepted by *all* the parties to the treaty, not only for the reservation to be permissible, but even for the reserving state to be a party to the treaty.[152] The rule was simple, objective and easy to apply. It was also inflexible, and allowed one or a small number of states to prevent another state from becoming a party to a treaty even though its reservation was viewed by most contracting states as being compatible with the treaty's object and purpose.[153]

The increasing importance of the multilateral treaty as a means of international lawmaking — particularly in the field of human rights — led the Court, as well as influential commentators, to view the traditional rule as no longer being well-suited to the requirements of international relations.[154] The Court therefore introduced considerable flexibility into the law of reservations. This approach was in line with the view of the Soviet Union and its allies, a minority within the United Nations.[155] While its opinion addressed only reservations to the Genocide Convention, it formed the basis of the Vienna Convention's provisions on reservations, which are of general applicability. Further, according to Oppenheim, the opinion "must be considered as having a distinct bearing upon the general rules of customary international law relating to reservations."[156]

A final and important point regarding the "compatibility test" of Article 19(c) concerns the effect of a reservation's failing this test. It will be recalled that Article 19 provides that a state may formulate a reservation, inter alia, "unless" the reservation is incompatible with the treaty's object and purpose. The plain meaning of this language would seem to be that a state simply may not formulate, or make, a reservation that fails this test. But what if it does? Does the reservation simply not exist? Can the reserving state still be a party to the treaty? And who determines whether the reservation fails the test? The reserving state or the other contracting states?

In his first report the ILC's special rapporteur on reservations identifies two schools of thought on this question: the "permissibility" school and the "opposability" school.[157] The former holds the view that a reservation

---

[152] *See, e.g.*, SINCLAIR, *supra* note 20, at 54-55; Jose Maria Ruda, *Reservations to Treaties*, 146 RECUEIL DES COURS (1975-III) 105, at 112; and subsection [e] below. Sinclair notes that "The traditional unanimity rule governing the admissibility of reservations to multilateral conventions was closely linked with the traditional unanimity rule applying to the establishment of the text of such conventions." SINCLAIR, *supra* note 20, at 56.

[153] *See* OPPENHEIM, *supra* note 13, at 1245.

[154] *Id. See also* RESTATEMENT 3d, *supra* note 18, § 313, Reporters' Note 1.

[155] *See* REUTER, *supra* note 1, at 61.

[156] OPPENHEIM, *supra* note 13, at 1245. Note that this respected work stops short of saying that the opinion reflects customary international law.

[157] Alain Pellet, First Report on the Law and Practice relating to Reservations to Treaties, U.N. Doc. A/CN.4/470, at 49, para. 102. *See also* [1995] Y.B. Int'l L. Comm'n, pt. 2., 101, giving an account of Prof. Pellet's treatment of this subject in his report.

which is incompatible with the object and purpose of the treaty is impermissible; it is null and void. Incompatibility is determined by reference to the treaty, not the reactions of other states.[158] According to the latter school, the opposite is the case: "the validity of a reservation depends solely on the acceptance of the reservation by another contracting State."[159] For adherents of the permissibility school, the question of whether a reservation was "opposable" to — i.e., could be invoked against — another party would arise only in respect of permissible reservations.[160] Pellet observes that these two schools of thought could produce very different results. For example, if the permissibility doctrine is followed, another state could assert the invalidity of a reservation before an international tribunal or in a diplomatic exchange, for example, even if it had not objected to it; the reservation fails automatically, it self-destructs, due to its incompatibility with the treaty's purpose. The opposability theory, on the other hand, would not automatically invalidate such a reservation. It could even be argued that a tribunal should "refrain from ruling on the permissibility of a reservation if there is no objection by the other parties"[161] because the reservation's status would depend solely upon the reactions of other contracting states.

This still leaves the question of the effect of the impermissibility of a reservation. Does the reservation simply disappear, so that the reserving state is a contracting party without it? Or does the invalidity of the reservation vitiate the very consent to be bound of the reserving state, so that *that state* "disappears" from the list of contracting parties? Or are there other possibilities? This issue will be addressed in the following subsection.

[e] Acceptance of and Objection to Reservations[162]

The traditional concept of a multilateral treaty was of an agreement between a number of states, all of whom agreed upon all of its terms. However, with the increased use and significance of multilateral treaties as a means of international lawmaking, it became important to allow as many states as possible to join them. The idea that a state could adhere to such treaties subject to reservations thus came to be generally accepted.[163] What experienced a great evolution in the 20th century was the effect of objections to reservations.

The development of the law and practice in this area may be summarized as follows: The starting point is typified by the approach adopted by the League of Nations in 1927, under which it was "essential" that a

---

[158] *See, e.g.,* Derek W. Bowett, *Reservations to Non-Restricted Multilateral Treaties*, 1976-1977 BRITISH Y.B. INT'L L. 88.

[159] Ruda, *supra* note 152, at 190.

[160] Pellet, *supra* note 157, at 48, para. 101.

[161] *Id.* at 49-50, para. 104.

[162] *See generally* AUST, *supra* note 38, at 112-116.

[163] The exceptions to the general permissibility of reservations are those listed in art. 19 of the Vienna Convention, quoted above.

reservation be "accepted by all contracting parties to be valid, as would have been the case if it had been put forward in the course of the negotiations."[164] If it was not so accepted, the reservation, and the signature to which it was attached, was null and void.[165]

A more flexible approach was proposed in 1932 by the Pan American Union (PAU), the predecessor of today's Organization of American States (OAS). Under that approach, which was followed by Latin American countries in their treaty relations with each other, there could be different legal regimes for different parties to a multilateral treaty. In particular, as between a reserving state and a state accepting the reservation, the treaty would be in force, as modified by the reservation. But as between a reserving state and a state that did not accept the reservation, the treaty would not be in force.[166]

It was the Pan American Union approach rather than that of the League of Nations that proved to be the trail-blazer for the development of the law. The ICJ in the 1951 *Genocide* case,[167] the ILC in its 1966 draft articles on the law of treaties,[168] and the 1969 Vienna Convention in its provisions on reservations all followed variants of the PAU approach. Thus, in the absence of a provision in a treaty to the contrary, the day would seem to be gone when a reservation must be accepted by all of the contracting states.

We will focus, as usual, on the approach of the Vienna Convention. For convenience, let us assume that there is a multilateral treaty called the Astrology Convention, negotiated by States A, B, C, D, and E. Assume further that State A enters a reservation regarding Article 5 of the Convention, entitled "Gemini," and that the other negotiating states respond as follows:

- State B does nothing;

- State C expressly accepts State A's reservation;

- State D objects to State A's reservation, on the ground that it is incompatible with the object and purpose of the Convention; and

- State E also objects to State A's reservation, on the ground that it is incompatible with the object and purpose of the Convention, but also opposes the entry into force of the Convention between itself and State A.

What is the legal status of the parties vis-à-vis each other? The answer to this question may be gleaned from Articles 20 and 21 of the Vienna Convention. (It will be assumed the State A's reservation is permissible under Article 19(a) and (b).)

---

[164] Report of the League of Nations Committee of Experts for the Progressive Codification of International Law, 8 L.N.O.J. 880, 881 (1927).

[165] *Id.*

[166] Reservations to Multilateral Conventions, U.N. Doc. A/1372, p. 11.

[167] 1951 I.C.J. 15.

[168] For the final report of the ILC on the Law of Treaties, *see* [1966] 2 Y.B. Int'l L. Comm'n 9-38.

A key threshold issue is raised by the fact that only five states negotiated the Astrology Convention. The issue, which is raised by any treaty with a small number of negotiating states, is whether the agreement falls within paragraph 2 of Article 20. That provision deals with what have come to be called "plurilateral" or restricted multilateral treaties, expressions that distinguish this special kind of agreement from other multilateral treaties. Determining whether a treaty is a "plurilateral" one is important because if it is, all parties must accept any reservation. According to Article 20(2), these treaties have two characteristics: (1) there is a limited number of negotiating states;[169] and (2) it appears from that limited number, and the object and purpose of the treaty, that "the application of the treaty in its entirety between all the parties is an essential condition of the consent of each one to be bound by the treaty. . . ." If these two characteristics are present, all parties must accept any reservation. Examples of plurilateral treaties might include the treaties establishing the European Union[170] and other basic European Community treaties, the NAFTA[171] and the Antarctic Treaty of 1959.[172]

Is the Astrology Convention a plurilateral treaty? There are five negotiating states, which on its face would qualify as a limited number. As to the second characteristic, given the very few facts at our disposal, it is difficult to determine whether this is satisfied. The fact that Article 5 concerns "Gemini" suggests that there may be a separate provision for each of the twelve signs of the zodiac; if application of all of these provisions between all the parties is an essential condition of the consent of each one to be bound by the Convention (which seems plausible), then the treaty is "plurilateral" and falls under Article 20(2). Any reservation, such as that of State A, would therefore have to be accepted by all other parties.

Having resolved the plurilateral treaty issue to the extent we can, let us assume the Astrology Convention is not a plurilateral treaty for the purposes of the following analysis. We may begin with State B: This state's failure to act raises the question of the effect of silence: does it constitute tacit acceptance or acquiescence? If so, may acquiescence amount to acceptance of a reservation? That question is answered by Article 20(5), which tells us in essence that unless the treaty otherwise provides (and we will assume the Astrology Convention does not), a state will be considered to have accepted a reservation if it has not objected to it within 12 months of having been notified of the reservation or by the date on which it expressed its consent to be bound, whichever is later.[173] Whenever this

---

[169] This was originally the ILC's sole criterion: "where the treaty is one concluded between a small group of States, unanimous agreement to the acceptance of a reservation must be presumed to be necessary in the absence of any contrary indication." ILC commentary on the preliminary set of draft articles on reservations, [1962] 2 Y.B. Int'l L. Comm'n 179.

[170] 7 Feb. 1992, 298 U.N.T.S. 11, 32 I.L.M. 289 (1993).

[171] 8 Dec. 1992, 32 I.L.M. 289 (1993).

[172] 402 U.N.T.S. 71.

[173] If it is the expression of consent to be bound that comes later, the state must therefore be sure it has reviewed all reservations before expressing its consent so that it may object in

constructive acceptance takes effect, State A will be regarded as a contracting state in relation to the Convention, regardless of whether any other state accepts its reservation, by virtue of Article 20(4)(c).

But we know that one state did expressly accept A's reservation: State C. This would have the effect just described of making State A a contracting state under Article 20(4)(c). The result, as between States A and C, would be that after the treaty's entry into force for those states, Article 5 would not be applicable *as between those two states*. Since the Vienna Convention's approach permits different legal relations to exist between different parties to a multilateral treaty, we must examine separately the legal relations between A and each of the other contracting states.

State D objects to State A's reservation on the ground that it is incompatible with the object and purpose of the Astrology Convention. Does this mean (a) that the reservation is invalid but that there are treaty relations between A and D, (b) that there are no treaty relations between A and D, or possibly even (c) that A may not become a party to the treaty with respect to any other state? Article 20(4)(b) provides a negative answer to all of these questions. The treaty may still enter into force as between States A and D. Perhaps more surprising is the effect of D's objection on the applicability of A's reservation to D. According to Article 21(3), since State D has not opposed the entry into force of the Astrology Convention between itself and State A, Article 5 *does not apply* as between States A and D. That is to say, State A gets the benefit of its reservation despite the fact that State D objected to it, and objected not on general grounds of policy but because it viewed the reservation as being incompatible with the object and purpose of the treaty. We saw earlier that to be permissible under Article 19, a reservation must not be incompatible with the object and purpose of the treaty. Yet Article 21(3) gives State A the benefit of its reservation despite State D's objection on this ground. How can this be?

The answer lies in the nature of the international system. While there is general agreement on the compatibility test for determining the permissibility of reservations, there would normally be no tribunal or other body vested with competence to interpret the treaty in question — i.e., to determine what the "object and purpose" of the treaty is, and whether a given reservation is incompatible with it. In the absence of a rule of treaty law to the contrary, this would leave it to each contracting state to judge for itself whether another state's reservation fails the compatibility test. However, while the judgment of a given state on this question might influence the views of other contracting states, it would not be binding upon either them or the reserving state — again, in the absence of a rule to the contrary. When the International Law Commission initially tackled this conundrum in 1962, it considered various possible solutions, including a "collegiate" system "under which the reserving State would only become a

---

a timely fashion. Sinclair emphasizes the importance played by tacit consent, especially because "Governments tend to be sluggish in their reaction to reservations. . . ." SINCLAIR, *supra* note 20, at 63. In his view, "The most significant feature of international practice concerning reservations is the part played by tacit consent." *Id.*

party if the reservation were accepted by a given proportion of the other States concerned."[174] It ultimately rejected this approach in favor of one that was more flexible, under which each state would decide for itself whether to accept a reservation.[175]

This is the basic approach reflected in the Vienna Convention, and in particular, in Article 21(3). However, while the ILC had proposed that an objection to a reservation, without more, would preclude the entry into force of the treaty between the objecting and reserving states, the Convention requires that in order to avoid treaty relations with the reserving state, the objecting state must declare affirmatively that it opposes the entry into force of the treaty between itself and the reserving state.[176] Thus since State D failed to oppose the entry into force of the Astrology Convention as between itself and State A, not only may the treaty come into force between those two states, but Article 5 — "the provision[ ] to which the reservation relates" — does not apply as between them.

This is not the case, however, with regard to State E. That state not only objected to State A's reservation on the ground that it fails the compatibility test, but also opposed the entry into force of the Astrology Convention between itself and State A. Thus under Article 20(4)(b), State A will not be a party to the Convention with State E, because State E "definitely expressed" its intention that the Convention not enter into force as between it and State A. This result is also implied by Article 21(3).

The effect of Articles 20 and 21 of the Vienna Convention is thus that there can be different legal relationships between different parties to a multilateral treaty. In fact, as far as reservations are concerned, a multilateral treaty may be viewed as a network of bilateral agreements. In our example, States B through E will have treaty relations with each other as to the entire Astrology Convention, while there are no treaty relations at all as between States A and E, and as between State A and States B, C and D, there are treaty relations but Article 5 does not apply. The law of reservations established by the Vienna Convention is thus flexible, but it can result in a patchwork of legal relationships.

[C] The Legal Effect and Interpretation of Treaties[177]

Once a treaty has been concluded and has entered into force, what is its legal effect on the parties? The answer to this question is found in Part III

---

[174] SINCLAIR, *supra* note 20, at 61, referring to [1962] 2 Y.B. Int'l L. Comm'n 180.

[175] [1962] 2 Y.B. Int'l L. Comm'n 180. But in contrast to the Convention, under the ILC's approach, an objection to a reservation would mean that the treaty could not come into force between the objecting and reserving states.

[176] This change was made by the Conference at which the Convention was negotiated, on the basis of a proposal by the Soviet Union. *See* SINCLAIR, *supra* note 20, at 62. Sinclair points out that by putting the onus on the "innocent" party to declare publicly that it does not wish to have treaty relations with the reserving state, the Convention may put smaller states in a difficult position when the reserving state is larger and more powerful.

[177] *See, e.g.*, OPPENHEIM, *supra* note 13, at 1248-1260; REUTER, *supra* note 1, ch. 3, at 73; and RESTATEMENT 3d, *supra* note 18, ch. 3, §§ 321-326.

of the Vienna Convention, which is entitled "Observance, Application and Interpretation of Treaties."

[1] *Pacta Sunt Servanda*

Perhaps the most fundamental principle of the law of treaties[178] — and indeed of international law as a whole[179] — is set forth in Article 26, "*Pacta sunt servanda.*" This Latin expression, which is not found in the text of the article itself, simply means that agreements are binding and must be performed. Or, as Article 26 puts it, "Every treaty in force is binding upon the parties to it and must be performed by them in good faith."[180] This may seem a statement of the obvious, but it lays to rest any notion that because a state is sovereign it may choose to disregard its treaty obligations.[181] And, as the ICJ found in the *Gabčíkovo-Nagymaros* case, the requirement that a treaty be performed in good faith may mean that "the purpose of the Treaty, and the intentions of the parties in concluding it, . . . should prevail over its literal application."[182] The Court continued: "The principle of good faith obliges the Parties to apply [the treaty] in a reasonable way and in such a manner that its purpose can be realized."[183]

Importantly, once a state becomes bound by a treaty it cannot assert justifications based on its internal law as a defense to its failure to perform the agreement.[184] Thus if State A's legislature passes a law requiring its government to do something that would cause it to violate a treaty, and State A follows that legislative directive, it may not plead the law in defense of its breach of the treaty.[185] In the *PLO Mission Case*, for example, the U.S. government was required by the 1987 Anti-Terrorism Act (ATA) to close all offices of the Palestine Liberation Organization (PLO) in the United States, apparently including the PLO's Permanent Observer

---

[178] The ILC called art. 26 "a definition of the very essence of treaties." [1982] 2 Y.B. Int'l L. Comm'n, pt. 2, 38.

[179] RESTATEMENT 3d, *supra* note 18, § 321 comment *a*.

[180] Vienna Convention, *supra* note 22, art. 26.

[181] In the *Wimbledon Case*, the Permanent Court of International Justice made the following statement regarding the relationship between sovereignty and treaty obligations: "The Court declines to see in the conclusion of any Treaty by which a State undertakes to perform or refrain from performing a particular act an abandonment of its sovereignty. No doubt any convention creating an obligation of this kind places a restriction upon the exercise of the sovereign rights of the State, in the sense that it requires them to be exercised in a certain way. But the right of entering into international engagements is an attribute of State sovereignty." 1923 P.C.I.J., (ser. A) No. 1, at 25. *See generally* Lord McNair, *Treaties and Sovereignty*, SYMBOLAE VERZIJL (1958), *reprinted in* LORD (ARNOLD D.) MCNAIR, LAW OF TREATIES, Appendix A, at 754 (1961).

[182] *Case concerning the Gabčíkovo-Nagymaros Project*, 1997 I.C.J. 7, 79.

[183] *Id.*

[184] Vienna Convention, *supra* note 22, art. 27.

[185] "This rule is without prejudice to article 46," according to Article 27 of the Vienna Convention. Article 46 provides that a state may not invoke its internal law as invalidating its consent to be bound by a treaty except in certain circumstances. Article 46 will be discussed in subsection [D], below.

Mission to the United Nations in New York. Closure of that office would have violated the Headquarters Agreement of 26 June 1947 between the U.S. and the U.N.[186] International law, and in particular Article 27 of the Vienna Convention, would not permit the United States to assert the ATA as a justification for violating the Headquarters Agreement. A federal district court avoided the problem by construing the ATA not to require closure of the PLO Mission.[187]

[2] Non-retroactivity and Territorial Scope

Treaties are generally non-retroactive.[188] Their legal effect is prospective unless a different intention appears, as in the case of certain tax and extradition treaties of the United States which state expressly that they apply retroactively.[189] The non-retroactivity rule is consistent with the *Ambatielos* case, in which the ICJ refused to give retroactive effect to a 1926 treaty under which Greece had attempted to present a claim concerning acts that had occurred in 1922 and 1923.[190]

With regard to territorial scope, a treaty is generally binding on a party in respect of its entire territory, as would be expected.[191] The rule does have implications for countries with overseas territories, however.[192]

[3] Successive Treaties Relating to the Same Subject Matter

The sharp increase in the number and variety of multilateral treaties since the Second World War has significantly multiplied the chances that a state will enter into successive agreements relating to the same subject matter.[193] These treaties typically do not cover precisely the same topic but instead overlap or conflict with each other to some degree. Thus, "the problem of incidental conflict between successive treaties has become more acute."[194] In such a case, is there a legal presumption that either the earlier or the later treaty prevails in the event that they are inconsistent? The answer is in the affirmative. The Vienna Convention provides that the later treaty generally prevails — specifically, that "the earlier treaty applies only to the extent that its provisions are compatible with those of the later

---

[186] 61 Stat. 3416, 11 U.N.T.S. 11.

[187] United States v. Palestine Liberation Organization, 695 F.Supp. 1456 (S.D.N.Y 1988). The United States Government did not appeal the district court's decision. *See* the discussion of this case in § 2.03 above.

[188] Vienna Convention, *supra* note 22, art. 28.

[189] *See, e.g.*, the agreements referred to in RESTATEMENT 3d, *supra* note 18, § 322, Reporters' Note 1.

[190] *Ambatielos* case (Preliminary Objection), 1952 I.C.J. 28, 40.

[191] Vienna Convention, *supra* note 22, art. 29.

[192] Some of these implications are explored in SINCLAIR, *supra* note 20, at 87-92.

[193] SINCLAIR, *supra* note 20, at 93, calls this a "particularly obscure aspect of the law of treaties". He concludes that the way in which it is dealt with in Article 30 of the Vienna Convention "is in many respects not entirely satisfactory." *Id.* at 98.

[194] *Id.* at 93.

treaty."[195] When the parties are the same this makes sense as a matter of treaty interpretation[196] since it is natural to assume, in the absence of evidence to the contrary, that states would intend a later agreement to override an earlier inconsistent one. That will not always be the case, however, as when the states concerned did not foresee the conflict.[197]

There is an important exception to the general later-in-time principle and it involves the United Nations Charter, effectively the constitution, or "basic law,"[198] of the international community. Article 103 of the Charter provides that in the event of a conflict between states' obligations under the Charter and those under "any other international agreement," whether concluded earlier or later, their obligations under the Charter prevail. The drafters of the Charter believed that it was critically important that performance by U.N. member states of their obligations under the Charter not be hindered in any way by their obligations under other agreements, even if those agreements were with non-member states.[199] The Covenant of the League of Nations contained a similar provision.[200]

[4] Interpretation

Just as is true of statutes in domestic law, treaty provisions may require interpretation to clarify how they apply in a particular case. Of course, if the meaning of a treaty's terms is clear, there is theoretically no need to resort to interpretation;[201] in such a case, the treaty "is 'applied,' not 'interpreted.'"[202] But often, terms that appear clear on their face become less so when an attempt is made to apply them to concrete facts and

---

[195] *Id.*, art. 30(3). This assumes, of course, that the parties to the two agreements are the same, that there is no provision to the contrary in the later treaty, and that the earlier treaty is still in force.

[196] *See* McNAIR,, *supra* note 181, at 219; and SINCLAIR, *supra* note 20, at 93.

[197] This may be the case, for example, with multilateral environmental agreements (MEAs) and the 1994 General Agreement on Tariffs and Trade (GATT), 33 I.L.M. 1125 (1994), which have come into conflict in several instances. For example, the 1987 Montreal Protocol on Substances that Deplete the Ozone Layer, S. TREATY DOC. No. 100-10, 1522 U.N.T.S. 3, and the 1973 Washington Convention on International Trade in Endangered Species of Flora and Fauna (CITES), 27 U.S.T. 1087, 993 U.N.T.S. 243, both use trade measures to effectuate their purposes, trade measures that may conflict with the GATT.

[198] LELAND M. GOODRICH, ET AL., CHARTER OF THE UNITED NATIONS, COMMENTARY AND DOCUMENTS 614 (3d ed. 1969).

[199] United Nations Conference on International Organizations, Report of the Rapporteur of Committee IV/2, Doc. 933, IV/2/42 (2).

[200] Covenant of the League of Nations, *available at* http:://www.yale.edu/lawweb/ avalon/leagcov, art. 20, providing that the members agree that the Covenant abrogates "all obligations or understandings inter se which are inconsistent with the terms thereof, and solemnly undertake that they will not hereafter enter into any engagements inconsistent with the terms thereof." Parties also pledged to "take immediate steps to procure [their] release from . . . obligations" entered into prior to becoming members of the League that were inconsistent with the Covenant. *Id.*, art. 20, second para.

[201] Vattel goes further: "it is not allowable to interpret what has no need of interpretation." 2 EMERICH VATTEL, LE DROIT DES GENS § 263 (1773).

[202] McNAIR, *supra* note 181, at 365 n. 1.

circumstances. It may well be that clarity can only be arrived at through the process of interpretation.[203]

The approach of international law to interpretation is in theory quite different from that generally followed in the United States. While U.S. courts and lawyers are often quick to resort to the legislative history of a statute to determine the intent of its drafters, international law mandates a focus on the ordinary meaning of the terms in question. As the International Law Commission put it, "the starting point of interpretation is the elucidation of the meaning of the text, not an investigation *ab initio* into the intentions of the parties."[204] International law by no means precludes reference to the preparatory work of a treaty (*travaux prépara-toires*) but relegates it to treatment as a "supplementary means of interpretation."[205] "The primacy of the text," as Reuter puts it, "is the cardinal rule for any interpretation."[206]

The doctrinal controversy swirling around the subject of interpretation of treaties is such that one of the great figures in the field of treaty law, Lord McNair, allowed that "there is no part of the law of treaties which [he] approaches with more trepidation than the question of interpretation."[207] Controversial though it may be, the law of treaty interpretation has not changed radically in several centuries: "in the seventeenth century Grotius set out the principles of treaty interpretation in terms not unlike those of the 1969 Vienna Convention on the Law of Treaties. . . ."[208] Rather than immersing ourselves in the complexities of the scholarly debate,[209] we will attempt simply to arrive at a basic understanding of the approach of the Vienna Convention to this important subject.

[a] The General Rule

The basic rules of the Vienna Convention on treaty interpretation are contained in Article 31. While the touchstone of interpretation of a treaty is the "ordinary meaning" of its terms, Article 31 begins by stating a still

---

[203] *See* OPPENHEIM, *supra* note 13, § 629, where it is pointed out that one does not know whether the meaning of a treaty is clear in relation to the case at hand without interpretation.

[204] [1966] 2 Y.B. Int'l L. Comm'n 220.

[205] Vienna Convention, *supra* note 22, art. 32.

[206] REUTER, *supra* note 1, at 74.

[207] McNAIR, *supra* note 181, at 364. Sinclair agrees with this observation. SINCLAIR, *supra* note 20, at 114.

[208] REUTER, *supra* note 1, at 1.

[209] A good overview of the various positions is given in SINCLAIR, *supra* note 20, at 114-15. They range from an effective denial of any rules of treaty interpretation (*see, e.g.,* Stone, *Fictional Elements in Treaty Interpretation*, 1 SYDNEY L. REV. 344 (1955)) to advocacy of a search for the "genuine shared expectations" of the parties (MYRES S. MCDOUGAL, HAROLD. LASSWELL & JAMES C. MILLER, INTERPRETATION OF AGREEMENTS AND WORLD ORDER (1967)). See also the review of the various schools of thought in Gerald Fitzmaurice, *The Law and Procedure of the International Court of Justice 1951-4: Treaty Interpretation and Other Treaty Points*, 33 BRIT. Y.B. INT'L L. 204 (1957).

more fundamental principle: that a treaty is to be interpreted *in good faith*.[210] Words should not be twisted to suit the convenience of a party nor, as Article 31 goes on to make clear, should they be wrenched out of their context. Good faith requires neutrality, or something close to it.

The starting point, as the ILC puts it, for the actual process of interpretation, is the "ordinary meaning" of the treaty's terms. But the ordinary meaning is to be determined not in the abstract, but in the terms' "context and in the light of [the treaty's] object and purpose."[211] As we have seen in relation to reservations, determining a treaty's object and purpose is not always an easy undertaking. But the task may be facilitated by reference to the treaty's preamble,[212] which normally recites the considerations that motivated the contracting states to conclude the agreement. In any event, reference to the object and purpose of a treaty may be seen as a second step, a method of testing an initial determination of a term's ordinary meaning.[213]

Paragraph 1 of Article 31 provides that a treaty is to be interpreted in conformity with "the ordinary meaning to be given to the terms of the treaty in their context. . . ." Thus the meaning of terms should not be sought by considering them in isolation or in the abstract. They must be taken in context. For example, in Article 1 of the Comprehensive Nuclear-Test-Ban Treaty (CTBT) each party "undertakes not to carry out any nuclear weapon test explosion or any other nuclear explosion. . . ."[214] The promise not to carry out "any other nuclear explosion," if read in isolation, could be taken as a commitment not to use nuclear weapons. However, when viewed in context, including the preamble's emphasis on nuclear disarmament and the very title of the treaty, it becomes clear that this is not the case.[215] Of course, if the parties intend to assign a special meaning to a term, this will be respected.[216]

But how broad is a treaty's "context" for the purpose of Article 31(1)? Paragraph 2 of the article provides a rather restrictive definition, containing the following elements: (1) The text of the treaty, including its

---

[210] This follows from art. 26 of the Vienna Convention, discussed above. *See* [1966] 2 Y.B. Int'l L. Comm'n 221.

[211] Vienna Convention, *supra* note 22, art. 31(1).

[212] The ICJ has done this on a number of occasions. *See, e.g., United States Nationals in Morocco,* 1952 I.C.J. 176, 196.

[213] According to Sinclair, "it is *in the light of* the object and purpose of the treaty that the initial and preliminary conclusion must be tested and either confirmed or modified." SINCLAIR, *supra* note 20, at 130. For Aust also, "in practice, having regard to the object and purpose is more for the purpose of confirming an interpretation." AUST, *supra* note 38, at 188.

[214] CTBT, art. 1, 35 I.L.M. 1443 (1996).

[215] The author is grateful to Anthony Aust for this example. *See* AUST, *supra* note 38, at 189.

[216] Vienna Convention, *supra* note 22, art. 31(4).

preamble and annexes.[217] It is clear that the text of a treaty, no less than that of a contract, statute or constitution, must be read as a whole, not piecemeal. (2) Any agreement relating to the treaty that was made between all the parties in connection with the conclusion of the treaty.[218] These agreements may be, but need not have been made at the same time the treaty was concluded. "'Connected agreements'; often form part of a network of treaties which can be viewed together as a whole,"[219] and referred to in order to provide a wider context for understanding the meaning of a particular term.[220] (3) Finally, any instrument made by one or more of the parties in connection with the conclusion of the treaty and accepted by the other parties as an instrument related to the treaty.[221] Note that such an instrument may be made by as few as "one" of the parties, so long as it is accepted by the others as being related to the treaty. The use of such instruments in connection with both bilateral and multilateral treaties is not uncommon.[222] They should be distinguished from "interpretative declarations"[223] states may make when signing or ratifying a treaty, however, which do not require acceptance.

A treaty may be modified, or the meaning of its terms illuminated, through the practice of the parties subsequent to its conclusion. This practice may take the form of subsequent agreements or simple conduct. Paragraph 3 of Article 31 recognizes that such practice is relevant to interpretation of the treaty's terms and states that it "shall" be taken into account, "together with"[224] the context. Specifically, paragraph 3 lists the following matters that are to be taken into account: (a) any subsequent agreement between the parties regarding the interpretation or application of the treaty, (b) any subsequent practice establishing agreement of the parties regarding the treaty's interpretation, and (c) any relevant rules of international law applicable in the relations between the parties.[225] A subsequent "agreement" need not be a treaty. It may take various forms, including a document adopted by the parties or a decision they adopt at a

---

[217] *Id.*, art. 31(2), chapeau.

[218] *Id.*, art. 31(2)(a).

[219] OPPENHEIM, *supra* note 13, at 1274.

[220] *See, e.g., Rights of United States Nationals in Morocco*, 1952 I.C.J. 176, 189; and *Rights of Passage Case*, 1960 I.C.J. 6, 38.

[221] Vienna Convention, *supra* note 22, art. 31(2)(b).

[222] Aust gives the examples of instruments produced by one or more member states of the European Union (EU) in connection with an EU treaty, the texts of which were agreed during the negotiation of the treaty; and the "many assurances and explanations in correspondence between the parties and in joint and national declarations" that accompanied the 1991 "START" treaty between the U.S. and the U.S.S.R. (Treaty on the Reduction and Limitation of Strategic Offensive Arms, 31 July 1991, 31 I.L.M. 246 (1992)). AUST, *supra* note 38, at 190.

[223] Interpretative declarations are discussed in § 4.05[B][2][c], *supra*.

[224] OPPENHEIM, *supra* note 13, at 1274 n. 17, states that the words "together with" indicate that "the stipulations which follow are to be taken as incorporated in the basic statement of the rule, and not as norms of an inferior character."

[225] Vienna Convention, *supra* note 22, art. 31(3)(a)-(c).

meeting.[226] Such subsequent interpretative agreements are not terribly common, however.[227]

More prevalent are instances of subsequent practice[228] relevant to a treaty's interpretation. How the parties actually apply a treaty can shed considerable light on their understanding of the meaning of its terms, as international tribunals have often recognized.[229] The parties' practice under a treaty can actually change what is apparently the plain meaning of the text. A well-known example of this relates to Article 27(3) of the U.N. Charter, which provides that decisions of the Security Council on non-procedural matters are to be made "by an affirmative vote of nine members including the concurring votes of the permanent members." This would appear to mean that all five permanent members of the Security Council must cast affirmative votes for such a decision to be made. However, the consistent practice of the Security Council since 1946 has been to treat an abstention or even a failure to vote due to absence[230] as the equivalent of a "concurring" vote within the meaning of Article 27(3).[231] As the International Court of Justice declared in the *Namibia* case, in upholding this practice, if a permanent member wishes to prevent the adoption of a non-procedural resolution, it "has only to cast a negative vote,"[232] generally known as a veto.

One interpreting a treaty is also to take into account relevant rules of international law, according to Article 31(3)(c). States may be presumed to have negotiated a treaty against the background of the rules of international law that existed at the time and thus it makes sense to interpret the treaty in light of those rules.[233] But it may also be necessary to have regard to developments in the law subsequent to the treaty's conclusion.

---

[226] Aust gives the example of a statement adopted at a meeting of the heads of state and government of EU countries which provided that the term Euro would henceforth be used instead of the term "ECU" (European currency unit) that is used in the Treaty of Rome, and that this was the agreed and definitive interpretation of the relevant provisions of the Rome treaty. AUST, *supra* note 38, at 192.

[227] *Accord*, SINCLAIR, *supra* note 20, at 136.

[228] Sinclair defines a "practice" as "a sequence of facts or acts [which] cannot in general be established by one isolated fact or act or even by several individual applications." *Id.* at 137.

[229] *See, e.g.*, the *Corfu Channel Case*, 1949 I.C.J. 25; the *Temple of Preah Vihear Case*, 1962 I.C.J. 34-35; *Certain Expenses of the UN*, 1962 I.C.J. 157-61; and other decisions referred to in OPPENHEIM, *supra* note 13, at 1274 n. 20.

[230] This was the case in 1950, early in the Korean War, when the Soviet representative did not attend Security Council meetings but was not thereby able to prevent the Council from taking action.

[231] *See* Constantin A. Stavropoulos, *The Practice of Voluntary Abstentions by Permanent Members of the Security Council under Article 27 Paragraph 3 of the Charter of the United Nations*, 61 AM. J. INT'L L. 737 (1967). *See also* SINCLAIR, *supra* note 20, at 137.

[232] *Legal Consequences for States of the Continued Presence of South Africa in Namibia*, Advisory Opinion, 21 June 1971, 1971 I.C.J. 16, 22.

[233] This is sometimes called inter-temporal law. *See* Rosalyn Higgins, *Some Observations on the Inter-Temporal Rule in International Law*, in J. Makarczyk ed., THEORY OF INTERNATIONAL LAW AT THE THRESHOLD OF THE 21ST CENTURY 173 (1996).

This would be the case where concepts embodied in an agreement are of an evolutionary nature. In such a case, as the ICJ recognized in the *Namibia* case, "interpretation cannot remain unaffected by the subsequent development of law."[234] The Court in that case went even further when it declared that "an international instrument has to be interpreted and applied within the framework of the entire legal system prevailing at the time of the interpretation."[235] Similarly, the terms of a treaty may in effect make it, or certain of its provisions, organic, so that newly developed norms of international law are relevant for its implementation. Thus, the ICJ found in the *Gabčíkovo-Nagymaros* case that the treaty involved there "is not static, and is open to adapt to emerging norms of international law."[236]

[b] Supplementary Means of Interpretation

Anything beyond the "context" of the terms of a treaty, as defined in Article 31(2), and the subsequent agreements and practice and relevant rules referred to in Article 31(3), is considered a "supplementary means of interpretation"[237] and may only be resorted to under Article 32 for specific, limited purposes. Article 32 provides that such supplementary means "include" — but they are not limited to[238] — the preparatory work of the treaty, such as a set of draft articles prepared by the International Law Commission, and the circumstances of the treaty's conclusion. That article makes clear that these interpretative aids may be referred to in only two situations: first, in order to *confirm* the meaning of a term derived from an application of the basic rule in Article 31; and second, to *determine* the meaning of a term when an interpretation under Article 31:

"(a) leaves the meaning ambiguous or obscure; or

(b) leads to a result which is manifestly absurd or unreasonable."[239]

Thus, while reference to the preparatory work of a treaty is not excluded, if the text is sufficiently clear there is no occasion to resort to that interpretative aid.[240]

---

[234] *Namibia (Legal Consequences)*, Advisory Opinion, *supra* note 232, 1971 I.C.J. at 31. *See also* the *Agean Sea Continental Shelf Case*, 1978 I.C.J. 3, 32.

[235] *Id.*

[236] 1997 I.C.J. 7, 68.

[237] Vienna Convention, *supra* note 22, art. 32.

[238] OPPENHEIM, *supra* note 13, at 1277-82, lists eleven supplementary means of interpretation.

[239] *Id.*, art. 32.

[240] *See Admission of a State to the United Nations*, 1948 I.C.J. 63, where the Court said, "there is no occasion to resort to preparatory work if the text of a convention is sufficiently clear in itself."

In reading the literature of international law one often finds mention of various maxims.[241] These are only aids to interpretation that may be relevant in a given case, not controlling rules. A sampling of those often referred to is as follows:

- *Ejusdem generis* — general language following special words are limited to the *genus*, or class, indicated by the special words.

- *Expressio unius est exclusio alterius* — the expression of one thing excludes others that are not expressed.

- *Lex posterior derogat legi priori* — a later rule prevails over an earlier one applicable to the same question.

- *Lex specialis derogat legi generali* — a specific rule prevails over a general one.

The first two maxims are in essence grammatical rules of construction. Another common principle of interpretation is that where two meanings are possible, the one least advantageous to the proponent, drafter or beneficiary of the provision — i.e., the interpretation *contra proferentem* — is preferred.

[c] Treaties in More than One Language

It is common today for treaties to be adopted in more than one language.[242] Article 33 of the Vienna Convention addresses problems of interpretation that may result from different language versions. Many "plurilingual" treaties[243] provide that all language texts are equally authentic,[244] and even if there is no such provision Article 33(1) provides that where a treaty has been authenticated in more than one language, the text is equally authoritative in each language. A treaty's terms are presumed to have the same meaning in each authentic text.[245] Unfortunately, this does not provide much assistance in resolving conflicting interpretations based on different language versions. Obviously, if the treaty provides that a particular language version is to prevail in the case of inconsistency, that rule will be respected. But otherwise, how are differing interpretations based on different language versions to be resolved?

---

[241] *See* the more extensive lists of maxims and other supplementary means of interpretation in OPPENHEIM, *supra* note 13, at 1277-82; and AUST, *supra* note 38, at 200-01.

[242] Aust gives the "extreme" example of the 1997 Protocol to the 1980 Eurocontrol Convention, of which there are nineteen equally authentic language versions, although it provides that the French text is to control in the case of any inconsistency. AUST, *supra* note 38, at 203.

[243] *See generally* OPPENHEIM, *supra* note 13, at 1283-84; SINCLAIR, *supra* note 20, at 147-52; AUST, *supra* note 38, at 202-06; and Dinah Shelton, *Reconcilable of Differences? The Interpretation of Multilingual Treaties*, 20 HASTINGS INT'L & COMP. L. REV. 611 (1997).

[244] Sometimes a third, neutral, language is designated as controlling in the case of inconsistency, as in the case of English in the 1994 Treaty of Peace between Israel and Jordan, whose texts in Arabic, Hebrew and English are equally authentic. 34 I.L.M. 43 (1995).

[245] Vienna Convention, *supra* note 22, art. 33(3).

That question is answered by Article 33(4), which provides that where a difference of meaning cannot be resolved through the application of the rules of interpretation in Articles 31 and 32, "the meaning which best reconciles the texts, having regard to the object and purpose of the treaty, shall be adopted." In the end, therefore, the interpreter will have to wrestle with the two language versions, keeping an eye on the object and purpose of the treaty and taking into account such factors as whether a particular language was dominant in the negotiations.[246]

[5]   Treaties and Third States

Just as contracts are not binding on non-parties under domestic law, treaties do not create rights or obligations for a "third state" — i.e., one "not a party to the treaty"[247] — without its consent.[248] It follows from this that if a treaty does purport to impose an obligation on a third state, the latter is bound only if it "expressly accepts that obligation in writing."[249] Rights are a different matter, of course, and the Vienna Convention's regime regarding rights of a third state under a treaty is correspondingly more liberal. In order to acquire a right under a treaty, the third state must assent thereto, but its assent is presumed absent a contrary indication.[250] Treaties that merely *benefit* third states — such as pollution control agreements — are another matter and do not confer rights on them.[251] However, treaties that create obligations *erga omnes* (owed to all) do, by definition, create rights in third states. An example of such an agreement is the 1959 Antarctic Treaty,[252] which creates a special, or "objective," regime for Antarctica.[253]

---

[246] *See* Sinclair's discussion of the *Young Loan* arbitration (Belgium et al. v. Federal Republic of Germany, 59 ILR 495 (1980)), in which he states that "some weight ought to be given to the original language text on which the negotiators agreed if it is apparent from the *travaux préparatoires* . . . that other language versions are mere translations." SINCLAIR, *supra* note 20, at 152.

[247] Vienna Convention, *supra* note 22, art. 2(1)(h).

[248] *Id.*, art. 34.

[249] *Id.*, art. 35, requiring also that the parties to the treaty intend the provision in question to be the means for establishing the obligation. Even if these two conditions are satisfied, the third state does not become a party to the treaty.

[250] *Id.*, art. 36(1) which, like art. 35, requires that the parties to the treaty intend to accord the right — in this case, "either to the third State, or to a group of States to which it belongs, or to all States. . . ." If the state exercises the right, it must comply with any conditions for its exercise provided for or established under the treaty. *Id.*, art. 36 (2). Aust points out that "Peace treaties concluded after the two World Wars provided for the defeated states to waive claims arising out of the wars in favor of certain states which were not parties to the peace treaties." AUST, *supra* note 38, at 208.

The issue of revocation or modification of obligations or rights of third states is governed by art. 37 of the Vienna Convention.

[251] *See* AUST, *supra* note 38, at 208.

[252] 402 U.N.T.S. 71.

[253] For other examples, *see* AUST, *supra* note 38, at 208-09.

Although they do not qualify as exceptions to the general rule, treaties that codify norms of customary international law may seem to create obligations for third states. Of course, it is the customary norm, not the treaty that codifies it, which obligates the third state.[254] But codification conventions, like the Vienna Convention itself, have proved quite useful to the ICJ[255] and others in giving customary norms a degree of precision they might otherwise lack. For example, in its Advisory Opinion in *Legal Consequences of the Construction of a Wall in the Occupied Palestinian Territory*,[256] the Court stated that it "considers that the provisions of the Hague Regulations [Respecting the Laws and Customs of War on Land, annexed to the Fourth Hague Convention of 18 October 1907] have become part of customary law. . . ."[257] The norms they expressed were therefore applicable to Israel which was not a party to the Fourth Hague Convention of 1907.

[D] Amendment and Modification of Treaties

"As a question of law, there is not much to be said upon the revision of treaties."[258] Treaties may be amended by agreement of the parties.[259] This is not surprising. It caused Lord McNair to observe that since "no State is legally obliged to conclude a treaty . . . treaty revision is a matter for politics and diplomacy . . ." [260] rather than law. An amendment of a treaty is, *pro tanto*, a new treaty. It must accordingly be made in accordance with the normal rules for making treaties,[261] including any applicable rules under domestic law. What makes the procedures for amendment especially significant is the difficulty of escaping treaty obligations, as detailed in the following section. If it were easier to terminate a treaty, the incentive of a party advantaged by its provisions to agree to amend it would presumably be greater. But, with Lord McNair, it must be acknowledged that "we touch here one of the weakest spots in the now existing system of States, and it must be admitted that no national society which is not equipped with legislative and administrative machinery for effecting changes could hope to hold together for long."[262]

Modern multilateral treaties often address this "weak spot" by establishing their own, self-contained procedures for amendment.[263] Probably

---

[254] Vienna Convention, *supra* note 22, art. 38.

[255] Among numerous examples, *see, e.g.,* the *Gabčíkovo-Nagymaros* case, 1997 I.C.J. 7, 38, para. 46 (Vienna Convention on the Law of Treaties).

[256] 9 July 2004, 2004 I.C.J. 131.

[257] *Id.*, para. 89.

[258] McNair, *supra* note 181, at 534.

[259] Vienna Convention, *supra* note 22, art. 39, which goes on to provide that the rules of the Convention on conclusion and entry into force of treaties apply to any such amendment unless the treaty provides otherwise.

[260] McNair, *supra* note 181, at 534.

[261] *Id.*

[262] *Id.*

[263] *See* the examples given in Aust, *supra* note 38, at 215-18.

the best known example is Article 108 of the U.N. Charter, which provides as follows:

> "Amendments to the present Charter shall come into force for all Members of the United Nations when they have been adopted by a vote of two thirds of the members of the General Assembly and ratified in accordance with their respective constitutional processes by two thirds of the Members of the United Nations, including all the permanent members of the Security Council."[264]

It will be noted that an amendment adopted in accordance with this procedure is binding on *all members* of the United Nations, whether or not they voted for or ratified it. Other treaties contain similar provisions on amendment.[265]

Provided the other party agrees, there is no particular difficulty in amending a bilateral treaty. This is not the case with multilateral treaties, which may have as many as 150 parties or more. Moreover, since they often have no set duration, multilateral treaties are likely to reach a stage where they require amendment. Amendment and modification of multilateral treaties is governed by Articles 40 and 41 of the Vienna Convention, which address the difficulties inherent in attempting to make changes to an instrument in which many countries have a stake. This subsection will briefly describe the rules set forth in those provisions.

Article 40 deals with "amendment" of multilateral treaties, while Article 41 concerns "modification" of such agreements. As used in the Convention, "amendment" refers to changes intended to apply to all parties, while a "modification" is an agreement between two or more of the parties to alter the treaty as between themselves alone. Understandably, somewhat different regimes apply to each of these forms of changing the text of a treaty.

For "amendments," Article 40 requires that unless the treaty otherwise provides, all contracting states must be notified of a proposal to amend the treaty and have the right to participate in both the decision on the action to be taken on the proposal and the negotiation and conclusion of any amending agreement. The treaty as amended would be effective only as between the states that become parties to the amending agreement. A party to the original treaty only would remain so vis-à-vis another state that had also accepted the amending agreement, since the original agreement is the one to which both are parties.[266] If a state becomes a party to the treaty after the amending agreement has entered into force, unless it expresses a different intention it will be regarded as a party to the treaty as amended; as to states that were only parties to the unamended treaty,

---

[264] U.N. CHAPTER, art. 108.

[265] *See* AUST, *supra* note 38, at 215-18 for other examples.

[266] Vienna Convention, *supra* note 22, art. 40(4), referring to art. 30(4)(b) on the case in which the parties to a successive treaty relating to the same subject matter as an earlier one do not include all the parties to the earlier one.

it would be considered as a party to that treaty.[267] It will be recalled that the parties to an agreement can also, in effect, amend it through practice under it.[268]

As to "modifications" effected by a limited number of parties to a multilateral treaty, a key question is whether such changes would adversely affect other parties to the treaty. Article 41 protects such other parties by requiring that where the possibility of a modification is neither provided for nor prohibited by the treaty, a modification may be made so long as it does not affect the enjoyment of the rights or the performance of the obligations of the other parties to the treaty and is not incompatible with the treaty's object and purpose. Again, other parties must be notified of the intent to modify and of the modification.[269]

[E] Invalidity and Termination of Treaties

It has already been suggested that it is very hard to get out of a treaty, at least if the other party or parties do not wish that to happen. And as the international community becomes increasingly integrated and interdependent it is ever more difficult for a state to simply walk away from its treaty obligations without suffering unpleasant consequences. This is perhaps not such a bad state of affairs in a world that for the most part lacks tribunals with compulsory jurisdiction that can decide whether a state's claims regarding a treaty or its observance by other parties are legitimate. It stands to reason that since a state cannot routinely go to court to enforce a treaty, or to escape from one, the rules for terminating treaties must of necessity be highly strict and clear, admitting of very little room for argument from the other side as to whether they have been complied with. Nevertheless, argue states do, as we will see.

This subsection will first consider possible grounds for impeaching the very validity of the treaty. It will then go through the main ways in which a treaty may be terminated. As to all of these methods of challenging the validity of or terminating a treaty, certain procedural rules apply. These rules, which are set forth in Articles 65 and following of the Vienna Convention, essentially require prior notification of the claim in question; then, if a timely objection to the claim is made, they require that the parties seek a solution through the means for peaceful settlement of disputes indicated in Article 33 of the U.N. Charter[270] or through other means that they have accepted. In the *Gabčíkovo-Nagymaros* case, the parties were

---

[267] *Id.*, art. 40(5).

[268] *See id.*, art. 31(3)(a). AUST, *supra* note 38, at 214, notes that the Convention on International Trade in Endangered Species (CITES), 999 U.N.T.S. 243, was "effectively modified by a resolution of the Conference of the Parties in 1986 despite an amendment procedure having been built into the Convention."

[269] *Id.*, art. 41(2).

[270] These are: "negotiation, enquiry, mediation, conciliation, arbitration, judicial settlement, resort to regional agencies or arrangements, or other peaceful means of their own choice." U.N. CHARTER, art. 33(1).

not bound by the Vienna Convention in respect of the treaty involved there. Nevertheless, the ICJ emphasized the importance of procedural principles in the following terms:

> "Both Parties agree that Articles 65 to 67 of the Vienna Convention on the Law of Treaties, if not codifying customary law, at least generally reflect customary international law and contain certain procedural principles which are based on an obligation to act in good faith. As the Court stated in its Advisory Opinion on the Interpretation of the Agreement of 25 March 1951 between the WHO and Egypt (in which case the Vienna Convention did not apply):
>
>> 'Precisely what periods of time may be involved in the observance of the duties to consult and negotiate, and what period of notice of termination should be given, are matters which necessarily vary according to the requirements of the particular case. In principle, therefore, it is for the parties in each case to determine the length of those periods by consultation and negotiation in good faith.'"[271]

Thus even where the parties to a dispute are not bound by the Vienna Convention, the basic procedural principles it embodies will be binding on them as rules of customary international law.

[1] Invalidity

It has been observed by a seasoned practitioner in the field that the subject of the invalidity of treaties "is not of the slightest importance in the day-to-day work of a foreign ministry."[272] Nevertheless, the Vienna Convention contains nine articles on the subject (Articles 46-53 and 64), which justifies a brief review of the main grounds for finding a treaty invalid or void. Those grounds include lack of competence, error, fraud, corruption, coercion and conflict with a peremptory norm of international law (*jus cogens*).

[a] Lack of Competence

We have already seen that a state cannot assert justifications based on its internal law as a defense to its failure to perform the agreement.[273] The same is true of an assertion that its consent to be bound was expressed in violation of a provision of its internal law regarding competence to conclude treaties.[274] The only exception to this rule is for the case in which the violation was manifest and concerned a rule of its internal

---

[271] 1997 I.C.J. 7, 66 (quoting 1980 I.C.J. 96, para. 49)).

[272] AUST, *supra* note 38, at 252. That author goes on to say that he "does not recall during more than thirty years of practice a single serious suggestion that an existing treaty might be invalid." *Id.*

[273] Vienna Convention, *supra* note 22, art. 27.

[274] *Id.*, art. 46(1).

[275] *Id.*

law of fundamental importance.[275] Likewise, a state may not invoke the failure of its representative to observe a restriction it imposed on his or her authority to express its consent to be bound unless the state had notified the other negotiating states of the restriction prior to the representative's expression of consent.[276]

[b] Error

It makes sense to allow a state to invalidate its consent to be bound to a treaty where it was based on a fact or situation that turns out not to exist. This ground is recognized by the Vienna Convention, subject to several conditions: the mistake must relate to a fact or situation that formed an essential basis of the state's consent to be bound by the treaty; the state in question must not have contributed by its own conduct to the error; and the circumstances must not have been such as to have put the state on notice of a possible error.[277] Most cases of this kind involve incorrect maps.[278]

[c] Fraud

A state may invoke fraud as invalidating its consent to be bound by a treaty where it was induced to conclude the treaty by the fraudulent conduct of another negotiating state.[279]

[d] Corruption

If a state's consent to be bound by a treaty is procured by the corruption of its representative by another negotiating state, the state may invoke the corruption as invalidating its consent to be bound.[280] "Corruption" for the purpose of this rule refers not to small courtesies or favors but to something that is calculated to influence the representative in a substantial way.[281]

[e] Coercion

As with corruption, expression of consent to be bound due to coercion is invalid. Where a state's representative has been coerced, through acts or threats directed against him or her, to express the state's consent to be bound, the consent is without any legal effect.[282] By the same token, where the state itself is coerced into concluding a treaty by an unlawful threat or use of force, the treaty is void.[283]

---

[276] *Id.*, art. 47.

[277] *Id.*, art. 48(1) and (2).

[278] OPPENHEIM, *supra* note 13, at 1288. *See also* AUST, *supra* note 38, at 254.

[279] Vienna Convention, *supra* note 22, art. 49. Oppenheim observes that examples of such fraud "are happily very rare." OPPENHEIM, *supra* note 13, at 1289.

[280] Vienna Convention, *supra* note 22, art. 50.

[281] [1966] 2 Y.B. Int'l L. Comm'n 245.

[282] Vienna Convention, *supra* note 22, art. 51.

[283] *Id.*, art. 52. That provision refers to a threat or use of force in violation of the U.N. Charter, but since these acts are prohibited by general international law the principle applies to non-members of the U.N. as well. *See* AUST, *supra* note 38, at 256.

[f]   *Jus Cogens*

The concept of a norm of *jus cogens*, or a peremptory norm of international law, is defined in Article 53 of the Vienna Convention as:

> "a norm accepted and recognized by the international community of States as a whole as a norm from which no derogation is permitted and which can be modified only by a subsequent norm of general international law having the same character."[284]

These are, then, norms of general, or customary, international law of the highest order. Unfortunately, there is no generally accepted list of *jus cogens* norms. But it is safe to say that the U.N. Charter's prohibition of the use of force, in Article 2(4) qualifies as such a norm. In addition, it is likely that including genocide in the list would not encounter objections. Other possible candidates are slavery, torture, colonialism and *apartheid*.

The Vienna Convention provides in Article 53 that a treaty is void if it conflicts with a norm of *jus cogens* at the time of its conclusion. In Article 64 the Convention further provides that if a new peremptory norm emerges, any treaty that is in conflict with it "becomes void and terminates."[285] Thus, states' "freedom to contract," through entering into treaties, is limited by norms of *jus cogens*. It should be emphasized that this is a very small group of norms and, indeed, that beyond one or two members of the group there is no agreement on its composition. Thus, care should be taken in asserting this basis for invalidity.

[2]   Termination

Today many treaties contain provisions on duration and termination. In the absence of such a provision, the party wishing to suspend or terminate a treaty has the burden of establishing that a ground exists for doing so. And not just any ground will do: only the few that are contained in the Vienna Convention may be invoked. In the *Gabčíkovo-Nagymaros* case, the International Court of Justice noted that it had in several cases held that some of the rules laid down in the Vienna Convention might be considered as codifications of existing customary international law.[286] It declared that in many respects this applies to the rules of the Vienna Convention concerning the termination and suspension of the operation of treaties, set forth in Articles 60-62.[287] The Court therefore held that the treaty involved in that case "could be terminated only on the limited

---

[284] Vienna Convention, *supra* note 22, art. 53.

[285] *Id.*, art. 64.

[286] 1997 I.C.J. 7, 38.

[287] *Id.* (citing Legal Consequences for States of the Continued Presence of South Africa in Namibia (South-West Africa) notwithstanding Security Council Resolution 276 (1970)), Advisory Opinion, 1971 I.C.J. 47 and Fisheries Jurisdiction (United Kingdom v. Iceland), Jurisdiction of the Court, Judgment, 1973 I.C.J. Reports 18; *see also* Interpretation of the Agreement of 25 March 1951 between the WHO and Egypt, Advisory Opinion, 1980 I.C.J. Reports 95-96.

grounds enumerated in the Vienna Convention."[288] No others may be invoked.[289] Those grounds are: material breach (Article 60), supervening impossibility of performance (Article 61), fundamental change of circumstances (Article 62), and — although it was not involved in the *Gabčíkovo* case — emergence of a new norm of *jus cogens* (Article 64). These are not easy to establish, and for good reason: the international community places great weight in the stability of treaty relations, which requires that it not be easy for states to escape their treaty obligations.

This principle was recently confirmed in resounding fashion by the ICJ in the *Gabčíkovo* case.[290] In that case, all of the grounds of termination enumerated above save *jus cogens* were asserted. The Court found that none was applicable. The essential facts of the *Gabčíkovo* case were as follows: Hungary and Czechoslovakia entered into a treaty in 1977 providing for the construction and operation of the Gabčíkovo-Nagymaros project, a system of dams and related works on the Danube River. Many of the works were on a stretch of the Danube that forms the border between the two states. In the late 1980s and early 1990s, Hungary suspended and subsequently abandoned work on the project, citing financial, environmental and other concerns. In May, 1992, Hungary unilaterally issued a declaration of termination of the 1977 treaty, referring to the grounds listed above as alternative justifications for its action. Czechoslovakia rejected Hungary's attempt to terminate the treaty. In October of that year, Czechoslovakia unilaterally implemented the upstream portion of the project by means of a dam it constructed on a portion of the Danube that is wholly within Czechoslovak territory, referred to as Variant C. On January 1, 1993, Slovakia became an independent state. The non-Hungarian portions of project are located in what then became Slovak territory. In April 1993 Hungary and Slovakia agreed to submit the case to the Court. The Court's judgment in this case will be referred to below, for purposes of illustration, in discussing grounds for termination. Before taking up the grounds that may be invoked unilaterally to terminate a treaty, several other possibilities will be addressed.

First, as is perhaps obvious, a treaty may be terminated, or a party may withdraw, in accordance with the terms of the treaty.[291] As mentioned above, treaties — especially multilateral ones — increasingly contain such provisions. Equally obvious is that a treaty may be terminated or a party may withdraw at any time with the consent of all the parties.[292]

---

[288] 1997 I.C.J. at 63.

[289] This follows from the *Gabčíkovo* judgment in respect of customary international law, and from art. 42(2) of the Vienna Convention in cases where that treaty is binding on the parties. As discussed below, Hungary's assertion of the defense of necessity was treated by the Court not as a ground for terminating the treaty but as a circumstance that might preclude the wrongfulness of Hungary's breach of the treaty. 1997 I.C.J. at 38-39.

[290] 1997 I.C.J. 7.

[291] Vienna Convention, *supra* note 22, art. 54(a).

[292] *Id.*, art. 54(b).

Somewhat more subtle is the consequence of the reduction of the parties to a multilateral treaty below the number necessary for its entry into force: does the treaty continue in force or does it terminate? Article 55 provides that under these circumstances the treaty does not terminate.

A key provision on termination is Article 56, which deals with the situation in which a treaty contains no provision on termination, denunciation or withdrawal. A slight digression is necessary here to address terminology. "Denunciation" is a unilateral act by which a party seeks to terminate its participation in a *bilateral* treaty. "Withdrawal" is the counterpart of denunciation for *multilateral* treaties. Whereas lawful denunciation will terminate a bilateral treaty, withdrawal from a multilateral treaty will not normally terminate it.

Returning now to Article 56, that article provides that a treaty containing no provision on termination, denunciation or withdrawal is *not generally subject to denunciation or withdrawal*. This is a crucial point because it means that in the absence of an agreement to terminate or an applicable provision in the treaty, a party wishing to escape its treaty obligations must be able to place itself within one of the four narrow grounds for termination. It cannot simply announce that it is terminating and walk away. The exceptions contained in Article 56 will generally not be of much comfort to such a state. They are that the parties intended to admit the possibility of denunciation or withdrawal;[293] or a right of denunciation or withdrawal may be implied by the nature of the treaty.[294]

[a] Material Breach

Article 60 of the Vienna Convention provides that a state may "invoke" a material breach by another party to a treaty as a ground for terminating the treaty or suspending its operation in whole or in part. The use of the term "invoke" signifies that a unilateral declaration of termination does not bring the treaty, or the state's participation in it, to an end.[295] Rather, the state invoking a material breach by another state must follow the procedures set out in Articles 65-68 of the Convention, or their counterparts under customary international law as discussed above.

The situation is obviously different as between bilateral and multilateral treaties. Article 60 accordingly provides for them separately. In the case of a bilateral treaty, a material breach by one party entitles the other party to invoke the breach as a ground for terminating or suspending it.[296] As the ICJ noted in the *Gabčíkovo* case, the breach

---

[293] *Id.*, art. 56(1)(a).

[294] *Id.*, art. 56(1)(b). Article 56(2) provides that at least twelve months' notice must be given of a party's intention to denounce or withdraw from a treaty under art. 56(1).

[295] To this effect, *see* OPPENHEIM, *supra* note 13, at 1300; and AUST, *supra* note 38, at 237.

[296] Vienna Convention, *supra* note 22, art. 60(1).

must be of the treaty the state is seeking to terminate; alleged breaches of other treaties or rules of general international law do not constitute a ground for termination under the law of treaties.[297] The Court also pointed out in that case that one party to a bilateral treaty cannot assert the other party's breach as a ground for termination if the breach was a result of the first party's own prior wrongful conduct.[298] Thus Hungary could not invoke Czechoslovakia's wrongful act of putting Variant C into operation as a ground for termination because that had been done in response to Hungary's having wrongfully stopped work on the project.

A more complex set of possibilities arises from the material breach of a multilateral treaty by one of the parties. Responsive action may be taken by all of the other parties together or by individual states. First, all of the other parties to the treaty may, by unanimous agreement, suspend the operation of the treaty in whole or in part, or terminate it, either (i) as between themselves and the defaulting state, or (ii) as between all of the parties to the treaty.[299] Second, a party specially affected by the breach may invoke it as a ground for *suspending* the operation of the treaty in whole or in part in the relations between itself and the defaulting state.[300] And there is a third possibility, relating to a special category of treaty. This kind of agreement is described in Article 60 as being "of such a character that a material breach of its provisions by one party radically changes the position of every party with respect to the further performance of its obligations under the treaty." Disarmament agreements are the classic examples of such treaties, since a breach by one party could mean that other parties would want to protect their interests by re-arming, at least provisionally. In the case of such treaties, any party may invoke the defaulting state's breach as a ground for suspending the operation of the treaty in whole or in part with respect to itself.[301]

In order for a party to have the right to terminate or suspend in the above circumstances the breach must be "material." Article 60 defines material breach as:

"(a) a repudiation of the treaty not sanctioned by the present Convention; or

(b) the violation of a provision essential to the accomplishment of the object or purpose of the treaty."[302]

---

[297] 1997 I.C.J. 7, 65. The Court noted, however, that such breaches of other treaties or rules of general international law may justify the injured state in taking countermeasures against the breaching state. *Id.*

[298] *Id.* at 67.

[299] Vienna Convention, *supra* note 22, art. 60(2)(a)(i) and (ii).

[300] *Id.*, art. 60(2)(b).

[301] *Id.*, art. 60(2)(c).

[302] *Id.*, art. 60(3)(a) and (b).

An example of the latter might be the refusal of a party to the Chemical Weapons Convention to allow international inspections to verify its compliance, since such inspections are a cornerstone of the regime established by the treaty.

In any case, it would be absurd to permit a party to a human rights or humanitarian treaty to terminate it or suspend its operation in response to a material breach by another state. Article 60(5) recognizes this, referring in particular to provisions of such agreements prohibiting any form of reprisal against persons protected by this kind of treaty, such as prisoners of war.

[b] Impossibility

It seems reasonable that a state should be allowed to terminate an agreement if it becomes impossible to perform. Article 61 of the Vienna Convention, "Supervening Impossibility of Performance," recognizes this possibility but restricts it severely.[303] To entitle a state to invoke impossibility as a ground for terminating or withdrawing from a treaty, the impossibility must result from "the permanent disappearance or destruction of an object indispensable for the execution of the treaty."[304] If the impossibility is temporary, the state may only invoke it to justify suspending the treaty's operation. In its commentary, the International Law Commission acknowledged that there are few examples in state practice of termination of a treaty on this ground.[305] As examples of situations that would fit the narrow requirements of Article 61 the Commission gave the following: "the submergence of an island, the drying-up of a river or the destruction of a dam or hydro-electric installation indispensable for the execution of a treaty."[306]

The requirement that an "object" be involved has drawn criticism on the basis that many treaties can become impossible to perform but do not involve objects of the kind referred to in Article 61.[307] Indeed, in the *Gabčíkovo* case, Hungary asserted impossibility as a ground for terminating the 1977 treaty but was unable to identify a physical object that had disappeared or been destroyed. Hungary was therefore left to contend that "the essential object of the Treaty — an economic joint investment which was consistent with environmental protection and which was operated by the two contracting parties jointly — had permanently disappeared and that the Treaty had thus become impossible to perform."[308]

---

[303] The Restatement notes that Article 61's definition of the doctrine of impossibility does not reach situations produced by *force majeure* (acts of God) or war and is therefore "narrower than the analogous doctrines of impossibility and frustration in international trade law or in domestic contract law." RESTATEMENT 3d, *supra* note 18, § 336, Reporters' Note 3.

[304] Vienna Convention, *supra* note 22, art. 61(a).

[305] [1966] 2 Y.B. Int'l L. Comm'n 256.

[306] *Id.*

[307] *See* SINCLAIR, *supra* note 20, at 191, referring to criticism by Capotorti.

[308] 1997 I.C.J.7, 63.

The Court observed, however, that "Hungary's interpretation of the wording of Article 61 is . . . not in conformity with the terms of that article, nor with the intentions of the Diplomatic Conference which adopted the Convention."[309] While a proposal had been made at the conference to include in the scope of the article cases such as the impossibility to repay loans due to serious financial difficulties, the participating states were not prepared to include such situations within the article, preferring a much narrower scope.[310] The Court concluded by saying that it was not necessary for it to determine whether the term "object" could be understood to embrace a legal regime as well as something physical since even if it could the regime had not definitively ceased to exist; the 1977 treaty remained in force and allowed the parties to adjust its terms. Furthermore, the Court pointed out, if joint operation of the project was no longer possible this was "originally because Hungary did not carry out most of the works for which it was responsible under the 1977 Treaty; . . . ."[311] And Article 61(2) expressly provides that a party may not invoke impossibility when it results from the party's own breach of an obligation under the treaty.

The Restatement does not contain a separate section on impossibility, treating it as a "particular application of *rebus sic stantibus* since the disappearance of an indispensable object would ordinarily constitute a 'fundamental change of circumstances.'"[312] We will now turn to that latter ground.

[c]　Fundamental Change of Circumstances

A fundamental change in the circumstances that existed at the time a treaty was concluded may entitle a party to terminate or withdraw from the treaty, but only under very limited conditions. The Latin expression *rebus sic stantibus* is often used to refer to this doctrine.[313] As Oppenheim explains,

> "it is the function of the law to enforce contracts or treaties even if they become burdensome for the party bound by them. This explains why, in almost all cases in which the doctrine *rebus sic stantibus* has been invoked before an international tribunal, the latter, while not rejecting it in principle, has refused to admit that it could be applied to the case before it."[314]

---

[309] *Id.*

[310] *Id.*

[311] *Id.* at 64.

[312] RESTATEMENT 3d, *supra* note 18, § 336 cmt. c.

[313] Thus the idea that all treaties include an implied clause, a *clausula rebus sic stantibus*, providing that the obligations they contain terminate with a change of circumstances. *See* RESTATEMENT 3d, *supra* note 18, § 336 cmt. a. The International Law Commission rejected this notion of an implied term as undesirable "since it increased the risk of subjective interpretation and abuse." [1966] 2 Y.B. Int'l L. Comm'n 258. The expression *rebus sic stantibus* remains in common use, however.

[314] OPPENHEIM, *supra* note 13, at 1307.

Indeed, in the *Gabčíkovo* case, Hungary invoked as a ground for termination what was surely one of the greatest changes of circumstances in the twentieth century: the collapse of the Soviet Union.[315] But even this was unavailing due to the restrictions on the use of the doctrine contained in Article 62. Those begin with the negative formulation of the general rule: "A fundamental change of circumstances . . . may *not* be invoked as a ground for terminating or withdrawing from the treaty unless. . . ."[316] This emphasizes the highly restrictive nature of this ground for termination: a change may not be invoked unless the conditions are satisfied. The two conditions laid down in Article 62 are that: (a) the existence of the circumstances that have allegedly changed must have constituted an essential basis of the consent of the parties to be bound by the treaty; and (b) the effect of the change of circumstances must have been to radically transform the extent of obligations still to be performed under the treaty.[317]

In the *Gabčíkovo* case, the Court noted that the treaty involved there "provided for a joint investment programme for the production of energy, the control of floods and the improvement of navigation on the Danube."[318] It then stated: "In the Court's view, the prevalent political conditions were thus not so closely linked to the object and purpose of the Treaty that they constituted an essential basis of the consent of the parties and, in changing, radically altered the extent of the obligations still to be performed."[319] It found that the same was true of the economic system that prevailed when the treaty was concluded.[320] The Court added an exclamation point in summing up its discussion of this ground for termination:

> "The negative and conditional wording of Article 62 of the Vienna Convention on the Law of Treaties is a clear indication . . . that the stability of treaty relations requires that the plea of fundamental change of circumstances be applied only in exceptional cases."[321]

Thus it is clear that an assertion of *rebus sic stantibus* as a ground of termination will be examined very closely indeed to determine whether the two conditions mentioned above are satisfied. Yet even if they are, Article 62 imposes two additional hurdles.

First, *rebus* may not be invoked if the treaty involved establishes a boundary.[322] And second, a fundamental change may not be invoked if it is the result of a breach by the party invoking it either of an obligation under the treaty involved or of any other international obligation owed to

---

[315] 1997 I.C.J. 7, 64.

[316] Vienna Convention, *supra* note 22, art. 62(1) (emphasis added).

[317] *Id.*, subparas. (a) and (b).

[318] 1997 I.C.J. at 64.

[319] *Id.*

[320] *Id.*

[321] *Id.* at 65.

[322] Vienna Convention, *supra* note 22, art. 62(2)(a).

any other party to the treaty. Thus the party asserting the change must, in effect, have clean hands.

[d] *Jus Cogens*

Article 64 of the Vienna Convention is entitled "Emergence of a New Peremptory Norm of General International Law (*Jus Cogens*)." It provides that the effect of the emergence of such a norm is that a treaty that is in conflict with it "becomes void and terminates."[323] It will be recalled that the concept of *jus cogens* is defined in Article 53, which provides that a treaty is void if it conflicts with a norm of *jus cogens* at the time it is concluded.[324] It is only logical that a treaty should suffer the same fate if after it is concluded a new norm of *jus cogens* emerges which conflicts with it. A point made in connection with the discussion of Article 53, above, bears repeating here: there are only a very few norms of *jus cogens*, which means that states are free to contract out of the overwhelming majority of rules of general international law. Moreover, as Aust reminds us, "There are no reported instances of Articles 53 or 64, as such, being invoked."[325]

§ 4.06   THE RELATIONSHIP BETWEEN TREATIES AND STATE RESPONSIBILITY

Article 73 of the Vienna Convention provides that the provisions of the Convention "shall not prejudge any question that may arise in regard to a treaty from . . . the international responsibility of a State. . . ."[326] The "international responsibility of a state" is governed by the law of state responsibility, which deals with the circumstances under which a state is responsible for an internationally wrongful act and the consequences of that responsibility. The law of state responsibility is part of customary international law.[327] The breach of a treaty constitutes an internationally wrongful act, and gives rise to a new set of obligations on the part of the breaching state. Those obligations fall under the heading of "reparation," which all states that have committed a breach of an international obligation have a duty to make. State responsibility is the subject of Chapter 7, below.

But could a state terminate a treaty under the law of state responsibility, even if it were not possible to do so under the law of treaties? In the

---

[323] *Id.*, art. 64.

[324] *See* § 4.05[E][1][f], *supra.*

[325] AUST, *supra* note 38, at 258.

[326] Vienna Convention, *supra* note 22, art. 73. That article also provides that it does not prejudge questions arising from a succession of states or hostilities between states.

[327] The International Law Commission has adopted a set of draft articles on Responsibility of States for Internationally Wrongful Acts, 2001 ILC Rep. 43, 56 UN GAOR, Supp. No. 10, U.N. Doc. A/56/10, and annex to General Assembly resolution 56/83 of 12 Dec. 2001. The draft articles are available on the ILC's website, at http://www.un.org/law/ilc/texts/State_responsibility/responsibilityfra.htm.

Gabčíkovo-Nagymaros case, the International Court of Justice answered that question resoundingly in the negative. Referring to the law of treaties and the law of state responsibility, the Court noted that "those two branches of international law obviously have a scope that is distinct."[328] The Court explained:

> "A determination of whether a convention is or is not in force, and whether it has or has not been properly suspended or denounced, is to be made pursuant to the law of treaties. On the other hand, an evaluation of the extent to which the suspension or denunciation of a convention, seen as incompatible with the law of treaties, involves the responsibility of the State which proceeded to it, is to be made under the law of State responsibility.
>
> Thus the Vienna Convention of 1969 on the Law of Treaties confines itself to defining — in a limitative manner — the conditions in which a treaty may lawfully be denounced or suspended; while the effects of a denunciation or suspension seen as not meeting those conditions are, on the contrary, expressly excluded from the scope of the Convention by operation of Article 73. It is moreover well established that, when a State has committed an internationally wrongful act, its international responsibility is likely to be involved whatever the nature of the obligation is has failed to respect. . . ."[329]

Thus, whether the obligation that was breached had its source in customary or treaty law, the breaching state would be internationally responsible and consequently under a duty to make reparation.

The first of the five arguments made by Hungary in support of the lawfulness of its notification of termination of the 1977 treaty concerned the existence of a "state of necessity."[330] As we will see in Chapter 7, necessity is a defense to a breach of international obligations. The Court responded as follows:

> "[E]ven if a state of necessity is found to exist, it is not a ground for the termination of a treaty. It may only be invoked to exonerate from its responsibility a State which has failed to implement a treaty. Even if found justified, it does not terminate a Treaty; the Treaty may be ineffective as long as the condition of necessity continues to exist; it may in fact be dormant, but — unless the parties by mutual agreement terminate the Treaty — it continues to exist. As soon as the state of necessity ceases to exist, the duty to comply with treaty obligations revives."[331]

---

[328] 1997 I.C.J. 7, 38.

[329] *Id.*

[330] *Id.* at 58.

[331] *Id.* at 63.

Thus, the doctrine of a state of necessity — a defense or "circumstance precluding wrongfulness"[332] — belongs in the domain of state responsibility which, while preserved by Article 73 of the Vienna Convention, cannot intrude into the domain of the law of treaties. Even if a state can make out a defense to the breach of an international obligation having its source in a treaty, that does not terminate the treaty. As noted earlier, the Court left no doubt that a treaty can "be terminated only on the limited grounds enumerated in the Vienna Convention."[333] The law of state responsibility determines the available remedies for the breach of a treaty[334] but has no bearing on termination of the treaty itself.

§ 4.07   THE LAW OF TREATIES AND UNITED STATES LAW

The subject of treaties in the domestic law of the United States has been touched upon in earlier chapters.[335] This section will consider the following topics: the position of the United States on the Vienna Convention; the meaning of the term "treaty" in U.S. domestic law; authority to make treaties under U.S. law; authority to interpret treaties under U.S. law; and authority to suspend or terminate a treaty under U.S. law. The reader interested in further detail is invited to consider other works on the subject.[336]

[A]   The Position of the United States on the Vienna Convention

The United States is not a party to the Vienna Convention, although it participated actively in its negotiation[337] and the President submitted the Convention to the Senate for its advice and consent.[338] In fact, the State Department, in submitting the text of the Vienna Convention to the President, stated that although it was not yet in force at the time, "the Convention is already generally recognized as the authoritative guide to

---

[332] Circumstances precluding wrongfulness are in effect defenses to the commission of an internationally wrongful act. They are covered in ch. V of the ILC's draft articles on Responsibility of States for Internationally Wrongful Acts, *supra* note 327.

[333] 1997 I.C.J. 7, at 63.

[334] *See* the discussion of remedies for breach of treaties in AUST, *supra* note 38, ch. 21, at 300.

[335] *See* ch. 2 and, in particular, § 2.05, Self-Executing Treaties.

[336] *See, e.g.*, the sections of the Restatement referred to in this section; and Robert E. Dalton, *National Treaty Law and Practice: United States*, in AMERICAN SOCIETY OF INTERNATIONAL LAW, NATIONAL TREATY LAW AND PRACTICE (AUSTRIA, CHILE, COLOMBIA, JAPAN, NETHERLANDS, U.S.), ch. 6, Studies in Transnational Legal Policy, No. 30 (Monroe Leigh, Merritt R. Blakeslee & L. Benjamin Ederington eds. 1999), *available at* http://www.asil.org/dalton.pdf.

[337] *See* the President's Letter of Transmittal of the Vienna Convention to the Senate, S.Exec.Doc.L., 92d Cong., 1st sess. (1971), at 9, describing the preparations for the negotiation and listing the members of the U.S. delegation; and Kearney & Dalton, *supra* note 39.

[338] S.Exec.Doc.L., 92d Cong., 1st sess. (1971).

current treaty law and practice."[339] The State Department has since stated that it "follows most of the rules [of the Vienna Convention] in its conduct of its treaty business since most of the rules reflect customary law."[340] However, the Senate — presumably in order to preserve its constitutional prerogatives — wished to align the definition of the term "treaty" in the Convention with the meaning of that term in the U.S. Constitution (discussed in the following subsection). Thus it proposed that the United States' ratification of the Vienna Convention be made subject to an understanding and interpretation that no treaty, as defined in the Convention, would be "valid with respect to the United States, and the consent of the United States may not be given regarding any such treaty, unless the Senate of the United States has given its advice and consent to such treaty, or the terms of such treaty have been approved by law, as the case may be."[341]

This condition of Senate advice and consent, the rationale for which has since largely disappeared,[342] would have limited the President's power to conclude executive agreements, and would have prevented him entirely from entering into sole executive agreements on his own authority. Executive agreements, which are discussed in subsection [C], below, are instruments to which the Vienna Convention would otherwise apply and which constitute a large majority of the international agreements of the United States. The State Department therefore refused to accept the Senate's proposed condition.[343] Since the President need not "make," or ratify a treaty even if the Senate has given its advice and consent,[344] approval of the Convention by the Senate subject to its proposed condition would have been futile; the Convention therefore went no further in the Senate.

Even though the Vienna Convention is not a treaty of the United States, however, as already noted the State Department has indicated that the Convention "is generally regarded as reflecting current international law on the subject . . ."[345] and follows it in its treaty practice.

---

[339] *Id.* at 1.

[340] Statement of Mary V. Mochary, Deputy Legal Adviser, in hearings on the Vienna Convention in the Senate Foreign Relations Committee, 11 June 1986, in 1 Marian Nash (Leich), CUMULATIVE DIGEST OF UNITED STATES PRACTICE IN INTERNATIONAL LAW 1981-1988 1230 (1993).

[341] Proposed interpretation and understanding contained in a resolution of advice and consent reported out by the Senate Committee on Foreign Relations, 7 Sept. 1972, *quoted in* [1974] DIGEST OF U.S. PRACTICE IN INT'L L. 195.

[342] "The enactment of the Case-Zablocki Act [of 1972] and the establishment of consultative procedures with both the Senate and the House of Representatives concerning the form that international agreements would take have resolved the problem." Mochary, *supra* note 340, at 1232.

[343] *See supra* note 341, at 196-97.

[344] *See* U.S. CONST., Art. II, Sect. 2. *See generally* RESTATEMENT 3d, *supra* note 18, § 303 comment *d*.

[345] Charles I. Bevans, Assistant Legal Adviser for Treaty Affairs, Department of State, Memorandum of Law, 5 August 1974, responding to questions from Senator Thomas F. Eagleton of Missouri, as quoted in WHITEMAN, *supra* note 47, at 198.

As a result, the situation is that although the Vienna Convention is not binding on the United States as a treaty, since it largely reflects customary international law and has been accepted by the United States as such, the Convention is effectively binding on the U.S. by this route.[346]

[B]   The Meaning of the Term "Treaty" in U.S. Domestic Law

The term "treaty" has a different and more restricted meaning in United States law than it does in international law. The U.S. definition of the term derives from Article II, section 2, of the Constitution, which provides that the President "shall have the Power, by and with the Advice and Consent of the Senate, to make Treaties, provided two thirds of the Senators present concur; . . . ."[347] This is to be contrasted with the definition of the term "treaty" in Article 2 of the Vienna Convention, which as we know speaks of "an international agreement concluded between States in written form and governed by international law, whether embodied in a single instrument or in two or more related instruments and whatever its particular designation; . . . ."[348]

Thus the term "treaty" as it is used in the U.S. Constitution would seem to cover only some of the agreements that are contemplated by the same term as defined in the Vienna Convention. For example, if the President concludes an agreement with another country but does not submit it to the Senate for advice and consent, it would appear at least on the surface that there would be a "treaty" in the international sense but not in the U.S. constitutional sense.[349] Is such an agreement valid as a matter of United States law? If not, is it still valid on the international plane? This section will examine these questions, among others. For now, we can content ourselves with brief answers: yes, such an agreement may be valid under U.S. law, if it is made within the President's authority under the constitution; and yes, if all the requirements for the conclusion of a treaty under

---

[346] This probably cannot be said of the entire Convention, word for word, but is at least true of the Convention's principal provisions. In connection with hearings on the Vienna Convention held in the Senate Foreign Relations Committee in 1986, the Committee submitted a number of questions to the State Department, including the following: "Are there any conflicts between treaty law and practice as set out in the Convention and present U.S. law and practice?" As quoted in Dalton, *supra* note 336 n. 41. The State Department responded: "Although there are a few differences on matters of detail, there are no conflicts between treaty law and practice as set out in the Convention and present U.S. law and practice." *Id.* Material on the 1986 hearings on the Vienna Convention may be found in 1 Marian Nash (Leich), CUMULATIVE DIGEST OF UNITED STATES PRACTICE IN INTERNATIONAL LAW 1981-1988, at 1229-39 (1993).

[347] U.S. Const., art. II § 2.

[348] Vienna Convention, *supra* note 22, art. 2(1)(a).

[349] This is of course subject to art. 46 of the Vienna Convention, concerning the circumstances under which a state may invoke the provisions of its internal law to establish the invalidity of its consent to be bound. But as the head of state, the President would have presumptive authority to conclude treaties with other states; thus the likelihood of invalidity on the international plane is minimal.

international law are satisfied the treaty will be valid on that level and binding on the United States even if it is not valid under U.S. domestic law.

A final point concerns the fact that there are different kinds of international agreements in United States law, many of which — perhaps confusingly — are called "treaties." We will look at one of these forms, the executive agreement, in § 4.07[C][2], below. The term "treaties" is used in three different provisions of the Constitution. First, there are the treaties that may be made by the President with the advice and consent of the Senate under Article II § 2 of the Constitution. Second, there are the treaties mentioned in Article III § 2, in connection with the judicial power. And third, there are the treaties mentioned in the Supremacy Clause of the Constitution, Article 6 § 2. The term "treaties" is also used in federal statutes, such as the Circuit Court of Appeals Act (mentioned in the Supreme Court's opinion in the *Belmont*[350] case, discussed in subsection [C][2][c], below). Does the term "treaty" bear the same meaning in all three cases?

It seems clear that it does not. Article II § 2 treaties are the narrowest class but their coverage extends to the widest limit of the treaty power. Article VI § 2 treaties certainly include those of the Article II variety, but do they include executive agreements? *Belmont*[351] and *Pink*,[352] discussed in subsection [C][2][c] below, answered this question resoundingly in the affirmative as to the supremacy of the executive agreement involved there over state law. However, it is uncertain whether an executive agreement should benefit from the "last-in-time" rule governing conflicts between international agreements and acts of Congress, both of which are potentially "supreme" under Article VI. (The last-in-time rule is discussed in subsection [F], below.) The Supreme Court has not ruled on this question, but there is authority suggesting that an earlier statute may prevail over a later executive agreement.[353] Finally, when used in a federal statute, the term "treaty" may embrace both Article II treaties and executive agreements, as *Belmont* makes clear.

Let us now look directly at the question of the President's authority to make treaties under the law of the United States.

[C] Authority to Make International Agreements Under U.S. Law

Although Article II of the Constitution makes reference only to one kind of treaty — that which is made by the President with the advice and consent of the Senate under Article II section 2 — the President actually has authority to make three other kinds of international agreements, all of

---

[350] United States v. Belmont, 301 U.S. 324, 57 S.Ct. 758, 81 L.Ed. 1134 (1937).

[351] *Id.*

[352] United States v. Pink, 315 U.S. 203, 62 S.Ct. 552, 86 L.Ed. 796 (1942).

[353] *See* United States v. Guy W. Capps, Inc., 204 F.2d 655 (4th Cir. 1953), *aff'd on other grounds*, 348 U.S. 296, 75 S.Ct. 326, 99 L.Ed. 329 (1955).

which are called "executive agreements."[354] These are: (1) Congressional-Executive agreements; (2) agreements made pursuant to other treaties of the United States; and (3) sole executive agreements. In this subsection we will focus on these forms of international agreements, which are of considerable importance not least because they are far more numerous than Article II treaties.[355] The term "treaty" will be used in this subsection only in reference to Article II section 2 treaties; the term "international agreement" will be used to refer to the three kinds of executive agreements just mentioned.

The issue of whether the President has authority to make a treaty or executive agreement is one of constitutional law. The President's authority in this regard may be visualized as an inverted, four-layered pyramid, with Article II treaties — with respect to which the President's authority is at its broadest — in the top layer, followed by the three forms of executive agreement in the order listed above, ending with sole executive agreements in the bottom, smallest layer. Before taking up executive agreements, we should dwell for a moment on the top layer: the extent of the President's authority to make, or the permissible subjects of, Article II treaties.

[1] Article II Treaties

In short, the authority of the President to make a treaty with the advice and consent of the Senate is plenary in the sense that, subject to certain constitutional restrictions such as the guarantees contained in the Bill of Rights, it covers agreements on any subject.[356] The ultimate proof of this proposition is perhaps that Article II treaties may even deal with matters that could not be addressed by federal legislation. This principle, which may seem rather surprising on its face, follows from *Missouri v. Holland*.[357] The issue there was whether the Migratory Bird Treaty[358] and its implementing statute, the Migratory Bird Treaty Act,[359] were void as an interference with the rights reserved to the States under the Tenth Amendment. A similar statute, enacted before the conclusion of the treaty, had been held unconstitutional on the federal district court level.[360] Writing for the Court, Justice Holmes observed that "Acts of congress are the supreme law of the land only when made in pursuance of the

---

[354] *See generally* RESTATEMENT 3d, *supra* note 18, § 303.

[355] *See* Treaties and other International Agreements: The Role of the United States Senate, S.Rep.No. 205, 98th Cong., 2d sess. at 38 (1984), indicating that as of 1983 there were 906 treaties and 6571 executive agreements to which the United States was a party.

[356] *See* RESTATEMENT 3d, *supra* note 18, § 303(1), and cmt. b.

[357] 252 U.S. 416, 40 S.Ct. 382, 64 L.Ed. 641 (1920).

[358] Convention between the United States and Great Britain (for Canada) for the Protection of Migratory Birds, 39 Stat. 1702, T.S. 628.

[359] July 3, 1918, c. 128, 40 Stat. 755, 16 U.S.C. §§ 703-712.

[360] United States v. Shauver, 214 F. 154 (D.C. Ark. 1914); United States v. McCullagh, 221 F. 288 (D. Kan. 1915).

Constitution, while treaties are declared to be so when made under the authority of the United States."[361] He continued:

> "We do not mean to imply that there are no qualifications to the treaty-making power; but they must be ascertained in a different way. It is obvious that there may be matters of the sharpest exigency for the national well being that an act of Congress could not deal with but that a treaty followed by such an act could, and it is not lightly to be assumed that, in matters requiring national action, 'a power which must belong to and somewhere reside in every civilized government' is not to be found."[362]

After observing that Missouri's claim of exclusive authority over the migratory birds rested on "the presence within their jurisdiction of birds that yesterday had not arrived, tomorrow may be in another State and in a week a thousand miles away,"[363] Justice Holmes declared: "Here a national interest of very nearly the first magnitude is involved. It can be protected only by national action in concert with that of another power. . . . But for the treaty and the statute there soon might be no birds for any powers to deal with."[364]

Thus, the subject matter — migratory birds — was found to be a permissible subject of the Article II treaty power despite (a) Congress' lack of authority to legislate on the subject, and (b) the Tenth Amendment claims of authority over the birds by the State of Missouri. Since the Tenth Amendment reserves to the States only those powers that are not delegated to the United States, and since the treaty-making power is one of those that are so delegated, the Tenth Amendment does not limit the authority of the President to make treaties or other international agreements.[365] In *Holland*, Justice Holmes went so far as to suggest that the Article II treaty power is limited only by the "authority of the United States," which may exceed that vested in Congress and the States by the Constitution.[366] As noted above, however, the treaty power does remain subject to constitutional limitations, such as those contained in the Bill of

---

[361] 252 U.S. at 433.

[362] *Id.* (quoting Andrews v. Andrews, 188 U. S. 14, 33, 23 S.Ct. 237, 47 L. Ed. 366 (1903)).

[363] 252 U.S. at 434.

[364] *Id.* at 435.

[365] *See* RESTATEMENT 3d, *supra* note 18, § 302 cmt. d.

[366] During the 1950's Senator Bricker of Ohio attempted to change this situation through a constitutional amendment, the effect of which would have been that a treaty would become effective as U.S. law only through legislation that would be lawful in the absence of treaty. This effort came to naught. On the Bricker Amendment, *see, e.g.,* RESTATEMENT 3d, *supra* note 18, § 111, Reporters' Note 8; and WILLIAM W. BISHOP, JR., INTERNATIONAL LAW 112 (3d ed. 1971), and sources there cited. *See also* Louis Henkin, *U.S. Ratification of Human Rights Conventions: The Ghost of Senator Bricker*, 89 AM. J. INT'L L. 341 (1995). Concern has also been expressed more recently about the *Holland* doctrine. *See* John C. Yoo, *Globalism and the Constitution: Treaties, Non-Self-Execution, and the Original Understanding*, 99 COLUM. L. REV. 1955, 2238-39 (1999). *But see* Martin S. Flaherty, *History Right?: Historical Scholarship, Original Understanding, and Treaties as "Supreme Law of the Land,"* 99 COLUM. L. REV. 2095 (1999); and Jordan J. Paust, *Self-Executing Treaties*, 82 AM. J. INT'L L. 760 (1988).

Rights:[367] "The view, once held, that treaties are not subject to constitutional restraints is now definitely rejected."[368]

A final point regarding Article II treaties concerns reservations and understandings.[369] As we have seen, these may be added by the Senate as conditions of its advice and consent. If the Senate does so, and if the President decides to go forward with the ratification of (or accession to) the treaty,[370] the President must inform the other party or parties (ordinarily by notifying the depositary in the case of multilateral treaties) of the Senate's conditions. Reservations, understandings or other declarations of the Senate conditioning its advice and consent are normally referred to in the instrument of ratification and copied in an attachment to the instrument as well as in the presidential proclamation of the treaty. Those relating to the relevant agreements may be found on the website maintained by the United Nations, Status of Multilateral Treaties Deposited with the Secretary-General.[371]

Let us now turn to the three varieties of executive agreements.

[2]　Executive Agreements

[a]　Congressional-Executive Agreements

While only the President, not Congress, has the constitutional authority to negotiate and conclude international agreements, Congress may become involved in such ways as indicating the need for an agreement or authorizing the President to conclude an agreement on a particular subject that is outside the President's independent constitutional powers. But the President will sometimes decide that approval by both houses of Congress is necessary to ensure the effectiveness of an international agreement. This is often the case with trade agreements,[372] such as the North American Free Trade Agreement (NAFTA).[373] In such cases, the agreement is approved by a joint resolution of Congress. It is generally thought that this method may constitutionally be used as an alternative to the Article II treaty method for international agreements on any subject,[374] since the authority to make such agreements is composed of at least the sum of the powers of the President and Congress.[375]

---

[367] *See* Reid v. Covert, 354 U.S. 1, 77 S.Ct. 1222, 1 L.Ed.2d 1148 (1957).

[368] RESTATEMENT 3d, *supra* note 18, § 302 cmt. b.

[369] *See generally id.,* § 314.

[370] As we have seen, the President may decide not to proceed with the ratification of a treaty. *See* RESTATEMENT 3d, *supra* note 18, § 303 cmt. d.

[371] *See* http://untreaty.un.org (the user must have an account to gain full access).

[372] *See* RESTATEMENT 3d, *supra* note 18, § 302, Reporters' Note 9.

[373] 17 Dec. 1992, T.I.A.S..

[374] *See* RESTATEMENT 3d, *supra* note 18, § 302 cmt. e and Reporters' Note 8. The latter states: "Congressional-Executive agreements have . . . been made on a wide variety of subjects, and no such agreement has ever been effectively challenged as improperly concluded."

[375] It may be that such authority is even broader — that the whole is greater than the sum of its parts — on the theory that together, the President and Congress possess all of the powers inherent in the sovereignty of the United States. *See id.,* Reporters' Note 7.

[b] Agreements Made Pursuant to Other Treaties

Presidential authority to make an international agreement may derive from a treaty of the United States.[376] Such a treaty may itself indicate the need for implementation by an international agreement. Alternatively, an executive agreement may be a proper means of implementing a treaty. In any case, presidential authority to make such an agreement derives from the treaty pursuant to which it is made. While the authority of the President to make such agreements is well-established, this kind of executive agreement is less common than the other two varieties.

[c] Sole Executive Agreements

The President has certain independent powers under the Constitution that support his authority to conclude international agreements without any participation by Congress. These powers include, but are not necessarily limited to,[377] those flowing from his position as commander in chief,[378] those deriving from his power to make treaties[379] and appoint[380] and receive[381] ambassadors, and those based on his duty to "take Care that the Laws be faithfully executed."[382]

The authority of the President to make sole executive agreements was confirmed in two cases involving the assignment by the Soviet Union of claims to the United States by agreement incident to recognition of the government of the Soviet Union, *United States v. Belmont*[383] and *United States v. Pink*.[384] Both cases involved the so-called Litvinov Assignment, under which Soviet claims against American nationals were assigned to the United States in order "to eliminate all possible sources of friction between these two great nations."[385] The Soviet claims arose from nationalizations by the Soviet Union of corporations and their property and assets, wherever situated, including assets and bank accounts in the United States.[386]

---

[376] *See* Wilson v. Girard, 354 U.S. 524, 77 S.Ct. 1409, 1 L.Ed.2d 1544 (1957) (involving an Administrative Agreement with Japan made pursuant to a Security Agreement with that country).

[377] For a discussion of the authority of the President to make sole executive agreements, including possible authority under the Executive Power clause (Art. II, Sect. 1), *see* RESTATEMENT 3d, *supra* note 18, § 303 cmt. g.

[378] U.S. CONST., Art. II, Sect. 2.

[379] *Id.*

[380] *Id.*

[381] *Id.*, Art. II, Section 3.

[382] *Id.*

[383] 301 U.S. 324, 57 S.Ct. 758, 81 L.Ed. 1134 (1937).

[384] 315 U.S. 203, 62 S.Ct. 552, 86 L.Ed. 796 (1942).

[385] 315 U.S. at 224.

[386] Justice Frankfurter, concurring, explained: "One needs to be no expert in Russian law to know that the expropriation decrees intended to sweep the assets of Russian companies taken over by that government into Russia's control no matter where those assets were credited. Equally clear is it that the assignment by Russia meant to give the United States as part of the comprehensive settlement everything that Russia claimed under its law against Russians." *Id.* at 241-42.

Disputes arose between the Soviet government and the American holders of the property, who claimed that the Soviet nationalization decrees lacked extraterritorial effect or, if they had such effect, were confiscatory and in violation of due process. In *Pink*, the Court explained that "the existence of unpaid claims against Russia and its nationals which were held in this country and which the Litvinov Assignment was intended to secure, had long been one impediment to resumption of friendly relations between these two great powers."[387] Justice Frankfurter, concurring, added: "The two chief barriers to renewed friendship with Russia — intrusive propaganda and the effects of expropriation decrees upon our nationals — were at the core of our negotiations in 1933, as they had been for a good many years."[388]

The Assignment was effected through a sole executive agreement that took the form of an exchange of notes between the the United States and the Soviet Union — the so-called Roosevelt-Litvinov agreement.[389] Specifically, in a letter of 16 November 1933 to the President of the United States, Maxim Litvinov, People's Commissar for Foreign Affairs, stated that the Soviet government released and assigned to the United States all amounts due it from American nationals. The President acknowledged Litvinov's letter on the same date.[390] Coincident with the Assignment, the President recognized the Soviet government[391] and normal diplomatic relations were established between the two states, followed by an exchange of ambassadors.

Writing for the Court in *Belmont*, Justice Sutherland declared: "That the negotiations, acceptance of the assignment and agreements and understandings in respect thereof were within the competence of the President may not be doubted."[392] He explained that power over external affairs is vested exclusively in the national government, and that "in respect of what was done here, the Executive had authority to speak as the sole organ of that government."[393] Justice Sutherland then addressed the fact that the agreement between the United States and the Soviet Union had not been submitted to the Senate for its advice and consent: "The assignment and the agreements in connection therewith did not, as in the case of treaties, as that term is used in the treaty making clause of the Constitution (Art. 2, §2), require the advice and consent of the Senate. . . . [A]n international compact, as this was, is not always a treaty which requires the participation of the Senate. There are many such compacts, of which a protocol, a modus vivendi, a postal convention, and agreements like that now under

---

[387] *Id.* at 225.

[388] *Id.* at 241.

[389] The text of the notes is set forth in *U.S. v. Pink*, 315 U.S. at 212-213.

[390] *Id.*

[391] *See* Establishment of Diplomatic Relations with the Union of Soviet Socialist Republics, Dept. of State, Eastern European Series, No. 1 (1933), cited in *Pink* at note 1.

[392] 301 U.S. 324, 330 (1937).

[393] *Id.* at 330.

consideration are illustrations."[394] Justice Sutherland went on to explain that although an agreement of this kind "might not be a treaty requiring ratification by the Senate, it was a compact negotiated and proclaimed under the authority of the President,[395] and as such was a 'treaty' within the meaning of the Circuit Court of Appeals Act . . . , the construction of which might be reviewed upon direct appeal to this court."[396]

It is thus clear that the President has authority to conclude sole executive agreements. What is not clear is precisely how far that authority extends. The Supreme Court has left little doubt that the President can do many things via sole executive agreement in the implementation of important foreign policy decisions. To help it keep track of the executive agreements of all types made by the President, Congress enacted the Case Act.[397] The Act requires that all "international agreements" — defined to exclude Article II treaties — be published annually and submitted to Congress within sixty days of their entry into force.

[D] Authority to Interpret Treaties and Other International Agreements Under U.S. Law

The need to interpret an international agreement may arise in different contexts, including in the United States' relations with other parties to the agreement and in cases before courts in the United States. As to the former cases, the President, as the "sole organ of the nation in its external relations,"[398] has authority to interpret any kind of international agreement of the United States — be it an Article II treaty or an executive agreement. With respect to questions of interpretation that arise in cases before federal or state courts, if an international agreement constitutes the applicable law, the court has "final authority"[399] to interpret the agreement though it will give great weight to any interpretation by the President.[400] Since international agreements are the supreme law of the land under Article VI of the Constitution, their interpretation is a matter of federal law which is binding on state courts.[401]

---

[394] *Id.*

[395] As to that authority, *see* United States v. Curtiss-Wright Export Corp., 299 U.S. 304, 57 S.Ct. 216, 81 L.Ed. 255 (1936), in which Justice Sutherland, again writing for the Court, referred to "the very delicate, plenary and exclusive power of the President as the sole organ of the federal government in the field of international relations. . . ." 299 U.S. at 320, 57 S.Ct. at 221, 81 L.Ed. at 262. (Author's footnote.)

[396] 296 U.S. at 331.

[397] Public Law 92-403, as amended by Public Law 95-426, 1 U.S.C.A. § 112b.

[398] United States v. Curtiss-Wright Export Corp., 299 U.S. 304, 319, 57 S.Ct. 216, 81 L.Ed. 255 (1936).

[399] RESTATEMENT 3d, *supra* note 18, § 326(2).

[400] *Id.* The Executive Branch often provides its views on the interpretation of international agreements to the courts, usually through *amicus* briefs. *See id.,* cmt. c and Reporters' Note 2. The interpretation of international agreements has not been treated by the courts as a political question. *See id.,* Reporters' Note 3.

[401] *Id.,* cmt. d.

[E] Authority to Suspend or Terminate Treaties and Other International Agreements under U.S. Law

Does the President have sole authority to suspend or terminate international agreements of the United States or do the Senate or the Congress have a role to play with respect to this matter where they have participated in the agreement's formation? While the constitution is silent on this question there is little doubt that it is for the President, as the "sole organ of the Federal government in the field of international relations,"[402] to suspend or terminate international agreements of the United States and to make all findings and decisions connected therewith.[403]

[F] Conflict between Treaty and Federal Statute: The Last-in-Time Rule

Earlier in this section we touched on the possibility that a treaty or executive agreement might be inconsistent with a federal statute. This is not a common occurrence, but the issue does arise occasionally.[404] How to resolve such a conflict might be thought to pose an interesting dilemma, since treaties and federal statutes appear to be given equal status under the Supremacy Clause of the U.S. Constitution (Article VI § 2). But in *Whitney v. Robertson*,[405] the Supreme Court cut this Gordian knot by deciding that where a statute is inconsistent with a treaty, the latter in time shall prevail:

> "By the Constitution, a treaty is placed on the same footing, and made of like obligation, with an act of legislation. Both are declared by that instrument to be the supreme law of the land, and no superior efficacy is given to either over the other. When the two relate to the same subject, the courts will always endeavor to construe them so as to give effect to both, if that can be done without violating the language of either; but, if the two are inconsistent, the one last in date will control the other. . . ."[406]

Chief Justice Marshall's more general pronouncement in *Murray v. Schooner Charming Betsy* also applies to treaties: "an Act of Congress ought never to be construed to violate the law of nations if any other possible construction remains. . . ."[407] And Justice Brandeis added an additional layer of protection for treaties when he said in *Cook v. United States*

---

[402] United States v. Curtiss-Wright Export Corp., 299 U.S. 304, 320, 57 S.Ct. 216, 81 L.Ed. 255 (1936).

[403] RESTATEMENT 3d, *supra* note 18, § 339 and cmt. a. Such findings and decisions would include those relating to the various grounds for suspension and termination under the Vienna Convention, Part V, Section 3.

[404] *See generally* RESTATEMENT 3d, *supra* note 18, §§ 114 & 115.

[405] 124 U.S. 190, 8 S.Ct. 456, 31 L.Ed. 386 (1888).

[406] 124 U.S. at 194.

[407] 6 U.S. (2 Cranch) 64, 118, 2 L.Ed. 208 (1804).

that "a treaty will not be deemed to have been abrogated or modified by a later statute unless such purpose on the part of Congress has been clearly expressed."[408]

A case that gave full effect to this doctrine is *United States v. Palestine Liberation Organization*,[409] discussted in Chapter 2, § 2.03, above. Section 5202(3) of the Anti-Terrorism Act (ATA)[410] makes it unlawful for the PLO, "notwithstanding any provision of law to the contrary, to establish or maintain an office, headquarters, premises, or other facilities or establishments within the jurisdiction of the United States." The federal district court held that this broad language did not include the PLO's Permanent Observer Mission to the United Nations in New York, since closure of that office would have violated the United Nations Headquarters Agreement,[411] a treaty of the United States. The court found that the Headquarters Agreement "places an obligation upon the United States to refrain from impairing the function of the PLO Observer Mission to the United Nations," and that "[t]he ATA and its legislative history do not manifest Congress' intent to abrogate this obligation."[412] It held that it was "therefore constrained to interpret the ATA as failing to supersede the Headquarters Agreement and inapplicable to the Mission."[413] This case demonstrates that before it will find that a subsequent statute overrides a prior treaty obligation, the court will require a showing of clear congressional intent that the statute have this effect.

---

[408] 288 U.S. 102, 120, 53 S.Ct. 305, 311, 77 L.Ed. 641 (1933).

[409] 695 F.Supp. 1456 (S.D.N.Y. 1988).

[410] 22 U.S.C.A. §§ 5201-5203.

[411] 26 June 1947, 61 Stat. 3416, 11 U.N.T.S. 11.

[412] 695 F.Supp. at 1471.

[413] *Id.*

Chapter 5

TO WHOM IS INTERNATIONAL LAW ADDRESSED? STATES AND OTHER SUBJECTS OF INTERNATIONAL LAW

Synopsis

§ 5.01   INTRODUCTION

This chapter addresses the question, to whom is international law addressed? Or, put more traditionally, who are the "subjects" of international law? What entities possess international legal personality? On the level of domestic law, the subjects of law are primarily individuals and corporations — natural and legal persons. There are important exceptions, of course: the Bill of Rights, for example, imposes obligations on government. But the subjects of the domestic legal order all possess legal personality and thus have the capacity to enjoy rights and powers and to bear obligations and, generally, to act on the national plane.

International law, in contrast, is addressed principally to states. As we saw in Chapter 1, international law may be seen as the body of norms that governs the relations between nations[1] — hence the more traditional expression, law of nations. As is true of the subjects of law on the domestic level, states and other subjects of international law possess legal personality and thus the capacity to enjoy rights and powers, to bear obligations and, generally, to act on the international plane.[2] International organizations may also possess international legal personality, depending on whether and to what extent it is conferred on them by the international agreements by which they are established.

What about individuals? Classically, individuals were not subjects of international law; whether they were protected or not depended upon whether the state of their nationality chose to take up their claims against another state. Especially since World War II and the founding of the United Nations, however, individuals have enjoyed the protection of international human rights law. This body of law confers rights directly on individuals which must be observed by their governments. Beginning in this same period, with the Nuremberg trials, international law has also been applied to individuals who have committed serious offenses such as war crimes and crimes against humanity. And, of course, the pirate has for centuries been considered an arch criminal under international law. Have corporations, like individuals, been increasingly recognized as persons under international law? Not to the same extent as individuals, certainly, but there is no reason why corporations and other legal persons under domestic law cannot be accorded rights and duties, as well as legal status and capacity, by international law or agreement.[3]

We begin by considering the state in international law (§ 5.02): what is a "state;" does a state's existence depend on recognition by other states; what are the rules governing state succession — i.e., the situation that occurs when a state splits into two or more new states, when two or more states join to become a single state, when a territory that was formerly non-self-governing becomes a state, etc.; and finally, with regard to the non-self-governing territories just mentioned, how may they become states through self-determination? We then turn to other subjects of

---

[1] *See* § 1.02.

[2] *See generally* 1 OPPENHEIM'S INTERNATIONAL LAW § 33, at 119-120 (R. Jennings & A. Watts 9th ed. 1992) (hereinafter OPPENHEIM).

[3] To this effect, *see* RESTATEMENT (THIRD) OF THE FOREIGN RELATIONS LAW OF THE UNITED STATES, Introductory Note to Part II, at 70 (1987) (hereinafter RESTATEMENT 3d), which notes that "Corporations frequently are vehicles through which rights under international economic law are asserted." *Id.* at 71.

international law (§ 5.03), including territorial entities other than states, international organizations, and natural and legal persons.

§ 5.02 STATES

"State" is the term used in modern international law to refer to a nation-state or country. The state is the principal and most traditional subject of international law. As we saw in Chapter 1, it was the emergence of the independent and secular nation-state following the Peace of Westphalia in 1648 that marked the birth of what we know today as international law.[4]

There are many questions that surround the concept of statehood. For example: How are states created? If I purchased an old oil platform situated on the high seas — i.e., outside the territory of any state — and declared it the State of Oceana,[5] would it qualify as a state under international law? Would it matter whether I actually lived there, and whether I was accompanied by others? Whether any other state recognized Oceana as a state? Whether Oceana was allowed to join the United Nations? Getting back to the more traditional conception of the state, what legal consequences flow from the division or uniting of states? These and related questions will be considered in the following subsections.

[A] Statehood: Objective Requirements

The generally accepted definition of what constitutes a state is set forth in the 1933 Montevideo Convention on the Rights and Duties of States: "The State as a person of international law should possess the following qualifications: (a) a permanent population; (b) a defined territory; (c) government; and (d) capacity to enter into relations with other States."[6] While there is general agreement on the definition, however, its application to concrete situations can present problems. Moreover, as the Restatement puts it, "issues of statehood have been resolved by the practice of states reflecting political expediency as much as logical consistency."[7] But as a matter of law, the starting point is always the four criteria enumerated in the Montevideo Convention. Even when recognition is accorded as a matter of political expediency, the recognizing state will virtually always seek to justify its action on the basis of the Montevideo requirements. Let us then take a closer look at the four characteristics of statehood set forth in the Montevideo Convention.

---

[4] *See* § 1.04.

[5] *Cf.* the Principality of Sealand, an abandoned World War II-era anti-aircraft platform situated six miles off the English coast in the North Sea that was occupied in 1967 by Paddy Roy Bates. *See, e.g.,* Gary Slapper, *How A Law-less "Data haven" Is Using Law To Protect Itself,* THE TIMES, 8 Aug. 2000, at 3; and Marjorie Miller & Richard Boudreau, *A Nation for Friend and Faux,* L.A. TIMES, 7 June 2000, at A-1. Information on the Principality of Sealand, *available at* http://www.wordiq.com/definition/Sealand.

[6] Art. 1, 49 Stat. 3097, T.S. No. 881, 165 L.N.T.S. 19. *See also* the very similar definition in RESTATEMENT 3d, *supra* note 3, § 201.

[7] RESTATEMENT 3d, *supra* note 3, § 201 cmt. a.

[1]　Permanent Population

A state does not consist simply of territory; otherwise, Antarctica could qualify for statehood. In addition to territory and the other requirements, in order to qualify as a state an entity must possess what Oppenheim refers to as a *people*.[8] This criterion, which is defined as "an aggregate of individuals who live together as a community,"[9] is somewhat more abstract and potentially more difficult to satisfy than the concept of a "permanent population" since it raises the question of what constitutes a "community." There are certainly a number of entities in the world today whose status as states is unquestioned but whose populations include elements that cannot be said to form one community, in the ordinary sense of that term.[10] But they are nevertheless acknowledged to be states, at least in part for political reasons. Perhaps the more objective criterion of a "permanent population" would better fit actual conditions on the ground.

Yet it is obvious even at first blush that both elements of this requirement — permanence and a population — raise significant questions. What constitutes "permanence?" Surely it cannot mean that members of the population cannot emigrate or reside abroad. But some degree of stability of the population is implied. What about the requirement of a "population?" Is a quantitative aspect implied in this term? Harris states that "There is no lower limit to the size of a state's population," citing the example of Nauru, with less than 13,000 inhabitants.[11] Reference could also be made to The Vatican, which is generally regarded as a state but has a population of only around 1,000.[12] The Restatement, on the other hand, maintains that an entity's population must be "significant" for it to qualify as a state.[13] What is "significant" may lie in the eye of the beholder, but certainly the number of inhabitants would have to be sufficient to enable the entity to comply with requirements (c) and (d) if it is to qualify as a state. Ultimately it may be that as Justice Potter Stewart said of obscenity, while it is difficult to define exactly what is meant by the "population" element, we know it when we see it.[14]

How does my State of Oceana measure up to this criterion? It may be assumed for purposes of analysis that I, and some friends and members of my family, have taken up residence on Oceana. Let us also assume that

---

[8] OPPENHEIM, *supra* note 2, at 121.

[9] *Id.*

[10] Sudan and Iraq come immediately to mind in this connection.

[11] D.J. HARRIS, CASES AND MATERIALS ON INTERNATIONAL LAW 103 (5th ed. 1998) (hereinafter HARRIS). According to the CIA World Factbook, Nauru's population as of July 2004 was estimated to be 12, 809, http://www.cia.gov/cia/publications/factbook/geos/nr.html#People.

[12] *See, e.g.,* JAMES CRAWFORD, THE CREATION OF STATES IN INTERNATIONAL LAW 152-160(1979); and RESTATEMENT 3d, *supra* note 3, § 201, Reporters' Note 7, noting that "The Vatican . . . is generally accepted as a state, and the Holy See (the central administration of the Catholic Church) as its government." Regarding the status of the Vatican City and the Holy See in international law, *see* 1 OPPENHEIM, *supra* note 2, at 327-329.

[13] RESTATEMENT 3d, *supra* note 3, § 201 comt. c.

[14] Jacobellis v. Ohio, 378 U.S. 184, 197 (1964) (Stewart, J., concurring).

my friends, family members and I consider Oceana to be our permanent home, in the sense that we have no other home elsewhere and intend to remain on Oceana indefinitely. These facts could lead us to conclude that the "permanence" requirement is satisfied. What about the requirement of a "population?" It could be argued that the "permanent" presence on Oceana of my friends, family members and I satisfies this requirement. Yet surely there must be some quantitative requirement; the Restatement requires a "significant" population and even states with the smallest number of inhabitants have much larger populations than Oceana. Certainly my friends, family and I would argue that we are not insignificant, in number or otherwise. Does the answer lie in political expediency?

[2] Defined Territory

Once again, a requirement that appears clear enough on its face may raise questions on closer examination. For example, how "defined" must the territory be? Many states in the world today have borders that are not precisely defined and that may in fact be the subject of disputes and even conflicts with their neighbors.[15] This evidently has not called into question their statehood. In fact, once a state has been established, occupation of a significant part or even all of its territory will not usually affect its status as a state.[16] It is probably sufficient for statehood that the territory of an entity be reasonably consistent, even if its boundaries have not been authoritatively determined.[17] Size of the territory evidently does not matter: the Vatican City, for example, comprises only some 100 acres, yet it is generally considered a state.[18]

How does my state of Oceana fare with respect to this requirement? The boundaries of Oceana would appear to be those of the oil platform, plus applicable maritime zones (a territorial sea of 12 miles and an exclusive economic zone of 200 nautical miles). Thus Oceana would seem to satisfy this criterion.

[3] Government

The need for a government has an internal and an external aspect. Internally, a state is "the legal organization of a community, [which] is determined by the state's internal constitutional order."[19] Externally, as a purely practical matter, it would be difficult for countries to deal

---

[15] India's ongoing dispute with Pakistan over Kashmir, Iraq's war with Iran in the 1980s, as well as its invasion of Kuwait in 1990, and Ethiopia's war with Eritrea in the 1990s, all involve or involved border disputes, at least in part. Another well-known example is Israel, whose borders have not been finally settled.

[16] *See* RESTATEMENT 3d, *supra* note 3, § 201 cmt. b and § 202, Reporters' Note 5. The situation of Lebanon, significant portions of whose territory were long occupied by Syria and Israel, comes to mind in this connection.

[17] *See* Deutsche Continental Gas-Gesellschaft v. Polish State, 5 ANN. DIG. 11, 15 (1929).

[18] OPPENHEIM, *supra* note 2, at 327, acknowledging that "the constituent elements of state hood are . . . highly abnormal or reduced to a bare minimum."

[19] *Id.* at 130.

with a "state" that had no government — at least no unitary government. How would such an entity interact with the other members of the international community? How would other states enter into agreements with it and hold it to its obligations under those agreements or under customary international law? It would be virtually impossible. Thus there is good reason for requiring that an entity claiming statehood have a government. The form of government does not matter, so long as it is effective in performing governmental functions — i.e., is able to speak for the country and ensure that international engagements are complied with.

In the *Aaland Islands* case,[20] a preliminary question concerned the date on which Finland became a state. Finland, which had been part of the Russian Empire, fell into "revolution and anarchy"[21] after its Diet, or parliament, declared independence in 1917 as permitted by the new Soviet government. The International Committee of Jurists appointed by the Council of the League of Nations to examine the situation and submit their opinion to the Council had the following to say about the conditions that had to obtain for Finland to constitute a state:

> "In the midst of revolution and anarchy, certain elements essential to the existence of a State . . . were lacking for a fairly considerable period. Political and social life was disorganized; . . . the Diet , the legality of which had been disputed by a large section of the people, had been dispersed by the revolutionary party, and the Government had been chased from the capital and forcibly prevented from carrying out its duties; . . . and Russian troops, and after a time Germans also, took part in the civil war. . . . It is, therefore, difficult to say at what exact date the Finnish Republic . . . actually became a definitely constituted sovereign State. This certainly did not take place until a *stable political organization had been created, and until the public authorities had become strong enough to assert themselves throughout the territories of the State* without the assistance of foreign troops."[22]

These qualities of political stability and general control by public authorities over the entity's territory would ordinarily have to be present for the entity to claim statehood. It is perhaps obvious, however, that once an entity becomes a state, strict adherence to these characteristics has generally not been required in state practice.[23]

---

[20] Report of the International Committee of Jurists on the Legal Aspects of the Aaland Islands Question, League of Nations Official Journal, Special Supp. No. 3 (1920).

[21] *Id.* at 3.

[22] *Id.* (emphasis added).

[23] *See* OPPENHEIM, *supra* note 2, at 122, pointing out that once a state is established, even civil war or belligerent occupation have not been treated as being inconsistent with its continued status as a state. Lebanon is one example of a country whose status as a state was never questioned despite the occupation of its territory by Syria and Israel, and the sectarian conflict that ravaged the country for many years.

Does Oceana satisfy the requirement that the entity have a government? Unless my family and friends are riven by feuds, which does not appear in the facts that have been posited, it seems a fair assumption that the group might "govern" the entity, perhaps through direct democracy and by electing a head of state for the conduct of relations with other states. There is no showing that such a "government" would not have control over the entity, including its territory and population. Thus this requirement could be said to be satisfied.

[4]   Capacity to Enter into Relations with Other States

This requirement has also been referred to as sovereignty[24] and independence.[25] Its essence is that the entity not be under the legal authority of another state, and that it thus have the capacity, independently, to conduct relations with other states. However, as Judge Anzilotti explained in his separate opinion in the *Austro-German Customs Union Case*,[26] "restrictions upon a State's liberty, whether arising out of ordinary international law or contractual [treaty] engagements, do not as such in the least affect its independence."[27] The fact that a state voluntarily entrusts control of its foreign relations to another state, as in the case of Liechtenstein, does not affect its "capacity" to conduct those relations, and thus its statehood.

As far as we know from the meager facts at our disposal, Oceana has the capacity to enter into relations with other states. It would appear to be independent of other states and not under any state's legal authority.

[5]   Summation

We have now gone through all four requirements and have sought to apply them to my "State" of Oceana. We have seen that it is at least arguable that Oceana satisfies all four requirements, with the possible exception of that of a population. And yet, would other governments really consider it to be a state? As we will see in the following subsection, it is now generally accepted that statehood does not depend upon recognition by other states;[28] satisfaction of the four Montevideo Convention requirements is all that is necessary. Still, one must ask whether Oceana is not an illustration of the role played by political considerations in the determination of statehood. If Oceana is not treated as a state by other members of the international community, it would be impossible as a practical matter for it to function as a state on the international plane.

Let us now look more closely at the question of the role of recognition.

---

[24] *Id.*

[25] *Id. See also* HARRIS, *supra* note 11, at 107 n. 1.

[26] Advisory Opinion, 1931 P.C.I.J. (ser. A/B) No. 41.

[27] *Id.* at 57 (separate opinion).

[28] RESTATEMENT 3d, *supra* note 3, § 202 cmt. b.

[B] Recognition of States and Governments

We have just considered the "objective" requirements of statehood, as set forth in the Montevideo Convention. It is necessary that an entity meet all of these requirements in order to have a legitimate claim to statehood. But is it sufficient? Are there what might be called "subjective" requirements, as well? That is, does an entity's statehood also depend upon how it is viewed by other members of the international community? This is the first issue the present subsection will consider. It will then take up the related subject of recognition of governments.

[1] Recognition of States

The Restatement explains that recognition of a state "is a formal acknowledgment by another state that an entity possesses the qualifications for statehood . . . and implies a commitment to treat that entity as a state."[29] It is generally accepted today that statehood does not depend upon recognition by other states. It is enough if the four requirements listed in the Montevideo Convention, discussed in the previous subsection,[30] are satisfied. However, in order for an entity to realize the full potential of statehood it must, as a practical matter, be treated as a state by other members of the international community.[31] Such treatment is in fact required for entities that meet the Montevideo criteria.[32] This obligation, to treat as a state an entity that meets the objective requirements of statehood, renders the question of the effect of recognition of less importance than it would have if recognition were necessary to statehood.

Yet for many years scholars debated whether recognition was "constitutive" of an entity's statehood or whether it was merely "declaratory" of a status that had already been achieved through the satisfaction of the Montevideo requirements. Today most writers subscribe to the declaratory view of statehood,[33] which also finds support in the practice of states[34] and international arbitral tribunals.[35]

---

[29] *Id.* § 202 cmt. a. The Restatement adds that "states often treat a qualified entity as a state without any formal act of recognition." *Id.*

[30] *See* § 5.02[A], *supra.*

[31] *See* RESTATEMENT 3d, *supra* note 3, § 202 cmt. b.

[32] *Id.* § 202(1).

[33] *See, e.g.,* J.L. BRIERLY, THE LAW OF NATIONS 139 (Humphrey Waldock, 6th ed. 1963). *See also* RESTATEMENT 3d, *supra* note 3, whose § 202 "tends towards the declaratory view," while noting that "the practical differences between the two theories have grown smaller." *Id.* at Reporters' Note 1.

[34] Brierly refers to the claim made by Britain against Israel, before it had recognized the latter, relating to British airplanes shot down over Egypt in 1949 by Jewish pilots. BRIERLY, *supra* note 33, at 139 n. 1.

[35] *See, e.g.,* Arbitration Commission, E.C. Conference on Yugoslavia, *Opinion No. 1,* 29 Nov. 1991, 92 INT'L L. REP. 162 ("the existence or disappearance of the State is a question of fact; . . . the effects of recognition by other States are purely declaratory. . . ."). Compare the *Tinoco* Arbitration, discussed in text at notes 49-50, *infra.* While that case involved recognition *vel non* of a government, the declaratory theory is generally thought to apply to both. *See, e.g.,* HARRIS, *supra* note 11, at 146.

However, states have been known to grant[36] or withhold[37] recognition to further a national policy, as when a state is recognized "in order to establish the very independence of which recognition is supposed to be a mere acknowledgment. . . ."[38] The constitutive and declaratory theories of statehood are of less significance today, given the acceptance of the obligation to treat as a state an entity that fulfills the Montevideo requirements.[39] However, it is for each state to decide whether it will formally recognize an entity as a state,[40] as opposed to simply dealing with it as such in its practice.

An exception to the duty to treat a qualified entity as a state applies when the entity has met the requirements for statehood through a threat or use of force in violation of international law. For example, State A may intervene in an internal conflict in State B through an unlawful use of force, resulting in part of State B claiming to have become new State C.[41] In such a case, other states are in fact required *not* to recognize the entity's statehood.[42] An entity ("State C") should not benefit from a violation of international law of this seriousness, nor should other states (State A) whose illegal acts have brought the situation about.

---

[36] This seems to have been the case with the United States' recognition in 2004 of a former Yugoslav republic as the Republic of Macedonia, despite Greece's protests over the use of that name. Greece contends use of that name implies territorial ambitions regarding a northern Greek province of the same name. The State of Macedonia is a member of the military coalition in Iraq. *See* Anthee Carassava, *U.S. to Recognize Ex-Yugoslav Republic as Macedonia*, N.Y. Times, 5 Nov. 2004, at A8.

[37] Taiwan, which has not sought recognition as a separate state, also has not been recognized as such by the United States due to the U.S. policy regarding China. Both the U.S. and Taiwan regard the latter as part of China. *See* Restatement 3d, *supra* note 3, § 201 comment *f* and Reporters' Note 8.

[38] Brierly, *supra* note 33, at 140, citing the examples of the United States recognition of Panama "only three days after it had revolted from Colombia" and Israel "within a few hours of its proclamation of independence." *Id.*

[39] Oppenheim, *supra* note 2, at 133, states: "Recognition, while declaratory of an existing fact, is constitutive in its nature, at least so far as concerns relations with the recognizing state." But those relations would exist on some level in any event, given the obligation to treat the entity as a state; formal recognition may carry with it certain additional prerogatives. *See* Restatement 3d, *supra* note 3, § 202 comment *c*.

[40] *See, e.g.*, Oppenheim, *supra* note 2, at 132-133; and Restatement 3d, *supra* note 3, § 202 comment *a*, pointing out that "states often treat a qualified entity as a state without any formal act of recognition."

[41] Compare India's intervention in Bangladesh, which some states viewed as unlawful and others as a lawful use of force in support of self-determination or as humanitarian intervention. *See id.* § 202, Reporters' Note 5.

[42] *Id.* § 202(2). A historical antecedent of this principle is the Stimson Doctrine, set forth in a note of 7 Jan. 1932 by US Secretary of State Henry Lewis Stimson, according to which situations brought about by actions contrary to the 1928 Kellogg-Briand Pact would not be recognized. It was articulated in the context of the Japanese invasion of Manchuria and setting up of the puppet state of "Manchukuo." *See generally* Robert Langer, Seizure of Territory: The Stimson Doctrine and Related Principles in Legal Theory and Diplomatic Practice (1947).

Premature recognition of an entity as a state can also entail international responsibility.[43] This issue often arises in cases of internal conflict in which a portion of a state attempts to secede, against the will of the state of which it forms a part. Clearly, recognition of such an entity as a new state would greatly enhance its status but at the same time deal a blow to the interests of the state from which the entity seeks to secede. Premature, or "precipitate" recognition of the entity as a new state is an unlawful act which could well amount to intervention.[44] According to Oppenheim, the test is whether the new state has "really already safely and permanently established itself, or only makes efforts to this end without having already succeeded."[45] This is a question of fact in each case, and it is up to each state to make the determination for itself (absent an authoritative determination by the United Nations Security Council). As might be expected, this regime does not always produce consistent results, relying as it does on individual judgments as to whether an entity has "safely and permanently established itself" as a new state.

[2] Recognition of Governments

According to the Restatement, "[r]ecognition of a government is formal acknowledgment that a particular regime is the effective government of a state and implies a commitment to treat that regime as the government of that state."[46] As in the case of states, while there is no requirement of formal recognition of governments, states are obligated to treat a regime that is the government in fact as the government.[47]

But how do we know when a particular regime is the government in fact? According to Oppenheim, this question is governed by the principle of effectiveness: "A government which is in fact in control of the country and which enjoys the habitual obedience of the bulk of the population with a reasonable expectancy of permanence, can be said to represent the state in question and as such to be deserving of recognition."[48] In the *Tinoco* arbitration,[49] the sole arbitrator, William Howard Taft (then Chief Justice of the United States Supreme Court), rejected Costa Rica's argument that

---

[43] *See* OPPENHEIM, *supra* note 2, at 143-146, which points out that there is a basic difference between recognizing insurgents as a belligerent authority (which is lawful if the belligerents meet certain conditions) and recognizing them and the portion of the country they control as a new state; and RESTATEMENT 3d, *supra* note 3, § 202 cmt. f.

[44] *See* OPPENHEIM, *supra* note 2, at 143-144, citing as instances of recognition that have been regarded as precipitate the United States recognition of Panama in 1903 immediately after it seceded from Colombia; the U.S. recognition of Israel on 14 May 1948, the same day that Israel's Act of Independence became effective; and India's recognition of Bangladesh in early December, 1971, when most of East Pakistan was still under Pakistani control.

[45] *Id.* at 143.

[46] RESTATEMENT 3d, *supra* note 3, § 203 cmt. a.

[47] *Id.* at cmt. b.

[48] OPPENHEIM, *supra* note 2, at 150.

[49] Great Britain v. Costa Rica, award of 18 Oct. 1923, 1 UNRIAA 369 (1923), 18 AM. J. INT'L L. 147 (1924).

the Tinoco government was not a *de facto* or *de jure* government according to international law. While Costa Rica pointed, inter alia, to the fact that many leading powers, including the United States and its allies in the First World War, refused to recognize the Tinoco government, Taft held that the facts were determinative: "Such non-recognition . . . cannot outweigh the evidence disclosed by this record before me as to the *de facto* character of Tinoco's government, according to the standard set by international law."[50]

The United States, in determining whether to recognize *de facto* governments, has followed criteria similar to those identified by Oppenheim but has also looked to other factors, including "whether the new government has indicated its willingness to comply with its international obligations under treaties and international law."[51] But over the years the recognition criteria of the United States became increasingly complex, creating "the impression among other nations that the United States approved of those governments it recognized and disapproved of those from which it withheld recognition."[52]

To avoid this implication, the United States changed its practice. An article published in the Department of State *Bulletin* in 1977 explains: "In recent years, U.S. practice has been to deemphasize and avoid the use of recognition in cases of changes of governments and to concern ourselves with the question of whether we wish to have diplomatic relations with the new governments."[53] Recognition of a government is not the same as maintaining diplomatic relations with it, however. A state may recognize the government of another state but choose not to have diplomatic relations with it.[54] In the United States, the Constitution gives exclusive authority to the President to determine whether to recognize a government or maintain diplomatic relations with it.[55]

As in the case of recognition of states, recognition of governments can in certain circumstances be unlawful. This would be the case, for example,

---

[50] *Id.* at 157.

[51] 2 M. WHITEMAN, DIGEST OF INTERNATIONAL LAW 72-73 (1963) (hereinafter WHITEMAN). For a description of other criteria that have been applied by the U.S. government, *see* 1977 DIGEST OF UNITED STATES PRACTICE IN INTERNATIONAL LAW 20 (1979) (hereinafter 1977 DIGEST).

[52] *See* 1977 DIGEST, *supra* note 51, at 20.

[53] *Diplomatic Recognition*, 77 DEPT. OF STATE BULL. 462-463 (1977), *reprinted in* 1977 DIGEST, *supra* note 51, at 19-20. This does not mean the United States will never refuse to recognize a government, however. Nor does it imply that it will always recognize the results of an election, even one sanctioned by the existing government. *See, e.g.,* C.J. Chivers, *Ukraine Premier Is Named Winner; U.S. Assails Move,* N.Y. TIMES, 25 Nov. 2004, at A1, and Steven R. Weisman, *Powell Says Ukraine Vote Was Full of Fraud, id.* at A10 (*quoting* Secretary of State Colin L. Powell as stating, in reference to the Ukrainian government's certification of the prime minister as president-elect: "We cannot accept this result as legitimate because it does not meet international standards and because there has not been an investigation of the numerous and credible reports of fraud and abuse.").

[54] *See* RESTATEMENT 3d, *supra* note 3, § 203 cmt. d.

[55] *Id.* § 204.

where a new government was installed by another state through the threat or use of force in violation of Article 2(4) of the United Nations Charter, or where an insurgent group was recognized as the government of a state while the existing government was still in control.[56]

[C] State Succession

A succession of states occurs when one state takes the place of another.[57] This can happen in a variety of ways,[58] including the break-up of a state (such as occurred with the Soviet Union, Yugoslavia and Czechoslovakia), the secession of a part of a state (as in the case of Bangladesh) and decolonization. In all of these cases, one state succeeds another with regard to a particular territory.

It is important to distinguish clearly between succession of *states* and succession of *governments*.[59] Since it is the state that is the international legal person, and hence the entity to which rights and obligations attach under international law, a succession of governments has no effect on those rights and obligations. This subsection concerns only the succession of states.

State succession raises a number of legal issues, most of which involve the general question, to what extent do the rights and obligations of the predecessor state pass to the successor state? Assuming this question is not regulated by treaty, the answers to it depend upon a number of factors, including the manner in which the new state was formed and what it is the succession to which is at issue. But state practice has varied, according to "the historical circumstances of the time, and the major preoccupations of the leading members of the international community in the situations which at the time most frequently give rise to cases of

---

[56] *See id.* § 203 comments *e* and *g*.

[57] Art. 2 of both the 1978 Vienna Convention on Succession of States in respect of Treaties, 17 I.L.M. 1488 (1978), and the 1983 Vienna Convention on Succession of States in respect of State Property, Archives and Debts, 22 I.L.M. 298 (1983), defines "succession of states" to mean "the replacement of one State by another in the responsibility for the international relations of territory." D.P. O'Connell defines state succession as "the factual situation which arises when one State is substituted for another in sovereignty over a given territory."1 D.P. O'CONNELL, STATE SUCCESSION IN MUNICIPAL LAW AND INTERNATIONAL LAW 3 (1967) (hereinafter O'CONNELL). According to Oppenheim: "A succession of international persons occurs when one or more international persons takes the place of another international person, in consequence of certain changes in the latter's condition." OPPENHEIM, *supra* note 2, at 208-209.

[58] In this connection Oppenheim discusses absorption or merger, dismemberment, separation and secession, transfer of territory and former dependent territories. *See* OPPENHEIM, *supra.* note 2, at 210-234. The 1978 Vienna Convention on Succession of States in respect of Treaties, *supra* note 57, treats instances of succession as falling into two categories: newly independent states (Part III) and uniting and separating of states (Part IV).

[59] While the Soviet Union initially claimed it was not only a new government but a new state and was thus free from the international obligations of Czarist Russia, and repeated this claim from time to time, it also made contradictory claims (when succession would be favorable to it). It was generally treated by other states as a new government, not a new state. *See generally* RESTATEMENT 3d, *supra* note 3, § 208 cmt. a and Reporters' Note 2.

succession."[60] Indeed, Brierly cautions against thinking about the succession of states under international law as being in any way analogous to succession to the estate of an individual under private law. As that author points out, "states do not die in any literal sense; their population and their territory do not disappear, but merely suffer political change."[61] This basic difference helps to explain the very different legal regimes of "succession" as between domestic and international law, and also the fact that there is no one regime under international law governing all issues or cases.[62]

There are two[63] multilateral treaties dealing with issues of state succession: the 1978 Vienna Convention on Succession of States in respect of Treaties,[64] and the 1983 Vienna Convention on Succession of States in respect of State Property, Archives and Debts.[65] While these agreements were the product of preparatory work by the International Law Commission and thus may to some extent reflect customary law, they have not been particularly well received by states.[66] This subsection will therefore not generally rely upon the 1978 and 1983 Vienna Succession Conventions. The titles of those agreements do, however, give a sense of the kinds of issues raised by a succession of states. Brierly uses the following categories, which are somewhat more inclusive: "treaties, membership of international organizations, property, contracts, and wrongs."[67] Each raises distinct issues and must be analyzed separately. This subsection will focus upon succession to treaties, an issue that arises quite frequently.

Like the different categories of issues involved, the factual situations giving rise to a succession of states are also unique. While they, too, may be arranged in categories,[68] state practice does not allow us to say that a succession falling into a particular category will give rise to clear legal consequences.[69] In fact, according to Oppenheim, "the extent to which the rights and duties of the predecessor devolve on the successor is uncertain and

---

[60] OPPENHEIM, *supra* note 2, at 210.

[61] BRIERLY, *supra* note 33, at 152.

[62] OPPENHEIM, *supra* note 2, at 210: "no general rule can be laid down concerning all the cases in which a succession occurs. . . ."

[63] There is also a third, between members of the former Yugoslavia, which is not relevant for our purposes. Agreement on Succession Issues, Vienna, 29 June 2001, 41 I.L.M. 3 (2002).

[64] 17 I.L.M. 1488 (1978).

[65] 22 I.L.M. 298 (1983).

[66] The 1978 Convention is in force, but has only 18 parties, none of which is a permanent member of the U.N. Security Council. Only six states (all from Central and Eastern Europe) have signed and ratified the 1983 Convention, which is not yet in force. *See* Multilateral Treaties Deposited with the Secretary-General, *available at* http://untreaty.un.org.

[67] BRIERLY, *supra* note 33, at 153.

[68] For example, issues of state succession may be thought of as arising in the following three ways: part of the territory of State A becomes the territory of existing State B; State A is absorbed by existing State B; or part of State A becomes new State B.

[69] *See* OPPENHEIM, *supra* note 2, at 209, discussing the example of the partition of the former British India into the "newly independent State of India" and the "new State of Pakistan."

controversial."[70] But it seems clear enough that while "no *general* succession takes place according to international law[,] . . . certain rights and duties do devolve upon an international person from its predecessor."[71] Again, what those rights and duties are must be determined on a case-by-case basis.[72]

General rules have, however, been asserted and applied in some situations. The "clean slate" theory, as the name implies, holds that the new state begins afresh, having received no rights or obligations from its predecessor.[73] Also self-defining is the older "universal succession" theory, the clean slate theory's polar opposite, according to which all of the predecessor's rights and obligations pass to the successor.[74] Both the Restatement[75] and the 1978 Vienna Succession Convention[76] generally follow the clean slate theory with respect to international agreements, but apply it to different categories of state succession. While the Restatement applies the approach to both newly independent states emerging from colonialism and new states that were formerly a part of other states, the 1978 Convention applies it only to newly independent states. The Restatement rejects this distinction on the ground that "it does not reflect consistent practice and would be difficult to apply."[77] Thus under the Restatement's version of the clean-slate approach, new states, whether formerly part of another state or newly independent, are free to pick and choose the agreements by which they wish to be bound. Agreement or acquiescence of the other party or parties would also be necessary.

Another way of looking at the problem of succession to treaties is to view treaty rights and obligations as attaching not to the *territories* of the states that concluded the agreement but to the contracting *states* themselves.[78] Thus, "when considering the effect of a change in the sovereignty of

---

[70] *Id.* Some commentators have gone so far as to contend that a true "succession of international persons never takes place. Their argument was that the rights and duties of an international person disappeared with the extinguished person, or became modified, according to the modifications an international person underwent through losing part of its sovereignty." *Id.* at 209-210.

[71] *Id.* at 210 (emphasis in original).

[72] *Id.*

[73] *See* RESTATEMENT 3d, *supra* note 3, § 210(3) cmt. f and Reporters' Note 3. When the United States became independent, for example, it refused to be bound by the treaties applicable to its territory that had been concluded by Great Britain. The same was generally true of Latin American states that had been colonies of Spain. *See* 2 O'CONNELL, *supra* note 57, at 91.

[74] *See* O'CONNELL, *supra* note 57, at 9. The 1978 Vienna Succession Convention applies a similar principle, that of continuity, to cases in which a part of the territory of a state separates to form one or more states. *See* 1978 Vienna Succession Convention, *supra* note 57, art. 34. In the *Gabčíkovo-Nagymaros* case, Slovakia argued, and Hungary denied, that art. 34 reflected customary international law. The ICJ did not find it necessary to rule on the question. *See* 1997 I.C.J. 7, 71.

[75] RESTATEMENT 3d, *supra* note 3, § 210(3) cmt. f and Reporters' Note 3.

[76] 1978 Vienna Succession Convention, *supra* note 57, arts. 16-30.

[77] *See* RESTATEMENT 3d, *supra* note 3, § 210, Reporters' Note 4.

[78] *See* BRIERLY, *supra* note 33, at 153.

territory on treaty rights and obligations, the key to the matter is to have regard to the personalities of the contracting states and to see if these have in any material way changed their identity."[79] If territory is transferred from one state to another, or becomes a new state, it in effect passes out of the treaty system of the former state and into that of the state of which it is newly a part.[80] This is consistent with a "clean-slate" approach to succession. It appears that at least one exception to this general rule has now been established, however, as discussed in the following paragraphs.

The exception to the general, or "clean-slate," rule concerns so-called "dispositive" treaties, or "treaties of a territorial character." Such agreements are said to attach to the territories of the contracting states rather than to the states, or legal persons, that concluded them. By virtue of being attached to the territory, they would bind the state that succeeded to that territory. In the *Gabčíkovo-Nagymaros* case,[81] Slovakia cited this exception in support of its argument that it became a party to the 1977 Treaty there involved as a successor to Czechoslovakia.[82] Hungary had maintained that there was "'no rule of international law which provides for automatic succession to bilateral treaties on the disappearance of a party' . . . ;"[83] such a treaty would not survive, according to Hungary, unless the new state succeeded to it by express agreement between itself and the remaining party. Slovakia, for its part, while acknowledging that there was no agreement between itself and Hungary on succession to the 1977 Treaty, referred in particular to "the principle of *ipso jure* continuity of treaties of a territorial or localized character,"[84] which it said is embodied in Article 12 of the 1978 Vienna Succession Convention. That article provides in relevant part as follows:

Article 12

Other Territorial Regimes

. . .

2. A succession of States does not as such affect:

(*a*) Obligations relating to the use of any territory, or to restrictions upon its use, established by a treaty for the benefit of a group of States or of all States and considered as attaching to that territory;

(*b*) rights established by a treaty for the benefit of a group of States or of all States and relating to the use of any territory, or to restrictions upon its use, and considered as attaching to that territory.[85]

---

[79] *Id.*

[80] *Id. See also* RESTATEMENT 3d, *supra* note 3, § 210.

[81] 1997 I.C.J. 7.

[82] *Id.* at 70, paras. 122.

[83] *Id.* at 69.

[84] *Id.* at 70.

[85] 1978 Vienna Succession Convention, *supra* note 57, art. 12, as quoted in 1997 I.C.J. at 71.

Slovakia argued that the 1977 Treaty fell within the scope of this provision. As discussed in Chapter 4,[86] that treaty provides for the construction and operation of the Gabčíkovo-Nagymaros project, a system of dams and related works, many of which were on a stretch of the Danube River that forms the border between Hungary and what was then Czechoslovakia. On January 1, 1993, Slovakia became an independent State and succeeded to the portion of territory of the former Czechoslovakia whose boundary with Hungary is formed by the Danube. Slovakia's position was that the 1977 Treaty is "'a dispositive treaty, creating rights *in rem*, independently of the legal personality of its original signatories.'"[87]

The Court found that:

> "the content of the 1977 Treaty indicates that it must be regarded as establishing a territorial regime within the meaning of Article 12 of the 1978 Vienna Convention. It created rights and obligations 'attaching to' the parts of the Danube to which it relates; thus the Treaty itself cannot be affected by a succession of States [and] became binding upon Slovakia on 1 January 1993."[88]

The Court pointed in particular to the fact that the Treaty provided for the construction and operation of a "large, integrated and indivisible complex of structures and installations on specific parts of the respective territories of Hungary and Czechoslovakia along the Danube."[89] The Court also noted that the Treaty established a navigational regime for an important sector of the Danube, thus implicating the interests of other users of that international waterway.[90]

Hungary was not a party to the 1978 Vienna Succession Convention but Slovakia argued that the relevant provisions of that agreement amounted to codifications of customary international law. The Court agreed that "Article 12 reflects a rule of customary international law,"[91] noting that "neither of the Parties disputed this."[92] It further observed that the International Law Commission, in its commentary on the draft articles that formed the basis of the 1978 Convention, "indicated that 'treaties concerning water rights or navigation on rivers are commonly regarded as candidates for inclusion in the category of territorial treaties'. . . ."[93]

On the basis of the ICJ's decision in the *Gabčíkovo-Nagymaros* case, therefore, we may conclude that there is indeed a separate category of

---

[86] *See* § 4.05[E][2].

[87] 1997 I.C.J. 7, at 71.

[88] *Id.* at 72.

[89] *Id.* at 71.

[90] *Id.* at 71-72.

[91] *Id.* at 72.

[92] *Id.*

[93] *Id.*

treaties, known as treaties of a territorial character, which "attach to" the parts of territory to which they relate and are unaffected by a succession of states. These treaties, or obligations originally created by them,[94] would thus be binding on the successor state.

[D] Self-Determination

While it is closely connected with human rights law, the principle of self-determination is treated here because the exercise by a people of its right to self-determination may culminate in the formation of a new state. It is perhaps more likely that it will not, however, as we will see in the balance of this subsection. A major distinction between human rights law and the principle of self-determination is that while the former protects rights of individuals, the latter is a right pertaining to a "people," or group.

It is difficult to argue with the abstract proposition that a people should have the right to self-determination.[95] It is in the application of that principle to concrete fact situations that problems are encountered. One need only think of the U.S. Civil War to understand how strongly held the convictions on both sides of a secession battle can be, or of the states emerging from the former Yugoslavia to realize how difficult it is to define concepts such as a "people"[96] and self-determination itself. Many contemporary examples of secession attempts or similar civil conflict could also be cited, including Chechnya, the southern and Darfur regions of Sudan, Kashmir, the Tamils in Sri Lanka and the Kurdish region in northern Iraq (extending into southeastern Turkey and western Iran).[97] There is an inevitable tension between two opposing considerations that are often involved in cases raising questions of self-determination: countries do not like to lose

---

[94] The ICJ noted in the *Gabčíkovo* case that art. 12 of the 1978 Vienna Succession Convention refers only to succession in relation to rights and obligations, rather than to the treaty itself. It concluded that the article was formulated in this way to take into account the fact that in many cases treaties that established boundaries or territorial regimes are no longer in force. If they were, they would bind a successor state, despite the language of art. 12, according to the Court. *See id.* at 72.

[95] On self-determination, *see generally* 2 OPPENHEIM, *supra* note 2, at 712-715. *See also, e.g.,* ANTONIO CASSESE, SELF-DETERMINATION OF PEOPLES: A LEGAL REAPPRAISAL (1995) (hereinafter CASSESE); K. Doehring, *Self-Determination,* in Bruno Simma, ed., THE CHARTER OF THE UNITED NATIONS: A COMMENTARY 70 (1994) (hereinafter Doehring); THOMAS M. FRANCK, FAIRNESS IN INTERNATIONAL LAW AND INSTITUTIONS ch. 5, at 140-169 (1995) (hereinafter FRANCK); and HURST HANNUM, AUTONOMY, SOVEREIGNTY AND SELF-DETERMINATION: THE ACCOMMODATION OF CONFLICTING RIGHTS (1990).

[96] The precise meaning of this term is not entirely settled. *See* the discussion of the question in *Reference re Secession of Quebec,* Supreme Court of Canada, 20 Aug. 1998, paras. 123-125, 37 I.L.M. 1340 (1998). Speaking of self-determination, a Briton writing in the 1950s offered the following perspective: "On the surface, it seemed reasonable: let the people decide. It was in fact ridiculous, because the people cannot decide until someone decides who are the people." SIR IVOR JENNINGS, THE APPROACH TO SELF-GOVERNMENT 55-56 (1956) (hereinafter JENNINGS).

[97] Other difficult cases include Western Sahara, Tibet and Gibraltar. East Timor achieved independence from Indonesia in May, 2002 following a 1999 referendum and transitional administration by the United Nations.

territory; and minority groups may aspire to have autonomy over their affairs.[98] In part because of this conflict, and analogous ones where there is no effort to secede, the meaning of the concept of self-determination is controversial. The principle itself is well recognized, however.

The United Nations Charter refers in Articles 1 and 55 to "the principle of equal rights and self-determination of peoples."[99] Article 1(1) of both of the 1966 Human Rights Covenants reads as follows: "All peoples have the right of self-determination. By virtue of that right they freely determine their political status and freely pursue their economic, social and cultural development."[100] The principle is also recognized in a number of UN General Assembly resolutions.[101] But these instruments often simply give expression to the conflicting values referred to above rather than resolving them. For example, the 1960 Declaration on the Granting of Independence to Colonial Countries and Peoples proclaims both that "All peoples have the right to self-determination" (paragraph 2) and that "Any attempt aimed at the partial or total disruption of the national unity and the territorial integrity of a country is incompatible with the purposes and principles of the Charter of the United Nations" (paragraph 6).[102] The combination of these two statements suggests support for decolonization but only so long as colonial boundaries remain intact.

While self-determination became the cornerstone of the UN's decolonization policy, the idea is considerably older than the United Nations. It has in fact been said to date at least from the Hebrews' exodus from Egypt circa 1000 BC.[103] The philosophy underlying the concept is a powerful one. The notion that the legitimacy of governmental authority is based on the consent of the governed may be traced to the English, French and American revolutions. But "[w]hile democracy invokes the right of each *person* to participate in governance, self-determination is about the social right of a *people* to constitute a nation state."[104]

---

[98] For a case illustrating this tension, *see* the *Western Sahara Case*, Advisory Opinion, 1975 I.C.J. 12.

[99] U.N. CHARTER, arts. 1(2) and 55.

[100] International Covenant on Economic, Social and Cultural Rights, 19 Dec. 1966, art. 1(1), GA Res. 2200 (XXI), 21 U.N. GAOR, Supp. (No. 16) 49, UN Doc. A/6316 (1967), 6 I.L.M. 360 (1967); International Covenant on Civil and Political Rights, 19 Dec. 1966, art. 1(1), GA Res. 2200 (XXI), 21 U.N. GAOR, Supp. (No. 16) 52, U.N. Doc. A/6316 (1967), 6 I.L.M. 368 (1967).

[101] Among the most important of these are Resolution 637 A (VII) of 16 Dec. 1952; the Declaration on the Granting of Independence to Colonial Countries and Peoples, 14 Dec. 1960, GA Res. 1514 (XV), 15 U.N. GAOR Supp. (No. 16) 66, UN Doc. A/4684 (1961); and the Declaration of Principles of International Law concerning Friendly Relations and Co-operation Among States in Accordance with the Charter of the United Nations, 24 Oct. 1970, GA Res. 2625 (XXV), 25 U.N. GAOR, Supp. (No. 28) 121, UN Doc. A/8028 (1971), 9 I.L.M. 1292 (1970) (hereinafter Friendly Relations Declaration).

[102] 14 Dec. 1960, Paras. 2 and 6, GA Res. 1514 (XV), 15 U.N. GAOR Supp. (No. 16) 66, U.N. Doc. A/4684 (1961).

[103] FRANCK, *supra* note 95, at 93.

[104] FRANCK, *supra* note 95, at 92 (emphasis in original), adding that "many of the contemporary standards for a democratic entitlement have their origins in the *process* by which persons were consulted, in internationally supervised or observed elections and plebiscites, to

The idea of conducting plebiscites in connection with cessions or acquisition of territory gained traction in 19th century Europe,[105] but was interrupted by a resurgence of annexation by conquest in Africa, Asia and Europe after 1870.[106] During World War I President Woodrow Wilson "proposed a post-war order informed by the notion that ethnically identifiable peoples or nations would govern themselves."[107] This concept in fact played an important role in the post-war territorial settlement, which dealt with the fate of territories freed from the Central Powers, including those in the Austro-Hungarian, German and Russian empires. Two elements of that settlement were that identifiable peoples would be granted statehood and that those in disputed border areas would determine their allegiance by plebiscite.[108] Vladimir Lenin of the Soviet Union was also a proponent of the principle, albeit chiefly in the context of colonialism rather than within the Soviet Union and Soviet bloc countries themselves.

Despite its role in organizing political geography in the post-World War I era, self-determination was not mentioned in the Covenant of the League of Nations and, as of 1920, probably did not form part of international law. In that year, the International Committee of Jurists formed by the League to deal with the *Aaland Islands Question*, stated in its report: "The recognition of [the principle of self-determination] in a certain number of international treaties cannot be considered as sufficient to put it upon the same footing as a positive rule of the Law of Nations. . . . Positive International Law does not recognize the right of national groups, as such, to separate themselves from the State of which they form part by the simple expression of a wish. . . ."[109]

---

determine whether and how they wished to emerge from a pre-existing political context and to establish a new civil association" (emphasis in original).

[105] *See* Anthony Whelan, *Wilsonian Self-determination and the Versailles Settlement*, 43 Int'l & Comp. L.Q. 99, 100 (1994) (hereinafter Whelan). Thomas Franck points out that the 1814-15 Congress of Vienna "had utterly disregarded ethnic sensibilities in redrawing the map of post-Napoleonic Europe." Franck, *supra* note 95, at 93. This must have provided an impetus for the use of plebiscites in Europe later in the century.

[106] Whelan, *supra* note 105, at 100.

[107] *Id.*

[108] *Id.*, noting also that "ethnic groups too small or too dispersed to be eligible for either course of action were to benefit from the protection of special minorities regimes, supervised by the Council of the new League of Nations." *Id.* at 100-101. The "Wilsonian principle" of basing settlements on "facts" of nationality and ethnicity was applied to allow Northern Schleswig to revert to Denmark; in the creation of Czechoslovakia; in opposing French efforts to create a buffer "Rhenish Republic;" in creating an independent Poland; and in dividing Upper Silesia along ethnic lines. Thomas M. Franck, *Legitimacy in the International System*, 82 Am. J Int'l L. 705, 743-744 (1988) (hereinafter Franck, *Legitimacy*).

[109] Report of the International Committee of Jurists on the Legal Aspects of the Aaland Islands Question, League of Nations Official J., Special Supp. No. 3 (1920). *See also* Whelan, *supra* note 105, at 103-104; Franck, *Legitimacy*, *supra* note 108, at 744; and Leslie C. Green, *Self-Determination and the Settlement of the Arab-Israeli Conflict*, 65 Am. J. Int'l L. 40 (1971).

But the principle of self-determination has developed considerably since 1920, particularly in the context of decolonization.[110] As already indicated, however, its application in specific cases can raise difficult questions; it can also produce different results.[111] The experience of the decolonization movement of the 1960s and 1970s, together with other state practice, suggests that the principle has the following aspects. First, it applies in the context of decolonization and the gaining of independence by other dependent territories.[112] Here self-determination means that the inhabitants of these territories have the right to determine their political future, through "a free and genuine expression of the will of the peoples concerned."[113] This right is limited, however, by the principle of *uti possidetis*, according to which colonial boundaries should not change when independence is achieved.[114] That doctrine finds expression as the principle of territorial integrity in paragraph 6 of the U.N. General Assembly's 1960 Declaration on the Granting of Independence to Colonial Countries and Peoples, set forth above[115] — a resolution that Franck cites as evidence of the "[i]ncreasing incoherence" of the principle of self-determination.[116] The *uti possidetis* doctrine has also been applied outside the context of decolonization, in cases involving the break-up of Yugoslavia[117] and, in the form of the principle of territorial integrity, in other cases of attempted secession.[118]

---

[110] Judge (now President) Higgins has characterized the development of the principle this way: "It seems that many governments have come all the way from an insistence in the 1950s that self-determination was not a legal right (the Western view); and from an insistence that it had no application beyond decolonization (the Third World view); to an assumption, by many European leaders at least, that self-determination is a right that authorizes minorities to break away." ROSALYN HIGGINS, PROBLEMS & PROCESS: INTERNATIONAL LAW AND HOW WE USE IT 124 (1994) (hereinafter HIGGINS).

[111] Franck points out that the international system has taken at least three different approaches to implementing the principle of self-determination, citing the cases of the disintegration of Spain's American empire, the defeat of the Central Powers in World War I, and the anti-colonialism and nationalist movements in Africa, Asia and the Caribbean. FRANCK, *supra* note 95, at 147.

[112] On dependent territories generally, *see* 1 OPPENHEIM, *supra* note 2, at 275-295. According to that work, "colonies and similar dependent territories possess no separate statehood or sovereignty: it is the parent state alone which possesses international personality and has the capacity to exercise international rights and duties." *Id.* at 275-276.

[113] Western Sahara Case, Advisory Opinion, 1975 I.C.J. 12, para. 55.

[114] In the Frontier Dispute case, a Chamber of the I.C.J. stated: "The essence of the principle [of *uti possidetis juris*] lies in its primary aim of securing respect for the territorial boundaries at the moment when independence is achieved." Burkina Faso v. Mali, 1986 I.C.J. 554, para. 23. For other cases applying the principle, *see* the Land, Island and Maritime Frontier Dispute case, El Salvador v. Honduras, 1992 I.C.J. 351; and, outside a post-colonial context, Opinions No. 2 and No. 3, Arbitration Commission, E.C. Conference on Yugoslavia, 1992, 92 I.L.R. 167, 170. *See generally* FRANCK, *supra* note 95, at 146-147.

[115] *See* text at note 102, *supra*.

[116] Franck, *Legitimacy*, *supra* note 108, at 746, where the author states that "the principle of self-determination began its descent into incoherence . . . almost from the moment of its greatest apparent ascendance [in the decolonization era]." *Id.*

[117] *See* Opinions No. 2 and No. 3, Arbitration Commission, E.C. Conference on Yugoslavia, 1992, 92 I.L.R. 167, 170.

[118] Franck cites the examples of Katanga, Cyprus and Mayotte, in which the U.N. "actively sided with the authorities to prevent the success of a secessionist movement." FRANCK, *supra* note 95, at 147.

A second aspect of the contemporary principle of self-determination relates to the rights of a minority within a country. Both paragraph 6 of the 1960 Declaration and the principle of *uti possidetis* suggest that secession in fulfillment of self-determination is, if not prohibited, at least strongly discouraged.[119] This attitude is echoed by the 1970 Friendly Relations Declaration which, after defining the elements of "the principle of equal rights and self-determination of peoples," states:

> "Nothing in the foregoing paragraphs shall be construed as authorizing or encouraging any action which would dismember or impair, totally or in part, the territorial integrity or political unity of sovereign and independent States conducting themselves in compliance with the principle of equal rights and self-determination of peoples as described above and thus possessed of a government representing the whole people belonging to the territory without distinction as to race, creed or color."[120]

The Canadian Supreme Court, in its advisory opinion on the *Secession of Quebec*, put it this way: "international law expects that the right to self-determination will be exercised by peoples within the framework of existing sovereign states and consistently with the maintenance of the territorial integrity of those states."[121] The court found that "international law does not specifically grant component parts of sovereign states the legal right to secede unilaterally from their 'parent' state."[122]

International law does not entirely exclude the possibility of secession, however. The last clause of the above passage of the Friendly Relations Declaration (". . . States conducting themselves in compliance . . .") signals that secession may be permissible under what the Canadian Supreme Court has called "exceptional circumstances."[123] These include situations in which peoples are under colonial rule, are oppressed by such means as foreign military occupation,[124] or "where a definable group is denied meaningful access to government to pursue their political, economic, social and cultural development."[125] Put another way, "when a people is blocked from the

---

[119] U.N. practice has sometimes supported this position. See the examples cited by Franck, referred to in note 118, *supra*, in which the U.N. worked to prevent the success of secessionist movements.

[120] Friendly Relations Declaration, *supra* note 101.

[121] Reference re Secession of Quebec, para. 122, Supreme Court of Canada, 20 Aug. 1998, 37 I.L.M. 1340 (1998).

[122] *Id.*, para. 111. *See also* HIGGINS, *supra* note 110, at 124: "minorities *as such* do not have a right of self-determination. That means, in effect, that they have no right to secession, to independence, or to join with comparable groups in other states." (Emphasis in original.)

[123] *Reference re Secession of Quebec, supra* note 121, paras. 122, 138.

[124] *Id.*, paras. 131 (citing CASSESE, *supra* note 95, at 334), 133. The Court referred in this connection to peoples who are "subject to alien subjugation, domination or exploitation outside a colonial context." *Id.*, para. 133. *See also* Legal Consequences of the Construction of a Wall in the Occupied Palestinian Territory, Advisory Opinion, 9 July 2004, 2004 I.C.J. 131, 43 I.L.M. 1009 (2004), paras. 87 and 88.

[125] *Reference re Secession of Quebec, supra* note 121, para. 138.

meaningful exercise of its right to self-determination internally, it is entitled, as a last resort, to exercise it by secession."[126] But this would only be the case where a state's government failed to represent "the whole people belonging to the territory without distinction as to race, creed or color,"[127] i.e., where it was impossible for the people in question to pursue its political, economic, social and cultural development within the framework of the state.

A distinction is sometimes made between internal and external self-determination. The former refers to a people's pursuit of its various development goals within the context of an existing state. It assumes that this would be possible given the state's governmental structure, as indicated in the preceding paragraph, which the Canadian Supreme Court found to be the case as to Quebec.[128] External self-determination may take either of two forms. It may be interpreted to mean "the expression of a people's external political status through the government of the existing state;"[129] or, in the highly exceptional kinds of cases referred to above,[130] it may take the form of unilateral secession by a people from a state.[131]

In sum, the right of a people to self-determination may be considered to be a general principle of international law.[132] In most cases this does not imply a right of unilateral secession, however. Instead, peoples must generally pursue their political, economic, social and cultural development goals through the government and within the framework of the state in which they are located.

§ 5.03   OTHER "SUBJECTS" OF INTERNATIONAL LAW

In addition to states, there are other entities that may enjoy international legal personality, to varying degrees. These include territorial entities other than states, international organizations, and natural and legal persons. Each will be taken up in turn in the following subsections.

[A]   Territorial Entities Other than States

There are a number of remaining dependent territories[133] that are administered in varying degrees by a variety of states including Australia, Denmark, France, Netherlands, New Zealand, Norway, South Africa, the United Kingdom and the United States. (The fact that a state transfers to

---

[126] *Id.*, para. 134.

[127] Friendly Relations Declaration, *supra* note 101.

[128] *Id.*, paras. 136-137.

[129] *Reference re Secession of Quebec, supra* note 121, para. 129.

[130] *See* text at notes 123-127, *supra*.

[131] *Reference re Secession of Quebec, supra* note 121, para. 126.

[132] *See, e.g.,* CASSESE, *supra* note 95, at 171-172; Doehring, *supra* note 95, at 70; and *Reference re Secession of Quebec, supra* note 121, para. 114.

[133] On dependent territories generally, *see* 1 OPPENHEIM, *supra* note 2, at 275-295. A list of the many existing dependent territories is available at http://en.wikipedia.org/wiki/Dependent_area.

another state responsibility for its foreign relations, as in the case of Liechtenstein, does not affect its statehood.[134]) There are also a number of disputed or occupied territories, including the West Bank, Gibraltar, Kashmir, Nagorno-Karabakh, the Senkaku and Spratly Islands, Taiwan, Tibet and Western Sahara.[135] Antarctica, a continent, is perhaps in a class by itself although it too is subject to conflicting territorial claims;[136] these are effectively placed in a "state of suspense" under the Antarctic Treaty.[137]

Dependent territories would generally not qualify as states. Even assuming the population and territory requirements were satisfied, and that they possessed their own government, they would usually not have the capacity to enter into relations with other states. This is another way of saying that they would not be independent.

Taiwan is something of an anomaly insofar as statehood is concerned. While it fulfills the Montevideo criteria, it does not claim to be a state since it regards itself as part of China. Since the United States shares this view, and because an entity must claim to be a state in order to be one, the U.S. does not recognize Taiwan as a state.

[B] International Organizations

After states, the entities that may be thought of as potentially having the most complete international legal personality are international organizations. However, international organizations are creatures of states. They therefore possess legal personality only to the extent that states have conferred it upon them. The nature and extent of the legal personality of an international organization is chiefly dependent upon its founding charter, a treaty between the states that establish it. We will explore this point further below. Certain of an organization's characteristics may also derive from customary international law and other sources but the organization as an international legal person is for the most part defined by the agreement that creates it. International organizations may be intergovernmental or non-governmental. This section deals only with intergovernmental international organizations.[138]

Though they are hardly a recent phenomenon,[139] international organizations have played an increasingly important role on the world stage

---

[134] *See generally* RESTATEMENT 3d, *supra* note 3, § 201, Reporters' Note 4.

[135] A full list is available at http://en.wikipedia.org/wiki/List_of_disputed_or_occupied_territories, listing 35 such territories.

[136] Such claims have been made by Argentina, Australia, Brazil, Chile, France, New Zealand, Norway and the United Kingdom.

[137] Washington, D.C., 1 Dec. 1959, 402 U.N.T.S. 71. *See generally* 2 OPPENHEIM, *supra* note 2, § 257, at 694-696 (referring to the "state of suspense" at 694).

[138] A list of the many intergovernmental international organizations is available at http://www.library.northwestern.edu/govpub/resource/internat/igo.html.

[139] Paul Reuter has described the Central Commission of the Navigation of the Rhine, established at the time of the Congress of Vienna, 1814-15, as the "*doyen*" of international institutions. PAUL REUTER, INTERNATIONAL INSTITUTIONS 207 (1961) (hereinafter REUTER). Some international river commissions, however, are considerably older.

since the Second World War.[140] States have found it convenient to form international organizations to institutionalize and facilitate their cooperation in a variety of fields. These bodies provide needed forums for discussion of and action on common problems, assist states with the implementation of treaties, enter into agreements with states and other international organizations and may even contribute to the making of international law.[141] The functions international organizations are established to perform are nearly as many and varied as the fields of human endeavor.[142]

An international organization, as that term is used here, is established by an international agreement.[143] Its members are normally states, although they may include other international organizations, dependent territories and other non-state entities.[144] The agreement establishing the organization — its charter or constituent instrument[145] — provides for its organs as well as their functions and procedures. The organs ordinarily include a secretariat or permanent staff, headed by an executive officer, a decision-making body and sometimes a technical support body. Other organs are of course possible, as the United Nations itself demonstrates, depending on the functions to be served by the organization. The constituent instrument typically provides for the headquarters and finances of the organization, as well.

---

[140] On the law of international organizations generally, *see* HAGUE ACADEMY OF INTERNATIONAL LAW, A HANDBOOK ON INTERNATIONAL ORGANIZATIONS (René-Jean Dupuy, 2nd ed. 1998); DEREK BOWETT, THE LAW OF INTERNATIONAL INSTITUTIONS (4th ed. 1982); 1 OPPENHEIM, *supra* note 2, § 7, at 16-22; RESTATEMENT 3d, *supra* note 3, ch. 2, §§ 221-223; REUTER, *supra* note 139; PAUL REUTER & J. COMBACAU, INSTITUTIONS ET RELATIONS INTERNATIONALES (1980); and H.G. SCHERMERS, INTERNATIONAL INSTITUTIONAL LAW (2nd ed. 1980).

[141] *See* the discussions of the role of U.N. General Assembly resolutions in international lawmaking in chapter 3, § 3.03[B][1], *supra*.

[142] *See, e.g.*, the list of international organizations referred to in note 138, *supra*. A short list will perhaps make the point: they range from the United Nations itself to the International Labor Organization (ILO) and the Universal Postal Union, both of which pre-date the UN; the United Nations Educational, Social and Cultural Organization (UNESCO), the World Health Organization (WHO) and the International Civil Aviation Organization (ICAO), all among the specialized agencies of the UN under arts. 57-59 of the U.N. Charter; and the World Trade Organization (WTO) and World Bank, international economic organizations.

[143] The agreement may take various forms, but should constitute a "treaty" within the meaning of art. 2 of the Vienna Convention on the Law of Treaties. In *Qatar v. Bahrain*, the ICJ found that signed minutes of a meeting constituted a treaty because the requisite intent to create international obligations was present. 1994 I.C.J. 112. *See also* the *Aegean Sea Continental Shelf Case* (Jurisdiction), 1978 I.C.J. 1, 39, in which the Court stated that "it knows of no rule of international law which might preclude a joint communiqué from constituting an international agreement," although it concluded that the communiqué in question did not have that effect.

[144] *See* RESTATEMENT 3d, *supra* note 3, § 221 cmt. c, noting that the membership of the Universal Postal Union includes territories and possessions of member states and that an organization such as the European Union may be a member of another international organization.

[145] The Restatement uses the term "constitutive" agreement, which has the same meaning. *See, e.g.*, RESTATEMENT 3d, *supra* note 3, § 222(1).

Once the organization is established, it may itself enter into agreements with states and other international organizations, assuming it has the capacity to do so. It would normally conclude a headquarters agreement with the state in which its permanent seat and secretariat are located.[146] It may also conclude a separate agreement with its member states on privileges and immunities of the organization, its staff and officials, as well as those of representatives of members when participating in meetings of the organization.[147] Privileges and immunities of an organization and its personnel are generally functional in nature, i.e., they include those necessary to discharge the functions of the organization and its personnel.[148]

As indicated earlier in this subsection, the nature and extent of the legal personality of an international organization are defined in its charter. Its legal capacity, privileges and immunities and other qualities may be further defined in additional agreements, as in the case of the United Nations.[149] In the *Reparation Case*,[150] the U.N. General Assembly requested an advisory opinion from the International Court of Justice on the question whether the United Nations had the legal capacity to bring an international claim against a government seeking reparation for injuries suffered by itself, its agent or persons entitled through the agent, even where the U.N. Charter failed to provide expressly for such capacity. The relevant facts of the case were as follows: In 1948 the General Assembly appointed Count Folke Bernadotte of Sweden as U.N. Mediator in Palestine. Bernadotte was assassinated on 17 September 1948 in the

---

[146] *See, e.g.*, the Headquarters Agreement of 26 June 1947 between the U.S. and the U.N, 61 Stat. 3416, 11 U.N.T.S. 11.

[147] *See, e.g.*, the Convention on the Privileges and Immunities of the United Nations, 13 Feb. 1946, 1 U.N.T.S. 15, 21 U.S.T. 1418, T.I.A.S. No. 6900; and the Convention on Privileges and Immunities of the Specialized Agencies, 33 U.N.T.S. 261. On immunities of international organizations generally, *see* RESTATEMENT 3d, *supra* note 3, §§ 467-470.

[148] Although they are based upon the privileges and immunities of states, those of international organizations differ because such organizations are not sovereign and because of the lack of the reciprocity that exists between states. *See* RESTATEMENT 3d, *supra* note 3, ch. 6, subch. B, Immunities of International Organizations, Introductory Note, at 492. Beginning in 1976, the International Law Commission considered the topic of the status, privileges and immunities of international organizations and their officials, experts and other persons engaged in their activities who are not representatives of states. It decided, in 1992, not to pursue work on the topic further during the current term of office of its members. The General Assembly endorsed this decision in resolution 47/33 of 25 Nov. 1992. No action has since been taken on the topic. *See* 1 UNITED NATIONS, THE WORK OF THE INTERNATIONAL LAW COMMISSION 148-151 (6th ed. 2004).

[149] *See* the Convention on the Privileges and Immunities of the United Nations, *supra* note 147., which provides in art. 1(1) that: "The United Nations shall possess juridical personality. It shall have the capacity: (a) to contract; (b) to acquire and dispose of immovable and movable property; (c) to institute legal proceedings." The Convention goes on to provide, *inter alia*, for the privileges and immunities of representatives of members (art. IV), officials (art. V) and experts on missions for the United Nations (art. VI).

[150] Reparation for Injuries Suffered in the Service of the United Nations, Advisory Opinion, 1949 I.C.J. 174.

Israeli-controlled zone of Jerusalem by men in Israeli uniform.[151] Speaking of the U.N., the Court said:

> "the Organization is an international person. That is not the same thing as saying that it is a State, which it certainly is not, or that its legal personality and rights and duties are the same as those of a State. . . . What it does mean is that it is a subject of international law and capable of possessing international rights and duties, and that it has capacity to maintain its rights by bringing international claims."[152]

The Court went on to address the specific question whether the U.N. had the capacity to bring the claim in question.

> "Whereas a State possesses the totality of international rights and duties recognized by international law, the rights and duties of an entity such as the Organization must depend upon its purposes and functions as specified or implied in its constituent documents and developed in practice. The functions of the Organization are of such a character that they could not be effectively discharged if they involved the concurrent action, on the international plane, of fifty-eight or more Foreign Offices [then the number of U.N. member states], and the Court concludes that the Members have endowed the Organization with capacity to bring international claims when necessitated by the discharge of its functions."[153]

The Court concluded that the United Nations has the capacity to bring an international claim against a *de jure* or *de facto* government of either a member state or one that is not a member of the U.N. With regard to non-member states, the Court reasoned that states "representing the vast majority of the members of the international community, had the power . . . to bring into being an entity possessing objective international personality. . . ."[154] Being "objective," such personality would allow the U.N. to enter into legal relations with non-member states, and thus to bring claims against them. In addition, the Court found that claims could be brought not only for injury to the U.N. itself, but also for injury to the victim or persons entitled through the victim. Thus, it is clear that an international organization may possess international legal personality.[155] However, an international organization does not possess the full panoply of rights and duties of a state.[156] In fact, the legal capacity of most international organizations generally does not

---

[151] *See* 1 PUBLIC PAPERS OF THE SECRETARIES-GENERAL OF THE UNITED NATIONS 163 (1969). The Provisional Government of Israel had proclaimed Israeli statehood on May 14, 1948.

[152] *Reparation Case, supra* note 150, at 179.

[153] *Id.* at 180.

[154] *Id.* at 185.

[155] *See* OPPENHEIM, *supra* note 2, at 18.

[156] For example, they do not possess sovereignty (though they may be given immunity by agreement), they do not exercise dominion over territory (though they may be given the right to occupy territory for headquarters and other offices under headquarters agreements and similar instruments) and they do not generally exercise governmental functions (though some, such as the European Union, do exercise such functions to a large extent).

begin to approach even that of the United Nations, which is *sui generis* in the universe of such organizations. It is doubtful whether any other international body would be found to possess objective legal personality of the kind attributed to the United Nations by the Court. Still, international organizations have become important and in some cases indispensable actors on the international scene.

[C] Natural and Legal Persons

As we have seen, traditionally states were the sole subjects of international law. The previous subsection showed, however, that over time states found it increasingly useful and necessary to accord international legal personality to international organizations. Has a similar development occurred with respect to natural and legal persons? That is the subject of the present subsection.

[1] Natural Persons

The focus of this subsection is upon individuals as subjects of international law. However, it will also touch briefly upon a topic considered earlier in connection with the principle of self-determination, namely, that of the concept of a "people."

[a] Individuals

[i] The Individual as an "Object" of International Law

Individuals were traditionally viewed as "objects" rather than subjects of international law.[157] They did not enjoy international rights and duties directly, but only through the states of which they were nationals. An injury to a national of State A caused by State B was regarded as an injury to State A, not the individual directly suffering the injury. The fate of the individual's claim was thus in the hands of the state of his or her nationality, which could choose to press it against the other state or not, in its sole discretion.[158] Individuals were thus, at best, the object of efforts by the states of their nationality to protect them against harm by other states. This attitude is reflected in Article 34(1) of the ICJ Statute, which provides: "Only states may be parties in cases before the Court."

---

[157] *See generally* OPPENHEIM, *supra* note 2, § 7 and ch. 8. The Restatement includes only states (ch. 1) and international organizations (ch. 2) in Part II, "Persons in International Law," while acknowledging that individuals and legal persons can in principle have rights and duties under international law. *See* RESTATEMENT 3d, *supra* note 3, Part II, and Introductory Note, at 70-71. *But see* Mark W. Janis, *Individuals As Subjects of International Law*, 17 CORNELL INT'L L.J. 61 (1984) (arguing that before eighteenth century positivism, and especially the work of Jeremy Bentham, the individual was considered a subject of international law).

[158] This is part of the law of state responsibility for injuries to aliens, dealt with in chapter 9, at § 9.01[B].

[ii] The Individual as a Subject of International Law

But especially since the end of World War II and the founding of the United Nations, state practice has increasingly recognized that individuals have certain rights and duties under international law. Thus, while the state remains the basic subject of international law, the proposition that individuals can directly possess international rights and duties continues to gain recognition. However, it is probably still wise to exercise caution before classifying individuals as subjects of international law since, as Brownlie points out, this may imply capacities that do not exist and in any event still requires distinctions to be drawn between the individual and other subjects.[159] It is more useful to examine the capacities that individuals actually possess.

On one view of the matter, states began to recognize the individual as being capable of possessing at least international duties when certain individuals became a menace to international order. These were pirates who, beginning in ancient times, preyed on international shipping and, for their troubles, were dubbed *"hostis humani generis"* — the enemy of all humankind.[160] They acted without the sanction of any state, which made it impossible for an injured state to claim reparation from another country. Because piracy posed a serious threat to international intercourse, it was recognized as an offense against the law of nations. And since piracy was regarded as a crime against all of humanity, rather than against any individual state, all states had jurisdiction to try and punish a pirate.[161] Thus did the individual enter the domain of international law. It was not a terribly auspicious beginning. It would be some time before the concept of the individual's possessing rights under international law would come into flower.

The trend of imposing international legal obligations on individuals who disrupt world order continued in the aftermath of World War II. But now the criminals were not fierce individual plunderers but state officials with the capacity to inflict much more widespread harm. Thus, the atrocities committed during the Second World War led to condemnation of the leaders of Nazi Germany and Japan and the establishment of the International Military Tribunals at Nuremberg and Tokyo. As in the case of piracy, the theory underlying the trials of these officials was that individuals can commit crimes under international law. Only here, the offenses were on a much larger scale — against not individual ships but the very peace and security of humankind: crimes against peace; war crimes; and crimes against humanity.

---

[159] IAN BROWNLIE, PRINCIPLES OF PUBLIC INTERNATIONAL LAW 65 (6th ed. 2003).

[160] *See generally* 2 OPPENHEIM, *supra* note 2, at 746-747, stating at 747 that the definition of the term "piracy" in the art. 15 of the 1958 Geneva Convention on the High Seas, 13 U.S.T. 2312, T.I.A.S. No. 5200, 450 U.N.T.S. 82, which is repeated verbatim in art. 101 of the 1982 U.N. Convention on the Law of the Sea, U.N. Doc. A/CONF.62/122, 21 I.L.M. 1261 (1982), "must be regarded as having great authority."

[161] As Judge Moore put it in his separate opinion in the *Lotus Case*, the pirate may be tried "by any nation into whose jurisdiction he may come." 1927 P.C.I.J. (ser. A.) No. 10, at 70.

The Nuremberg Tribunal explicitly rejected the argument that "international law is concerned with the actions of sovereign States, and provides no punishment for individuals," who are "protected by the doctrine of the sovereignty of the State." The Tribunal famously declared: "Crimes against international law are committed by men, not by abstract entities, and only by punishing individuals who commit such crimes can the provisions of international law be enforced."[162] The descendants of the Nuremberg and Tokyo Tribunals — those for the former Yugoslavia[163] and Rwanda,[164] and the International Criminal Court[165] — continue to operate on this principle.

By recognizing that individuals could commit, *inter alia* the crime of genocide under international law, states also recognized, at least implicitly, the other side of the coin: that individuals had rights under international law. This marked the beginning of a signal shift in the classic paradigm of states representing the interests of their nationals. That paradigm was obviously ill suited to situations in which individuals required protection from the very government that represented them under international law: their own. Protection in these cases had to be provided directly to individuals by international law, and had to be implemented by other states or international institutions. What the Nuremberg Charter and Tribunal recognized was a right not to be subjected to the most extreme forms of state abuse: crimes against humanity, including genocide. But recognition of other rights was not long in coming.

[iii]   International Human Rights Law

In 1945 states resolved in the United Nations Charter to promote "universal respect for, and observance of, human rights and fundamental freedoms for all without distinction as to race, sex, language, or religion."[166] But what were these rights? Did they consist only of protections against the most serious offenses such as the crimes against humanity condemned

---

[162] 6 F.R.D. 69, 110 (1946); 41 AM. J. INT'L L 172, 221 (1947). In 1946 the U.N. General Assembly unanimously affirmed the Nuremberg Principles. GA Res. 95 (I). For the Principles in code form, *see* [1950] 2 Y.B. Int'l L. Comm'n 374-378. *See also* the 1954 Draft Code of Offences against the Peace and Security of Mankind, [1954] 2 Y.B. Int'l L. Comm'n. 151-152; and the 1996 Draft Code of Crimes against the Peace and Security of Mankind, [1996] 2 Y.B. Int'l L. Comm'n, pt. 2, 17-56.

[163] Statute of the International Tribunal for the Prosecution of Persons Responsible for Serious Violations of International Humanitarian Law Committed in the Territory of the Former Yugoslavia Since 1991, U.N. Doc. S/25704, at 36, annex (1993), and S/25704/Add.1 (1993).

[164] Statute of the International Tribunal for Rwanda, S.C Res. 955, U.N. SCOR, 49th Sess., 3453d mtg. at 3, U.N. Doc. S/RES/955 (1994), 33 I.L.M. 1598, 1600 (1994).

[165] Rome Statute of the International Criminal Court, U.N. Doc. A/CONF.183/9 (17 July 1998), 37 I.L.M. 999 (1998). For an update on the Court and its activities, *see generally* the section entitled *Developments at the International Criminal Court*, 99 AM. J. INT'L L. 370-431 (2005), containing four articles on the ICC.

[166] U.N. Charter, art. 55(c). *See also id.*, art. 1(3).

by the Nuremberg Tribunal? Or did they extend further, to civil and political, and perhaps even to economic, social and cultural rights? The Charter itself does not provide an answer to these questions. The only light it sheds on them is negative: Article 2(7) provides that nothing in the Charter authorizes U.N. intervention in "matters which are essentially within the domestic jurisdiction of any state," except as authorized by the Security Council acting under Chapter VII of the Charter. To what extent are human rights matters of "domestic jurisdiction?"

This question will be pursued further in Chapter 9, but for now we may note that in 1948 the U.N. General Assembly adopted the Universal Declaration of Human Rights,[167] a resolution defining in some detail a wide range of civil, political, economic, social and cultural rights reflecting "a common understanding of [the] rights and freedoms"[168] referred to in the Charter. These rights were given legal force in the two 1966 Covenants on human rights, treaties that are binding on all parties.[169] Many of the provisions of the Universal Declaration and the Covenants have been said to reflect customary international law.[170] Both collectively and individually, these instruments indicate that human rights are matters of international concern and thus no longer within the domestic jurisdiction of states.

Despite these developments, however, the state remains the principal subject of international law. The implementation of international human rights law is proceeding slowly and, except in certain regional systems, individuals have few avenues through which to gain effective relief. Where they are harmed by a state other than that of their nationality, however, they may — and in fact must — depend upon their national state for protection, including the assertion of their claims against the harming state.[171] Thus an individual's nationality becomes critical.[172] These questions are governed by the law of "state responsibility for injuries to aliens," which is addressed in Chapter 9.[173]

[iv] Terrorists and Terrorism

A particular challenge to international law — not to mention domestic legal systems — has been posed by the phenomenon of terrorism, particularly as it

---

[167] 10 Dec. 1948, GA Res. 217A (III), U.N. Doc. A/810 at 71 (1948).

[168] *Id.*, preamble.

[169] International Covenant on Economic, Social and Cultural Rights, 19 Dec. 1966, GA Res. 2200 (XXI), 21 U.N. GAOR, Supp. (No. 16) 49, U.N. Doc. A/6316 (1967), 6 I.L.M. 360 (1967); International Covenant on Civil and Political Rights, 19 Dec. 1966, GA Res. 2200 (XXI), 21 U.N. GAOR, Supp. (No. 16) 52, U.N. Doc. A/6316 (1967), 6 I.L.M. 368 (1967).

[170] *See, e.g.,* Louis Sohn, *The New International Law: Protection of the Rights of Individuals Rather than States,* 32 AM. U. L. REV. 1, 16-17 (1982); and RESTATEMENT 3d, *supra* note 3, § 702.

[171] *See, e.g.,* RESTATEMENT 3d, *supra* note 3, Part II, Introductory Note, at 71. For such a case, *see* the ELSI case (U.S./Italy), 1989 I.C.J. 15.

[172] *See* 2 OPPENHEIM, *supra* note 2, § 376, "Nationality the link between individuals and international law," at 849.

[173] *See* chapter 9, § 9.01[B].

has manifested itself in the late 20th and early 21st centuries.[174] Terrorist groups or conspiracies such as Al Qaeda are loose but powerful affiliations of individuals that often do not operate under a central command structure. They are not states, state officials, pirates, transnational organized criminal groups or other entities that international law, as it has developed over the centuries, has addressed or is equipped to address. To this day there is no treaty containing a universally accepted definition of the concept of "terrorism." The controversy over the definition is captured in the adage, "one person's terrorist is another's freedom fighter."

However, probably as a result of the unprecedented threats posed by modern terrorism, the historic deadlock on this issue appears to be breaking. In a report submitted in December 2004, a broadly representative High-Level Panel on Threats, Challenges and Change convened by the U.N. Secretary General[175] finally succeeded in arriving at a definition of the term that was acceptable to all members of the group. According to that definition, terrorism consists of "any action . . . that is intended to cause death or serious bodily harm to civilians or non-combatants, when the purpose of such an act, by its nature or context, is to intimidate a population, or to compel a Government or an international organization to do or to abstain from doing any act."[176]

Despite this success at arriving at a generally acceptable definition of the term — which, it is to be hoped, will finally lead to the conclusion of a convention on the subject — much work needs to be done to make international law more responsive to the "new phenomenon"[177] of terrorism in its present-day form, which is "part crime and part combat, yet different from each."[178] For example, Thomas Franck has pointed out that the "prisoner of war" model developed to deal with members of regular armed forces of states is based on a logic — involving such considerations as reciprocity among states involved in armed conflicts and motivations of regular combatants — that does not apply comfortably to the phenomenon of modern terrorism.[179] Yet to argue that no law applies to captured alleged terrorists would be to reject what Professor Franck calls "the civilizing mission of the rule of law."[180] He thus calls for a rethinking of the international legal framework applicable to the treatment and protection of such detainees.[181]

---

[174] For a helpful commentary, see Thomas M. Franck, *Criminals, Combatants, or What? An Examination of the Role of Law in Responding to the Threat of Terror*, 98 AM. J. INT'L L. 868 (2004) (hereinafter Franck, *Threat of Terror*).

[175] See generally "A More Secure World: Our Shared Responsibility, Report of the High-Level Panel on Threats, Challenges and Change," U.N. Doc. A/59/565, 2 Dec. 2004, *available at* http://www.un.org/secureworld/.

[176] *Id.* at 49.

[177] Franck, *Threat of Terror*, *supra* note 174, at 688.

[178] *Id.*

[179] *Id.* at 687.

[180] *Id.* at 686.

[181] The present framework is that contained in the Third and Fourth Geneva Conventions of 1949. Convention Relative to the Treatment of Prisoners of War, 12 Aug. 1949, 6 U.S.T. 3316, T.I.A.S. No. 3364, 75 U.N.T.S. 135; and Convention Relative to the Treatment of Civilian Persons in Time of War, 12 Aug. 1949, 6 U.S.T. 3516, T.I.A.S. No. 3365, 75 U.N.T.S. 287.

[b] "Peoples"

As discussed in Subsection 5.02 [D] above, self-determination is a group right, not an individual right. It attaches to a "people," a term that is not without a certain ambiguity.[182] In *Reference re Secession of Quebec*, the Canadian Supreme Court reasoned that the term cannot refer to the entire population of an existing state because it would then be superfluous.[183] Instead the term refers to a portion of a state's population only. This group would ordinarily share a common language, culture and perhaps religion. The Wilsonian concept of self-determination referred to national or ethnic groups.[184] Beyond this it is difficult to go, however, and each case must be judged on its particular facts.

[2] Legal Persons

We have seen that individuals, or natural persons, are not traditional subjects of international law. The same is true of corporations, or legal persons. However, business and other organizations that are treated as legal entities under domestic legal systems[185] lag far behind individuals in gaining recognition as being capable of possessing rights and duties under international law. By definition, corporations are not "humans" and thus do not enjoy human rights. While a company would in theory be capable of committing offenses under international law such as piracy and crimes against humanity, this possibility has not yet been recognized in state practice, including instruments establishing the International Criminal Court[186] and other such tribunals.[187]

International law has been concerned with corporations chiefly in two kinds of situations: in international arbitrations between business organizations and states; and in claims between states regarding injuries to corporations. The latter category is the branch of international law known as state responsibility for injuries to aliens. It involves allegations by the state in which a company is incorporated that another state has injured

---

[182] *See, e.g.,* JENNINGS, *supra* note 96, at 55-56; and the sources cited in note 95, *supra.*

[183] *Reference re Secession of Quebec, supra* note 96, para. 124.

[184] *See* text at note 107, *supra,* quoting Whelan.

[185] The Restatement states that it "uses the term 'corporation' to refer to all legal entities created by the law of a state, whether in corporate form or otherwise, whether in corporate form or otherwise, whether for business, charitable or other non-profit purposes, and whether privately or state-owned." RESTATEMENT 3d, *supra* note 3, Part II, Introductory Note, note 2. *See also id.,* § 213 comment *a.* That definition serves present purposes, as well.

[186] Rome Statute of the International Criminal Court, U.N. Doc. A/CONF.183/9 (17 July 1998), 37 I.L.M. 999 (1998).

[187] Statute of the International Tribunal for the Prosecution of Persons Responsible for Serious Violations of International Humanitarian Law Committed in the Territory of the Former Yugoslavia Since 1991, U.N. Doc. S/25704, at 36, annex (1993), and S/25704/Add.1 (1993); Statute of the International Tribunal for Rwanda, S.C Res. 955, U.N. SCOR, 49th Sess., 3453d mtg. at 3, U.N. Doc. S/RES/955 (1994), 33 I.L.M. 1598, 1600 (1994).

the corporation in breach of international law. This topic is treated in Chapter 9, below,[188] but we will touch on one aspect of it here.

The former kind of situation, arbitrations between companies and states, frequently involves alleged interference by a state with a business activity operated by a foreign corporation in that state. Examples range from expropriation or nationalization of petroleum concessions[189] to so-called "creeping" or "constructive" expropriation[190] of foreign business enterprises. Concession agreements, by which a state authorizes a foreign corporation to exploit mineral or other forms of resources, normally contain a clause providing for referral of disputes regarding the concession to arbitration and further specifying the arbitral tribunal or the manner in which one is to be constituted.[191] Unless provided otherwise in the concession agreement, the tribunal would ordinarily apply the relevant rules of international law rather than the domestic law of the state effecting the expropriation.

The second kind of situation mentioned above, that involving a claim by one state against another regarding injuries to a corporation, is analogous to cases in which a state makes a claim against another state regarding injuries to an individual who is a national of the former state. Since a corporation is a legal fiction, an issue may arise as to which state is entitled to protect its interests. In the case of an individual this would be the state of the individual's nationality. But how is the nationality of a corporation determined?

This was the question before the International Court of Justice in the *Barcelona Traction* case.[192] The difficulty there was that while the company, Barcelona Traction, was organized under the laws of Canada and had its headquarters there, most of its shares — 88% according to Belgium — were owned by Belgian nationals. Belgium sought to represent the company in an action against Spain, essentially for causing the collapse of Barcelona Traction. The ICJ held that Belgium lacked standing, or *jus standi*, to claim reparation for Barcelona Traction's collapse because the corporation is a distinct legal entity and Barcelona Traction was not a Belgian national.[193] According to the Court, a corporation is a national of the country in which

---

[188] *See* chapter 9, § 9.01[B].

[189] *See, e.g., Texaco v. Libya*, 53 I.L.R. 389, 17 I.L.M. 1 (1978).

[190] For examples of this phenomenon, *see, e.g.,* Starrett Housing Corp. v. Iran (Interlocutory Award), 4 Iran-U.S.C.T.R. 122; 23 I.L.M. 1090 (1984); and Tippets v. TAMS-ATTA, 6 Iran-U.S.C.T.R. 219 (1985). Contrast the *ELSI* case, 1989 I.C.J. 14, 71, where the Court held that requisition of a company's plant for a limited period of six months did not amount to a "taking."

[191] Such clauses often refer to the International Center for the Settlement of Investment Disputes established by the 1965 Convention on the Settlement of Investment Disputes between States and Nationals of Other States, 575 U.N.T.S. 159, 4 I.L.M. 532 (1965).

[192] (Belgium v. Spain), 1970 I.C.J. 3.

[193] *Id.* at 43-45. This would be the case at least where Canada retained the capacity to extend diplomatic protection to the corporation, as it did in that case.

it is incorporated, not where the majority of its shareholders are nationals. Only on the corporation's "legal demise"[194] would the shareholders have no possibility of redress through the company, and only then would an independent right of action for them, and for their government (that of Belgium), arise.

In its analysis the Court delved into the characteristics of corporations under national law, emphasizing their separate legal existence. It noted that it "would lose touch with reality" if it were to "decide the case in disregard of the relevant institutions of municipal law. . . ."[195] The Court did not refer to the municipal law of a particular country, but to "rules generally accepted by municipal legal systems which recognize the limited company whose capital is represented by shares. . . ."[196] Thus it cannot be said that international law does not take cognizance of the corporation. It simply does not treat the corporation as a subject of international law in its own right. Rather, it requires that the corporation's interests be asserted by the state under whose laws it is organized.

Multinational corporations have no different status in international law than national ones. In fact, a multinational corporation, or enterprise, "generally consists of a group of corporations, each established under the law of some state,"[197] and is thus dependent for its existence on the national laws of various states. Thus, while the multinational enterprise has been the object of attention on the part of national and international bodies, sometimes taking the form of codes of conduct,[198] it remains a non-subject of international law.

---

[194] *Id.* at 41, para. 66.

[195] *Id.* at 37, para. 50.

[196] *Id.*

[197] RESTATEMENT 3d, *supra* note 3, § 213 cmt. f.

[198] Efforts during the 1970s, in particular, to regulate multinational enterprises on the international level did not produce a generally agreed text. On corporate codes of conduct generally, *see* the website of the United Nations Research Institute for Social Development (UNRISD), http://www.unrisd.org/unrisd/website/document.nsf/0/E3B3E78BAB9A886F80256B5E00344278 ?OpenDocument.

Chapter 6
THE ALLOCATION OF COMPETENCE
AMONG STATES: JURISDICTION

Synopsis

§ 6.01 INTRODUCTION

What is the extent of a state's authority under international law?[1]
Granted, it has well-nigh plenary authority within its territory —
although even this is subject to certain obligations under international law
such as those relating to human rights and transboundary pollution. But

---

[1] *See generally* 1 OPPENHEIM'S INTERNATIONAL LAW §136 (R. Jennings & A. Watts 9th ed.
1992) (hereinafter OPPENHEIM).

how far can a state extend its authority beyond its borders? Can it regulate the activities of its nationals or others abroad? Can it try a citizen of another country in its courts for a crime committed elsewhere? What about foreign states: may they be sued in its courts? Is the answer the same for diplomats of other countries? And finally, to what extent will U.S. courts defer to acts of foreign states within their own territories?

These and related questions are the subject of this chapter. Their importance has grown, and continues to do so, as the world becomes more interconnected and interdependent. These characteristics of contemporary international life make it increasingly likely that assertions of jurisdiction by two or more states will come into conflict. If this occurs, an important tool for the resolution of the conflict is the branch of international law dealing with state jurisdiction.

We will first look at the basic theoretical approach to state jurisdiction as framed by the Permanent Court of International Justice in 1927. We then take up the principal bases of jurisdiction recognized by states and followed by them in their practice. We turn next to a state's immunity from jurisdiction — in this case, the judicial jurisdiction of other states. Finally, we look at a doctrine which is chiefly a feature of United States practice according to which American courts refrain from examining the validity of acts of foreign states.

Throughout the chapter the reader should consider not so much *where* jurisdictional lines are drawn as *how* they are drawn under international law. What rules, or approaches, are used to avoid and accommodate conflicting assertions of jurisdiction by states?

§ 6.02 JURISDICTION OF STATES: GENERAL CONSIDERATIONS

In the *Lotus* case,[2] the Permanent Court of International Justice (PCIJ) was faced with the question of whether Turkey was entitled under international law to exercise criminal jurisdiction to try a French citizen who had charge of a French mail steamer, the *Lotus*, when it collided with a Turkish vessel, the *Boz-Kourt*, on the high seas, resulting in the sinking of the latter and the death of eight Turkish nationals. In holding that Turkey was so entitled, for lack of a prohibitory rule to the contrary, the Court made the following statement regarding state jurisdiction which is of present relevance:

> "Far from laying down a general prohibition to the effect that states may not extend the application of their laws and the jurisdiction of their courts to persons, property and acts outside their territory, it [i.e., international law] leaves them in this respect a wide measure of discretion which is only limited in certain cases by prohibitive

---

[2] (France v. Turkey) 1927 P.C.I.J. (ser. A) No. 10.

rules; as regards other cases, every state remains free to adopt the principles which it regards as best and most suitable."[3]

Within the bounds set by these "prohibitive rules" of international law, therefore, a state would be entitled to exercise jurisdiction based on its sovereignty. For the PCIJ, this followed from the overarching principle that "[r]estrictions upon the independence of states cannot . . . be presumed." Under this quintessentially positivist approach,[4] then, a state is free to exercise its jurisdiction whenever it is not prohibited from doing so by a positive rule of international law; more generally, whatever is not expressly prohibited is allowed — again, on the theory that restrictions on the sovereign independence of states may not be presumed.

While the general principles articulated by the PCIJ in the *Lotus* case have not been questioned by the PCIJ or its successor, the International Court of Justice, in practice states have generally justified exercises of jurisdiction by pointing to rules authorizing them. We will therefore approach the law of state jurisdiction by inquiring under what circumstances the exercise of jurisdiction by a state is permissible under international law. In this way we may gain an understanding of the limits imposed by international law upon state jurisdiction.

We may begin with the proposition, suggested at the outset of this chapter, that a state has jurisdiction, or authority, under international law to regulate conduct within its borders. This idea flows naturally enough from a state's sovereignty over its territory. There are exceptions even to a proposition as fundamental as this, however, as we will see: diplomats and embassies of other states enjoy immunity from jurisdiction. A state's jurisdiction over its citizens, whether they are at home or abroad, it also uncontroversial.[5] The main area of dispute, especially during the last half century or so, has been a state's authority to regulate the conduct of non-citizens abroad, through executive, legislative or judicial action. Just as a domestic court, in the United States, for example, must have a basis under its law for exercising personal jurisdiction over a defendant[6] or applying its law to a given fact situation,[7] so also should a state have a basis under international

---

[3] *Id.* at 19.

[4] On positivism generally, *see* Chapter 3, *supra*.

[5] The Restatement points out, however, that links of territoriality and nationality "are not in all instances sufficient conditions for the exercise of . . . jurisdiction" because in certain cases the exercise of jurisdiction even on these bases would be unreasonable and therefore unlawful. RESTATEMENT (THIRD) OF THE FOREIGN RELATIONS LAW OF THE UNITED STATES § 403 comment *a* (1987) (hereinafter RESTATEMENT 3D). And of course a state must exercise jurisdiction over its citizens consistently with international law, in particular, international human rights law, as noted earlier.

[6] For the United States, *see* International Shoe v. Washington, 326 U.S. 310 (1945), holding that a state court may constitutionally exercise personal jurisdiction over an absent defendant that has minimum contacts with the forum state.

[7] For the United States, *see* Home Ins. v. Dick, 281 U.S. 397, 50 S.Ct. 338 (1930), holding that it would be unconstitutional for a court to apply its law (the *lex fori*) in a case having little connection to the forum state.

law for exercising its jurisdiction to do such things as regulate conduct abroad and enforce compliance with its law outside its borders. The following section will examine the general bases of state jurisdiction under international law to regulate conduct and other matters at home and abroad.

§ 6.03   BASES OF STATE JURISDICTION

[A]   Introduction

This section examines the following bases of state jurisdiction: territoriality and the effects principle; nationality; the protective principle; universality; and other possible bases.[8] As we will see, more than one state may have jurisdiction in a given case, as when a national of one state conducts an activity in the territory of another. A state may exercise its jurisdiction in several different ways, each of which may purport to affect conduct or other matters not only at home but also abroad: through legislation or other action that purports to bind natural or legal persons (sometimes referred to as legislative jurisdiction); through action by its courts that asserts authority to adjudicate; and through action by its courts or executive to enforce compliance with its laws or regulations.[9] The Restatement describes these ways in which a state may assert its authority as jurisdiction to prescribe, jurisdiction to adjudicate and jurisdiction to enforce.[10] Each of these methods of asserting jurisdiction must have a valid basis in international law — which is another way of saying that it must not be prohibited by a rule of international law — as discussed in the following subsections.

[B]   Territoriality and the Effects Principle

As noted in § 6.02, a state has jurisdiction over its territory including the authority to regulate conduct and other matters within it. This authority is generally thought to carry with it the right to exercise jurisdiction with regard to effects within the territory caused by acts outside of it. These two situations will be taken up in turn.

[1]   Conduct and Other Matters Within a State's Territory

A state generally has jurisdiction over persons and things within its territory. Its authority there is at its strongest.[11] It is perhaps not surprising

---

[8] It should be noted that in the *Woodpulp Cases* the Report for the Hearing in the European Court of Justice took the position that "the only two legal bases of jurisdiction in international law are the principles of nationality and territoriality. . . ." 96 I.L.R. 148, 169. *See generally* IAN BROWNLIE, PRINCIPLES OF PUBLIC INTERNATIONAL LAW 301(6th ed.2003) (hereinafter BROWNLIE).

[9] *See* OPPENHEIM, *supra* note 1, at 456.

[10] RESTATEMENT 3D, *supra* note 5, §401.

[11] In his dissenting opinion in the *Lotus* case, Judge Moore stated as follows: "It is an admitted principle of international law that a nation possesses and exercises within its own

that most exercises of state jurisdiction are based on the principle of territoriality. Since states wish to have their own territorial jurisdiction recognized, they typically do not challenge exercises of jurisdiction by other states on this basis. Similar considerations of reciprocity have led states to recognize the jurisdictional immunity of other states and their property within their borders, to a large extent.[12] But this must be viewed as an exception to the principle of territoriality, or perhaps as an instance of consent to the immunity of the non-territorial state.[13]

However, as noted at the outset of this section it is possible that another state may have concurrent jurisdiction with the territorial state — e.g., where a national of State A was physically present in State B. In such cases the fact that the territorial state (State B) is capable in fact of enforcing its assertion of jurisdiction means that the jurisdiction of the territorial state would take primacy over the concurrent jurisdiction of another state (State A).[14] The Permanent Court of International Justice recognized this when it declared in the *Lotus* case that "the first and foremost restriction imposed by international law upon a State is that — failing the existence of a permissive rule to the contrary — it may not exercise its power in any form in the territory of another State."[15]

There are, however, two questions regarding the scope of the principle of territoriality. First, what is the physical extent of a state's territory? And second, when can a person or thing be regarded as being present in the territory of a state for jurisdictional purposes? As to the first question, it is obvious that a state's territory is coextensive with its land boundaries, whether these are actually on land or run through an international watercourse.[16] A state's territorial jurisdiction also extends to its territorial sea and the airspace above its territory.[17] As to the second question, international law generally requires that there be at least a reasonable relationship

---

territory an absolute and exclusive jurisdiction, and that any exception to this right must be traced to the consent of the nation, either express or implied *(Schooner Exchange v. McFaddon* (1812), 7 Cranch 116, 136). The benefit of this principle equally enures to all independent and sovereign States, and is attended with a corresponding responsibility for what takes place within the national territory." 1927 P.C.I.J. (ser. A) No. 10, at 65, 68.

[12] Foreign sovereign immunity is discussed in § 6.04, *infra*. Ambassadors, embassies and their staffs are also accorded immunity, under the 1961 Vienna Convention on Diplomatic Relations, art. 31, 23 U.S.T. 3227, T.I.A.S. No. 7502, 500 U.N.T.S. 95, *available at* http://www.un.org/law/ilc/texts/diplomat.htm.

[13] Indeed, the jurisdictional immunity of a foreign state does not mean that the law of a receiving state does not apply to a sending state's embassy and its staff, but simply that it cannot be enforced. On the question of the basis of immunity, if it is required by a rule of international law the consent of the territorial state would be superfluous.

[14] *See* OPPENHEIM, *supra* note 1, at 458. *See also* RESTATEMENT 3D, *supra* note 5, § 402 comment *b*.

[15] *S.S. Lotus*, (France v. Turkey) 1927 P.C.I.J. (ser. A) No. 10, at 18.

[16] On boundaries generally, *see* 2 OPPENHEIM, *supra* note 1, § 226.

[17] *See* Case Concerning Military and Paramilitary Activities In and Against Nicaragua (Nicaragua v. United States) (Merits), 1986 I.C.J. 14, ("sovereignty extends to internal waters and territorial sea of every state and to the airspace above its territory"); and OPPENHEIM, *supra* note 1, § 141, at 479.

between the person or thing and the state's territory before jurisdiction may be exercised. While this idea is expressed in the well-known "minimum contacts" test for personal jurisdiction laid down by the United States Supreme Court in *International Shoe Co. v. Washington*,[18] it applies more generally in international law.[19] Thus a state may have jurisdiction under international law to adjudicate or apply its law with respect to a natural or legal person not physically present in its territory but having an appropriate relationship with the state through, e.g., the ownership of property or doing of business there, so long as the particular assertion of jurisdiction is connected sufficiently closely with the thing or activity in question.

Even if a person is in a state's territory, questions may arise as to the state's jurisdiction to apply its law. To take the classic example, if a person fires a gun in State A, hitting another person in State B, does State A have jurisdiction under international law[20] to try the shooter for a criminal offense? Or must both the act and the harmful effect occur in State A in order for it to have jurisdiction based on the territoriality principle? It is obvious that the latter question must be answered in the negative, otherwise no state would have jurisdiction in a case involving this kind of transboundary crime (although the latter result did in fact obtain at one time in England[21]). Instead, state practice has extended the principle of territoriality to cover such cases, by applying it "subjectively" where the act occurs in the forum state and "objectively" where the injury occurs there.[22] Thus, according to the principle of subjective territoriality, State A would have jurisdiction under international law to try the shooter for the offense in question. Similarly, State B would have jurisdiction under the objective territoriality principle to apply its law to the shooter since the harmful effect occurred there. State B's jurisdiction in the latter case has also been explained in terms of the "constructive presence" of the shooter where the bullet takes effect.[23] Jurisdiction in the latter kind of case is often justified in terms of the "effects principle" but may also be

---

[18] 326 U.S. 310 (1945).

[19] *See* OPPENHEIM, *supra* note 1, at 457-58; and RESTATEMENT 3D, *supra* note 5, § 403 cmt. a.

[20] Whether State A would have jurisdiction under its own law is a separate question, which would be answered by the internal law of that state.

[21] As explained by Judge Moore in his dissenting opinion in the *Lotus* case, "In England it was once held that where a blow was struck in one county and death ensued in another county, the criminal could not be tried in either. This impotent result was due to the method of procedure, under which the grand jury could know only what took place in its own county; and in order to remedy the defect the *Statute of* 2 and *3 Edw. VI, c.* 24, A.D. 1549, was passed, to enable the criminal to be tried in either county." 1927 P.C.I.J. (ser. A) No. 10 at 65, 73.

[22] On subjective and objective territoriality *see* OPPENHEIM, *supra* note 1, at 459-460; and BROWNLIE, *supra* note 8, at 299-301.

[23] "[I]t appears to be now universally admitted that, where a crime is committed in the territorial jurisdiction of one State as the direct result of the act of a person at the time corporeally present in another State, international law, by reason of the principle of constructive presence of the offender at the place where his act took effect, does not forbid the prosecution of the offender by the former State, should he come within its territorial jurisdiction." 1927 P.C.I.J. (ser. A) No. 10 at 65, 73 (Moore, J., dissenting).

viewed as an aspect of territorial jurisdiction.[24] Jurisdiction based on effects within a state's territory is discussed in the following subsection.

[2]   Effects Within a State's Territory

According to the "effects principle," a state in which harmful effects have occurred has jurisdiction regarding activities outside the state that have resulted in those effects. Strictly speaking, this basis of state jurisdiction may be distinguished from that of objective territoriality, discussed in the preceding subsection. In the case of objective territoriality, the effect in the state is a constituent element of the tort or crime, whereas this is not strictly true of the effects principle.[25] This distinction is often not observed, however. Thus, it is common for all assertions of jurisdiction over activities abroad having harmful effects in a state to be referred to as being based on the effects principle. This may be due at least in part to the tendency to refer to elements of a tort or crime occurring in a state as "effects," as the PCIJ in fact did in the *Lotus* case.[26] It will be recalled that there, the PCIJ held that Turkey had not violated international law by prosecuting a French officer for an act committed on board the French vessel *Lotus* which had effects on the Turkish vessel *Boz-Kourt* while both vessels were on the high seas. The Court assimilated the ships to the territories of the respective states.

While assertions of jurisdiction based on the effects principle have generally been accepted in cases involving fact situations cognate to transboundary shooting (e.g., transboundary libel and product liability), such assertions have been controversial in the field of economic regulation, and especially where they have been made by United States courts with respect to business activities abroad by foreign nationals.[27] The theory in the latter class of cases is that U.S. courts have jurisdiction to apply American antitrust laws to foreign business activities on the basis of the economic effects of those activities in the United States, even though the activities are entirely consistent with the law of the state in which they are pursued.

The Restatement takes the position that a state has jurisdiction to regulate economic activities abroad under such circumstances, provided that the effect in the state is substantial and the exercise of jurisdiction is reasonable as determined through a factor analysis.[28] It thus attempts to minimize conflicts with the jurisdiction of other states.[29] But Oppenheim maintains that "[t]he justification for such assertions of jurisdiction on the

---

[24] *See* the discussion in the following subsection; and OPPENHEIM, *supra* note 1, at 460 n. 14.

[25] *See* OPPENHEIM, *supra* note 1, at 460 n. 14, 472-476.

[26] Among the many references to "effects," *see, e.g.,* 1927 P.C.I.J. (ser. A) No. 10, at 23.

[27] For a general discussion, *see* OPPENHEIM, *supra* note 1, at 472-478.

[28] RESTATEMENT 3D, *supra* note 5, § 402 cmt. d. Factors relevant to a determination of reasonableness in such cases are set out in § 403(2).

[29] *Id.* § 403 Reporters' Note 3.

basis of an alleged 'effects' principle of jurisdiction has not been generally accepted, and the matter is still one of controversy."[30] This on the ground that where the effects in the state are not constituent elements of a crime or tort, but "are mere consequences or repercussions of the act done, the legitimate bounds of the territorial principle of jurisdiction are over-stepped. . . ."[31]

The controversial nature of the effects principle has led some American courts to use a balancing test to determine whether it is proper for them to assert jurisdiction over activities abroad on that basis. Thus in *Timberlane Lumber Co. v. Bank of America*,[32] the Ninth Circuit Court of Appeals looked to see whether "the interests of, and links to, the U.S. — including the magnitude of the effects on American foreign commerce — are sufficiently strong, vis-à-vis those on other nations, to justify the assertion of extra-territorial authority."[33]

[C] Nationality

Along with territoriality, nationality is a venerable and well-recognized basis of jurisdiction under international law. In essence, the rationale for this jurisdictional basis is that an individual or legal person owes allegiance to the country of which he, she or it is a national. It is that country which issues a passport to a natural person and under whose laws a legal person is created. It is that country which is entitled under international law to represent the person's interests vis-à-vis other states and whose sovereignty gives it authority — albeit usually concurrent authority — over the person abroad.

In *Blackmer v. United States*,[34] the Supreme Court upheld the authority of the United States to require a U.S. national living in Paris to appear as a witness in a criminal trial in Washington, D.C. Writing for the Court, Chief Justice Hughes observed that though Blackmer had been living

---

[30] OPPENHEIM, *supra* note 1, at 474-475 (citing numerous writings in n. 43).

[31] *Id.* at 475.

[32] 549 F.2d 597 (9th Cir. 1976) (Honduran plaintiff alleged that American and Honduran defendants conspired to prevent it from milling lumber in Honduras and exporting to United States, thus directly and substantially affecting foreign commerce of the United States. *Held*, the Sherman Act is not limited to trade restraints which have both a direct and substantial effect on foreign commerce.). *See also* Mannington Mills, Inc. v. Congoleum Corp., 595 F. 2d 1287 (3d Cir. 1979) (American manufacturer brought an antitrust action against another American manufacturer alleging that foreign patents were secured by fraud. *Held*, acts and agreements occurring outside the territorial boundaries of the United States which adversely and materially affect American trade are not necessarily immune from U.S. antitrust laws). In United States v. Aluminum Co. of America, 148 F.2d 416 (2d Cir. 1945), Judge Learned Hand acknowledged that "we are not to read general words, such as those in [the Sherman] Act, without regard to the limitations customarily observed by nations upon the exercise of their powers. . . . We should not impute to Congress an intent to punish all whom its courts can catch, for conduct which has no consequences within the United States." *Id.* at 443.

[33] 549 F.2d at 613.

[34] 284 U.S. 421, 52 S.Ct. 252 (1932).

abroad for a number of years, "[h]e continued to owe allegiance to the United States. By virtue of the obligations of citizenship, the United States retained its authority over him, and he was bound by its laws made applicable to him in a foreign country. . . . [T]he United States possesses the power inherent in sovereignty to require the return to this country of a citizen, resident elsewhere, whenever the public interest requires it, and to penalize him in case of refusal."[35]

The country of a person's nationality therefore has jurisdiction to regulate that person's conduct, not only at home (where the person would also be subject to jurisdiction on the basis of the territoriality principle) but also abroad.[36] But when an individual is abroad, other states would clearly have jurisdiction as well, based on the individual's presence in their territory.[37] Jurisdiction in these cases would therefore be concurrent, with that of the territorial state often prevailing in the event of a conflict on the basis of that state's greater interest and ability to make effective the exercise of its jurisdiction.[38] In some instances, however, such as where the states of an individual's nationality and residence both apply their tax laws to him or her, there is no incompatibility, per se, between the two exercises of jurisdiction, and it is for the states involved to relieve the resulting hardship on the individual through treaties.[39]

There are other situations in which concurrent jurisdiction may exist,[40] as well, such as those involving ships and aircraft. These can get complicated, as for example when a national of State A is on board a vessel flagged by State B which is in the territorial waters of State C. Other variations of this hypothetical case can easily be imagined, as where the vessel is on the high seas, beyond the territorial jurisdiction of any state. Even in that case, the jurisdiction of the flag state and that of the individual's nationality would overlap.

For many purposes vessels are "assimilated" to the territory of the flag state.[41] The PCIJ treated the Turkish vessel in the *Lotus* case[42] in this way for the purpose of applying the principle of objective territoriality.

---

[35] 284 U.S. at 437, 52 S.Ct. at 255.

[36] For a list of laws that the United States applies to its nationals abroad, see RESTATEMENT 3d, *supra* note 5, § 402 Reporters' Note 1.

[37] Individuals in areas not subject to any state's jurisdiction, such as Antarctica, would of course remain subject to the jurisdiction of the state of their nationality.

[38] *See generally* OPPENHEIM, *supra* note 1, at 463.

[39] There are many treaties for the avoidance of double taxation. *See, e.g.*, Convention between the Government of the United States of America and the Government of the United Kingdom for the Avoidance of Double Taxation and the Prevention of Fiscal Evasion with respect to Taxes on Income and on Capital Gains, 24 July 2001, 21 TNT 143-18, 4 Tax Treaties (CCH) p. 10,900 at 44,505-11.

[40] Regarding conflicting exercises of jurisdiction, *see* RESTATEMENT 3d, *supra* note 5, §403 comment *e*.

[41] Care should be taken before treating a vessel as a piece of floating territory of a state, however. Clearly this is not the case for all purposes, and relying on such an assumption may lead to perverse results.

[42] *See, e.g.*, 1927 P.C.I.J. (ser. A) No. 10, at 23.

Assimilation of a vessel to the territory of the flag state would give that state a strong claim of authority in the event that assertions of jurisdiction by other states — such as the state of an individual passenger's or crew member's nationality — with respect to matters on board the ship came into conflict with the jurisdiction of the flag state.[43]

Finally, concurrent jurisdiction may also exist in cases of dual nationality. In this and other cases of overlapping jurisdiction, if the states involved wish to exercise jurisdiction in ways that conflict, "each state is required to evaluate both its interests in exercising jurisdiction and those of the other state,"[44] with the state whose interest is less strong deferring to the other state.[45]

Before leaving nationality as a basis of state jurisdiction it should be noted that states are increasingly exercising jurisdiction on the basis of other forms of settled connections that individuals have with them, namely, domicile and residence. This is the case in particular with regard to the application to non-nationals (aliens) of a state's law concerning such matters as status, including marriage and divorce, other family law matters, and the distribution of movables on death,[46] but may also be relied upon as to certain criminal matters having a direct and substantial connection with the state.[47]

[D] The Protective Principle

Also known as the "security principle," this basis of jurisdiction allows a state to assert jurisdiction over aliens abroad regarding conduct that threatens or otherwise affects the safety or security of the state, as well as certain other matters.[48] Although it is thus an exception to the principle of territoriality, and applies to offenses committed by non-nationals, it is generally accepted and widely applied. The principle applies not only to threats to physical security, through terrorist and other political acts, but also to other conduct that impairs governmental functions, such as counterfeiting of currency, drug trafficking, and conspiracy (e.g., on the high seas[49]) to commit immigration violations.[50]

---

[43] The 1982 United Nations Convention on the Law of the Sea, 10 December 1982, 1833 U.N.T.S. 3, 401, reprinted in 21 I.L.M. 1245, contains provisions regulating some of these questions but by no means all of them. *See, e.g.*, arts. 27, Criminal jurisdiction on board a foreign ship, and art. 28, Civil jurisdiction in relation to foreign ships, dealing with the jurisdiction of coastal states over vessels in their territorial seas or contiguous zones.

[44] RESTATEMENT 3d, *supra* note 5, § 403 cmt. e.

[45] Of course, the difficult case is that in which neither state's interest is clearly stronger. The Restatement provides little guidance in such cases, contenting itself with the observation that "states often attempt to eliminate the conflict so as to reduce international friction and avoid putting those who are the object of the regulations in a difficult situation."*Id.*

[46] *See generally* RESTATEMENT 3d, *supra* note 5, § 402 cmt. e.

[47] *See, e.g.*, OPPENHEIM, *supra* note 1, at 469 (referring to exchange control offenses that may be committed outside the U.K. by persons resident there), and sources there cited.

[48] *See generally id.*, at 470-471; BROWNLIE, *supra* note 8, at 302-303; and RESTATEMENT 3d, *supra* note 5, § 402(3) and cmt. f.

[49] *See* BROWNLIE, *supra* note 8, at 302, and precedents there cited.

[50] The Restatement gives other examples, including espionage and falsification of official documents. *See* RESTATEMENT 3d, *supra* note 5, § 402 cmt. f.

While a jurisdictional principle allowing a state to take measures to protect itself is clearly necessary and generally accepted, the elasticity of the concepts of "security" and "protection" may give rise to difficulties in the principle's application. The United States, in particular, has used economic measures that cannot be justified on the basis of the principles of territoriality or nationality to further its foreign policies, not merely to protect its security interests. For example, when the United States applied antiboycott measures under the Export Administration Act[51] to foreign subsidiaries of U.S. companies with a view to countering the Arab trade boycott of Israel, the United Kingdom protested in a series of diplomatic notes that this did not constitute a proper exercise of jurisdiction.[52]

Perhaps even more controversial were the sanctions imposed in 1982 by the United States on the Soviet Union in response to the latter's supporting the imposition of martial law in Poland, including repressive measures against the Solidarity movement. The 1982 measures were controversial principally because they affected U.S. allies in Western Europe in ways that the European countries claimed exceeded U.S. jurisdiction and impermissibly interfered with their territorial jurisdiction. The measures announced by President Reagan on June 18, 1982,[53] expanded sanctions that he had imposed in 1981[54] consisting of U.S. export controls on oil and gas technology to be used in the construction of the 12,000-mile Yamal gas pipeline from Western Siberia to Western Europe. In 1982 President Reagan extended those measures to foreign subsidiaries and foreign licensees of U.S. companies.[55] Moreover, the 1981 controls were extended to "foreign products of oil and gas technology exported from the United States prior to the December 1981 controls, if the technology was the subject of a licensing or royalty agreement with a U.S. person."[56]

---

[51] Export Administration Act of 1979, section 8, Pub. L. 96-72, 29 Sept. 1979, 93 Stat. 503, 521, 50 U.S.C.A. 2407.

[52] *See* 2 U.S. DEPARTMENT OF STATE, CUMULATIVE DIGEST OF UNITED STATES PRACTICE IN INTERNATIONAL LAW 1981-88, 2630-2637 (1994) (hereinafter CUMULATIVE DIGEST). The U.K. government stated in the context of debates in Parliament that the measures were "quite unjustified and contrary to international law." Parliamentary Debates (Commons), Hansard vol. 37, col. 548 (Written Answers, 25 Feb. 1983), as quoted in OPPENHEIM, *supra* note 1, at 471.

[53] *See* 21 I.L.M. 855, 864, 1098, 1115 (1982).

[54] For a description of the 1981 measures, *see* 3 CUMULATIVE DIGEST, *supra* note 52, at 2968-73.

[55] 47 Fed. Reg. 27250 (June 24, 1982), 15 C.F.R. 376.12, 379.8 and 385.2. For the president's announcement, *see* WEEKLY COMP. PRES. DOC., No. 24, 21 June 1982, at 820; Doc. 160, *Extension of Export Sanctions Against the Soviet Union*, AM . FOR. POL'Y: CURR. DOCS., 1982, 436 (1985). *See generally* CUMULATIVE DIGEST, *supra* note 52, at 2501-07.

[56] Remarks by Sherman E. Unger, General Counsel, Department of Commerce, at a panel on "Extraterritorial Application of U.S. Export Controls — Siberian Pipeline," 15 Apr. 1983, AMERICAN SOCIETY OF INTERNATIONAL LAW, PROCEEDINGS OF THE 77ᵀᴴ ANNUAL MEETING (APR. 14-16, 1983), 250, 251, excerpted in CUMULATIVE DIGEST, *supra* note 52, at 2503-05 (hereinafter Unger).

These aggressive sanctions drew the ire of European countries[57] and American companies alike. The U.S. sanctions were avowedly "taken as a foreign policy measure to apply pressure on the Soviet Union to permit relaxation of the repressive internal measures in effect in Poland."[58] They were thus not directed at protecting American security or the other interests traditionally covered by the protective principle. The predicament of affected U.S. companies is illustrated by the situation of Dresser-France, a French subsidiary of the American company Dresser Industries, Inc., which was subject simultaneously to the U.S. sanctions, prohibiting it from complying with a contract to supply compressors to the Soviet Union for the pipeline, and a French order compelling it to fulfill the contract.[59] The controversy was ultimately resolved when President Reagan lifted the sanctions on November 13, 1982.[60]

[E] The Universality Principle

Certain crimes are so heinous and threatening to international order that every state has an interest in punishing them. Jurisdiction regarding such crimes, and the individuals perpetrating them, is said to be universal, in the sense that any state having custody of the alleged offender has authority under customary international law to try and punish that person, whether or not the state was directly affected by the offense. The archetypal object of universal jurisdiction was the pirate, *hostis humani generis*, or enemy of all humankind. The same appellation has been applied more recently to the torturer[61] and the considerations supporting universal jurisdiction would also seem to apply to those committing or abetting at least serious terrorist acts,[62] such as the destruction of the Twin Towers of the World Trade Center in New York on September 11, 2001.[63] Other candidates for universal jurisdiction[64] include the slave trade, genocide,

---

[57] The diplomatic representations of the European Community in response to the measures are reprinted in 21 I.L.M. 891-904 (1982).

[58] Unger, *supra* note 56, at 251.

[59] *See* Dresser Industries, Inc. v. Baldridge, 549 F.Supp. 108 (D.D.C. 1982) (denial of injunctive relief against the imposition of sanctions on Dresser-France for violating regulations prohibiting the export of certain goods to the Soviet Union).

[60] For the text of the president's statement, *see* CUMULATIVE DIGEST, *supra* note 52, at 2506; 83 DEPT. OF ST. BULL. No. 2072 p. 28, Jan. 1983.

[61] *See* Filartiga v. Pena-Irala, 630 F.2d 876, 890 (2d Cir. 1980).

[62] It cannot presently be concluded that all acts of "terrorism" engender universal jurisdiction; the lack of a generally accepted definition of that term has impeded progress in regulating the crime, as discussed in Chapter 5. *See generally* OPPENHEIM, *supra* note 1, at 470 n. 22, and *id.* at 400 n. 42, and authorities there cited. A small number of American states, including the United States, are parties to the Convention to Prevent and Punish the Acts of Terrorism Taking the Form of Crimes against Persons and Related Extortion that are of International Significance, 27 U.S.T. 3949, T.I.A.S. No. 8413 (1976). And on April 13, 2005, the U.N. General Assembly adopted a treaty against nuclear terrorism. International Convention on the Suppression of Acts of Nuclear Terrorism, U.N. Doc. A/RES/59/290, 13 Apr. 2005.

[63] *See generally* NATIONAL COMMISSION ON TERRORIST ATTACKS UPON THE UNITED STATES, THE 9/11 COMMISSION REPORT (2004).

[64] *See, e.g.*, the lists in RESTATEMENT 3D, *supra* note 5, § 404; and OPPENHEIM, *supra* note 1, at 470. While most of the offenses listed here are identified in one or both of these sources,

crimes against humanity, war crimes, the hijacking and sabotage of aircraft, grave breaches of the 1949 Geneva Conventions on the law of war,[65] and *apartheid*.[66] It should be emphasized that where universal jurisdiction applies, it does so even where there is no other basis of jurisdiction.

The use by states of the universality principle and analogous bases of jurisdiction seems to be on the rise. A number of cases have been brought against foreign officials during the past decade on the basis of universal jurisdiction or similar grounds available under national law. Spain and Belgium have been particularly active, but France, Germany and the United States have also been involved in such matters. Thus, for example, a Spanish investigating judge issued an arrest warrant against General Augusto Pinochet, the former head of state of Chile,[67] as well as Argentine military officers, in connection with serious international crimes allegedly committed during the "dirty war" years in Chile and Argentina;[68] four Catholic nuns (the "Butare four") were tried, convicted and sentenced to long prison terms in Belgium for their complicity in the 1994 genocide in Rwanda under the Act Concerning the Punishment of Grave Breaches of International Humanitarian Law;[69] on the basis of the same Belgian law cases have been brought against former U.S. President George H.W. Bush, U.S. General Tommy Franks, who led the 2003 invasion of Iraq, and Israeli

---

there is no official, definitive list. Brownlie includes even "common crimes, such as murder, where the state in which the offence has occurred has refused extradition and is unwilling to try the case itself. . . ." BROWNLIE, *supra* note 8, at 303.

[65] 75 U.N.T.S. 31, 85, 135, 287.

[66] *See* the Convention on the Suppression and Punishment of the Crime of *Apartheid*, arts. III and IV, G.A. Res. 3068 (XXVIII) (1973).

[67] *See* Frederic L. Kirgis, *The Pinochet Arrest and Possible Extradition to Spain*, ASIL INSIGHT, October 1998, *available at* http://www.asil.org/insights/insigh27.htm. Pinochet was also the subject of a U.S. grand jury investigation into his role in the assassination of Orlando Letelier in Washington, D.C. in 1976. *See* Frederic L. Kirgis, *Possible Indictment of Pinochet in the United States*, ASIL INSIGHT, March 2000, *available at* http://www.asil.org/insights/insigh42.htm. Pinochet was ultimately indicted in Chile, where the Chilean Supreme Court had lifted his immunity from prosecution. *See* Frederic L. Kirgis, *Pinochet Arrest in Chile*, ASIL INSIGHT, December 2000, *available at* http://www.asil.org/insights/insigh58.htm.

[68] *See* Richard J. Wilson, *Argentine Military Officers Face Trial in Spanish Courts*, ASIL INSIGHT, December 2003, *available at* http://www.asil.org/insights/insigh122.htm.

[69] *See id.* for discussion. An unofficial translation of the Belgian law of 1993, as amended in 1999, may be found in 38 I.L.M. 918 (1999). *See also* 42 I.L.M. 1258 for an unofficial translation by the editor of the amendment to law of 7/15/93, containing detailed provisions on grave breaches. The law permitted the prosecution of individuals, *in absentia*, for genocide, war crimes and crimes against humanity on the basis of universal jurisdiction, regardless of whether the case had any connection with Belgium and whether the accused would ordinarily be entitled to immunity. (It has since been amended to soften its impact; *see* note 71, *infra*.) As of July, 2003, only one judgment had been rendered on the basis of the Belgian law but over forty claims had been filed. Stefaan Smis & Kim Van der Borght, *Belgian Law concerning The Punishment of Grave Breaches of International Humanitarian Law: A Contested Law with Uncontested Objectives*, ASIL INSIGHT, July 2003, *available at* http://www.asil.org/insights/insigh112.htm. On the law, *see* Stefan Smis & Kim Van der Borght, *Introductory Note on the Act Concerning the Punishment of Grave Breaches of International Humanitarian Law (10 February 1999)*, 38 I.L.M. 918 (1999).

Prime Minister Ariel Sharon,[70] and an arrest warrant was issued for the incumbent foreign minister of the Democratic Republic of Congo;[71] French judicial authorities have taken investigation and prosecution measures regarding a complaint for crimes against humanity and torture filed by various associations against officials of the Republic of Congo, including the president and minister of the interior;[72] and a criminal complaint was filed in Germany against U.S. Secretary of Defense Donald Rumsfeld and nine other governmental officials and military officers by a non-governmental organization and four Iraqi citizens who were allegedly detained and severely mistreated by U.S. forces in Iraq.[73]

---

[70] *See, e.g.,* BBC News, *Belgium Restricts 'Genocide Law,'* available at http://news.bbc.co.uk/1/hi/world/europe/2921519.stm. The case related to the 1982 massacres at the Sabra and Shatila Palestinian refugee camps in Lebanon.

[71] The issuance of the arrest warrant prompted the D.R. Congo to sue Belgium in the International Court of Justice, which ruled that Belgium's circulation of the arrest warrant failed to respect the immunity from criminal jurisdiction and the inviolability enjoyed by the incumbent minister for foreign affairs of Congo under international law. Case concerning the Arrest Warrant of 11 April 2000 (Democratic Republic of the Congo v. Belgium), 2002 I.C.J. 3, 41 I.L.M. 536 (2002) (Judgment of 14 Feb. 2002). Belgium has since moderated its universal jurisdiction law, at least in part in response to complaints from other states, to provide jurisdiction only where the violation is committed against Belgian nationals or habitual residents. The amendments also exclude prosecution regarding heads of state, heads of government, ministers of foreign affairs, and others with immunity under international law, presumably in response to the ICJ's decision in the *Arrest Warrant* case noted above. The amendments have retroactive effect. *See* Belgium's Amendment to the Law of June 15, 1993 (as Amended by the Law of February 10, 1999 and April 23, 2003) concerning the Punishment of Grave Breaches of Humanitarian Law, August 7, 2003, (unofficial English translation), 42 I.L.M. 1258 (2003); and BBC News, *Belgium Restricts 'Genocide Law,'* available at http://news.bbc.co.uk/1/hi/world/europe/2921519.stm. In September 2005, Belgium indicted Hissène Habré, the former president of Chad, charging him with large-scale violations of human rights. Belgium also filed a request for Habré's extradition from Senegal. *See* Marlise Simons, *Belgium Indicts Chad's Ex-Leader,* N.Y. Times, 30 Sept. 2005, at A 10.

In a related development, on 29 June 2005 a Belgian court sentenced two Rwandans to imprisonment for providing material assistance to the Hutu militia during the 1994 genocide. The defendants were tried under the 1993 Belgian law. A brief report is *available at* ASIL, International Law In Brief, http://www.asil.org/ilib/2005/07/ilib050719.htm#b1.

[72] As in the case of the D.R. Congo in relation to the Belgian arrest warrant, this case prompted the Republic of Congo (a different state) to sue France in the ICJ. Certain Criminal Proceedings in France (Republic of Congo v. France). For information on the case, *see* the ICJ's website, http://www.icj-cij.org/icjwww/idocket/icof/icofframe.htm.

[73] *See* Jan Arno Hessbruegge, *An Attempt to Have Secretary Rumsfeld and Others Indicted for War Crimes under the German Völkerstrafgesetzbuch,* ASIL Insight, December 2004, *available at* http://www.asil.org/insights/2004/12/insight041213.htm, calling the case "the first practical test for the universal jurisdiction clause contained in the *Völkerstrafgesetzbuch,* a criminal statute enacted in June, 2002." In anticipation of a planned visit to Germany by Secretary Rumsfeld the German Federal Prosecutor announced that he did not intend to indict him. *See* Eric Schmitt, *The Reach of War: Training, NATO and U.S. Plan Aid to Strengthen Iraqi Force,* N.Y. Times, 11 Feb. 2005, at A11; Elaine Sciolino, *"New" Rumsfeld is Seeking Stronger Ties With Europe,* N.Y. Times, 13 Feb. 2005, at A17.

Civil suits have also been attempted in the United States against present or former heads of state. In September and October, 2004, U.S. Federal Courts of Appeal for the Second and Seventh Circuits ruled respectively that Robert Mugabe, President of Zimbabwe, and Jiang Zemin, the former President of the People's Republic of China, enjoyed absolute immunity

Few of these complaints have actually come to trial, however, let alone resulted in punishment of the alleged offenders.[74] Moreover, some of the complaints gave rise to serious diplomatic friction between the states involved.[75] Another difficulty in cases based on universal jurisdiction is that by their very nature they involve offenses of such seriousness that they will often be brought against high-ranking state officials[76] — yet those officials normally enjoy immunity. This was the case with respect to Belgium's attempt to prosecute the foreign minister of the Democratic Republic of the Congo (DRC).

A Belgian investigating magistrate issued an "international arrest warrant in absentia" against the incumbent Foreign Minister of the Congo alleging grave breaches of the Geneva Conventions of 1949 and the Additional Protocols thereto, and crimes against humanity. The DRC sued Belgium before the International Court of Justice, challenging the Belgian law on the ground that by allowing prosecution of international crimes committed outside the state's territory it exceeded the permissible scope of national jurisdiction.[77] The DRC also argued that the arrest warrant issued by the Belgian court violated, *inter alia*, the "principle that a State may not exercise its authority on the territory of another State. . . ."[78] The DRC claim challenging the lawfulness of the Belgian law's provisions on universal jurisdiction was later withdrawn, leaving only the question of immunity.

The Court held, by a vote of 13 to three, that the issuance of the arrest warrant and its international circulation violated Belgium's obligations toward the DRC because these acts failed to respect the immunity from criminal jurisdiction and the inviolability enjoyed by the incumbent foreign minister of the DRC.[79] The Court noted that it had examined state practice carefully but had failed to find evidence of an exception under customary international law to the rule according immunity from criminal jurisdiction and inviolability to incumbent foreign ministers who are charged with responsibility for war crimes or crimes against humanity.

---

from U.S. jurisdiction. Tachiona v. United States, 386 F.3d 205, (2d Cir. 2004); Wei Ye v. Jiang Zemin, 383 F.3d 620, (7th Cir. 2004). *See generally* Sara Andrews, *Courts Rule on Absolute Immunity and Inviolability of Foreign Heads of State: The Cases against Robert Mugabe and Jiang Zemin,* ASIL INSIGHT, Nov. 2004, *available at* http://www.asil.org/insights/2004/11/insight041122.html.

[74] As of this writing the only case that has gone to trial and resulted in the imposition of punishment is that involving the four nuns prosecuted in Belgium for complicity in the Rwandan genocide. *See* note 69, *supra,* and accompanying text.

[75] This was true for example of the Belgian law and the use of the German law to charge Donald Rumsfeld and others.

[76] The most obvious exception is large-scale terrorist attacks, such as that on 9/11, but soldiers are obviously capable of committing war crimes that could qualify, as well.

[77] Case concerning the Arrest Warrant of 11 April 2000 (Democratic Republic of the Congo v. Belgium), judgment of 14 February 2002, available on the ICJ's website, http://www.icj-cij.org/icjwww/idocket/iCOBE/icobejudgment/icobe_ijudgment_20020214.PDF.

[78] Arrest Warrant of 11 April 2000, *Summary of the Judgment of 14 February 2002,* available on the ICJ's website, http://www.icj-cij.org.

[79] Para. 2 of the *dispositif,* set forth in *id.* at p. 12.

While the DRC revised its claim to eliminate the argument that Belgium's universal jurisdiction law was invalid, that very question is presented to the Court by the Republic of Congo's suit against France.[80] That case stemmed from investigations and prosecution measures taken by French judicial authorities regarding a complaint filed by various human rights organizations alleging that the president, the minister of the interior and other officials of the Republic of Congo (Congo-Brazzaville, as distinguished from the DRC) had committed crimes against humanity and torture in Congo-Brazzaville against nationals of that country.[81] In its application (equivalent to a complaint), the Republic of Congo contended that by "attributing to itself universal jurisdiction in criminal matters," France had violated "the principle that a State may not, in breach of the principle of sovereign equality among all Members of the United Nations . . . exercise its authority on the territory of another state."[82] The application thus raises the issue of the lawfulness of the assertion of universal jurisdiction by a state with regard to acts allegedly committed by foreigners abroad against non-nationals of the forum state. As of this writing the Court has not ruled in this case.

[F]   Other Possible Bases

Bases of state jurisdiction other than the ones already discussed are not as well recognized. The "passive personality principle" is perhaps the best known of these.[83] This principle would allow a state to exercise jurisdiction to punish aliens for acts committed abroad that harm its nationals. In a number of cases where it could have been invoked states have not had to because the cases were covered by other principles, chiefly those of protection and universality. While the passive personality principle has been invoked in several well-known cases, including the *Eichmann* case,[84] it

---

[80] Certain Criminal Proceedings in France (Republic of Congo v. France). For information on the case, *see* the ICJ's website, http://www.icj-cij.org/icjwww/idocket/icof/icofframe.htm. *See generally* Pieter H.F. Bekker, *Prorogated and Universal Jurisdiction in the International Court:* The Congo v. France, ASIL INSIGHT, April 2003, *available at* http://www.asil.org/insights/insigh103.htm.

[81] *See* the description of the history of the case in the Court's Press Release 2003/21, available at http://www.icj-cij.org/icjwww/ipresscom/ipress2003/ipresscom2003-21_cof_20030714.htm.

[82] *Id.* at 1. Doubtless inspired at least in part by the Court's ruling in the DRC's suit against Belgium (on which *see* note 77, *supra*), the Republic of Congo also argued that by issuing a warrant instructing police officers to examine its president as a witness in the case, France had violated "the criminal immunity of a foreign Head of State. . . ." *Id.* at 2.

[83] *See generally* BROWNLIE, *supra* note 8, at 302; OPPENHEIM, *supra* note 1, at 471 (stating that "[i]t is sometimes claimed" that a state has jurisdiction under these circumstances); and RESTATEMENT 3D, *supra* note 5, § 402 cmt. g.

[84] Attorney-General of the Government of Israel v. Eichmann, 36 I.LR. 5 (1961). Eichmann had been the Head of the Jewish Office of the German Gestapo and in charge of Nazis' "the final solution." He was abducted from Argentina and brought to Israel, where he was tried for war crimes, crimes against the Jewish people and crimes against humanity, convicted, sentenced to death and executed. Unlike the usual case in which the passive personality principle is invoked, the State of Israel did not exist when the acts in question occurred.

has not been accepted widely except as to certain offenses such as war crimes and the hijacking of aircraft. Recently, however, it has gained some support in cases involving terrorist acts against a state's nationals and assassinations of its officials.[85]

§ 6.04   IMMUNITY FROM JURISDICTION

[A]   Introduction

We have already seen that certain high state officials enjoy immunity from the jurisdiction of other states, and indeed inviolability, including immunity from arrest, other forms of coercion such as subpoenas, and the like.[86] The same is generally true of diplomats[87] and, to a lesser extent, consular officials.[88] However, we have not yet considered the extent to which the *state* itself may be brought before the courts of another state. That question is the principal subject of this section.[89]

[B]   Historical Development

Questions of the immunity of states from the judicial jurisdiction of other states did not arise often before the 20th century, perhaps for a combination of two reasons: first, the immunity of states and their property from the jurisdiction of the courts of other states was widely treated as being absolute; and second, states themselves engaged in only limited trade and other activities that would bring them into contact with private parties. There were exceptions, however.[90] As early as 1873, when *The Charkieh*, a vessel owned by the Khedive of Egypt but used as an ordinary merchant

---

[85] *See* RESTATEMENT 3D, *supra* note 5, § 402 cmt. g and Reporters' Note 3.

[86] *See* especially Case concerning the Arrest Warrant of 11 April 2000 (Democratic Republic of the Congo v. Belgium), 2002 I.C.J. 3, 41 I.L.M. 536 (2002) (Judgment of 14 Feb. 2002).

[87] Ambassadors and other diplomats, as well as their families, enjoy immunity under customary international law, as largely reflected in the 1961 Vienna Convention on Diplomatic Relations, 18 April 1961, 500 U.N.T.S. 95, 23 U.S.T. 3227, T.I.A.S. No. 7502.

[88] Consular immunity is governed by the 1963 Vienna Convention on Consular Relations, 24 April 1963, 596 U.N.T.S. 261, 21 U.S.T. 77, T.I.A.S. No. 6820.

[89] *See generally* the reports of the special rapporteur of the U.N. International Law Commission, Sompong Sucharitkul, on Jurisdictional Immunities of States and their Property, [1979] 2 Y.B. Int'l L. Comm'n 227, pt. 1; 1980 *id.*, at 199, 1981 *id.*, at 125, 1982 *id.* at 199, 1983 *id.* at 25, 1984 *id.* at. 5, 1985 *id.* at 21, and 1986 *id.* at 21; the draft articles with commentaries on Jurisdictional Immunities of States and their Property adopted by the International Law Commission in 1986, [1986] 2 Y.B. Int'l L. Comm'n 8, pt. 2,; the 2004 U.N. Convention on Jurisdictional Immunities of States and their Property, U.N. Doc. A/RES/59/38 (2 Dec. 2004); OPPENHEIM, *supra* note 1, §§ 109-110; BROWNLIE, *supra* note 8, ch. 16, at 319; RESTATEMENT 3D, *supra* note 5, ch. 5, §§ 451-460; International Law Association, The ILA Montreal Draft Convention on State Immunity, Montreal, 4 Sept. 1982; and CHRISTOPH H. SCHREUER, STATE IMMUNITY: SOME RECENT DEVELOPMENTS (1988).

[90] In addition to the following British case, *see* the late nineteenth century decisions of the Italian and Belgian courts discussed in Claim Against the Empire of Iran, German Constitutional Court, decision of 30 April 1963, translated in 45 ILR 57 (1972).

trading vessel, became involved in a collision on the Thames River in England, Sir Robert Phillimore had the following to say in the ensuing case:

> "No principle of international law, and no decided case, and no dictum of jurists of which I am aware, has gone so far as to authorize a sovereign prince to assume the character of a trader, when it is for his benefit; and when he incurs an obligation to a private subject to throw off, so to speak, his disguise, and appear as a sovereign, claiming for his own benefit, and to the injury of a private person, for the first time, all the attributes of his character. . . . Assuming the privilege to exist, it has been waived with reference to this ship by the conduct of the person who has claimed it."[91]

The notion that when the state deals with individuals it cannot claim immunity underlies the modern "restrictive" approach to foreign sovereign immunity discussed below.

But lack of immunity from judicial jurisdiction was and remains the exception. It follows from the basic principle of the sovereign equality of states, which is enshrined in Article 2(1) of the United Nations Charter, that one state generally cannot subject another to its jurisdiction — a principle expressed in the maxim *par in parem jurisdictionem non habet*[92] and by Chief Justice Marshall in *The Schooner Exchange v. M'Faddon* when he referred to the "perfect equality and absolute independence of sovereigns. . . ."[93]

The difficulty with this principle is precisely that described so graphically by Sir Robert Phillimore: it makes sense when only states are involved, but when a state deals with a private person it does not seem fair to allow the state to shield itself behind a cloak of immunity. As the Austrian Supreme Court put it in a case involving an accident caused by a U.S. embassy driver while picking up mail, "[t]o deny the liability of a foreign State arising from the operation and management of motor vehicles would lead to intolerable results and hardships for private citizens."[94] Granting immunity in such cases would mean that the foreign state could sue the citizen, but the citizen could not sue the foreign state.

---

[91] *The Charkieh*, (1873) L.R. 4 A. & E. 59. *See also Parlement Belge*, (1879) L.R., Probate Division, vol. IV, p. 129, in which Sir Robert Phillimore found that this vessel was not entitled to immunity. This decision was reversed by the Court of Appeal, (1880) L.R., vol. IV, p. 197. The rationale for lifting immunity is also captured nicely in the following metaphor: "So if a sovereign descend from the throne and become a merchant, he submits to the law of the country. If he contract private debts, his private funds are liable. So if he charter a vessel, the cargo is liable for the freight." The Schooner Exchange v. McFaddon, 7 Cranch 116, 123 (1812). *See also* Sompong Sucharitkul, Fourth Report on Jurisdictional Immunities of States and their Property, [1982] 2 Y.B. Int'l L. Comm'n 199, 213 n. 64, pt. 1 ("When a sovereign 'descended into the market place, he should be treated on a par with a private trader'").

[92] This is a specific application of the more general maxim, *par in parem, imperium non habet*.

[93] 11 U.S. (7 Cranch) 116, 137, 3 L.Ed. 287, 294 (1812).

[94] Collision with a Foreign Government-Owned Motor Car, Supreme Court of Austria, 10 Feb. 1961, 40 I.L.R. 73 (1970).

These considerations began to take on special force in the first half of the 20th century with the emergence of the Soviet Union and its socialist allies in Central and Eastern Europe. By definition, since they were socialist countries, all business between them and persons in other countries was done by the state, often through state agencies or instrumentalities. If the state could not be sued in such transactions the situation would be intolerably asymmetrical, as the Austrian Supreme Court observed. In the field of shipping — in which many states have long operated publicly owned merchant vessels, as *The Charkieh* illustrates — the problem was addressed in the 1926 Brussels Convention on the Immunity of State-Owned Vessels.[95] This treaty confined immunity to public ships "used at the time a cause of action arises exclusively on Governmental and non-commercial service. . . ."[96] A number of important trading nations became parties to this agreement, and while the United States did not, it has long followed a policy of not claiming immunity for its publicly-owned merchant vessels.[97] While the Soviet Union did not recognize exceptions to jurisdictional immunities except in treaties, of which there were a significant number,[98] state trading organizations of the Soviet Union and eastern bloc countries developed the practice of routinely including arbitration clauses in contracts with private companies.[99]

Meanwhile, support continued to increase, especially among western industrialized countries, for a *restrictive* — as opposed to the classical *absolute* — approach to state jurisdictional immunity. As already indicated, this approach would restrict foreign sovereign immunity to those cases in which the state acts in its public, sovereign capacity (acts *jure imperii*), as opposed to those in which it acts in the private sphere, in ways in which a private person could act (acts *jure gestionis*). This so-called "restrictive theory" of sovereign immunity was expressly adopted by the United States in 1952, as announced in the "Tate Letter" from the Acting Legal Adviser of the State Department, Jack B. Tate, to the Acting Attorney General,[100] which was circulated to embassies in Washington. In that letter, Tate wrote:

---

[95] International Convention for the Unification of Certain Rules relating to the Immunity of State-owned Vessels, 10 Apr. 1926, 176 L.N.T.S. 200.

[96] *Id.* art. 3, §1.

[97] *See* the "Tate Letter," 26 Dept. State Bull. 984 (1952), 6 MARJORIE M. WHITEMAN, DIGEST OF INTERNATIONAL LAW 569, 570 (1968), discussed below.

[98] *See* the agreements between the Soviet Union and France of 1951 and India of 1953 referred to in the International Law Commission's commentary to its draft articles on Jurisdictional Immunities of States and their Property, adopted on second reading in 1991, [1991] Y.B. Int'l L. Comm'n, vol. 2, pt. 2, 39; and in RESTATEMENT 3D, *supra* note 5, § 451, Reporters' Note 1. The agreements related to the non-immunity of state enterprises or trading organizations in respect of commercial relations, not that of the state itself.

[99] *See* Howard Holtzmann, *Settlement of Disputes: the Role of Arbitration in East-West Trade*, in Starr, ed., EAST-WEST BUSINESS TRANSACTIONS 554 (1974).

[100] Letter from the Acting Legal Adviser (Jack B. Tate) to the Acting Attorney General (Philip B. Perlman), 26 Dept. State Bull. 984 (1952). For the text of the letter, *see* 6 MARJORIE M. WHITEMAN, DIGEST OF INTERNATIONAL LAW 569-571 (1968) (hereinafter WHITEMAN).

"The newer or restrictive theory of sovereign immunity has always been supported by the courts of Belgium and Italy. It was adopted in turn by the courts of Egypt and of Switzerland. In addition, the courts of France, Austria, and Greece, which were traditionally supporters of the classical theory, reversed their position in the [19]20's to embrace the restrictive theory. Rumania, Peru, and possibly Denmark also appear to follow this theory."[101]

Thus by the middle of the 20th century the restrictive theory had been accepted at least by the courts, if not in the legislation, of a number of countries, and eleven states had relinquished immunity in respect of public merchant vessels either by treaty or through their practice.[102]

Two decades after the issuance of the Tate Letter, member states of the Council of Europe adopted the 1972 European Convention on State Immunity and Additional Protocol,[103] which follows the restrictive approach. Thereafter a number of countries, some non-western, codified the restrictive theory in their legislation in relatively rapid succession: the United States in 1976,[104] the United Kingdom in 1978,[105] Singapore in 1979,[106] Pakistan[107] and South Africa in 1981,[108] Canada in 1982,[109] and Australia in 1985.[110]

Interestingly, however, while the concept of non-immunity for acts *jure gestionis* has won increasing acceptance, this has not been true to the same extent of non-immunity with respect to enforcement of any resulting judgment against state property. As we will see, although the United States announced in the 1952 Tate Letter that it would adhere to the restrictive theory of immunity from jurisdiction, it continued to follow its traditional view that foreign state property is absolutely immune from execution. Even if a country's courts apply the restrictive theory to

---

[101] WHITEMAN, *supra* note 100, at 570.

[102] The states in this category listed in the Tate Letter are: Brazil, Chile, Estonia, Germany, Hungary, Netherlands, Norway, Poland, Portugal, Sweden and the United States. *Id.* For a thorough survey of state practice, *see* Claim Against the Empire of Iran, German Constitutional Court, decision of 30 April 1963, translated in 45 I.L.R. 57 (1972).

[103] 16 May 1972, Council of Europe, Eur. T.S. No. 74 (1972), 11 I.L.M. 470 (1972), reproduced in UNITED NATIONS, MATERIALS ON JURISDICTIONAL IMMUNITIES OF STATES AND THEIR PROPERTY 156 (1982) (hereinafter UN MATERIALS ON JURISDICTIONAL IMMUNITIES).

[104] Foreign Sovereign Immunities Act of 1976, Public Law 94-583, 90 Stat. 2891 (hereinafter FSIA).

[105] State Immunity Act 1978, 17 I.L.M. 1123 (1978), UN MATERIALS ON JURISDICTIONAL IMMUNITIES, *supra* note 103, at 41.

[106] State Immunity Act, 1979, 1979 Supplement to the Statutes of the Republic of Singapore, UN MATERIALS ON JURISDICTIONAL IMMUNITIES, *supra* note 103, at 28.

[107] State Immunity Ordinance, 1981, Gazette of Pakistan, 11 March 1981, UN MATERIALS ON JURISDICTIONAL IMMUNITIES, *supra* note 103, at 20.

[108] Foreign Sovereign Immunity Act (1981), UN MATERIALS ON JURISDICTIONAL IMMUNITIES, *supra* note 103, at 34.

[109] State Immunity Act, 22 June 1982, 21 I.L.M. 798 (1982).

[110] Foreign States Immunities Act 1985, 25 I.L.M. 715 (1986).

enforcement against state property, when they find it difficult to distinguish between property that serves sovereign purposes and that which does not, they may decide to grant protection generously to state property.[111] And the issue of enforcement was sufficiently controversial in Europe that the 1972 European Convention on State Immunity relies on the defendant-state, assuming it is a party to the Convention, to "give effect to a judgment given against it by a court of another Contracting State."[112] This obligation is, moreover, subject to a number of exceptions, including the rather subjective and potentially broad one that giving effect to the judgment would be manifestly contrary to the defendant-state's public policy.[113]

Despite these hesitations in the area of enforcement, the development of the restrictive theory has thus been steady, if it was somewhat uncertain in its early stages.[114] In 2004 the U.N. General Assembly adopted without a vote the United Nations Convention on Jurisdictional Immunities of States and Their Property,[115] a treaty negotiated on the basis of preparatory work by the U.N. International Law Commission.[116] Both the Commission's draft and the U.N. Convention follow a restrictive approach to state jurisdictional immunity and permit enforcement against state property that is used for "other than government non-commercial purposes".[117] This, together with the trend in state practice referred to above, suggests that a rule of customary international law reflecting the restrictive approach is at least nearing maturity, if it has not already crystallized. The fact that no state called for a vote on the U.N. Convention, a universal agreement, lends support to this proposition and provides some indication of how much less controversial this subject has become since the end of the Soviet era.[118]

---

[111] *See, e.g.,* Philippine Embassy Bank Account (X. v. Republic of Philippines), German Constitutional Court, 13 Dec. 1977, U.N. MATERIALS ON JURISDICTIONAL IMMUNITIES, *supra* note 103, at 297 (Philippine embassy bank account immune from execution).

[112] European Convention, *supra* note 103, art. 20(1).

[113] *Id.,* art. 20(2)(a).

[114] The commentary of the International Law Commission aptly characterizes "the movement of State practice in its progressive evolution towards the 'restrictive' view of State immunity [as having] taken the character of a snake, which can move sideways by swinging and swaying its body to the left and right with intermittent ups and downs in a zigzagging pattern." [1983] 2 Y.B. Int'l L. Comm'n, pt. 2, 82.

[115] General Assembly Resolution 59/38, 2 Dec. 2004, Annex, U.N. Doc. A/RES/59/38 (hereinafter 2004 UN Convention).

[116] For the full set of draft articles adopted on second reading by the ILC, with commentaries, *see* [1991] 2 Y.B. Int'l L. Comm'n, pt. 2, 13.

[117] 2004 UN Convention, *supra* note 115, art. 19(c).

[118] The ILC's draft articles were reported to the General Assembly in 1991, but the restrictive theory was evidently still too controversial at that time to permit states to negotiate a treaty on the basis of that draft. It ultimately took until 2004 for member states to agree on a text.

[C] The United States Foreign Sovereign Immunities Act of 1976

[1] Introduction

In 1976 Congress adopted the Foreign Sovereign Immunities Act (FSIA),[119] codifying the American version of the restrictive theory of sovereign immunity[120] which had characterized U.S. practice at least since the 1952 Tate Letter. The FSIA went beyond this, however. It provided that not only would the United States continue to follow the restrictive theory, but that henceforth U.S. courts, rather than the State Department, would determine whether a foreign state enjoys jurisdictional immunity. Until the enactment of this statute, quasi-judicial hearings had often been held in the State Department to determine whether to issue a "suggestion of immunity" to a court in which a suit involving a sovereign immunity claim was pending. As the FSIA's legislative history recognizes, these hearings were subject to diplomatic influence and could thus result in determinations that were at least in part political.[121] "A principle purpose" of the FSIA, according to the legislative history, was "to transfer the determination of sovereign immunity from the executive branch to the judicial branch, thereby reducing the foreign policy implications of immunity determinations and assuring litigants that these often crucial decisions are made on purely legal grounds and under procedures that insure due process."[122]

The most important provisions of the FSIA are the "commercial activities exception" to immunity, set forth in § 1605(a)(2), the "noncommercial tort exception" contained in § 1605(a)(5), and the Act's provisions on enforcement, found in § 1610. These will be discussed briefly in the following subsections. Also worthy of brief mention is an exception added in 1996 by Congress for suits seeking money damages "for personal injury or death that was caused by an act of torture, extrajudicial killing, aircraft sabotage, [or] hostage taking"[123] if the foreign state has been designated as a state sponsor of terrorism under the Export Administration Act of 1979[124] or the Foreign Assistance Act of 1961.[125]

---

[119] Foreign Sovereign Immunities Act of 1976, Public Law 94-583, 90 Stat. 2891 (hereinafter FSIA).

[120] *See* the legislative history of the FSIA, House Rep. No. 94-1487, reproduced in UN MATERIALS ON JURISDICTIONAL IMMUNITIES, *supra* note 103, at 98 (hereinafter House Report), which rather optimistically states that the bill, as it then was, "would codify the so-called 'restrictive' principle of sovereign immunity, as presently recognized in international law." *Id.*

[121] *Id.* at 99.

[122] *Id.*

[123] FSIA, *supra* note 119, §1605(a)(7).

[124] 50 U.S.C. App. 2405(j).

[125] 22 U.S.C. 2371.

[2]　The Commercial Activities Exception

The commercial activities exception may be said to be the principal driving force behind the development of the restrictive theory (notwithstanding the importance of the tort exception, discussed below).[126] In essence, codifications of this exception take two different approaches: they either carve out one broad exception, as in the case of the FSIA; or they provide for a number of discrete exceptions for different forms of commercial or trading activities, which is the approach taken by, e.g., the European Convention, the British 1978 State Immunity Act and the 2004 UN Convention.

As indicated above, the FSIA's commercial activities exception is contained in § 1605(a)(2).[127] The term "commercial activity" is defined in §1603(d) to mean "either a regular course of commercial conduct or a particular commercial transaction or act. *The commercial character of an activity shall be determined by reference to the nature of the course of conduct or particular transaction or act, rather than by reference to its purpose*."[128] The major difficulty the courts have had with the definition is that it does not define what is meant by the pivotal term "commercial."[129]

The final sentence of the definition is crucial. It sets forth the "nature vs. purpose" test used by most, if not all, countries following the restrictive approach. Thus, for example, if State A enters into a contract with Arms, Inc., a private company, for the purchase of boots for the State A Army, it would be the *nature* of the contract, not its *purpose* which would control as to the question of immunity. Accordingly, while the purpose of the contract, acquiring boots for the State A Army, is clearly sovereign or governmental, its nature is that of a contract for the sale of goods, a transaction that could be entered into by any private person.

---

[126] In 1982 the special rapporteur for the work of the International Law Commission on sovereign immunity concluded: "The most common place or common ground for an apparent exception to the rule of State immunity is likely to be classified as trading or commercial activities." Sompong Sucharitkul, Fourth Report on Jurisdictional Immunities of States and their Property, [1982] 2 Y.B. Int'l L. Comm'n, 199, 210, pt. 1. *See* the historical survey of case law regarding the "trading or commercial activity exception" in Italy, Belgium, Egypt, France, Germany, Netherlands, Austria, the United States, the United Kingdom, Pakistan, Argentina, Chile and the Philippines, in *id.* at 212-222.

[127] That section reads as follows:

"(a) A foreign state shall not be immune from the jurisdiction of courts of the United States or of the States in any case —

　. . .

(2) in which the action is based upon a commercial activity carried on in the United States by the foreign state; or upon an act performed in the United States in connection with a commercial activity of the foreign state elsewhere; or upon an act outside the territory of the United States in connection with a commercial activity of the foreign state elsewhere and that act causes a direct effect in the United States; . . ."

FSIA, *supra* note 119, §1605(a)(2).

[128] *Id.* § 1603(d) (emphasis added).

[129] *See, e.g.,* Republic of Argentina v. Weltover, Inc., 504 U.S. 607, 612, 122 S.Ct. 2160, 119 L.Ed.2d 394 (1992).

U.S. courts have generally applied this test quite strictly, finding no immunity even in some cases in which, at first blush, the foreign state's act seemed to be of a *jure imperii* nature. Thus, in *Republic of Argentina v. Weltover, Inc.*,[130] the Supreme Court held that Argentina's issuance of government bonds as part of a plan to stabilize its currency was a "commercial activity" within the meaning of § 1605(a)(2) of the FSIA.[131] Argentina was therefore not immune from suit for breach of contract by private parties holding some of the bonds when it defaulted on payment. The Court, calling the bonds "almost in all respects garden-variety debt instruments,"[132] reasoned that "there is nothing distinctive about the state's assumption of debt (other than perhaps its purpose) that would cause it always to be classified as *jure imperii*. . . ."[133] It explained that "when a foreign government acts, not as a regulator of a market, but in the manner of a private player within it, the foreign sovereign's actions are 'commercial' within the meaning of the FSIA."[134] On the other hand, "a foreign government's issuance of regulations limiting foreign currency exchange is a sovereign activity, because such authoritative control of commerce cannot be exercised by a private party;. . . ."[135] The Court thus focused narrowly on the nature of the state's act, rejecting Argentina's argument that viewing it in "context" would reveal that it was not commercial.[136] The Court drew a bright line between regulation of markets or other private activity — something only a government can do — and participation in such activity.

The nature/purpose test does not unfailingly result in findings of non-immunity, however. Thus in *MOL v. Bangladesh*,[137] the Ninth Circuit Court of Appeals found that a licensing agreement by Bangladesh for the export of rhesus monkeys was not a commercial activity and thus that Bangladesh was immune from suit when it unilaterally terminated the contract. While MOL, the private party to the contract, argued that the court should focus on "Bangladesh's contracting to sell monkeys,"[138] the court responded that "Bangladesh was terminating an agreement only a sovereign could have

---

[130] *Id.*

[131] The Court also held that the FSIA's requirement of a "direct effect" in the United States was satisfied by Argentina's *failure* to make payments on the bonds into plaintiffs' New York bank accounts. *Id.* at 618-619. The court further rejected the suggestion in the FSIA's legislative history that the effect in the United States must be both "substantial" and "foreseeable." *Id.* at 618.

[132] 504 U.S. at 615.

[133] *Id. See also* the definition of "commercial transaction" in the 2004 U.N. Convention: "'commercial transaction' means: . . . (ii) any contract for a loan or other transaction of a financial nature, including any obligation of guarantee or of indemnity in respect of any such loan or transaction;. . . ." 2004 U.N. Convention, *supra* note 115, art. 2(1)(c).

[134] *Id.* at 614.

[135] *Id.*

[136] *Id.* at 615-616 ("even in full context, there is nothing about the issuance of these [bonds] (except perhaps its purpose) that is not analogous to a private commercial transaction.").

[137] 736 F.2d 1326 (9th Cir. 1984).

[138] *Id.* at 1328.

made. . . . It concerned Bangladesh's right to regulate imports and exports, a sovereign prerogative."[139] For good measure, the court added that the contract "concerned Bangladesh's right to regulate its natural resources, also a uniquely sovereign function"[140] — despite MOL's objection that "this conclusion relies on the *purpose* of the agreement, in contradiction of the FSIA."[141] This result, and the reasoning on which it is based, seem questionable given the nature/purpose test and the Supreme Court's narrow focus on the nature of the act in question, regardless of its context. *MOL* was decided eight years before *Weltover*, however; it is interesting to speculate as to whether the result would have been different if the case had come before the Ninth Circuit after the Supreme Court's decision in *Weltover*.

[3]   The Non-Commercial Tort Exception

The non-commercial tort exception is codified in § 1605(a)(5) of the FSIA.[142] While this exception is also well established in a number of countries,[143] at least until recently it has perhaps been somewhat more controversial in certain regions of the world. In fact, the International Law Commission's special rapporteur concluded, on the basis of a thorough survey of state practice, that "the basis for actual exercise of jurisdiction when the act or omission complained of is attributable to a foreign State cannot be found in customary international law. . . . [T]he exercise of jurisdiction [in such cases] is not warranted in the traditional practice of States."[144] But the 2004 U.N. Convention includes a provision on "Personal injuries

---

[139] *Id.* at 1329.

[140] *Id.*

[141] *Id.* (emphasis in original).

[142] That section provides:

"(a) A foreign state shall not be immune from the jurisdiction of courts of the United States or of the States in any case —

. . .

(5) not otherwise encompassed in paragraph (2) above, in which money damages are sought against a foreign state for personal injury or death, or damage to or loss of property, occurring in the United States and caused by the tortious act or omission of that foreign state or of any official or employee of that foreign state while acting within the scope of his office or employment; except this paragraph shall not apply to —

(A) any claim based upon the exercise or performance or the failure to exercise or perform a discretionary function regardless of whether the discretion be abused, or

(B) any claim arising out of malicious prosecution, abuse of process, libel, slander, misrepresentation, deceit, or interference with contract rights; . . ."

FSIA, *supra* note 119, §1605(a)(5).

[143] *See, e.g.,* Collision with a Foreign Government-Owned Motor Car [Holubek v. Government of the United States], decision of 10 Feb. 1961, Supreme Court of Austria, translated in 40 ILR. 73 (1970), reproduced in UN MATERIALS ON JURISDICTIONAL IMMUNITIES, *supra* note 103, at 203; and the survey of state practice in Sompong Sucharitkul, Fifth Report on Jurisdictional Immunities of States and their Property, [1983] 2 Y.B. Int'l L. Comm'n, pt. 1, 25, 41-45.

[144] Sucharitkul, *supra* note 143, at 39.

and damage to property"[145] which reproduces the draft article adopted by the ILC[146] and constitutes some evidence of the emergence of this exception as part of customary international law.

The principal issues under this exception have been its applicability to transboundary torts, the discretionary function exception, and enforcement of tort judgments. The latter will be discussed in the following subsection. Transboundary torts are generally not covered by this exception in international practice,[147] and the same is true of the FSIA. In fact, the tort exception is often said to be "directed primarily at the problem of traffic accidents. . . ."[148] An initial reading of the FSIA's tort exception might suggest otherwise, however, since § 1605(a)(5) only requires that the *injury* ("personal injury or death, or damage to or loss of property") have occurred in the United States. It might be assumed that this would not preclude suits against foreign states where the act causing the injury occurred outside U.S. territory. But the FSIA's legislative history makes clear that "the tortious *act or omission* must occur within the jurisdiction of the United States. . . ."[149] While, rather oddly, the legislative history mentions only the location of the tortious act, while the FSIA refers only to the location of the injury, the courts have put the two together to require that, as one court put it, "the tort, in whole, must occur in the United States."[150]

---

[145] Article 12 of the U.N. Convention, "Personal injuries and damage to property," reads as follows:

> "Unless otherwise agreed between the States concerned, a State cannot invoke immunity from jurisdiction before a court of another State which is otherwise competent in a proceeding which relates to pecuniary compensation for death or injury to the person, or damage to or loss of tangible property, caused by an act or omission which is alleged to be attributable to the State, if the act or omission occurred in whole or in part in the territory of that other State and if the author of the act or omission was present in that territory at the time of the act or omission."

2004 UN Convention, *supra* note 115, art. 12.

[146] *See* draft art. 12, Personal injuries and damage to property, [1991] 2 Y.B. Int'l L. Comm'n, pt. 2, 44.

[147] *See, e.g.,* art. 12 of the 2004 U.N. Convention, *supra* note 115, which requires that the act or omission in question have "occurred in whole or in part in the territory of [the forum] State and [that] the author of the act or omission was present in that territory at the time of the act or omission."

[148] House Report, *supra* note 120, in UN MATERIALS ON JURISDICTIONAL IMMUNITIES, *supra* note 103, at 112. *See also* the ILC's commentary to its draft articles on jurisdictional immunities as adopted on second reading in 1991, [1991] 2 Y.B. Int'l L. Comm'n, pt. 2, 45 ("The areas of damage envisaged in article 12 are mainly concerned with accidental death or physical injuries to persons . . . involved in traffic accidents. . . .").

[149] House Report, *supra* note 120, in UN MATERIALS ON JURISDICTIONAL IMMUNITIES, *supra* note 103, at 112 (emphasis added).

[150] In re Sedco, Inc., 543 F.Supp. 561, 567 (S.D. Texas 1982) (Pemex, the Mexican government-owned oil company, was immune in a suit seeking compensation for damage to the Texas coast resulting from the blowout of an exploratory oil well in the Bay of Campeche, Mexico). This decision was vacated on other grounds, 610 F. Supp. 306 (1984) (order dismissing Pemex from the litigation vacated in order to hear more evidence regarding the applicability of the commercial activities exception of the FSIA; defendant Permargo's motions for an order directing arbitration and stay of proceedings pending arbitration

In fact, some courts seem quite willing to find that a tort has been committed in U.S. territory even though some aspects of the allegedly tortious conduct occurred abroad. Thus in *Olsen v. Mexico*,[151] the Ninth Circuit held that Mexico was not immune from suit for the wrongful death of plaintiffs' parents in a plane crash near San Diego, California, even though the crash occurred during a flight from Monterrey to Tijuana, Mexico, as the plane was approaching an airport in Tijuana from United States airspace, and some of the negligent conduct was alleged to have occurred in Mexico. The court held that "if plaintiffs allege at least one entire tort occurring in the United States, they may claim under section 1605(a)(5)."[152]

The discretionary function "exception" is found in § 1605(a)(5)(A) of the FSIA. It is actually an exception to the non-commercial tort exception, which is a rather roundabout way of saying that if it applies, the defendant state will be immune. This exception, which is not found in the 2004 U.N. Convention, is based on a similar provision of the Federal Tort Claims Act (FTCA).[153] The Supreme Court has stated that the discretionary function exception of the FTCA "marks the boundary between Congress' willingness to impose tort liability upon the United States and

---

denied). On appeal from the latter decision, the 5th Circuit remanded with instructions to the district court to order the parties (Sedco and Permargo) to perform the arbitration agreement contained in their contract. Sedco, Inc. v. Petroleos Mexicanos Mexican National Oil Co., 767 F.2d 1140 (5th Cir. 1985).

[151] 729 F.2d 641 (9th Cir. 1984), *cert. denied*, 469 U.S. 917, 105 S. Ct. 295, 83 L. Ed. 2d 230 (1984).

[152] *Id.* at 646.

[153] House Report, *supra* note 120; UN Materials on Jurisdictional Immunities, *supra* note 103, at 112, referring to the Federal Tort Claims Act, 28 U.S.C. § 2671. 28 U. S. C. § 2680(a) provides that the Act shall not apply to "[any] claim based upon an act or omission of an employee of the Government, exercising due care, in the execution of a statute or regulation, whether or not such statute or regulation be valid, *or based upon the exercise or performance or the failure to exercise or perform a discretionary function or duty on the part of a federal agency or an employee of the Government, whether or not the discretion involved be abused.*" (Emphasis added.) Congress' intent in enacting this provision was described as follows:

"'[It is] designed to preclude application of the act to a claim based upon an alleged abuse of discretionary authority by a regulatory or licensing agency — for example, the Federal Trade Commission, the Securities and Exchange Commission, the Foreign Funds Control Office of the Treasury, or others. It is neither desirable nor intended that the constitutionality of legislation, the legality of regulations, or the propriety of a discretionary administrative act should be tested through the medium of a damage suit for tort. The same holds true of other administrative action not of a regulatory nature, such as the expenditure of Federal funds, the execution of a Federal project, and the like.

'On the other hand, the common law torts of employees of regulatory agencies, as well as of all other Federal agencies, would be included within the scope of the bill.' Hearings on H. R. 5373 and H. R. 6463 before the House Committee on the Judiciary, 77th Cong., 2d Sess., 28, 33 (1942) (statement of Assistant Attorney General Francis M. Shea)."

As quoted in United States v. S.A. Empresa de Viacao Aerea Rio Grandense (Varig Airlines), 467 U.S. 797, 809, 104 S.Ct. 2755, 2762, 81 L.Ed.2d 660, 672 (1984).

its desire to protect certain governmental activities from exposure to suit by private individuals."[154] The same can probably be said, substituting "foreign sovereigns" for "the United States," of the role of the exception in the FSIA.

On the basis of the Supreme Court's interpretation of the FTCA's version of the exception,[155] the Ninth Circuit Court of Appeals has held that a two-pronged test determines whether the FSIA's discretionary function exception applies in a foreign sovereign immunity case. "First, the court must examine '"the nature of the conduct, rather than the status of the actor."' . . . Second, the court must inquire whether the governmental acts at issue were '"grounded in social, economic, and political policy."'"[156] The Ninth Circuit explained: "In other words, the court should avoid second-guessing policy decisions through the medium of a tort action. . . . The execution of policy decisions by subordinates, even those subordinates at the operational level, comes under the discretionary function exception if the acts involved the exercise of policy judgment."[157] The court applied these standards to hold that the while the acquisition (by lease) and operation of a residence by the Nigerian consulate in San Francisco was "a discretionary policy decision,"[158] the "purely destructive acts"[159] that gave rise to the landlord's tort claims were non-discretionary. "Destruction of property can hardly be considered as part of a policy decision to establish a consular residence."[160] Moreover, the court found that "the exercise of jurisdiction over the instant lawsuit [will not] encroach on the ability of foreign sovereigns to make policy decisions regarding their consular buildings."[161] It therefore concluded that the discretionary function exception did not apply.[162]

[4] Enforcement of Judgments

Finally, let us turn to the FSIA's provisions on enforcement of judgments against foreign sovereigns, found in § 1610. In general, the FSIA makes it more difficult to enforce judgments against the foreign state itself

---

[154] *Id.* at 808.

[155] *See* the *Varig* case, *id.*

[156] Joseph v. Office of the Consulate General of Nigeria, 830 F.2d 1018, 1026 (1987) (quoting Begay v. United States, 768 F.2d 1059, 1064 (9th Cir. 1985); and Varig, *supra* note 153, 467 U.S. at 813)).

[157] *Id.* at 1026 (citing Red Lake Band of Chippewa Indians v. United States, 800 F.2d 1187, 1196 (D.C. Cir. 1986)).

[158] *Id.* at 1027.

[159] *Id.* Plaintiff-Joseph alleged "'extensive damage to appliances, fixtures, and landscaping; removal of appliances, furniture, light fixtures, solid wood doors, the glass shower door; removal of shutters and drapes from thirty-three windows, removal of fully grown trees; the removal of wood framing from windows and floor boards, the removal of a built-in barbecue.'"*Id.* at 1020 n. 1.

[160] *Id.* at 1027.

[161] *Id.*

[162] *Id.*

than against the foreign state's agencies or instrumentalities.[163] As we have seen, the position of the United States, even after the Tate Letter, had traditionally been that "the property of foreign states is absolutely immune from execution."[164] Thus, the approach of the FSIA is to lower the barrier of immunity from execution, but not to eliminate it altogether.

Let us first look at enforcement of judgments against a foreign state itself. Under the exception to immunity from execution that will be applicable most often,[165] judgments may be enforced against foreign state property "used for a commercial activity in the United States," but only if "the property is or was used for the commercial activity *upon which the claim is based*"[166] Since the non-diplomatic[167] property of foreign states in the United States will often consist of bank accounts, it will in many cases be difficult to establish the requisite nexus between the property and the claim.[168]

The other notable aspect of these provisions is that they refer only to "commercial" activity upon which the claim was based, not tortious activity. In *Letelier v. Republic of Chile*,[169] the worst fears of the successful plaintiff regarding this omission were confirmed. The Second Circuit held that as to a tort judgment against a foreign state, "Congress did in fact

---

[163] The FSIA defines "agency or instrumentality of a foreign state" to mean:

(b) " . . . any entity:

(1) which is a separate legal person, corporate or otherwise, and

(2) which is an organ of a foreign state or political subdivision thereof, or a majority of whose shares or other ownership interest is owned by a foreign state or political subdivision thereof, and

(3) which is neither a citizen of a State of the United States as defined in section 1332 (c) and (d) of this title, nor created under the laws of any third country."

FSIA, *supra* note 119, § 1603(b).

[164] House Report, *supra* note 120; UN MATERIALS ON JURISDICTIONAL IMMUNITIES, *supra* note 103, at 118 (citing Dexter and Carpenter, Inc. v. Kunglig Jarnvagsstyrelsen, 43 F.2d 705 (2d Cir. 1930)); and Weilamann v. Chase Manhattan Bank, 21 Misc. 2d 1086, 192 N.Y.S.2d 469, 473 (Sup. Ct. N.Y. 1959).

[165] § 1610 creates other exceptions for explicit or implicit waiver ((a)(1)), judgments establishing rights in property taken in violation of international law ((a)(3)), acquired by succession or gift ((a)(4)(A)), or which is immovable and situated in the United States (provided it is not used for diplomatic purposes) ((a)(4)(B)), and proceeds from automobile or other liability or casualty insurance policies ((a)(5)).

[166] FSIA, *supra* note 119, § 1610 (a) and (a)(2) (emphasis added).

[167] As indicated above, diplomatic property — using that expression broadly to cover most property of diplomatic and consular missions — is immune from execution under the 1961 Diplomatic and 1963 Consular Conventions. *See* notes 87 and 88 and accompanying text, *supra*.

[168] *But see* Birch Shipping Corp. v. Embassy of United Republic of Tanzania, 507 F.Supp. 311 (D.D.C. 1980) (motion to quash writ of garnishment against embassy bank account denied; if embassy wishes accounts to be immune, it must segregate them into public purpose funds and commercial activity funds). However, the same court later declined to follow that decision. Liberian Eastern Timber v. Liberia, 659 F.Supp. 606 (D.D.C. 1987).

[169] 748 F.2d 790 (2d Cir. 1984), *cert. denied*, 471 U.S. 1125 (1985).

create a right without a remedy"[170] by failing to provide for enforcement of such judgments. The court reasoned that reading the FSIA against its historical background of absolute immunity in U.S. practice and a 1972 European Convention that "left the availability of execution totally up to the debtor state"[171] makes plain that "it was not Congress' purpose to lift execution immunity wholly and completely. . . ."[172] Therefore, in the absence of waiver or another rarely available exception,[173] judgments may be enforced against foreign states only where the claim was based on the commercial activities exception, and even then only against state property used for the commercial activity on which the claim was based.

The FSIA's rules regarding enforcement of judgments against state agencies or instrumentalities are more liberal.[174] In contrast with judgments against the state itself, the kinds of property available for execution are not narrowly restricted and there is no requirement that property be linked with the claim. Thus, "*any* property of an agency or instrumentality of a foreign state engaged in commercial activity in the United States" is subject to execution provided, inter alia,[175] that the judgment relates to a claim for which the entity is not immune under the commercial activities *or* non-commercial tort exception, among others, "*regardless* of whether the property is or was used for the activity upon which the claim is based."[176] The principal restriction is therefore that the agency or instrumentality be engaged in commercial activity in the United States. The legislative history also makes clear that a judgment against one agency or instrumentality may not be enforced against property of another that is unrelated to the first.[177]

§ 6.05   THE ACT OF STATE DOCTRINE

We have seen that it is not uncommon for the jurisdiction of two or more states to overlap and also that the jurisdiction of the territorial state will ordinarily prevail in the event of conflict. This section deals with a policy developed chiefly[178] by courts in the United States, known as the act of state doctrine, which is consistent with that principle. According to this doctrine, American courts will generally refrain from examining the validity of acts of foreign governments taken in their own territories.

---

[170] *Id.* at 798.

[171] *Id.* at 799.

[172] *Id.*

[173] *See* note 165, *supra.*

[174] *See* FSIA, *supra* note 119, § 1610(b).

[175] The waiver exception applies here, as well as to the state itself. *See* § 1610(b)(1).

[176] *Id.* § 1610(b) and (b)(2) (emphasis added).

[177] House Report, *supra* note 120; UN MATERIALS ON JURISDICTIONAL IMMUNITIES, *supra* note 103, at 120, *citing* Prelude Corp. v. Owners of F/V Atlantic, 1971 A.M.C. 2651 (N.D. Calif.).

[178] This section will focus on the act of state doctrine as developed in U.S. case law. However, other countries follow similar doctrines of judicial restraint, and the House of Lords has in effect aligned British practice with that of the U.S. *See* Buttes Gas & Oil Co. v.

Several rationales have been advanced for the act of state doctrine, ranging from respect for the sovereignty of foreign states to considerations relating to the separation of powers to theories of choice of law. However, the United States Supreme Court has stated clearly that the doctrine is required neither by international law nor by the Constitution.[179] On the other hand, the Court has concluded that it does have "'constitutional' underpinnings"[180] in the sense that "[i]t arises out of the basic relationships between branches of government in a system of separation of powers."[181]

The act of state doctrine is generally not embraced by the business community or the international law bar, because it may effectively insulate from judicial scrutiny in the United States acts of other governments that take the property of, or otherwise injure, foreign nationals (often U.S. corporations or individuals) — even in violation of international law. The classic statement of the theory behind this seemingly harsh result, and indeed of the act of state doctrine itself, was uttered by the Supreme Court in its 1897 decision in *Underhill v. Hernandez*:

> "Every sovereign state is bound to respect the independence of every other sovereign state, and the courts of one country will not sit in judgment on the acts of the government of another, done within its own territory. Redress of grievances by reason of such acts must be obtained through the means open to be availed of by sovereign powers as between themselves."[182]

In other words, the injured party should seek to have the claim taken up by the U.S. government and asserted on the international plane, under international law, against the government of the state that allegedly caused the injury. Or, as the Court put it somewhat more specifically in *Banco Nacional de Cuba v. Sabbatino*, "[b]ecause of [the] peculiar nation-to-nation character [of international law] the usual method for an individual to seek relief is to exhaust local remedies and then repair to the executive authorities of his own state to persuade them to champion his claim in diplomacy or before an international tribunal."[183]

However, there are difficulties with this procedure (which is discussed in Chapter 9, § 9.01[B]), some of which are obvious. First, the claimant must exhaust remedies in the very state that is alleged to have committed the wrong. If that state has an independent judiciary it may well be possible for the claimant to obtain relief. In a significant number of cases, however, this does not occur. The claimant would then be left to

---

Hammer, [1982] A.C. 888, 936-38 (H.L.(E.)). *See generally* RESTATEMENT 3D, *supra* note 5, § 444, Reporters' Note 12.

[179] *See* Banco Nacional de Cuba v. Sabbatino, 376 U.S. 398, 421-23, 84 S.Ct. 923, 11 L.Ed.2d 804 (1964).

[180] *Id.* 376 U.S. at 423.

[181] *Id.*

[182] 168 U.S. 250, 252 (1897).

[183] 376 U.S. 398, at 422-23.

"persuade" the U.S. government to espouse the claim, because the government is not obligated by either U.S. or international law to do so. Even if the government does take up the claim, the vigor with which it pursues it will depend on a variety of factors, ranging from domestic political considerations to those of a diplomatic nature. In fact, since it becomes the state's claim once it is taken up,[184] the state can compromise it or even waive it altogether. If the government pursues the claim, prevails and secures compensation from the foreign state, it is not required by international law to pass the recovery along to the private claimant (though it would usually do so).[185]

The theory behind this cumbersome procedure, fraught as it is with obstacles and uncertainties, is that when a state injures a foreign natural or legal person, that is regarded by international law as an injury to the person's state of nationality.[186] This is all well and good for the "injured" state, but may not be of much help to the person who actually suffered the harm. Thus the motivation of the private party to take a more direct route, pursuing redress against the foreign state through U.S. courts. The frustration such a person might feel upon being informed that this avenue, too, is closed — this time because of the act of state doctrine (or sovereign immunity) — is understandable.

Nevertheless, that is exactly what has happened in a number of well-known cases.[187] Several examples will perhaps suffice to illustrate the point. In *Underhill*,[188] an American citizen claimed that he had been unlawfully assaulted and detained in Venezuela by Hernandez, a revolutionary military commander whose government was later recognized by the United States. In *Oetjen v. Central Leather Co.*,[189] plaintiff sought to recover a large shipment of hides that had allegedly been seized in violation of international law by Mexican armed forces from a Mexican citizen through whom plaintiff claimed title. In *Ricaud v. American Metal Co.*,[190] lead bullion belonging to an American citizen was seized, again by the

---

[184] Mavrommatis Palestine Concessions, 1924 P.C.I.J. (ser. A) No. 2, at 12. *See also* the Chorzow Factory Case, 1928, PCIJ, Series A, No. 17, at pp. 25-29. When one state injures a national of another, international law treats the injury as being to the state of the person's nationality. That state may then pursue redress against the state causing the harm, but usually after the harmed person (natural or legal) exhausts local remedies in the state where the harm occurred. *See generally* RESTATEMENT 3D, *supra* note 5, Part VII, Introductory Note; and Chapter 9, *infra*.

[185] *See generally* RESTATEMENT 3D, *supra* note 5, §713.

[186] *See* note 184, *supra*.

[187] *See, e.g.,* Underhill v. Hernandez, 168 U.S. 250 (1897); American Banana Co. v. United Fruit Co., 213 U.S. 347 (1909); Oetjen v. Central Leather Co., 246 U.S. 297 (1918); Ricaud v. American Metal Co., 246 U.S. 304 (1918); Shapleigh v. Mier, 299 U.S. 468 (1937); United States v. Belmont, 301 U.S. 324 (1937); United States v. Pink, 315 U.S. 203 (1942); and Banco Nacional de Cuba v. Sabbatino, 376 U.S. 398 (1964).

[188] Underhill v. Hernandez, 168 U.S. 250 (1897).

[189] 246 U.S. 297 (1918).

[190] *Id.* at 304.

Mexican army as a military levy. And in *Shapleigh v. Mier*,[191] the Mexican government expropriated an American citizen's land in Mexico. In all of these cases, the Court refused to examine the validity of the act of the foreign state, leaving the plaintiff without a judicial remedy. The rationale in each case was along the lines of that stated in the passage from *Underhill* quoted above.[192]

In the *Sabbatino*[193] case, a landmark 1964 decision of the Supreme Court, the Court indicated that there might be circumstances in which the act of state doctrine would not tie the courts' hands — but then held once more that it would not examine the validity of the foreign governmental act in question. At issue there was an expropriation by Cuba in August, 1960 — in retaliation for the United States' reduction of the Cuban sugar import quota — of the property, rights and interests, including sugar, of a Cuban company (C.A.V.) largely owned by Americans.[194] Banco Nacional de Cuba, an instrumentality of the Cuban government, sued the New York receiver of the expropriated company's assets in the Federal District Court for the Southern District of New York to recover funds paid for a shipment of the sugar.[195] The District Court and Court of Appeals both found the act of state doctrine to be inapplicable when the act in question violated international law, which they concluded the Cuban expropriation did because it was motivated by a retaliatory purpose, discriminated against American nationals and failed to provide adequate compensation.[196]

---

[191] 299 U.S. 468 (1937).

[192] Underhill v. Hernandez, 168 U.S. 250 (1897). *See* text at note 182, *supra*.

[193] 376 U.S. 398, 84 S.Ct. 923, 11 L.Ed.2d 804 (1964).

[194] More specifically, the Cuban law "provided for the compulsory expropriation of all property and enterprises, and of rights and interests arising therefrom, of certain listed companies, including C.A.V., wholly or principally owned by American nationals." *Id.* at 403.

[195] The sale of the sugar had been arranged by a New York commodities broker (Farr, Whitlock) before the expropriation. It was a typical documentary sales transaction, whereby the buyer pays for documents provided by the seller (mainly one or more bills of lading) giving title to the goods. The expropriation occurred on the day the loading of the sugar onto a ship for transport commenced. In order to obtain permission for the ship to leave Cuban waters the commodities broker entered into contracts with a Cuban government bank (Banco Exterior, which stood in the position of C.A.V. under the Cuban expropriation law) identical to those it had made with C.A.V. Banco Exterior received the bills of lading from the vessel and assigned them to plaintiff Banco Nacional, another government bank. Banco Nacional sent the bills of lading, together with a sight draft, to its agent in New York for delivery to the commodities broker for payment. The broker negotiated the bills of lading to its customer, the buyer, and received payment for the sugar. But it was ultimately ordered by the New York Supreme Court, which had appointed Sabbatino as Temporary Receiver of C.A.V.'s New York assets, to transfer the funds to Sabbatino. Plaintiff Banco Nacional then sued Sabbatino in federal court to recover the proceeds of the bills of lading.

[196] 376 U.S. 398, at 406-07. To be legal under international law, an expropriation must be for a public purpose, non-discriminatory, and accompanied by adequate compensation. The Court of Appeals also relied on two letters from the State Department, not before the District Court, which it regarded as indicating that the Executive Branch had no objection to a judicial examination of the Cuban decree's validity. *Id.* at 407.

The Supreme Court reversed, holding that the act of state doctrine applied. It concluded that the doctrine is not "compelled either by the inherent nature of sovereign authority . . . or by some principle of international law,"[197] and further that "[t]he text of the Constitution does not require the act of state doctrine; it does not irrevocably remove from the judiciary the capacity to review the validity of foreign acts of state."[198] It found, however, that the doctrine does "have 'constitutional' underpinnings," since it "arises out of the basic relationships between branches of government in a system of separation of powers."[199] In particular, the court found that the doctrine "expresses the strong sense of the Judicial Branch that its engagement in the task of passing on the validity of foreign acts of state may hinder rather than further this country's pursuit of goals both for itself and for the community of nations as a whole in the international sphere."[200]

Thus the Court found that the act of state doctrine is "compelled by neither international law nor the Constitution. . . ."[201] Indeed, it observed that "the greater the degree of codification or consensus concerning a particular area of international law, the more appropriate it is for the judiciary to render decisions regarding it. . . ."[202] Then, in a passage that has been quoted repeatedly in subsequent decisions, the Court articulated its understanding of the act of state doctrine as it applied in cases of expropriation of foreign-owned property:

> "[R]ather than laying down or reaffirming an inflexible and all-encompassing rule in this case, we decide only that the Judicial Branch will not examine the validity of a taking of property within its own territory by a foreign sovereign government, extant and recognized by this country at the time of suit, in the absence of a treaty or other unambiguous agreement regarding controlling legal principles, even if the complaint alleges that the taking violates customary international law."[203]

The Court found no such "unambiguous agreement" on controlling legal principles in the field of expropriation. Indeed, it declared that "[t]here are few if any issues in international law today on which opinion seems to be so divided as the limitations on a state's power to expropriate the property of aliens."[204] It was thus not appropriate for the "judiciary to render decisions regarding" this "area of international law."[205] The act of state doc-

---

[197] *Id.* at 421.

[198] *Id.* at 423.

[199] *Id.*

[200] *Id.*

[201] *Id.* at 427.

[202] *Id.* at 428.

[203] *Id.*

[204] *Id.*

[205] *Id.* (quoted above).

trine therefore applied, requiring the Court not to examine the validity of the act of the foreign government but to accept the act as the rule of decision in the case before it.[206]

The case is particularly interesting because of the historical context in which it was decided. Fidel Castro had taken power in Cuba in January 1959, the year before the acts giving rise to the dispute. The United States military had supported the Cuban military dictator, Fulgencio Batista, ousted by Castro. This support, together with Castro's communist ideology and acts against American interests, soured relations between the two countries and led the United States to take acts such as the reduction of the Cuban sugar import quota. That the Supreme Court applied the act of state doctrine and thus refused to question the validity of Cuba's expropriation of American commercial interests, even in the face of U.S. enmity toward Cuba, shows how potentially powerful the doctrine is.

It should not be assumed that the act of state doctrine will automatically apply in all cases involving acts of foreign states, however, for several reasons. First, the Court's rule statement itself admits the possibility that a treaty between the United States and the foreign state concerned will establish "controlling legal principles," and the large and growing number of bilateral investment treaties (BITs) between the United States and other nations[207] increases the likelihood that such a treaty will be present.[208]

Second, from time to time the Executive Branch[209] writes a letter stating that it does not object to the adjudication of the case in question. Such "Bernstein letters"[210] have led courts to find the act of state doctrine inapplicable or have at least provided an alternative ground for doing so.[211] However, the courts have generally treated the letters as not being controlling upon them with regard to whether or not the doctrine is applied.[212]

---

[206] The Court quotes a passage from *Ricaud* stating that the foreign state's act "must be accepted by our courts as a rule for their decision." *Id.* at 418. *See also* RESTATEMENT 3D, *supra* note 5, § 443, Reporters' Note 1, "Act of state doctrine and conflict of laws."

[207] For a helpful discussion and links regarding the growing number of BITs, *see* the World Bank-International Center for the Settlement of Investment Disputes (ICSID) website, http://www.worldbank.org/icsid/treaties/intro.htm.

[208] In Kalamazoo Spice Extraction Co. v. Government of Socialist Ethiopia, 729 F.2d 422 (6th Cir. 1984), the federal Court of Appeals for the Sixth Circuit held that a standard clause in the applicable Friendship, Commerce and Navigation Treaty between the United States and Ethiopia, providing that property of nationals of the other state was not to be taken "without prompt payment of just and effective compensation," furnished a "controlling legal standard" which meant that the act of state doctrine did not apply. *Id.* at 427. *See generally* RESTATEMENT 3D, *supra* note 5, § 443, Reporters' Note 5.

[209] In particular, the letters are usually written by the State Department Legal Adviser.

[210] The name derives from Bernstein v. N.V. Nederlandsche-Amerikaansche Stoomvaart-Maatschappij, 173 F.2d 71 (2d Cir. 1949), 210 F.2d 375 (2d Cir. 1954).

[211] *See, e.g.,* Kalamazoo Spice Extraction Co. v. Government of Socialist Ethiopia, 729 F.2d 422 (6th Cir. 1984).

[212] *See, e.g.,* W.S. Kirkpatrick & Co., Inc., et al. v. Environmental Tectonics Corp., International, 493 U.S. 400, 404, 110 S.Ct. 701, 107 L.Ed.2d 816 (1990), discussed below.

And third, Congress reacted to the *Sabbatino* decision by enacting legislation, known as the Second Hickenlooper Amendment,[213] providing that the act of state doctrine is not to be applied by courts in the United States in cases involving claims that a foreign state confiscated property in violation of international law. However, the courts have generally interpreted the amendment to apply only where the claim is made to specific property that is before the court.[214]

Although *Sabbatino* and a number of the other well-known act of state cases involved expropriations, it should not be assumed that the doctrine applies only to this kind of governmental act.[215] For example, we have already seen that *Underhill*, a late nineteenth century decision, involved an allegedly unlawful assault and detention.[216] And a number of cases in which the doctrine was successfully invoked involved claims by one private party against another that the defendant was responsible for the loss of rights granted by a foreign government.[217] The latter kinds of cases are also significant because they demonstrate that an act of state defense may be raised in an action in which a foreign state is not a party.

While the act of state doctrine can be a potent defense, since the result of its application is that the court does not hear the case, the Supreme Court has recently indicated that it intends to confine the doctrine's application rather strictly. *W. S. Kirkpatrick & Co. v. Environmental Tectonics Corp., Int'l*,[218] another case between two private parties, involved a claim by plaintiff Environmental Tectonics that defendant Kirkpatrick had obtained the award of a contract from the Nigerian government through bribery.

---

[213] Foreign Assistance Act of 1961, § 620(e)(2), as amended, 22 U.S.C. § 2370(e)(2).

[214] *See, e.g.,* First National City Bank of New York v. Banco Nacional de Cuba, 431 F.2d 394, 399-402 (2d Cir. 1970), *reversed on other grounds*, 406 U.S. 759, 92 S.Ct. 1808, 32 L.Ed.2d 466 (1972); French v. Banco Nacional de Cuba, 242 N.E.2d 704 (N.Y. 1968); Banco Nacional de Cuba v. Chase Manhattan Bank, 658 F.2d 875, at 882 n. 10 (2d Cir. 1981). The federal circuits are split on whether the Second Hickenlooper Amendment applies to intangible property, the Second Circuit holding that it does not and the Ninth Circuit holding that it does. *Compare* Films by Jove, Inc. v. Berov, 341 F.Supp.2d 199 (E.D.N.Y. 2004); Zappia Middle East Constr. Co. v. Emirate of Abu Dhabi, No. 94 Civ.1942 (KMW), 1996 WL 413680 (S.D.N.Y. July 24, 1996); and French v. Banco Nacional de Cuba, 23 N.Y.2d 46, 295 N.Y.S.2d 433, 242 N.E.2d 704 (1968); *with* West v. Multibanco Comermex, S.A., 807 F.2d 820, 829-30 (9th Cir.1987) (noting that this exclusion is "contrary to the motivating policies of the Hickenlooper Amendment" and holding that in any event the "tangibleness" of property is not the dispositive factor). *See generally* Andreas Lowenfeld, *Act of State and Department of State: First National City Bank v. Banco Nacional de Cuba*, 66 AM. J. INT'L. L. 795, 801 (1972); and RESTATEMENT 3D, *supra* note 5, § 444 comment *e* and Reporters' Note 4.

[215] *See generally* RESTATEMENT 3D, *supra* note 5, § 443 comment *c* and and Reporters' Note 7.

[216] *See* text accompanying note 188, *supra*.

[217] *See, e.g.,* Occidental Petroleum Corp. v. Buttes Gas & Oil Co., 331 F.Supp. 92 (C.D. Cal. 1971), *aff'd*, 461 F.2d 1261 (9th Cir.), *cert. den.*, 409 U.S. 950, 93 S.Ct. 272, 34 L.Ed.2d 221 (1972); Hunt v. Mobil Oil Corp., 550 F.2d 68 (2d Cir.), *cert. den.*, 434 U.S. 984, 98 S.Ct. 608, 54 L.Ed.2d 477 (1977); and Clayco Petroleum Corp. v. Occidental Petroleum Corp., 712 F.2d 404 (9th Cir. 1983), *cert. denied*, 464 U.S. 1040, 104 S.Ct. 703, 79 L.Ed.2d 168 (1984).

[218] 493 U.S. 400, 110 S.Ct. 701, 107 L.Ed.2d 816 (1990).

Kirkpatrick and the other defendants[219] moved to dismiss plaintiff's complaint on the ground that the suit was barred by the act of state doctrine.

The trial court treated defendants' motion as one for summary judgment and dismissed.[220] It concluded that a finding that Nigerian government officials had demanded and accepted a bribe "would impugn or question the nobility of a foreign nation's motivations," and "result in embarrassment to the sovereign or constitute interference in the conduct of foreign policy of the United States."[221]

The Court of Appeals reversed.[222] It agreed with the District Court that "the award of a military procurement contract can be, in certain circumstances, a sufficiently formal expression of a government's public interests to trigger application"[223] of the act of state doctrine, but concluded that the doctrine's application was not warranted on the facts of the case. The Court of Appeals relied in particular on a letter from the State Department legal adviser[224] that had been requested by the District Court, while acknowledging that such letters "are not controlling on the courts."[225] The letter indicated that in the view of the State Department, dismissal of a complaint "merely because adjudication raises the bare possibility of embarrassment, constitutes an unwarranted expansion of the act of state doctrine and is contrary to the flexibility with which that doctrine should be applied."[226] In particular, according to the letter: "Judicial inquiry into the *purpose* of a foreign sovereign's acts would not require a court to rule on the *legality* of those acts, and a finding concerning purpose would not entail the particular kind of harm that the act of state doctrine is designed to avoid."[227]

The Supreme Court agreed with the Court of Appeals. Writing for the Court, Justice Scalia explained:

> "The act of state doctrine does not establish an exception [to the normal judicial function of deciding cases and controversies] for [those] that may embarrass foreign governments, but merely

---

[219] Defendants included the Chairman and CEO of Kirkpatrick and Benson "Tunde" Akindele, a Nigerian citizen with whom Carpenter made arrangements to secure the contract with the Nigerian government.

[220] Environmental Tectonics Corp., Int'l v. W.S. Kirkpatrick & Co., Inc., 659 F.Supp. 1381 (D.N.J. 1987).

[221] *Id.* at 1392-1393.

[222] 847 F.2d 1052 (3d Cir. 1988).

[223] *Id.* at 1058.

[224] Reprinted as an appendix to the Court of Appeals' opinion, *id.* at 1067-1069.

[225] *Id.* at 1061.

[226] *Id.* at 1068, quoting from a brief of the U.S. Government *amicus curiae* in support of petitions for a writ of *certiorari* in Industrial Investment Development Corp. v. Mitsui & Co., Ltd., 594 F.2d 48 (5th Cir. 1979), *cert. denied*, 445 U.S. 903, 100 S. Ct. 1078, 63 L. Ed. 2d 318 (1980); and in Hunt v. Mobil Oil Corp., 550 F.2d 68 (2d Cir. 1977), *cert. denied*, 434 U.S. 984, 54 L. Ed. 2d 477, 98 S. Ct. 608 (1977).

[227] *Id.* (emphasis added).

requires that, in the process of deciding, the acts of foreign sovereigns taken within their own jurisdictions shall be deemed valid.
That doctrine has no application to the present case because the
validity of no foreign sovereign act is at issue."[228]

Kirkpatrick thus focuses upon *validity* rather than *embarrassment*. That
is, dismissal on act of state grounds would be appropriate where adjudication would require inquiry into the validity of the act of a foreign state, but
not where it might merely result in embarrassment of the state. The
Court's interpretation of the doctrine seems to agree with that of the State
Department and represents a further refinement, and perhaps narrowing,
of the circumstances in which the doctrine applies.[229]

---

[228] 493 U.S. 400, 409 (1990).

[229] On *Kirkpatrick's* narrowing of the Act of State Doctrine, *see, e.g.*, Steven R. Swanson,
A Threshold Test for Validity: The Supreme Court Narrows the Act of State Doctrine,
23 VAND. J. TRANSNAT'L L. 889 (1991); Susan M. Morrison, Comment, *The Act of State
Doctrine and the Demise of International Comity*, 2 IND. INT'L & COMP. L. REV. 311 (1991); and
Mark Haugen & Jeff Good, *Evolution of the Act of State Doctrine: W.S. Kirkpatrick Corp v.
Environmental Tectonics Corp and Beyond*, 13 U. HAW. L. REV. 687 (Fall 1991).

Chapter 7
REMEDIES: INTERNATIONAL RESPONSIBILITY

Synopsis

§ 7.01 INTRODUCTION

This chapter is mainly concerned with the question, when State A breaches an obligation owed to State B, what remedies are available to State B? The question could also be framed as, what new obligations does the breach entail for State A? The chapter also touches on the criminal responsibility of individuals under international law, a topic that was considered from the perspective of jurisdiction in Chapter 6.[1]

The reader coming to this subject for the first time will likely be struck by the rather rudimentary nature of remedial or compliance mechanisms under international law, especially when compared to those available under national legal systems. However, taking the generally decentralized nature of the international legal system into account, the level of development of its remedial side is perhaps not so surprising. And of course, states have accepted treaty-based dispute resolution systems that are quite advanced in certain fields, such as trade[2] and human rights.[3]

---

[1] *See* ch. 6, § 6.03 [E].

[2] See, in particular, the system provided for under the World Trade Organization (WTO), applicable to the WTO's 148 members and described on the WTO website, http://www.wto.org/.

[3] *See* the systems described in ch. 9, § 9.02[A][4], especially that available in Europe.

The basic principles of the international law of remedies will probably not be particularly surprising to one with even a basic acquaintance with civil remedies available under domestic law; the most striking difference lies in way remedies are implemented. The legal principles themselves are rather straightforward: if State A breaches an obligation owed to State B (whether under a treaty[4] or under customary international law), State A must (a) stop doing whatever it was that caused the breach, (b) repair the situation by restoring it to the way it was before the breach or, if and to the extent that this is not possible, (c) compensate State B. International law recognizes that even these remedies might not be sufficient in some cases, and allows for additional remedies designed to make State B whole.[5] These new obligations of the breaching state are grouped under the heading of "reparation," which is the term used to refer to the obligations owed by a breaching state to the state injured by the breach.

Readers versed in comparative law will recognize that these principles of international law have more in common with the approach to remedies in the Civil Law system than that under the Common Law, especially as the latter is practiced in the United States: the first obligation is to restore, not to compensate; only if the situation resulting from the breach cannot be restored to what it was before the wrongful act is the defendant entitled to provide compensation to make good the plaintiff's loss. American law students and lawyers are used to the idea that if Mr. A commits a tort or breaches a contract, A will have to pay damages. The notion that A's first obligation would be to restore the situation to the *status quo ante*, and that A would only be entitled to pay the injured party money if restoration were not possible, is certainly different, and may even strike the American jurist as being rather strange. Nevertheless, that is the basic system in the Civil Law world and the one that generally applies under international law. That said, it is clear that in many instances restoration is not possible as a practical matter and the injured state will be compensated monetarily for its loss.

The reader might have noticed that thus far, remedies under international law have been discussed without regard to the nature of the obligation breached — whether analogous to a tort, a breach of contract, or other wrong in the field of civil law. This is for good reason, since international law generally does not differentiate between types of obligations in its rules on remedies (states are free, of course, to create specific remedial regimes for particular obligations)[6]. Whatever the source of the obligation breached, the wrongdoing state must make reparation. The exceptions to this general principle are matters of degree rather

---

[4] The explanation in the text assumes the treaty has no self-contained remedial regime.

[5] These additional remedies fall under the heading of "satisfaction," which will be discussed below.

[6] As noted at the outset of this chapter, it is not uncommon for treaties to contain their own remedial systems. The agreements in the field of international trade law are one example. *See* note 2, *supra*.

than kind and have more to do with how fundamental the obligation was and the seriousness of the breach[7] than with whether the obligation arose from, e.g., a trade agreement or rule of customary law prohibiting harmful transboundary pollution. And even in those exceptional cases, the obligation to make reparation still applies; it is the additional consequences of the breach that are different. Of course, the most fundamental obligations and the most serious breaches tend to involve the United Nations Charter, which contains its own enforcement regime, involving principally the Security Council.[8] The United Nations system of enforcement, or remedies, will be addressed in Chapter 8 on the Use of Force by States.

The ideas of fundamental obligations and serious breaches raise the question of criminal responsibility. The notion that a state might be criminally responsible has been a very controversial one.[9] It was originally proposed by the International Law Commission in Article 19 of its draft articles on State Responsibility, adopted in 1976. That article read:

"Article 19

International crimes and international delicts

1. An act of a State which constitutes a breach of an international obligation is an internationally wrongful act, regardless of the subject-matter of the obligation breached.

2. An internationally wrongful act which results from the breach by a State of an international obligation so essential for the protection of fundamental interests of the international community that its breach is recognized as a crime by that community as a whole, constitutes an international crime.

3. Subject to paragraph 2, and on the basis of the rules of international law in force, an international crime may result, *inter alia*, from:

    (*a*) a serious breach of an international obligation of essential importance for the maintenance of international peace and security, such as that prohibiting aggression;

    (*b*) a serious breach of an international obligation of essential importance for safeguarding the right of self-determination of peoples, such as that prohibiting the establishment or maintenance by force of colonial domination;

---

[7] *See* the discussion below (note 11, *infra,* and accompanying text) of serious breaches of obligations under general international law of a peremptory character.

[8] *See* CHARTER OF THE UNITED NATIONS, 26 June 1945, ch. VII, 59 Stat. 1031, T.S. No. 993, 3 Bevans 1153, 1976 U.N.Y.B. 1043.

[9] *See generally* JOSEPH WEILER, ANTONIO CASSESE & MARINA SPINEDI eds., INTERNATIONAL CRIMES OF STATES (1989); and N. JØRGENSEN, THE RESPONSIBILITY OF STATES FOR INTERNATIONAL CRIMES (2000).

(c) a serious breach on a widespread scale of an international
obligation of essential importance for safeguarding the
human being, such as those prohibiting slavery, genocide and
apartheid;

(d) a serious breach of an international obligation of essential
importance for the safeguarding and preservation of the
human environment, such as those prohibiting massive pollution of the atmosphere or of the seas.

4. Any internationally wrongful act which is not an international
crime in accordance with paragraph 2 constitutes an international
delict."[10]

It is likely that the notion of state crimes in general, and this provision in
particular, were informed in part by political considerations prevalent in the
1970s. In any event, the final version of the draft articles, adopted by the ILC
in 2001, does not recognize the idea of state crimes. Instead, it specifies additional consequences of a "serious breach of an obligation" arising under a
peremptory norm of general international law[11] — which is to say, a serious
breach of an obligation of fundamental importance to the international community. This approach to the consequences of particularly serious breaches of
international law will be discussed below. But the list of examples in paragraph 3 of the ill-fated Article 19, set forth above, affords an idea of the kinds
of wrongful acts of states that are considered to be particularly serious.

As to crimes under international law, since the Nuremberg Trials
they have been associated with individuals — chiefly state officials —
rather than states themselves. As the Nuremberg Tribunal famously
stated in 1946, "Crimes against international law are committed by
men, not by abstract entities, and only by punishing individuals who
commit such crimes can the provisions of international law be
enforced."[12] This tendency was reinforced in the 1990s by the establishment of *ad hoc* international criminal tribunals for the Former
Yugoslavia[13] and Rwanda,[14] and the first standing tribunal, the

---

[10] [1976] 2 Y.B. Int'l L. Comm'n, pt. 2, 95-96.

[11] *See* Draft Articles on Responsibility of States for Internationally Wrongful Acts,
adopted by the International Law Commission on second reading at its fifty-third session
(2001), ch. III, arts. 40 and 41, and commentaries, [2001] 2 Y.B. Int'l L. Comm'n, pt. 2,
277-292, *available at* http://www.un.org/law/ilc/ (hereafter ILC Draft Articles). The concept of
a peremptory, or overriding, norm of international law is discussed in ch. 4 on the Law of
Treaties, above.

[12] International Military Tribunal for the Trial of the Major War Criminals, judgment of
1 Oct. 1946, *reprinted in* 41 AM. J. INT'L. L. 172, 221 (1947).

[13] Statute of the International Tribunal for the Prosecution of Persons Responsible for Serious
Violations of International Humanitarian Law Committed in the Territory of the Former
Yugoslavia since 1991, 25 May 1993, U.N. Doc. S/25704 and Add.1, Annex, S.C. Res. 827 (1993),
as amended by Res. 1166 (1998) of 13 May 1998 and Res. 1329 of 30 Nov. 2000 (2000).

[14] Statute of the International Tribunal for the Prosecution of Persons Responsible for
Serious Violations of International Humanitarian Law Committed in the Territory of
Rwanda and Rwandan Citizens Responsible for such Violations Committed in the Territory
of Neighboring States, 8 Nov. 1994, approved by the U.N. Security Council in Res. 955 (1994).

International Criminal Court.[15] Thus while one can conceive of particularly reprehensible conduct of a state as being "criminal" in nature, international law has thus far confined itself to spelling out consequences of such conduct that amount to an aggravated form of international responsibility[16] and confining criminal responsibility to individuals.

A note on terminology: The title of this chapter begins with the word "remedies." While that is in effect the subject of the chapter, international law refers to this subject as "international responsibility" or "state responsibility." That nomenclature will generally be followed in this chapter. It is also worth foreshadowing a point made in Chapter 9: the field of "state responsibility" deals with the consequences of all kinds of internationally wrongful acts of states; "state responsibility for injuries to aliens," discussed in Chapter 9,[17] is a subset of the field of state responsibility, dealing only with the obligations owed by states to nationals of other states and the consequences of breaching those particular obligations.

§ 7.02　GENERAL PRINCIPLES

According to the International Law Commission's draft articles, there are two basic elements of an internationally wrongful act of a state. First, that the conduct in question, whether an act or an omission, is attributable to the state under international law; and second, that the conduct constitutes a breach of an obligation of the state under international law.[18] While the ILC's articles do contain some technical provisions concerning the legal requirements for establishing a breach of any obligation,[19] whether an actual breach occurred must be determined on a case-by-case basis — for example, whether imposing anti-dumping duties on imported steel constitutes a breach of an obligation under a trade agreement. As noted above, the rules of international law on state responsibility are general; they do not determine whether specific conduct has breached a particular rule, but are rather of generic applicability. On the other hand the first element, attribution, is in fact addressed by the law of state responsibility as discussed in the following paragraphs.

---

[15] Rome Statute of the International Criminal Court, 17 July 1998, art. 25(1), U.N. Doc. A/CONF.183/9.

[16] While not expressly called "criminal" or "penal" sanctions, the consequences for Iraq of its 1990 invasion of Kuwait set forth in U.N. Security Council resolution 687 may be viewed as having that character. *See* UNSC Res. 687, 3 Apr. 1991, which Professor Alvarez has dubbed the "mother of all resolutions." Jose E. Alvarez, *The Once and Future Security Council,* 18 THE WASHINGTON QUARTERLY, No. 2, at 3 (Spring 1995).

[17] *See* § 9.01[B].

[18] ILC Draft Articles, *supra* note 11, art. 2, at 43.

[19] *See id,* arts. 12-15, at 46. For example, art. 12, "Existence of a breach of an international obligation," provides: "There is a breach of an international obligation by a State when an act of that State is not in conformity with what is required of it by that obligation, regardless of its origin or character." *Id.*

[A]   Attribution

States, like corporations and other legal persons, are abstract entities. They cannot act by themselves. As the Permanent Court of International Justice put it in 1923, "States can act only by and through their agents and representatives."[20] But, as in the domestic law of corporations or agency, there will sometimes be a question as to whether the conduct of a particular individual or other entity can be attributed to the state. The law of state responsibility provides the general criteria for making this determination.[21] As the ILC explains, "the general rule is that the only conduct attributed to the State at the international level is that of its organs of government, or of others who have acted under the direction, instigation or control of those organs, i.e., as agents of the State."[22] Thus a state may be responsible for acts of its agencies, such as its central bank or ministry of energy. It may also be responsible for acts of individual state officials or employees, or of others who are acting under the authority, direction or control of the state.[23]

In the *Nicaragua* case, a pivotal issue was whether the breaches of international humanitarian law committed by the *contras*, irregular forces fighting against the Nicaraguan government, were attributable to the United States. The test used by the Court was one of control. The Court said:

> "There is no clear evidence of the United States having actually exercised such a degree of control in all fields as to justify treating the *contras* as acting on its behalf. . . . For this conduct [acts in violation of human rights and humanitarian law] to give rise to legal responsibility of the United States, it would in principle have to be proved that that State had effective control of the military or paramilitary operations in the course of which the alleged violations were committed."[24]

Thus the Court found that the conduct of the *contras* in question was not attributable to the United States "despite the heavy subsidies and other support provided to them by the United States. . . ."[25]

---

[20] German Settlers in Poland, 1923 P.C.I.J. (ser. B) No. 6, at 22.

[21] *See* ILC Draft Articles, *supra* note 11, arts. 4-11, at 44-45.

[22] ILC Draft Articles, *supra* note 11, commentary to Part One, Chapter II, at 80, para. 2. The ILC explains the rationale for limiting state responsibility in this way as follows: "In theory, the conduct of all human beings, corporations or collectivities linked to the State by nationality, habitual residence or incorporation might be attributed to the State, whether or not they have any connection to the government. In international law, such an approach is avoided, both with a view to limiting responsibility to conduct which engages the State as an organization, and also so as to recognize the autonomy of persons acting on their own account and not at the instigation of a public authority." *Id.*

[23] *Id,* art. 8, at 45.

[24] Military and Paramilitary Activities in and against Nicaragua (Nicaragua v. United States), Merits, 1986 I.C.J. 14, 62, and 64-65, paras. 109 and 115.

[25] *Id.* at 62.

While attribution rules are strict, there is an important exception to the general rule that "the conduct of a person or group of persons not acting on behalf of the State is not considered as an act of the State under international law."[26] The exception applies in cases where the state in effect ratifies the prior conduct — or, in the ILC's words, acknowledges the conduct and adopts it as its own. In the *Hostages* case, for example, the ICJ found that Iran became responsible for acts of the hostage-takers, despite the fact that they were not state officials or employees. The Court said: "The approval given to [the occupation of the Embassy and the detention of its diplomatic and consular staff as hostages] by the Ayatollah Khomeini and other organs of the Iranian State, and the decision to perpetuate them, translated continuing occupation of the Embassy and detention of the hostages into acts of that State."[27] While the ratification may take the form of words or conduct, it must be "clear and unequivocal;"[28] mere "approval" or "endorsement" does not necessarily involve any assumption of responsibility and is therefore not enough.[29]

A final point regarding attribution is that care should be taken not to confuse it with the effect of an international obligation. For example, if a rule of international law requires a state to protect embassies[30] or prevent transfrontier pollution,[31] it does not matter whether the person who damaged an embassy or caused the pollution was acting on behalf of the state. The rule itself requires the result, regardless of who prevented it from obtaining.[32]

[B] "Defenses" — Circumstances Precluding Wrongfulness

As we have seen, one of the elements of an internationally wrongful act of a state is that the conduct in question constitutes a breach of an obligation of the state under international law. If the state can show that its conduct did not actually amount to a breach because of the special circumstances of the case, the wrongfulness of its conduct, and thus its responsibility, will be precluded. The specific circumstances that have this effect thus serve as what we would call in domestic law a justification or excuse for failure to observe an obligation. However, it is important to note that the establishment by the state of one of these circumstances does not

---

[26] ILC Draft Articles, *supra* note 11, commentary to art. 11, at 119, para. 2.

[27] United States Diplomatic and Consular Staff in Tehran, 1980 I.C.J. 3, 35, para. 74.

[28] ILC Draft Articles, *supra* note 11, at 122, para. 8 of commentary to art. 11.

[29] *Id.* at 121, para. 6 of commentary to art. 11.

[30] *See* Vienna Convention on Diplomatic Relations, 18 Apr. 1961, art. 22(2), 500 U.N.T.S. 95, 23 U.S.T. 3227, T.I.A.S. No. 7502.

[31] *See* the Trail Smelter Arbitration (U.S. v. Canada), 3 U.N. Rep. Int'l Arb. Awards 1911, 1938 (1941).

[32] *Cf.* the former art. 21 of the ILC's draft articles, as adopted on first reading in 1980, entitled "Breach of An International Obligation Requiring the Achievement of a Specified Result." 1980 I.L.C. Rep., vol. 2, pt. 2, at 32.

make the obligation itself disappear; it is, in effect, held in abeyance for the duration of the circumstance in question — but only for that period, after which it becomes applicable once more.

The International Court of Justice brought the latter point home in the *Gabčíkovo-Nagymaros Project* case, in which Hungary had argued that the wrongfulness of its having discontinued work required under a 1977 treaty was precluded by a state of necessity. The Court answered that even if Hungary had succeeded in establishing a state of necessity, that "could not permit the conclusion that . . . it had acted in accordance with its obligations under the 1977 Treaty or that those obligations had ceased to be binding upon it. It would only permit the affirmation that, under the circumstances, Hungary would not incur international responsibility by acting as it did."[33] In other words, a state of necessity would excuse Hungary from performing its obligations under the treaty but would not eliminate them. They would subsist, and Hungary's obligation to perform them would resume once the state of necessity had passed.

The International Law Commission has identified six circumstances precluding wrongfulness and those will be the focus of our attention in this subsection. They are: consent, self-defense, countermeasures, *force majeure*, distress and necessity. The gist of many of these circumstances is suggested by their titles. However, international practice has established strict conditions for their applicability.[34] These requirements are particularly important in view of the general lack of compulsory dispute resolution in the international system, which means little room should be left to argue whether a particular circumstance applies. Let us look briefly at each of these circumstances.

Consent[35] by a state to an act by another state will generally preclude the wrongfulness of that act. Of course, the consent must be valid[36] and the act must conform to the scope of the consent.[37] Common examples of governmental consent to acts which would otherwise be wrongful include "transit through the airspace or internal waters of a State, the location of facilities on its territory or the conduct of official investigations or inquiries there."[38]

---

[33] Gabčíkovo-Nagymaros Project (Hungary/Slovakia), 1997 I.C.J. 7, 39, para. 48.

[34] In addition to the conditions applicable to each of these circumstances individually, an overarching condition is that the wrongfulness of a state's act that breaches a peremptory, or overriding, norm of general international law cannot precluded by any of the circumstances listed. *See* art. 26, ILC Draft Articles, *supra* note 11, at 50.

[35] *See* art. 20 of the ILC Draft Articles, *supra* note 11, at 48.

[36] Whether consent given by a state was valid has to do with issues such as whether it came from an authorized source and whether it was made under coercion. *See* ILC Draft Articles, *supra* note 11, at 174, para. 4 of the commentary to art. 20.

[37] *See* art. 20 of the ILC Draft Articles, *supra* note 11, at 48.

[38] *Id.* at 174, para. 2 of the commentary to art. 20.

Self-defense[39] is universally accepted as an exception to the prohibition against the use of force. We will examine this area in more detail in Chapter 8. If State A unjustifiably launches an armed attack against State B, thus violating the obligation to refrain from the threat or use of force under Article 2(4) of the U.N. Charter, State B is entitled by Article 51 of the Charter to use force against State A in self-defense. The fact that State B is acting in self-defense precludes what would otherwise be the wrongfulness of its use of force against State A. This does not mean that State B is subject to no other obligations in responding to State A's attack, however. The right to use force in self-defense is subject to the requirements of necessity and proportionality, and State B would remain subject to the obligations of international humanitarian law and human rights law.[40]

Countermeasures,[41] a subject we will revisit shortly, are very much like acts of self-defense, except that they do not involve the use of force. That is, a countermeasure, like a use of force in self-defense, is an act that would otherwise be unlawful except that it is a legitimate response to the prior wrongful act of another state. A common example is State A's raising of tariffs, beyond levels established in a trade agreement, on State B's goods in response to State B's breach of the agreement. In isolation, raising the tariffs would constitute a breach of State A's obligations under the trade agreement. But — assuming the requirements for a valid countermeasure are met — the fact that the tariff hike was a response to an unlawful act by State B precludes its unlawfulness. The problem here, as in much of international law, is that there is typically no authoritative determination of the prior breach; it is something that the "injured" state *alleges* to have occurred. This can lead to a spiral of acts and responses, as sometimes occurs in trade wars.[42] The conditions that must be fulfilled for a countermeasure to be legitimate will be discussed when we look at the law of countermeasures in greater detail, below.[43]

Force majeure[44] is an expression often used in the Civil Law system and in international commercial arbitration[45] to refer to an act of God or similarly unavoidable consequence. That is also the general sense in which it is used in international law. The expression has a particular meaning in the context of circumstances precluding wrongfulness, however. Since it is

---

[39] *See* art. 21 of the ILC Draft Articles, *supra* note 11, at 48.

[40] *See id.* at 178, para. 3.

[41] *See id.*, art. 22, at 48.

[42] *See, e.g.*, WTO Appellate Body Report on European Communities — Regime for Importation, Sale and Distribution of Bananas, WE/DS27/AB/R (9 Sept. 1997); and Todd Jatras, *Banana Wars Come to an End,* Forbes.com, 04.12.01, *available at* http://www.forbes.com/2001/04/12/0412bananas.html, reporting that " The European Union and the United States announced an accord [on 11 April 2001] resolving a long-running banana dispute that has been a source of constant friction between the transatlantic trading partners."

[43] *See* § 7.04, below.

[44] *See* ILC Draft Articles, *supra* note 11, art. 23, at 48-49.

[45] *See id.*, at 187, para. 8 of commentary to art. 23 and sources cited in note 381.

"quite often invoked"[46] by states to preclude the wrongfulness of their acts, it is necessary that the requirements for its proper invocation be restrictive. The ILC states the elements of *force majeure* as a countermeasure as follows:

> "1. The wrongfulness of an act of a State not in conformity with an international obligation of that State is precluded if the act is due to *force majeure*, that is the occurrence of an irresistible force or of an unforeseen event, beyond the control of the State, making it materially impossible in the circumstances to perform the obligation."[47]

Thus for a state to successfully invoke *force majeure* as an excuse for non-performance of an obligation, there must be an irresistible force or unforeseen event that is beyond the control of the state, making it actually impossible in the circumstances to perform the obligation.[48] Therefore it is not enough that the obligation has merely become more difficult to perform. *Force majeure* may take the form of a natural event, such as bad weather forcing an aircraft into another state's territory, or human conduct, such as that of an insurrectional movement.[49]

Distress,[50] a rather emotional term to apply to interstate relations, actually has to do with the conduct of individuals. The term refers to the circumstance where, due to a "situation of distress,"[51] an individual whose conduct is attributable to the state has no choice but to commit the act in question in order to save his or her own life or the lives of others for whom the actor is responsible. "In practice, cases of distress have mostly involved aircraft or ships entering State territory under stress of weather or following mechanical or navigational failure."[52] The entry of a state aircraft or vessel into the territory of another state without permission is an internationally wrongful act; the wrongfulness would be precluded if the entry were due to distress. The ILC's formulation of the doctrine of distress is "limited to cases where human life is at stake,"[53] and this indeed is the usual situation. However, arbitral tribunals have, on occasion, allowed the plea of distress when only a serious threat to health was involved.[54]

---

[46] *Id.* at 183, para. 1 of commentary to art. 23.

[47] Art. 23(1), *id.* at 48.

[48] Other conditions for the invocation of *force majeure* are set forth in para. 2 of art. 23, *id.* at 49, *viz.*, that the situation cannot be due to the conduct of the state invoking it, and that the state did not assume the risk that the situation would occur.

[49] *See id.* at 184, para. 3 of commentary to art. 23.

[50] *See id.*, art. 24, at 49.

[51] *Id.*, art. 24(1).

[52] *Id.* at 189, para. 2 of commentary to art. 24.

[53] *Id.* at 192, para. 6 of commentary to art. 24.

[54] This was the case in particular of the *Rainbow Warrior* arbitration, (New Zealand/France), 20 U.N. Rep. Int'l Arb. Awards 217 (1990), 82 I.L.R. 500 (1990), in which France entered a plea of distress to justify its removal, contrary to a prior agreement, of two of its officers who had been confined on the island of Hao for the bombing in a New Zealand harbor of the *Rainbow Warrior*, a Greenpeace vessel protesting French nuclear tests in the South Pacific.

Necessity[55] has the ring of a defense whose inherently subjective nature would allow the state relying upon it to do almost anything: "It is necessary that we place an embargo on your goods," or "arrest your ambassador," or "divert the entire river we once shared," or the like. The danger of allowing unbridled invocation of necessity has been confirmed by writers from Publius, ca. 42 B.C.,[56] to Milton in the 17th century.[57] International practice has therefore cabined its availability considerably, as reflected in this formulation of the defense by the ILC:

> "1. Necessity may not be invoked by a State as a ground for pre-cluding the wrongfulness of an act not in conformity with an international obligation of that State unless the act:
>
> (*a*) Is the only way for the State to safeguard an essential interest against a grave and imminent peril; and
>
> (*b*) Does not seriously impair an essential interest of the State or States towards which the obligation exists, or of the international community as a whole.
>
> 2. In any case, necessity may not be invoked by a State as a ground for precluding wrongfulness if:
>
> (*a*) The international obligation in question excludes the possibility of invoking necessity; or
>
> (*b*) The State has contributed to the situation of necessity."[58]

The meaning of "necessity" as a circumstance precluding wrongfulness is encapsulated in narrative form as follows: "The term 'necessity' . . . is used to denote those exceptional cases where the only way a State can safeguard an essential interest threatened by a grave and imminent peril is, for the time being, not to perform some other international obligation of lesser weight or urgency."[59] In the *Gabčíkovo-Nagymaros Project* case, a state of environmental necessity was invoked by Hungary as a ground for precluding the wrongfulness of its breach of the treaty involved in the dispute by discontinuing work on a dam project. The Court applied an earlier version of the ILC's draft article, observing that "such ground for precluding wrongfulness can only be accepted on an exceptional basis."[60] It ultimately rejected Hungary's plea as not satisfying a number of the requirements of the defense.[61]

---

[55] ILC Draft Articles, *supra* note 11, at 49.

[56] "Necessity knows no law except to conquer." Maxim 553, PUBLILIUS SYRUS (Darius Lyman transl.) (Ca. 42 B.C.).

[57] "And with necessity, The tyrant's plea, excus'd his devilish deeds." JOHN MILTON, PARADISE LOST, Book IV, line 393.

[58] ILC Draft Articles, *supra* note 11, at 49.

[59] *Id.* at 194, para. 1 of commentary to art. 25.

[60] Gabčíkovo-Nagymaros Project (Hungary/Slovakia), 1997 I.C.J. 7, 40, para. 51.

[61] *Id.* at 41-46, paras. 53-58.

§ 7.03   OBLIGATIONS OF THE WRONGDOING STATE

[A]   Introduction

When a state breaches an international obligation, new legal obligations arise. This is true regardless of the source of the obligation breached, whether a treaty or customary international law. It is akin to saying that when Mr. X breaches a contract or commits a tort, X has new legal obligations — i.e., to pay damages or to otherwise remedy the wrong done to the injured party. The new obligations for a breaching state that follow from its wrongful act fall into two main categories. They may be summed up as follows: the state committing the breach must cease any continuing wrongful conduct and offer the injured state any appropriate assurances of non-repetition;[62] and it must make full reparation for the injury caused by its breach.[63] Of course, breaching an obligation does not make it disappear, so in addition to its new obligations the wrongdoing state also has a continuing duty to perform that obligation.[64] Let us now look more closely at the law of reparation.

[B]   Reparation

As indicated earlier, the duty to make reparation is the principal consequence of breaching an international obligation. The leading case, or *locus classicus*, on the law of reparation is the *Chorzow Factory* case,[65] decided by the Permanent Court of International Justice in 1927. The Court stated the obligation to make reparation in the following terms: "It is a principle of international law that the breach of an engagement involves an obligation to make reparation in an adequate form. Reparation therefore is the indispensable complement of a failure to apply a convention and there is no necessity for this to be stated in the convention itself."[66] The Court was speaking of the breach of a treaty in that case, but the principle it articulated holds true for the breach of obligations under general international law, as well.

As to exactly what the obligation to make reparation entails, the Court had the following to say:

"The essential principle contained in the actual notion of an illegal act — a principle which seems to be established by international

---

[62] *See* art. 30 of the ILC Draft Articles, *supra* note 11, at 51. Regarding assurances that the wrongful act will not be repeated, art. 30(2) provides that the state responsible for the internationally wrongful act is under an obligation "[t]o offer appropriate assurances and guarantees of non-repetition, if circumstances so require." *Id.* Such assurances were sought by Germany in the *LaGrand* case and the ICJ upheld its jurisdiction to grant such relief. *See* LaGrand, (Germany v. United States), Merits, judgment of 27 June 2001, 2001 I.C.J. 466, paras. 48, 124 and 125.

[63] *See* art. 31 of the ILC Draft Articles, *supra* note 11, at 51.

[64] *See* art. 29 of the ILC Draft Articles, *id.* at 50.

[65] Factory at Chorzow, Jurisdiction, 1927 P.C.I.J (ser. A) No. 9.

[66] *Id.* at 21.

practice and in particular by the decisions of arbitral tribunals — is that reparation must, so far as possible, wipe out all the consequences of the illegal act and re-establish the situation which would, in all probability, have existed if that act had not been committed. Restitution in kind, or, if this is not possible, payment of a sum corresponding to the value which a restitution in kind would bear; the award, if need be, of damages for loss sustained which would not be covered by restitution in kind or payment in place of it — such are the principles which should serve to determine the amount of compensation due for an act contrary to international law."[67]

This famous passage lays out in a general way the components, or forms, of reparation. Let us now take a closer look at those elements, which are usually referred to as restitution, compensation and satisfaction.

[1] Restitution

The best way to "wipe out all the consequences of the illegal act and re-establish the situation which would, in all probability, have existed if that act had not been committed"[68] is to actually restore the situation to the *status quo ante* — the state of affairs that existed before the breach. This is what is contemplated by restitution, sometimes referred to as *restitutio in integrum*[69] or restitution in kind. In this sense, then, restitution does not mean the payment of compensation for harm resulting from the breach. It means undoing the harm, to the extent possible. Other than continuing to perform the obligation and ceasing any continuing wrongful conduct, restitution is the first obligation of the breaching state (sometimes called the "author" of the internationally wrongful act).

Clearly, however, not all situations are capable of being restored to their original state, and even those that are will not be precisely as they were prior to the breach. Thus international law does not require the breaching state to do the impossible[70] or even to bear burdens out of all proportion to the benefit to be received by the injured state.[71] If and to the extent that restoration of the situation is impossible or unduly burdensome, the breaching state is permitted to pay compensation. This is reflected in the ILC's draft article on restitution, according to which the wrongdoing state is obligated to "re-establish the situation which existed before the wrongful act was committed, provided and to the extent that restitution: (*a*) Is not materially impossible; (*b*) Does not involve a burden

---

[67] *Id.* at 47.

[68] *Id.*

[69] On the various definitions and meanings of this expression, *see* Gaetano Arangio-Ruiz, Preliminary Report on State Responsibility, [1988] 2 Y.B. Int'l L. Comm'n, pt. 1, 6, 21-23.

[70] Restoration to the *status quo ante* would be impossible, for example, where the object in question had been destroyed. For discussion and references *see* ILC Draft Articles, *supra* note 11, at 242-243, paras. 8-10 of commentary to art. 35.

[71] For a brief discussion and references, *see id.* at 243, para. 11 of commentary to art. 35.

out of all proportion to the benefit deriving from restitution instead of compensation."[72] Examples of restitution include evacuation of invaded territory, the release of diplomatic personnel or other persons wrongfully detained, the restoration of property, such as aircraft or ships, and the reversal of a governmental act that violates international law — so-called juridical restitution.[73]

[2] Compensation

As we have seen, the obligation to compensate the injured state arises in principle only if and to the extent that the wrongdoing state cannot re-establish the situation that existed prior to the breach — that is, to the extent that restitution is not possible. However, the injured state may elect to receive compensation rather than restitution,[74] as Germany did in the *Chorzow Factory* case.[75] In fact, according to the International Law Commission, "[o]f the various forms of reparation, compensation is perhaps the most commonly sought in international practice."[76]

Compensation is sometimes referred to as restitution by equivalent,[77] as distinguished from restitution in kind. This conveys well the purpose of compensation: to make the injured state whole, not by restoring the situation but by paying a sum of money that corresponds, or is equivalent, to the injured state's loss. Compensation, as so understood, covers only material damage, not moral injury. The latter kind of harm is the subject of the third form of reparation, satisfaction, which may also include the payment of exemplary damages as we will see presently. However, international practice amply supports the proposition that compensation covers "any financially assessable damage including loss of profits insofar as it is established."[78] Financially assessable damage[79] includes not only damage to the state itself but also damage to its nationals, whether individuals or legal persons.[80] In the *Corfu Channel* case,[81] in which the United

---

[72] *Id.*, art. 35, at 52.

[73] *Id.* at 240, para. 5 of commentary to art. 35. *See also* Arangio-Ruiz, Preliminary Report, *supra* note 69, at 23-24, para. 73.

[74] *See* ILC Draft Articles, *supra* note 11, art. 43(2)(b), at 54, and para. 6 of the commentary to that article, at 303-304.

[75] Factory at Chorzow, Jurisdiction, 1927 P.C.I.J. (ser. A) No. 9, at 17.

[76] ILC Draft Articles, *supra* note 11, at 244, para. 2 of commentary to art. 36.

[77] For a detailed discussion of reparation by equivalent, with full citations, *see* Gaetano Arangio-Ruiz, Second Report on State Responsibility, [1989] 2 Y.B. Int'l L. Comm'n, pt. 1, 8-30.

[78] ILC Draft Articles, *supra* note 11, art. 36(2), at 52.

[79] For a detailed discussion of financially compensable damage, including types of damage, methods of quantification, lost profits and interest, *see id.* at 248-263, paras. 8-34 of commentary to art. 36.

[80] *See id.* at 246, para. 5 of commentary to art. 36. The field of state responsibility for injuries to aliens, which is a subset of the law of state responsibility, is discussed in ch. 9, § 9.01[B]. It is there explained that a state may make a claim against another state on behalf of a national of the former that was wrongfully injured by the latter state.

[81] Corfu Channel case (Assessment of Compensation), 1949 I.C.J. 244.

Kingdom sued Albania to recover for damage to warships and crew from a minefield in the channel, the Court awarded the United Kingdom compensation for the total loss of one destroyer, damage sustained by another, and loss resulting from the deaths and injuries of naval personnel.

[3] Satisfaction

In some cases a combination of restitution and compensation will not provide full redress for a state's injuries. They also may not reflect adequately the culpability of the conduct of the state that committed the internationally wrongful act. Restitution and compensation may not even be appropriate in certain cases, as where the injury to the state is purely moral in character.[82] The function of satisfaction,[83] as the third form of reparation, is to address these cases.[84] Because such instances are not common, satisfaction is a "rather exceptional"[85] remedy.

Satisfaction may take various forms. According to the International Law Commission's draft articles, it "may consist in an acknowledgment of the breach, an expression of regret, a formal apology or another appropriate modality."[86] A former special rapporteur for the ILC's state responsibility project proposed a draft article providing that satisfaction would take the "form of apologies, nominal or punitive damages, punishment of the responsible individuals or assurances or safeguards against repetition, or any combination thereof."[87] A common form of satisfaction in cases where the state has suffered moral, but not material injury is a declaration by a competent tribunal that the act was wrongful.[88] There is support in state practice, judicial decisions and scholarly writings for all

---

[82] The arbitral tribunal in the *Rainbow Warrior* case observed that the "long established practice of States and international Courts and Tribunals of using satisfaction as a remedy or form of reparation . . . for the breach of an international obligation . . . relates particularly to the case of moral or legal damage done directly to the State. . . ." Rainbow Warrior (New Zealand/France), 20 UNRIAA 217, 272-273 (1990). *See also* ILC Draft Articles, *supra* note 11, at 264-265, para. 4 of commentary to art. 37.

[83] *See* ILC Draft Articles, *supra* note 11, art. 37, at 52-53.

[84] According to a draft article proposed by a special rapporteur of the International Law Commission, the form of satisfaction is to be determined by "taking into account the importance of the obligation breached and the existence and degree of wilful intent or negligence of the State which has committed the wrongful act." Arangio-Ruiz, Second Report, *supra* note 77, at 56, proposed draft art. 10(2).

[85] ILC Draft Articles, *supra* note 11, at 263, para. 1 of commentary to art. 37.

[86] *Id.*, art. 37(2), at 52.

[87] Arangio-Ruiz, Second Report, *supra* note 77, at 56, proposed draft art. 10(1).

[88] *See* ILC Draft Articles, *supra* note 11, at 266, para. 6 of commentary to art. 37; the Corfu Channel case, Merits, 1949 I.C.J. 4, 35-36 (the Court's finding that the British minesweeping operation violated Albanian sovereignty "is in itself appropriate satisfaction"); and the Rainbow Warrior case (New Zealand v. France), France-New Zealand Arbitration Tribunal, 82 I.L.R. 500, para. 123 (1990) ("the condemnation of the French Republic for its breaches of its treaty obligations to New Zealand, made public by the decision of the Tribunal, constitutes in the circumstances appropriate satisfaction for the legal and moral damage caused to New Zealand.").

of these forms[89] (though the International Law Commission takes the position that "satisfaction is not intended to be punitive in character, nor does it include punitive damages"[90]). However, while satisfaction serves an important function in the rather rare cases in which it is appropriate, it is also well recognized that if it is not to be counterproductive[91] it should "not be out of proportion to the injury and may not take a form humiliating to the responsible State."[92]

§ 7.04   COUNTERMEASURES

A countermeasure is a measure taken by an injured state in response to an internationally wrongful act. The term "countermeasure" is normally used to refer to such a responsive measure that would itself be unlawful but for the fact that it is taken in order to encourage the wrongdoing state to comply with its obligations of continued performance, cessation and reparation.[93] But to be lawful a countermeasure must be kept within permissible bounds, as we will see shortly. In the largely decentralized system of international law, countermeasures may be seen as a means of implementing norms of state responsibility. They are thus not frowned upon in the way self-help is in domestic legal systems. Taking the law into one's own hands could lead to anarchy on the national level but unless states were allowed to respond in an appropriate way to wrongs they suffer there might be no implementation or enforcement at all of many norms of international law. What is an "appropriate way" in which to respond to an internationally wrongful act is determined by the rules governing countermeasures.

Countermeasures are also referred to as "reprisals." The latter term is not preferred today, however, as it is liable to give rise to confusion. The confusion stems from the fact that the term reprisal was formerly used to refer to the use of armed force in response to an internationally wrongful act; hence the expression "armed reprisal." However, today armed reprisals that do not qualify as self-defense under Article 51 of the United Nations Charter, or are not permissible "belligerent reprisals" taken in time of armed conflict,[94] are unlawful. Countermeasures should also be

---

[89] *See* the ILC's commentary to art. 37, ILC Draft Articles, *supra* note 11, at 263-268; and Arangio-Ruiz, Second Report, *supra* note 77, at 31-42.

[90] ILC Draft Articles, *supra* note 11, at 268, para. 8 of commentary to art. 37.

[91] Humiliation of a state may arouse its population to demand retaliation or at least to resent strongly the injured state. Humiliating or disproportionate forms of satisfaction would also be inconsistent with the sovereign equality of states. *See id.* at 268, para. 8 of commentary to art. 37.

[92] *Id.*, art. 37(3), at 53.

[93] The ILC Draft Articles use the term in this way. *See id.* at 324, para. 1 of commentary to ch. II.

[94] A belligerent reprisal would be an otherwise unlawful response to a measure that was itself unlawful taken during armed conflict. Civilians enjoy protection from such reprisals. *See* 1977 Geneva Protocol I Additional to the Geneva Conventions of 12 August 1949, and Relating to the Protection of Victims of International Armed Conflicts, art. 51, 1125 U.N.T.S. 3 (1979) (prohibiting attacks on civilians).

distinguished from retorsion, an unfriendly but legal response (such as suspending aid or recalling an ambassador) to an act which may be unlawful.

The *locus classicus* on the law of countermeasures, then referred to as reprisals, is the 1928 *Naulilla* arbitration.[95] In that case, German troops attacked Naulilaa and other Portuguese outposts in Angola, then a Portuguese colony, in response to the killing of three Germans and confinement of two others who were members of a delegation visiting Naulilaa, a Portuguese border post. The German attack caused casualties and property damage. Portugal claimed damages and the two countries established an arbitral tribunal to adjudicate the claim.

The tribunal declared that the *sine qua non* of a right to resort to reprisals is the prior commission of an internationally wrongful act; that even then a reprisal is lawful only when it follows an unsatisfied demand; and that, while precise proportionality between act and response is not required, the response must not be out of all portion to the act. There was doctrinal debate at the time regarding whether there was in fact a requirement of proportionality. But the tribunal was of the view that "even if one were to admit that the law of nations does not require that the reprisal should be approximately in keeping with the offence, one should certainly consider as excessive and therefore unlawful reprisals out of all proportion to the act motivating them."[96] Applying these requirements, the tribunal found that the German responses could not be considered to be legal reprisals because Germany had made no prior demand and because its response was manifestly disproportionate to Portugal's act.

A more recent case dealing with countermeasures, and in particular the question of proportionality, is the *Air Services* arbitration of 1978.[97] In that case, the United States prohibited flights by certain French carriers to Los Angeles in response to France's having prevented passengers on a Pan American flight from disembarking in Paris. France claimed that Pan American's change of gauge, or transfer of passengers to a smaller plane, in London while en route from the west coast to Paris, violated the 1946 Air Services Agreement between the two countries and therefore that its refusal to allow the passengers to leave the plane in Paris was justified. The United States' rejection of this contention led it to respond as described above. The two countries agreed to submit the dispute to arbitration, following which the U.S. did not implement its ban.

On the question of proportionality, the tribunal stated that "[i]t is generally agreed that all counter-measures must, in the first instance, have some degree of equivalence with the alleged breach. . . ."[98] After

---

[95] "Naulilaa" (Responsibility of Germany for damage caused in the Portuguese colonies in the south of Africa) (Portugal/Germany), award of 31 July 1928, 2 UNRIAA 1013 (1949).

[96] *Id.* at 1028.

[97] Air Services Agreement of 27 March 1946 (United States/France), 18 UNRIAA 416, 54 I.L.R. 304 (1978).

[98] *Id.*, para. 83.

acknowledging that "judging the 'proportionality' of counter-measures is not an easy task,"[99] the tribunal concluded that "the measures taken by the United States do not appear to be clearly disproportionate when compared to those taken by France . . ." — even though the countermeasures "were rather more severe in terms of their economic effect on the French carriers than the initial French action."[100] Thus the tribunal did not require exact proportionality — something that usually would not be present[101] — but simply that the countermeasures not be "clearly disproportionate" to the internationally wrongful act.

The pendulum now seems to have swung fully back to the pre-*Naulilaa* days when proportionality was clearly a condition of a legitimate countermeasure. The International Law Commission's draft articles illustrate this, even couching the requirement in positive terms: "Countermeasures must be commensurate with the injury suffered, taking into account the gravity of the internationally wrongful act and the rights in question."[102] This language echoes that of the International Court of Justice in the *Gabčíkovo-Nagymaros Project* case: "In the view of the Court, an important consideration is that the effects of a countermeasure must be commensurate with the injury suffered, taking account of the rights in question."[103] The Court then found that "Czechoslovakia, by unilaterally assuming control of a shared resource, and thereby depriving Hungary of its right to an equitable and reasonable share of the natural resources of the Danube . . . failed to respect the proportionality which is required by international law. . . . The Court thus considers that the diversion of the Danube carried out by Czechoslovakia was not a lawful countermeasure because it was not proportionate."[104] Clearly, then, the countermeasure must be proportionate to the wrongful act. What other conditions must be observed for a countermeasure to be legitimate?[105]

We have already seen that one of these conditions is, as the *Naulilaa* tribunal found, an unsatisfied demand. If after such a demand, or notice of claim,[106] is made, the state to which it is addressed complies with the claim and fulfills the other obligations resulting from its wrongful act, the injured state may not take countermeasures. This is because the purpose of countermeasures would have been served, and there would no longer be a wrongful act to which it could lawfully

---

[99] *Id.*

[100] ILC Draft Articles, *supra* note 11, at 342, para. 3 of commentary to art. 51.

[101] Countermeasures would be exactly proportional when the same action was taken in response as had been taken initially — e.g., raising the same tariff by the same amount.

[102] ILC Draft Articles, *supra* note 11, art. 51, Proportionality, at 57.

[103] Gabčíkovo-Nagymaros Project (Hungary/Slovakia), 1997 I.C.J. 7, 56, para. 85.

[104] *Id.* at 56, paras. 85 and 87.

[105] The International Law Commission addresses this question in art. 52 of its draft articles, "Conditions relating to resort to countermeasures." *See* ILC Draft Articles, *supra* note 11, art. 52, at 57-58.

[106] *See id.*, art. 43, "Notice of claim by an injured State," at 54.

respond.[107] The ILC's draft requires not only that the injured state make a demand, but also that it offer to negotiate with the responsible state prior to resorting to countermeasures.[108] However, it would also allow the injured state to take "such urgent countermeasures as are necessary to preserve its rights"[109] notwithstanding the obligations to notify the responsible state and offer to negotiate.

An important aspect of the ILC's treatment of conditions for resort to countermeasures is that it would not allow countermeasures to be taken if "[t]he dispute is pending before a court or tribunal which has the authority to make decisions binding on the parties."[110] This issue had been debated in the International Law Commission and the *Air Services* tribunal was of the view that the injured state may take countermeasures even if the parties had agreed to settlement by a court or arbitral tribunal.[111] But this is not inconsistent with the Commission's position, which makes sense so long as the court or tribunal can actually take action on the dispute, alleviating the necessity for the injured party to act. The ILC's commentary makes clear that the injured state would not have to refrain from taking countermeasures unless this were the case.[112]

§ 7.05   ALTERNATIVES TO THE TRADITIONAL APPROACH: ACCOUNTABILITY AND COMPLIANCE

Recent treaties, especially in the field of the environment,[113] have developed new approaches to the implementation of international obligations. These approaches begin from the premise that the object of a system for dealing with breaches of international obligations is that the breaching state resume compliance with its obligations, not that it be punished or retaliated against in some way for breaching them. The new approaches also take into account states' well-known reluctance to submit to compulsory dispute resolution mechanisms that may produce an authoritative determination of wrongfulness, responsibility or liability. The principal techniques, which will be considered briefly in the following paragraphs, may be grouped under the headings of incentives and "sunshine" or spotlighting.[114]

---

[107] *See id.*, art. 52(3)(a), stating that the injured state may not take countermeasures if "[t]he internationally wrongful act has ceased. . . ." *Id.* at 58.

[108] *Id.*, art. 52(1)(b), at 57.

[109] *Id.*, art. 52(2).

[110] *Id.*, art. 52(3)(b).

[111] Air Services Agreement of 27 March 1946 (United States/France), 18 UNRIAA 416, 54 I.L.R. 304 (1978), para. 89.

[112] ILC Draft Articles, *supra* note 11, at 347-348, paras. 7 and 8 of commentary to art. 52.

[113] *See, e.g.,* Edith Brown Weiss, *Strengthening National Compliance with International Environmental Agreements,* 27 ENVTL. POL'Y & L. 297 (1997); and PETER SAND, LESSONS LEARNED IN GLOBAL ENVIRONMENTAL GOVERNANCE 31-34 (1990).

[114] *See* Brown Weiss, *supra* note 113.

Incentives may, of course, be either positive or negative. Since the more innovative method involves positive incentives, they will be focused upon here. The theory behind the use of positive incentives is that a noncomplying state in fact wishes to comply but for various reasons, usually relating to lack of adequate capacity or funding, is unable to. Such incentives "may take the form of training materials and seminars, special funds for financial or technical assistance, access to technology, or bilateral assistance outside the framework of the [treaty involved]."[115] Taking special funds as an illustration, funds to assist parties in complying with their treaty obligations have been established under a number of multilateral environmental agreements, including the 1972 World Heritage Convention,[116] and the Montreal Protocol on Substances that Deplete the Ozone Layer.[117] Funding to assist in meeting compliance costs is also provided for by the U.N. Framework Convention on Climate Change[118] and the U.N. Convention on Biological Diversity.[119]

A good illustration of the "sunshine" or spotlighting approach is provided by the citizen submission procedure under the North American Agreement on Environmental Cooperation (NAAEC)[120] concluded by Canada, Mexico and the United States in 1993. The Agreement requires each of the three countries to "ensure that its laws and regulations provide for high levels of environmental protection,"[121] and further to "effectively enforce its environmental laws and regulations through appropriate governmental action. . . ."[122] It also establishes the Commission for Environmental Cooperation (CEC),[123] which is composed of a Council, a Joint Public Advisory Committee, or JPAC, and a Secretariat.[124] The NAAEC provides for an innovative procedure, which — along with the JPAC — allows civil society to participate in the implementation of the agreement.

---

[115] *Id.* at 301.

[116] Convention concerning the Protection of the World Cultural and Natural Heritage, 16 Nov. 1972, 27 U.S.T. 37, 1037 U.N.T.S. 151.

[117] 16 Sept. 1987, *reprinted in* 26 I.L.M. 1550 (1987). For information and decisions on the Protocol's non-compliance procedures, *see* the website of the Secretariat, at the United Nations Environment Programme, http://www.unep.org/ozone/issues.shtml. According to the Secretariat, the non-compliance procedure has not been changed since the 1998 version reflected on the website, which is still in use. Personal communication from Ozone Secretariat, 1 Sept. 2005.

[118] U.N. Framework Convention on Climate Change, 5 June 1992, art. 14, 1771 U.N.T.S. 108, *reprinted in* 31 I.L.M. 849 (1992).

[119] U.N. Convention on Biological Diversity, 31 I.L.M. 818 (1992).

[120] 14 Sept. 1993, 32 I.L.M. 1480 (1993).

[121] *Id.*, art. 3.

[122] *Id.*, art. 5(1).

[123] *Id.*, art. 8. *See generally* the CEC website, http://www.cec.org/home/index.cfm?varlan=english.

[124] *Id.*, art. 8(2).

Article 14 of the NAAEC allows an individual or non-governmental organization to file a "submission" with the Secretariat "asserting that a Party is failing to effectively enforce its environmental law. . . ."[125] If the submission satisfies the rather straightforward criteria set out in the article, the Secretariat determines whether it merits requesting a response from the country in question. The Secretariat may then decide, in light of any response, whether the submission merits recommending to the Council that a "Factual Record" be prepared.[126] If the Secretariat makes such a recommendation, the Council may, by a two-thirds vote, instruct the Secretariat to prepare a factual record.[127] The final step in the process is the possibility of making the factual record publicly available, which the Council may decide to do, again by a two-thirds vote. As of August, 2005, the Secretariat had prepared ten of these factual records, all of which have been made public, and had submitted an eleventh to the Council for its decision on whether to make it publicly available.

Thus the citizen submission process allows citizens to participate in encouraging compliance with obligations under international law. It also brings to light failures to comply with international obligations. States typically would prefer to avoid being spotlighted in this way, which gives them an incentive to remain in compliance with their obligations.

---

[125] *Id.*, art. 14(1). *See generally* the CEC web page on citizen submissions on enforcement matters, http://www.cec.org/citizen/index.cfm?varlan=english.

[126] *Id.*, art. 15(1).

[127] *Id.*, art. 15(2)

Chapter 8
THE USE OF FORCE BY STATES

Synopsis

§ 8.01   INTRODUCTION

This chapter deals with the circumstances under which international law permits a state to use force against another state or states. The "use of force" is another way of referring to activities variously described as war, military activity, armed conflict, and the like. Since the end of the Second World War and the entry into force of the United Nations Charter, states have been prohibited from using force against other states except in self-defense. Like any apparently simple proposition, however, this one is not always easy to apply. Furthermore, arguments have recently been made that the prohibition should be relaxed or even that it is obsolete altogether in today's world. As is the case of other branches of international law, the state of the law today on the use of force as well where it might be going may be better understood through an understanding of its historical development.

[A]   Historical Development

One need only recall the practice of European powers of claiming title to territory by conquest, especially in the seventeenth and eighteenth centuries, to understand how far the international community has come today in the field of the use of force. As in most other branches of international law, the norms that were the precursors of today's legal order developed first in Europe then spread from there to other regions.

A moral basis for the regulation of the use of force was provided by St. Augustine in the fifth century, through his doctrine of just war.[1] According to this theory, war could be waged against a state that had caused injury under certain circumstances: "A just war is wont to be described as one that avenges wrongs, when a nation or state has to be punished, for refusing to make amends for the wrongs inflicted by its subjects, or to restore what it has seized unjustly."[2] Thus the intent, or purpose, behind the use of force were crucial for St. Augustine: "The passion for inflicting harm, the cruel thirst for vengeance, an unpacific and relentless spirit, the fever of revolt, the lust of power, and such things, all these are rightly condemned in war."[3]

But by the nineteenth century war had come to be viewed as a legitimate instrument of foreign policy, an "attribute of statehood,"[4] such that title to territory could be acquired by conquest.[5] This attitude persisted into the twentieth century and was, in effect, reflected in the Covenant of the League of Nations which was drawn up in 1919.[6] The Covenant established procedural mechanisms to encourage states to cool off before commencing hostilities[7] but, once the procedures were exhausted, a state could resort to war. This approach, while an improvement over non-regulation, seems through today's lenses to be unduly respectful of state sovereignty, only constraining minimally the use of force.

A breakthrough came in 1928 with the conclusion of the General Treaty for the Renunciation of War,[8] commonly known as the Kellogg-Briand Pact. In this treaty, which remains in force today, the "High Contracting Parties solemnly declare . . . that they condemn recourse to war for the solution of international controversies, and renounce it as an instrument of national policy in their relations with one another."[9] They also agree that the solution of

---

[1] *See* THOMAS AQUINAS, SUMMA THEOLOGICA, pt. II, ii, Q. 40, art. 1, at 1354 (Fathers of the English Dominican Province trans., Christian Classics, 1981), *available at* http://www.ccel.org/a/aquinas/summa/SS/SS040.html#SSQ40OUTP1.

For a discussion of the concept of just war in other cultural traditions *see* IAN BROWNLIE, INTERNATIONAL LAW AND THE USE OF FORCE BY STATES 3-50 (1963).

[2] THOMAS AQUINAS, *supra* note 1.

[3] *Id.*

[4] IAN BROWNLIE, PRINCIPLES OF PUBLIC INTERNATIONAL LAW 697 (6th ed. 2003).

[5] *Id.* (citing the example of the German conquest of Alsace-Lorraine, which even France then accepted as German territory).

[6] Covenant of the League of Nations, 28 June 1919, 2 Bevans 48; also in Treaty of Versailles, 28 June 1919, 225 C.T.S. 189, 22 U.S.T. 3410. A state had to exhaust procedural avenues under arts. 11-17 of the Covenant, but having done that could permissibly resort to war.

[7] Any dispute likely to lead to a "rupture" in relations was to be submitted to arbitration or to the Council of the League for inquiry. Members agreed not to resort to war until 3 months after rendition of an arbitral award, judgment or report by the Council. League of Nations Covenant, *id.*, art. 12.

[8] Treaty Providing for the Renunciation of War as an Instrument of National Policy, 27 Aug. 1928, 46 Stat. 2343, T.S. No. 796, 2 Bevans 732, 94 LNTS 57.

[9] *Id.*, art. I.

conflicts of any kind "shall never be sought except by pacific means."[10] Reservations were made by a number of important states concerning the use of force in self-defense and were accepted by the other parties.[11]

It is easy to write off the Kellogg-Briand Pact as the product of a euphoric era which was brought to an abrupt end just over a decade later by the outbreak of World War II. But the Pact laid the groundwork for the regime of the United Nations Charter concerning the use of force, and was "the foundation of State practice in the period 1928 to 1945"[12] relating to the use of force. The Kellogg-Briand pact was relied upon as one of the bases of the prosecution of the Major War Criminals before the International Military Tribunals in Nuremberg[13] and Tokyo.[14]

The United Nations Charter,[15] concluded in 1945, consolidated the practice under the Kellogg-Briand Pact and distilled it into two clear and quite specific provisions. As we will see, these provisions prohibited the threat or use of force (Article 2(4)), subject only to the "inherent right" of self-defense "if an armed attack occurs" (Article 51). They were, of course, part of a system that envisioned a Security Council able to act on behalf of the international community if need be, thus alleviating any necessity for individual states to have recourse to force except in self-defense.

[B] This Chapter

This Chapter will first examine the Charter's basic prohibition of the use of force. It will then look at self-defense as an exception to that prohibition. Finally, the chapter will consider use of force by, or with the permission of, the international community and pursuant to regional arrangements.

§ 8.02   THE BASIC PROHIBITION: ARTICLE 2(4)

Article 2, paragraph 4 of the United Nations Charter provides as follows:

> "All Members shall refrain in their international relations from the threat or use of force against the territorial integrity or political independence of any state, or in any other manner inconsistent with the Purposes of the United Nations."[16]

---

[10] *Id.*, art. II.

[11] *See* IAN BROWNLIE, INTERNATIONAL LAW AND THE USE OF FORCE 235-48 (1981). These states included Britain, Czechoslovakia, France, Japan, Romania, South Africa, and the United States.

[12] *Id.* at 698.

[13] *See* the Nuremberg Judgment, 6 F.R.D. 69 (1946).

[14] 1 THE TOKYO JUDGMENT: THE INTERNATIONAL MILITARY TRIBUNAL FOR THE FAR EAST 1 (November 1948) (BVA Roling & CF Ruter, eds. 1977).

[15] Charter of the United Nations, 26 June 1945, 59 Stat. 1031, T.S. No. 993, 3 Bevans 1153, 1976 U.N.Y.B. 1043 (hereafter UN Charter).

[16] *Id.* art. 2(4).

Further, paragraph 3 of Article 2 requires that states "settle their international disputes by peaceful mean. . . ."[17] This approach obviously represents a sharp departure from the pre-Kellogg-Briand Pact regime, in which the emphasis was not on prohibiting the use of force but on regulating the way it was used. The Pact and the U.N. Charter, born of two World Wars that produced unprecedented damage and suffering, added a strong component of *jus ad bellum* — the law governing the right to use force — to the *jus in bello* — the law applicable during wartime — that had already existed.[18]

In the *Nicaragua* case,[19] the International Court of Justice confirmed that "[t]he principle of non-use of force . . . may . . . be regarded as a principle of customary international law."[20] Both of the parties, Nicaragua and the United States, had in fact accepted this.[21] The point was important in that case because the Court could not apply the United Nations Charter due to a reservation by the United States to its acceptance of the Court's compulsory jurisdiction.[22] It is also important generally because as a customary norm, it is applicable to all states regardless of their membership in the United Nations. We will consider the *Nicaragua* case in greater detail in the following subsection.

The language of Article 2(4) is nearly absolute; the only exceptions are those contained in Article 51 (self-defense[23]) and in the Chapter VII (power of the Security Council to authorize the use of force[24]). It has occasionally been argued that the prohibition of the use of force against "the territorial integrity or political independence" of any state means that force is permissible so long as its object is not to deprive a state of territory or to interfere with its government in some way.[25] Thus, it could be contended, State A's

---

[17] *Id.* art. 2(3).

[18] The law applicable in wartime, referred to as international humanitarian law, is discussed in ch. 9, § 9.01[C], below.

[19] Military and Paramilitary Activities In and Against Nicaragua (Nicaragua v. United States), Merits, 1986 I.C.J. 14.

[20] *Id.* at 100, para. 188.

[21] *Id.* at 99, para. 187.

[22] The so-called multilateral treaty reservation provided that the United States did not accept the Court's jurisdiction with regard to "disputes arising under a multilateral treaty, unless all parties to the treaties affected by the decision are also parties to the case before the Court." 3 CUMULATIVE DIGEST OF UNITED STATES PRACTICE IN INTERNATIONAL LAW, 1981-88, 3351 (1995). Since this was obviously not the case with regard to the United Nations Charter (Nicaragua and the United States being the only states before the Court), the Court did not have jurisdiction to apply it. By letter of 7 Oct. 1985, the United States informed the U.N. Secretary General that the U.S. Declaration of acceptance of the Court's compulsory jurisdiction was terminated effective six months from that date. *See id.* at 3329, 86 DEPT. OF STATE BULL., No. 2106, Jan. 1986, at 67.

[23] *See* § 8.03, below.

[24] *See* § 8.04, below.

[25] Brownlie notes that "the United Kingdom employed this type of argument to defend the mine-sweeping operation to collect evidence within Albanian waters in the *Corfu Channel* case." BROWNLIE, *supra* note 11, at 700, citing Corfu Channel, 1949 I.C.J. 4.

troops may enter State B to protect State A against cross-border incursions by armed bands in State B provided State A withdraws when the job is done, annexes no territory and does not affect State B's political independence. However, this phrase was actually added at the San Francisco Conference in 1945 at the instance of smaller states to protect them against the more powerful states. Thus far from constituting an exception to the prohibition of force the phrase actually reinforces it.[26]

More recently it has been argued that events such as the invasions of Kosovo and Iraq (in 2003) demonstrate that the Charter's "grand attempt to subject the use of force to the rule of law ha[s] failed.[27] This frontal assault on Article 2(4)'s prohibition is based on the idea that the Charter's rules governing the use of force have "fallen victim to geopolitical forces too strong for a legalist institution to withstand"[28] — in particular, the "rise in American unipolarity. . . ."[29] Moreover, "[s]ince 1945, so many states have used armed force on so many occasions, in flagrant violation of the charter, that the regime can only be said to have collapsed."[30]

It is true that the world of today is different from that of 1945, and it is also true that force has been used on many occasions since the founding of the United Nations, in apparent violation of the Charter.[31] The fact remains, however, that all states continue to rely on the system of the Charter, probably because it is in their interest to do so. Apparent violations of Article 2(4) are defended not on the ground that the prohibition is not good law, but rather as exercises of self-defense, humanitarian intervention, or the like — that is to say, as uses of force that are permissible under the Charter, or at least in which the international community has acquiesced. In the *Nicaragua* case, the Court, speaking of the kind of state practice that is necessary to establish, or maintain, a rule of customary international law, had the following to say:

> "It is not to be expected that in the practice of States the application of the rules in question should have been perfect, in the sense that States should have refrained, with complete consistency, from

---

[26] *See, e.g.,* LELAND M. GOODRICH, ET AL., CHARTER OF THE UNITED NATIONS, COMMENTARY AND DOCUMENTS 103 and 104-105 (3d ed. 1969); and Albrecht Randelzhofer, *Article 2(4),* in BRUNO SIMMA, THE CHARTER OF THE UNITED NATIONS: A COMMENTARY 106 (1995).

[27] Michael J. Glennon, *Why the Security Council Failed,* 82 FOR. AFFAIRS 16 (2003). *See also* A.C. Arend, *International Law and the Preemptive Use of Military Force,* 26 WASH. QUARTERLY 89 (2003); and Jane E. Stromseth, *Law and Force After Iraq: A Transitional Moment,* 97 AM. J. INT'L. L. 628 (2003).

[28] Glennon, *supra* note 27.

[29] *Id.* at 18.

[30] *Id.* at 22.

[31] For a useful list of eight well-known instances of intervention (into Hungary (by the Soviet Union in 1956), Czechoslovakia (by the Soviet Union in 1958), Afghanistan (by the Soviet Union in 1979), Dominican Republic (by the United States in 1965), East Pakistan/Bangladesh (by India in 1971), Grenada (by the United States in 1983), Panama (by the United States in 1989) and Cyprus (by Turkey in 1974)), *see* DAVID J. HARRIS, INTERNATIONAL LAW 890-894 (5th ed. 1998).

the use of force or from intervention in each other's internal affairs. . . . [T]he Court deems it sufficient that the conduct of States should, in general, be consistent with such rules, and that instances of State conduct inconsistent with a given rule should generally have been treated as breaches of that rule, not as indications of the recognition of a new rule. If a State acts in a way prima facie incompatible with a recognized rule, but defends its conduct by appealing to exceptions or justifications contained within the rule itself, then whether or not the State's conduct is in fact justifiable on that basis, the significance of that attitude is to confirm rather than to weaken the rule."[32]

Thus perfect conformity with the prohibition of Article 2(4) is not necessary to the continued validity of the rule, nor should it be expected. Violations should be treated as such, and generally are,[33] and claims by states that a particular use of force was justified by an exception should be seen as reinforcing the rule rather than negating it. No state has yet directly challenged the continued legal validity of the Charter regime.[34] This is not to say that the system of the Charter cannot stand some updating to reflect contemporary realities, simply that it is premature to pronounce it dead.[35]

Having said this, it must be recognized that states have from time to time acquiesced in certain non-defensive uses of force, particularly to protect nationals in another state and in the case of "humanitarian intervention." Intervention to defend nationals suffering harm or the threat thereof in another state[36] is sometimes asserted as a ground for intervention. While it was generally accepted before 1945, its continued lawfulness is controversial.[37] Protection of nationals is still sometimes asserted as at

---

[32] Military and Paramilitary Activities In and Against Nicaragua, Merits, 1986 I.C.J. 14, 98, para. 186.

[33] Instances of intervention have usually been discussed both in the General Assembly and the Security Council. The former typically adopts a resolution condemning the action while the latter is often prevented from acting by the vetoes of one or more permanent members. For example, a draft Security Council resolution deploring the USSR's 1979 intervention in Afghanistan was vetoed by the USSR while the General Assembly adopted a resolution (by a vote of 104 to 18, with 18 abstentions) which "strongly deplored" the action (G.A. Res. ES-6/2, 6th Emerg. Sp. Sess., Supp. 1, at 2 (1980)); and a draft Security Council resolution condemning the US 1983 action in Grenada was vetoed by the US (SCOR, 2491st Meeting, 27 Oct. 1983) while the General Assembly adopted a resolution (by a vote of 108 to 9, with 27 abstentions) deploring the action (G.A. Res. 38/7, U.N. GAOR, 38th Sess., Supp. 47, at 19 (1983)).

[34] The doctrine of preemption announced by the United States in September 2002, discussed below, could be seen as an indirect challenge to the Charter system, but even the United States has avoided a frontal assault upon it.

[35] For earlier scholarship on this question, *see, e.g.*, Thomas Franck, *Who Killed Article 2(4)?*, 64 AM. J. INT'L. L. 809 (1970); and Louis Henkin, *The Reports of the Death of Article 2(4) Are Greatly Exaggerated*, 65 AM. J. INT'L. L. 544 (1971).

[36] *See generally* 1 OPPENHEIM'S INTERNATIONAL LAW 440-442 (R. Jennings & A. Watts 9th ed. 1992) (hereinafter OPPENHEIM).

[37] In support of such a right, *see, e.g.*, DEREK BOWETT, SELF DEFENSE IN INTERNATIONAL LAW 87 (1958); J.L. BRIERLY, THE LAW OF NATIONS 428 (Waldock 6th ed. 1963); 1 OPPENHEIM, *supra* note 36, at 440-442 ("there has been little disposition on the part of states to deny that

least one of the grounds justifying intervention.[38] However, it is a justification that is obviously prone to abuse,[39] particularly where the intervening state disagrees with the policies, or politics,[40] of the state that is the object of the intervention.

Like defense of nationals, humanitarian intervention[41] is a ground for the use of force that seems logical on its face but is subject to abuse and also suffers from the problem that Article 2(4) was intended to avoid: unilateral determinations to resort to force. Nevertheless, the international community may be said to have acquiesced, on occasion, to forcible intervention on humanitarian grounds, despite its *prima facie* unlawfulness under Article 2(4). There are very probably far more instances, however, in which humanitarian considerations have been cited as a justification for the use of force but have been generally rejected.

A recent and controversial example is the bombing of targets in Yugoslavia by NATO in 1999 to protect ethnic Albanians in Kosovo. While this action was defended as "an exceptional measure to prevent an overwhelming humanitarian catastrophe,"[42] it was not authorized by the U.N. Security Council and by its nature was not defensive in character. The concerns of weaker countries regarding intervention on this ground were reflected in a Ministerial Declaration adopted by the foreign ministers of the Group of 77 — a caucus of developing countries, now numbering many more than seventy-seven — several months after the NATO bombing campaign. In the declaration the ministers, from 132 African, Arab, Asian and

---

intervention properly restricted to the protection of nationals is, in emergencies, justified," *id.* at 440); and Spanish Zones of Morocco Claims (G.B. v. Spain), 2 UNRIAA 615, 640 (1925) (Huber, arbitrator). Opposed to a right of intervention to defend nationals after 1945 is, e.g., IAN BROWNLIE, INTERNATIONAL LAW AND THE USE OF FORCE BY STATES 301 (1963).

[38] When the United States sent troops into Grenada in 1983, it ultimately cited several grounds in justification of its action, including protection of its nationals. *See generally* Christopher Joyner, *Reflections on the Lawfulness of Invasion*, 78 AM. J. INT'L. L. 131 (1984). One of the best known post-1945 cases was the 1976 Israeli intervention at the Entebbe, Uganda airport to rescue mostly Israeli passengers on a hijacked aircraft. For the debate in the Security Council *see* 1976 U.N.Y.B. 315-320, 15 I.L.M. 1224 (1976). *See also* 1976 DIGEST OF UNITED STATES PRACTICE IN INTERNATIONAL LAW 149-154. More recently, France sent troops into Cote d'Ivoire (the Ivory Coast) following an insurrection there in September 2002 to protect and evacuate French nationals. *See French Evacuation Force Sent to Ivory Coast Amid Fighting*, N.Y. TIMES, 23 Sept. 2002, at A8.

[39] For example, Brierly warns that "the dispatch of troops to another state's territory to prevent an unlawful expropriation of the property of nationals and other acts of a similar kind are outside the principle and are forbidden by Article 2(4) of the Charter." BRIERLY, *supra* note 37, at 427.

[40] This appeared to be the case in the United States 1983 intervention in Grenada, where the government had established ties to Cuba and the USSR.

[41] *See generally* JOHN MURPHY, HUMANITARIAN INTERVENTION: THE UNITED NATIONS IN AN EVOLVING WORLD ORDER (1996); BROWNLIE, *supra* note 11, at 710-712; and 1 OPPENHEIM, *supra* note 36, at 442-444.

[42] Statement of Sir Jeremy Greenstock, Permanent Representative of the United Kingdom to the United Nations, 24 Mar. 1999, quoted in BROWNLIE, *supra* note 11, at 711.

Latin American states , "rejected the so-called right of humanitarian intervention, which has no basis in the UN Charter or international law."[43]

Especially when invoked by individual states to justify the otherwise unlawful use of force, humanitarian intervention "may be — and has been — abused for selfish purposes. . . ."[44] Also militating against the need for this exception is the increasing involvement of the international community, often but not always through the United Nations,[45] in the protection of individuals and groups against serious and widespread abuse by their governments. However, where the international community fails to act, as in Rwanda,[46] or does not respond with sufficient speed, as in Darfur, Sudan, there may still be some room for continued justification of at least collective intervention on humanitarian grounds.

§ 8.03 SELF-DEFENSE: ARTICLE 51

Article 51 of the United Nations Charter provides as follows:

"Nothing in the present Charter shall impair the inherent right of individual or collective self-defence if an armed attack occurs against a Member of the United Nations, until the Security Council has taken measures necessary to maintain international peace and security. Measures taken by Members in the exercise of this right of self-defence shall be immediately reported to the Security Council and shall not in any way affect the authority and responsibility of the Security Council under the present Charter to take at any time such action as it deems necessary in order to maintain or restore international peace and security."[47]

It is immediately evident that this provision does not so much create a right as preserve one: "Nothing . . . shall impair the inherent right. . . ." The description of the right as "inherent" reinforces the idea that it is something that all states possess, as an attribute of their statehood, of sovereignty.

---

[43] Ministerial Declaration of 24 Sept. 1999, para. 69, quoted in *id.*, at 712.

[44] 1 OPPENHEIM, *supra* note 36, at 443.

[45] Regional organizations as well as non-governmental organizations are often involved in the protection of human rights in cases of widespread abuse. This is the case of the humanitarian disaster (which the U.S. has called genocide) in Darfur, western Sudan, for example, where the African Union has sent troops and where many non-governmental organizations are providing humanitarian assistance. *See* Linnea D. Manashaw, *Genocide and Ethnic Cleansing: Why the Distinction? A Discussion of Atrocities Occurring in Sudan*, 35 CAL. W. INT'L L.J. 303, 327 (2005); and Somini Sengupta, *New Violence Hinders Relief Efforts in Western Sudan*, N.Y. TIMES, 3 Nov. 2004, at A9.

[46] *See, e.g.*, Philip Gourevitch, *The Genocide Fax: The United Nations Was Warned About Rwanda. Did Anyone Care?*, NEW YORKER, 11 May 1998, at 42. The Security Council did act, albeit belatedly, in adopting Resolution 929 of 1994, which authorized member states to cooperate with the Secretary-General and use "all necessary means" to conduct an operation with specified objectives in Rwanda. S.C. Res. 929, U.N. SCOR, 3392nd mtg., U.N. Doc. S/RES/929 (1994).

[47] U.N. Charter, *supra* note 15, art. 51.

In the *Nicaragua* case, the Court confirmed that the right of self-defense formed part of customary international law before the conclusion of the Charter:

> "[The Charter] itself refers to pre-existing customary international law; this reference to customary law is contained in the actual text of Article 51, which mentions the 'inherent right' (in the French text the 'droit naturel') of individual or collective self-defence, which 'nothing in the present Charter shall impair' and which applies in the event of an armed attack. The Court therefore finds that Article 51 of the Charter is only meaningful on the basis that there is a 'natural' or 'inherent' right of self-defence, and it is hard to see how this can be other than of a customary nature, even if its present content has been confirmed and influenced by the Charter."[48]

Despite its roots in pre-Charter custom, however, the right of self-defense[49] is placed under certain restrictions by Article 51. First and foremost, it is available only "if an armed attack occurs." Leaving aside for the moment the question whether an armed attack was necessary to trigger the right of self-defense before the Charter, the expression today raises a "particularly difficult issue of interpretation."[50] Second, the right only lasts "until the Security Council has taken measures necessary to maintain international peace and security." And third, any measures taken in the exercise of the right "shall be immediately reported to the Security Council. . . ." The United States ran afoul of this third condition in the *Nicaragua* case, the Court finding that although the Charter was not applicable per se for reasons discussed above, the United States' failure to report measures taken against Nicaragua "may be one of the factors indicating whether the State in question was itself convinced that it was acting in self-defence."[51]

It is also generally accepted that the use of force in self-defense is restricted by the requirements of necessity and proportionality under customary international law. The International Court stated in the *Nicaragua* case that the parties agreed that "whether the response to the attack is lawful depends on observance of the criteria of the necessity and the proportionality of the measures taken in self-defense."[52] And in its advisory opinion on the *Legality of the Threat or Use of Nuclear Weapons* the Court, in addressing the effect of environmental obligations on a state's freedom to use force in self-defense, said: "States must take environmental considerations into account when assessing what is necessary and proportionate in the pursuit of legitimate military objectives. Respect for the environment

---

[48] Military and Paramilitary Activities In and Against Nicaragua, Merits, 1986 I.C.J. 14, 94, para. 176.

[49] *See generally* BOWETT, *supra* note 37.

[50] BROWNLIE, *supra* note 11, at 700.

[51] Military and Paramilitary Activities In and Against Nicaragua, 1986 I.C.J. 14, 105, para. 200.

[52] *Id.* at 103, para. 194. The Court found that the criteria were not satisfied by the US actions. *Id.* at 122, para. 237.

is one of the elements that go to assessing whether an action is in conformity with the principles of necessity and proportionality."[53]

With regard to the "armed attack" requirement, many have questioned its continued justification in a world where an attack — especially a nuclear one — can eliminate a country's ability to defend itself. Should it not be enough that satellite photographs show missile silo doors opening and other intelligence indicates the targeting of a specific country, or even city? While this kind of logic is difficult to resist in a hypothetical world, we know all too well today that intelligence is not infallible; a mistake could start a nuclear war instead of defending against one. Furthermore, how far back can this logic be taken? To the placing of the missile in the silo? The development of the missile? The development of nuclear weapons?

The latter situation evokes the destruction of the Osiraq nuclear reactor near Baghdad, while it was still under construction, on June 7, 1981 by Israeli warplanes.[54] Israel stated: "The atomic bombs which that reactor was capable of producing whether from enriched uranium or from plutonium, would be of the Hiroshima size. Thus a mortal danger to the people of Israel progressively arose."[55] The U.N. Security Council did not accept this justification, adopting a resolution later that month stating that it "strongly condemns the military attack by Israel in clear violation of the Charter of the United Nations and the norms of international conduct."[56] While some scholars disagreed,[57] this was the position generally taken by states.

This kind of case raises the question of the permissibility of so-called anticipatory or pre-emptive self-defense. First of all, it will be helpful to distinguish between these two terms. Anticipatory self-defense may be described as that which is taken against action by another country that has not yet eventuated in an armed attack, but which is about to do so: massed troops are marching toward a border, warplanes are approaching a state's territory, and similar situations. Preemptive self-defense, on the other hand, may be understood as that which is applied well before an attack is about to occur, such as the Israeli strike on the Iraqi nuclear reactor. A policy of preemptive self-defense was recently announced in the U.S. National Security Strategy of September 2002[58] (e.g.: "as a matter of

---

[53] 1996 I.C.J. 226, 242, para. 30.

[54] *See, e.g.,* http://news.bbc.co.uk/onthisday/hi/dates/stories/June/7/newsid_3014000/-3014623.stm.

[55] *Id.*

[56] S.C. Res. 487, 36 U.N. SCOR (2288th mtg.), U.N. Doc. S/RES/487 (1981), *reprinted in* 75 AM. J. INT'L. L.724 (1981).

[57] *See, e.g.,* Anthony D'Amato, *Israel's Air Strike Upon the Iraqi Nuclear Reactor,* 77 AM. J. INT'L. L. 584 (1983).

[58] The National Security Strategy may be found at http://www.whitehouse.gov/nsc/nss.pdf. *See generally* Frederic L. Kirgis, *Pre-emptive Action to Forestall Terrorism,* ASIL *Insight,* June 2002, *available at* http://www.asil.org/insights/insigh88.htm; and Mary Ellen O'Connell, "The Myth of Preemptive Self-Defense," American Society of International Law, Task Force on Terrorism Essay, August 2002, *available at* http://www.-asil.org/taskforce/oconnell.pdf.

common sense and self-defense, America will act against such emerging threats before they are fully formed.;"[59] and "While the United States will constantly strive to enlist the support of the international community, we will not hesitate to act alone, if necessary, to exercise our right of self defense by acting preemptively against such terrorists, to prevent them from doing harm against our people and our country; . . ."[60]).

The permissibility of a particular instance of *anticipatory* self-defense is often analyzed in terms of the conditions laid down in Daniel Webster's correspondence with the British in relation to the *Caroline* incident.[61] The *Caroline* was an American vessel that had been used to supply Canadian rebels during an 1837 insurrection against Britain. In December of that year, British forces attacked the *Caroline* while it was in port on the American side of the Niagara River, killing at least one American, set the ship afire and released it into the river where it drifted over Niagara Falls. In the exchange of diplomatic notes that ensued, U.S. Secretary of State Daniel Webster stated in an 1842 note that the invasion of American territory was in principle unlawful, and "while it is admitted that exceptions growing out of the great law of self-defense do exist, those exceptions should be confined to cases in which *the necessity of that self-defense is instant, overwhelming, and leaving no choice of means and no moment for deliberation*, and must be limited by that necessity and kept clearly within it."[62]

This statement has been widely accepted as an authoritative statement relating to the customary law of self-defense and was referred to approvingly by the Nuremberg Tribunal. It would appear to countenance measures taken in anticipatory self-defense, but only under the strict conditions contained in Webster's note — namely, that the necessity of the use of force in self-defense be "instant, overwhelming, and leaving no choice of means and no moment for deliberation." This would appear to allow the use of force in self-defense when an invasion is imminent, leaving no time for taking any other steps to protect the country. It would thus not require the threatened state to wait for the "armed attack" to "occur" before taking defensive measures. The Webster formula would therefore appear to allow action to prevent an imminent nuclear missile attack, but not an attack to destroy missiles that were not targeted or being prepared for launch — and, *a fortiori*, not against an unfinished nuclear reactor that might produce weapons-grade material that might be used for nuclear weapons that might be targeted against a state.

---

[59] NATIONAL SECURITY STRATEGY OF THE UNITED STATES OF AMERICA, White House, Washington, D.C., September 2002, at 4, *available at* http://www.whitehouse.gov/nsc/nss.pdf.

[60] *Id.* at 12.

[61] 2 MOORE, DIGEST OF INTERNATIONAL LAW 412 (1906). For the documents, *see* Robert Jennings, *The Caroline and McLeod Cases*, 32 AM. J. INT'L. L. 82-99 (1938).

[62] *Id.* (emphasis added). In his response of 28 July 1842, Lord Ashburton did not dispute Webster's statement of the governing principles.

However, even as to anticipatory self-defense, it must be remembered that the *Caroline* standards were articulated in the middle of the nineteenth century, when circumstances were vastly different from those prevailing in the mid-twentieth century, when the U.N. Charter was drafted. As Brownlie has observed: "It is surely more appropriate to know the state of customary law in 1945 rather than 1842, and it is far from clear that in 1945 the customary law was so flexible."[63] That anticipatory self-defense, even as tightly restricted by the Webster formula, blurs the Charter's bright line may help to explain why states have generally opposed it since 1945.[64]

It follows from the foregoing that the use of force in pre-emptive self-defense does not appear to be permissible either under Article 51 or under customary international law.[65] But just as the requirement of an armed attack may seem outmoded in a nuclear age, the prohibition of forcible pre-emption may appear obsolete in a world plagued by terrorism. As already noted, the U.S. National Security Strategy issued in September, 2002, has explicitly adopted a policy of pre-emptive self-defense.[66] The document at one point states as follows:

> "For centuries, international law recognized that nations need not suffer an attack before they can lawfully take action to defend themselves against forces that present an imminent danger of attack. Legal scholars and international jurists often conditioned the legitimacy of preemption on the existence of an imminent threat — most often a visible mobilization of armies, navies, and air forces preparing to attack.

> "We must adapt the concept of imminent threat to the capabilities and objectives of today's adversaries."[67]

The document goes on to declare that "rogue states and terrorists" do not launch conventional attacks but may employ weapons of mass destruction that "can be easily concealed, delivered covertly, and used without warning."[68] It therefore reserves the right to take preemptive action "even if uncertainty remains as to the time and place of the enemy's attack,"[69] thus appearing to reject the requirement of imminence.

---

[63] BROWNLIE, *supra* note 11, at 702.

[64] *Id.*

[65] Brownlie states flatly that the "doctrine lacks a legal basis. . . ." BROWNLIE, *supra* note 11, at 702. *See also* Tom J. Farer, *Beyond the Charter Frame: Unilateralism or Condominium?*, 96 AM. J. INT'L. L. 359 (2002).

[66] The NATIONAL SECURITY STRATEGY is *available at* http://www.whitehouse.gov/nsc/nss.pdf. The United States also asserted preemption as a ground for its bombing raid on Libya on 15 April 1986. A draft Security Council resolution condemning the strike received 11 affirmative votes but was vetoed by the U.S., the U.K. and France. U.N. Doc. S/PV.2682, 21 Apr. 1986.

[67] NATIONAL SECURITY STRATEGY, *supra* note 66, at 15.

[68] *Id.*

[69] *Id.*

At the very least, the National Security Strategy seems to argue for a greatly expanded concept of "imminence," one that would allow the use of armed force to prevent "rogue states and terrorists"[70] from launching attacks against the United States, or perhaps even from acquiring the means to do so. While it may be questioned whether international law has recognized a right of anticipatory self-defense "for centuries," even assuming it has, the right claimed in the Strategy goes well beyond anticipation as Daniel Webster understood it. The problem with moving the concept of "imminence" back in time, of course, is that it becomes a far more subjective and uncertain test. This could open the door to the use of pre-emption as a pretext for forcible interventions into any state by which the state using force felt at all threatened, or even whose government, or leader, it did not happen to see eye to eye with for some reason.

Scholars have long debated whether the Charter's rules on the use of force should be construed strictly, to prevent the unilateral use of force except when an attack occurs, or more liberally, to permit the use of force to achieve objectives that will enhance world order.[71] The rationale behind the former approach is that if a state is to be permitted to decide unilaterally to use force, the circumstances under which that is permissible must be very tightly defined so as to minimize abuse. But the events of September 11, 2001 awakened the world to the carnage that could be unleashed by terrorists and the corresponding need to take reasonable preventive measures. They gave new force to the arguments of those who would construe the regime of the Charter in a liberal way, to permit the use of force in circumstances other than those permitted by a strict reading of Article 51.

It is undeniable that the world of today is different from that of 1945 when the Charter's rules on force were drafted. But in some ways the question today is much the same as the one facing the international community in the aftermath of World War II: should the decision to use force be left up to individual states, or should it, in all but the most extreme, bright-line cases, be made or at least sanctioned by the international community?

Each approach has its strengths and weaknesses. The former might make certain individual states feel more secure but could lead to increased levels of armed conflict around the globe, very possibly with stronger states often attacking weaker states. The latter approach would require

---

[70] Use of force against terrorists alone — e.g., on the high seas or in an aircraft — without affecting a state would presumably be analogous to similar acts against pirates, who, as the "enemy of all humankind" (*hostis humani generis*) have always been fair game under international law. It is when a state, such as Afghanistan, is affected that the rules of the Charter come into play.

[71] *See, e.g.*, Louis Henkin, *The Use of Force: Law and U.S. Policy*, in RIGHT V. MIGHT: INTERNATIONAL LAW AND THE USE OF FORCE 37 (1989) (arts. 2(4) and 51 should be construed strictly to limit the use of force); and W. Michael Reisman, *Criteria for the Lawful Use of Force in International Law*, 10 YALE J. INT'L L. 279 (1985) (force may be used to maintain and enhance public order objectives).

greater restraint on the part of individual states, which could not decide unilaterally to use force except in the face of an imminent and serious threat; but in theory, at least, the level of conflict worldwide would be lower since it would be managed by the international community through the Security Council.

The second approach is the one taken by the U.N. Charter, which remains the law today. While there have been, and will doubtless continue to be, violations of this regime, it seems unlikely that it will change cataclysmically, even in the face of global terrorism. States, especially weaker ones, like to feel some sense of security against an armed attack by stronger states. They may prefer to treat conduct that departs from the Charter regime as violations rather than reasons for change, and to avoid the slippery slope of introducing additional exceptions to the Charter's rules.

In any case, there still appears to be general acceptance of the Charter system. Even the United States did not reject it in deciding to invade Iraq in March 2003, but argued that it was authorized to do so by previous Security Council resolutions.[72] And one of the lessons of the war in Iraq seems to be that even a superpower cannot manage conflict singlehandedly.

§ 8.04   COLLECTIVE USE OF FORCE

Apart from its use in individual self-defense, force may be used consistently with the U.N. Charter in collective self-defense, as authorized by the Security Council, or under Regional Arrangements.

[A]   Collective Self-Defense

With regard to collective self-defense, the International Court of Justice found in the *Nicaragua* case that by referring to the "inherent right" of both individual and collective self-defense, the U.N. Charter "testifies to the existence of the right of collective self-defence in customary international law."[73] The Court further found that for an exercise of collective self-defense to be lawful, a state must declare itself to be the victim of an armed attack and it must request the assistance of the state or states purporting to exercise the right of collective self-defense.[74]

[B]   Action Under the Authority of the Security Council

While the design of the Charter gives the United Nations, and in particular the Security Council, a monopoly on the use of force except in

---

[72] *See* U.N. Doc. S/2003/351 (U.S. letter to the Security Council of 20 Mar. 2003). *See also* U.N. Doc. S/2003/350 (U.K. letter to the Security Council of 20 Mar. 2003).

[73] Military and Paramilitary Activities In and Against Nicaragua, 1986 I.C.J. 14, 102, para. 193.

[74] *Id.* at 104, para. 195; 105, para. 199.

cases of self-defense,[75] practice under the Charter has led to the Security Council's *authorizing* states to use force on behalf of the international community rather than using force itself. The first major instance of this form of action was in relation to Korea in 1950, when the Security Council first "[r]ecommend[ed] that the Members of the United Nations furnish such assistance to the Republic of Korea as may be necessary to repel the armed attack [by forces from North Korea] and to restore international peace and security in the area;"[76] then "[r]ecommend[ed] that all Members providing military forces . . . make such forces and other assistance available to a unified command under the United States;. . . ."[77] (The Security Council was able to adopt these resolutions because of the absence of the Soviet Union.) Sixteen member states sent forces, which engaged those of North Korea and, later, China. The hostilities ended when an armistice came into affect on July 27, 1953.

The next major action by the Security Council in authorizing the use of force related to the invasion of Kuwait by Iraq on August 2, 1990.[78] After adopting resolutions condemning the invasion[79] and imposing economic sanctions,[80] the Security Council "[a]uthorise[d] Member States cooperating with the Government of Kuwait . . . to use all necessary means to uphold and implement Security Council resolution 660 (1990) and all subsequent relevant resolutions and to restore international peace and security in the area; . . ."[81] Acting pursuant to this resolution, coalition forces acting under the command of the United States, in an operation lasting five days beginning on January 16, 1991, removed Iraq from Kuwait.

Questions have been raised about the "constitutionality" of the Security Council's action in these cases — i.e., its consistency with the U.N. Charter. After all, the Charter provides for the Security Council *itself* to take action involving the use of force, not for it to authorize member states to do so.[82] But practice under a treaty can give new meaning

---

[75] Art. 42 of the Charter provides in relevant part as follows:

"Should the Security Council consider that measures provided for in Article 41 [i.e., measures not involving the use of armed force] would be inadequate or have proved to be inadequate, it may take such action by air, sea, or land forces as may be necessary to maintain or restore international peace and security."

UN Charter, *supra* note 15, art. 42. This provision is premised on the existence of forces contributed to the Security Council by member states (art. 43) and a Military Staff Committee (art. 47) to advise and assist the Security Council, neither of which eventuated.

[76] S.C. Res. of 27 June 1950, SCOR, 5th Year, Resolutions and Decisions, 5.

[77] S.C. Res. of 7 July 1950, SCOR, 5th Year, Resolutions and Decisions, 5.

[78] *See generally* Thomas Franck and Faiza Patel, *UN Police Action In Lieu of War: "The Old Order Changeth*, 85 AM. J. INT'L. L. 63 (1991) (hereafter Franck & Patel).

[79] Resolution 660 (1990), 2 Aug. 1990, 29 I.L.M. 1325 (1990).

[80] Resolutions 661 (1990), 6 Aug. 1990, 29 I.L.M. 1325 (1990) and 665 (1990), 25 Aug. 1990, 29 I.L.M. 1329 (1990).

[81] Resolution 678 (1990), 29 I.L.M. 1565 (1990).

[82] *See* U.N. Charter, *supra* note 15, art. 42, quoted in relevant part in note 75, *supra*. *See generally* Chapter VII of the Charter, "Action with respect to Threats to the Peace, Breaches of the Peace, and Acts of Aggression."

to its provisions.[83] The design of the Charter's provisions on Security Council action through troops contributed by member states[84] may be elegant,[85] but it has never been implemented. The action of the Security Council in response to the invasion of Kuwait drew no protest except from Saddam Hussein's Iraq.[86] In short, there is nothing to suggest that the members of the United Nations do not accept the way in which the Security Council is authorizing force to be used on behalf of the international community. This suggests that the approach to the maintenance of international peace and security under the Charter has in fact changed. Contributed forces and the Military Staff Committee[87] have given way to action by states under the authorization of the Security Council on behalf of the international community. And if there is concern with respect to the propriety of the Security Council's authorizing coalition forces to dislodge Iraq from Kuwait in particular, the operation could be viewed as one of collective self-defense, which would require no Security Council authorization at all.[88]

[C] Regional Arrangements

In addition to collective self-defense and action under the authority of the Security Council, the Charter provides for action through "Regional Arrangements."[89] It allows these to address regional issues relating to the maintenance of international peace and security "provided that such arrangements or agencies and their activities are consistent with the Purposes and Principles of the United Nations."[90] It limits the autonomy of these bodies, however, by providing that "no enforcement action shall be taken under regional arrangements . . . without the authorization of the Security Council. . . ."[91]

---

[83] *See* Vienna Convention on the Law of Treaties, 1155 U.N.T.S. 331, 8 I.L.M. 679 (1969), art. 31(3)(a), providing that in interpreting a treaty, account is to be taken of any "subsequent agreement" between the parties regarding the interpretation or application of its provisions. Such an agreement does not have to be formal, but may take the form of practice under the treaty. For examples, *see* ANTHONY AUST, MODERN TREATY LAW AND PRACTICE 191-195 (2000).

[84] *See* U.N. Charter, *supra* note 15, arts.42-47.

[85] In this respect, Franck & Patel, *supra* note 78, at 63, call the Charter an "elegant, carefully crafted instrument."

[86] *See* U.N. Doc. S/PV.2963, at 19-20 (the Security Council could authorize the use of force only under arts. 42 and 43).

[87] *See* U.N. Charter, *supra* note 15, arts. 43 and 47. For a brief description of the system as originally conceived, *see* note 75, *supra*.

[88] To this effect, *see* Oscar Schachter, *United Nations Law in the Gulf Conflict*, 85 AM. J. INT'L. L. 452, 460 (1991) (arguing that res. 678 was necessary not to authorize the use of force but to obtain approval of Congress for the commitment of U.S. forces).

[89] U.N. Charter, *supra* note 15, ch. VIII.

[90] *Id.*, art. 52(1).

[91] *Id.*, art. 53(1).

While a number of these regional arrangements exist,[92] their role in maintaining international peace and security has been rather limited, except in the important field of peacekeeping.[93] Regional bodies sometimes become the default mechanism when powerful states and alliances such as NATO fail to become involved. For example, in the face of lack of action by the government of Sudan in response to Security Council resolutions on the situation in Darfur,[94] and a minimal response by Western governments, the African Union's Darfur Integrated Task Force (DITF)[95] is assisting with the quelling of the violence in that region, under the supervision of the Security Council.[96]

---

[92] Brownlie lists the Organization of American States, the Arab League, the African Union, the Organization for Security and Cooperation in Europe (OSCE) and the Organization of Eastern Caribbean States (OECS). BROWNLIE, *supra* note 11, at 705.

[93] Peacekeeping, an important activity of the U.N., is not mentioned in the Charter. It operates on the basis of the consent of the parties. Information on U.N. peacekeeping activities is available on the U.N. website, http://www.un.org/Depts/dpko/dpko/index.asp. As of August 2005, there were eight U.N. peacekeeping operations in Africa alone, in the following countries: Sudan, Burundi, Cote d'Ivoire, Liberia, Democratic Republic of Congo, Ethiopia and Eritrea, Sierra Leone, and Western Sahara. Expenditures to cover peacekeeping operations in the Congo and Middle East authorized by the General Assembly, but not the Security Council, were upheld as "expenses of the Organization" under art. 17(2) of the Charter in the advisory opinion of the I.C.J. in Certain Expenses of the United Nations (Article 17, Paragraph 2 of the Charter), Advisory Opinion of 20 July 1962, 1962 I.C.J. 151. The opinion established the legitimacy of U.N. peacekeeping operations despite the lack of an explicit basis for them in the Charter. On U.N. peacekeeping *see generally* Supplement to an Agenda for Peace, Position Paper of the Secretary-General on the Occasion of the Fiftieth Anniversary of the United Nations, U.N. Doc. A/50/60–S/1995/1, 3 Jan. 1995, in AN AGENDA FOR PEACE 1995 at 5 (2nd ed. 1995), U.N. Sales No. E.95.I.15.

[94] *See, e.g.,* UNSC Res. 1590 (2005), U.N. Doc. S/RES/1590 (2005), *inter alia*, referring to earlier resolutions, "*Commending* the efforts of the African Union, . . . acknowledging the progress made by the African Union in the deployment of an international protection force, police, and military observers, and calling on all member States to contribute generously and urgently to the African Union Mission in Darfur," and establishing the United Nations Mission in Sudan (UNMIS).

[95] For information, *see* the African Union website, http://www.africa-union.org/.

[96] A number of Security Council resolutions refer to the role of the African Union in Darfur. *See, e.g.,* S/RES/1556 (2004); S.RES/1564 (2004); and S/RES/1591 (2005).

Chapter 9
INTERNATIONAL HUMAN RIGHTS LAW

Synopsis

§ 9.01   INTRODUCTION

International Human Rights Law is that branch of international law that protects individuals, largely as against their own governments. As we have seen in Chapter 6, natural and legal persons are protected to some extent as against governments other than those of their nationality by the law of state responsibility for injuries to aliens. The latter field is more venerable than human rights law and in the case of individuals has been largely subsumed by it. We will return to state responsibility after a brief look at the background of today's system of international human rights law.

[A]   Background

The notion that international law had anything at all to say about the way in which a state treated its own citizens was largely unknown until the Second World War. But the genocide and other unthinkable atrocities committed during that conflict awakened the community of nations to the need for international protection of persons against acts of their own governments. This was an enormous step by the international community — a paradigm shift, really — because it meant that international law, which had up until then confined itself almost exclusively to regulating the relations *between* states, would now also regulate certain matters *within* states. For these purposes it would reach past the venerable barrier of sovereignty to regulate the way a state treated individuals within its own territory. What a state did within its jurisdiction had always been considered its own business, something that was not of international concern. This concept even appears to be enshrined in the United Nations Charter itself, which provides in Article 2(7) that: "Nothing contained in the present Charter shall authorize the United Nations to intervene in matters which are essentially within the domestic jurisdiction of any state. . . ."[1] The message of international human rights law is that how a state treats individuals subject to its jurisdiction is no longer a matter that is solely within its domestic jurisdiction. It is a matter of international concern.

The new consciousness following World War II led the international community to act quickly to lay the groundwork for a legal regime that would protect human rights. United States President Franklin D. Roosevelt had already paved the way through the "moral order" he called for in his famous "Four Freedoms" speech in 1941.[2] In 1948 the U.N. General Assembly adopted the Universal Declaration of Human Rights[3] — which refers to the four freedoms in its preamble[4] — and in the same year the Convention on the Prevention and Punishment of the Crime of Genocide[5] was concluded under United Nations auspices. Regional human rights instruments were also adopted beginning in that year,[6] as we will see below.

Human rights were discussed very generally in Chapter 5 in connection with the consideration of the individual as a subject of international law.

---

[1] Charter of the United Nations, 26 June 1945, art. 2(7), 59 Stat. 1031, T.S. No. 993, 3 Bevans 1153, 1976 U.N. Y.B. 1043 (hereinafter U.N. Charter).

[2] In his speech to Congress on 6 Jan. 1941, Roosevelt stated, "we look forward to a world founded upon four essential human freedoms," namely, "freedom of speech and expression," "freedom of every person to worship God in his own way," "freedom from want" and "freedom from fear." Franklin D. Roosevelt, The "Four Freedoms" Address, 87 CONG. REC. 44 (1941), *available at* http://www.libertynet.org/~edcivic/fdr.html.

[3] G.A. Res. 217 A (III), UN GAOR, 3d Sess., 1st plen. Mtg., UN Doc. A/810 at 71, (10 Dec. 1948).

[4] *Id.*, pmbl. ("the advent of a world in which human beings shall enjoy freedom of speech and belief and freedom from fear and want has been proclaimed as the highest aspiration of the common people, . . .").

[5] 9 Dec. 1948, 78 U.N.T.S. 277.

[6] For the first regional instruments adopted during the immediate postwar period, *see* the American Declaration of the Rights and Duties of Man, O.A.S. Res. XXX, adopted by the Ninth Int'l Conf. of American States, 30 Mar.-2 May 1948, Bogotá, O.A.S. Off. Rec. OEA/Ser. L/V/I.4 Rev. (1965), available on the OAS website, http://www.cidh.oas.-org/Basicos/basic2.htm; and the European Convention for the Protection of Human Rights and Fundamental Freedoms, 4 Nov. 1950, Eur. T.S. No. 5, *available at* the Council of Europe website, http://conventions.coe.int/treaty/en/Treaties/Html/005.htm.

We also saw in Chapter 6 that international law traditionally protected both natural and legal persons only against injuries caused by foreign states; and that it did this by treating the injury as one to the state of the person's nationality, thus giving that state a claim under international law against the state causing the harm. This body of law, known as state responsibility for injuries to aliens (in international law parlance, an "alien" is a national of another state) therefore afforded no protection to individuals against acts by their own governments, a gap filled by international human rights law. Because human rights law in some respects grew out of the field of state responsibility for injuries to aliens, and because corporations and other legal persons are protected by the law of state responsibility but not by human rights law, a few words about this field are in order to provide background and context for our consideration of human rights law.

[B] State Responsibility for Injuries to Aliens[7]

First, it is important to distinguish this body of international law from the broader one with a similar name of which it forms a part: that of state responsibility for internationally wrongful acts. The latter field is dealt with in Chapter 7. The two fields are related to each other in the following way: if a state unlawfully injuries an alien, it has committed an internationally wrongful act and is said to be internationally responsible. This responsibility entails an obligation to make reparation to the state of the alien's nationality in accordance with the law of state responsibility for internationally wrongful acts. That field of international law deals with such matters as attribution of conduct to a state, breach of an international obligation, circumstances precluding wrongfulness, the obligations that a state's international responsibility entails and how those obligations are given effect.[8] The rules on these issues govern the responsibility of a state that injuries an alien.

The law of state responsibility for injuries to aliens is considerably older than international human rights law, with many arbitral and claims commission decisions dating from the 19th century.[9] It proceeds from the traditional notion that only states are subjects of international law, and thus only states can have rights and duties under that legal

---

[7] See generally RESTATEMENT (THIRD) OF THE FOREIGN RELATIONS LAW OF THE UNITED STATES §§ 711-713 (1987) (hereinafter RESTATEMENT 3D); 1 OPPENHEIM'S INTERNATIONAL LAW §150 (R. Jennings & A. Watts 9th ed. 1992) (hereinafter OPPENHEIM); and IAN BROWNLIE, PRINCIPLES OF PUBLIC INTERNATIONAL LAW, ch. 24 (6th ed.2003) (hereinafter BROWNLIE).

[8] See generally Draft Articles on Responsibility of States for Internationally Wrongful Acts, adopted by the International Law Commission at its Fifty-Third Session (2001), 2001 I.L.C. Rep. 43, U.N. Doc. A/56/10 (2001); and chapter 7, above.

[9] Decisions in cases involving injuries to aliens are summarized in a number of international law digests and other works. See, e.g., JOHN BASSETT MOORE, HISTORY AND DIGEST OF INTERNATIONAL ARBITRATIONS (1898); GREEN HAYWOOD HACKWORTH, DIGEST OF INTERNATIONAL LAW 526-657 (1943); and 8 MARJORIE WHITEMAN, DIGEST OF INTERNATIONAL LAW 697-906 (1967).

order.[10] It followed that natural or legal persons enjoyed no rights and bore no obligations under international law. However, state practice developed the doctrine early that if a state injured a citizen, or national, of another state, that constituted under international law a legal injury to the state of the person's nationality.[11] Thus if Ms. X, a national of State A, were subjected to prolonged arbitrary imprisonment by State B, before the advent of international human rights law that would give rise only to a right in State A to make a claim for reparation from State B. The legal injury was to State A, not Ms. X, as far as international law was concerned, because individuals had no standing under international law. Since it was State A's right that had been violated, State A could decide whether or not to pursue a claim against State B. State A might decide, for example, that it would unduly strain its relations with State B to make such a claim. In such a case, Ms. X would be without a remedy unless the law of either State A or State B provided her with one.[12] Indeed, a person in Ms. X's position would often be required to exhaust any domestic remedies available in State B before State A could seek reparation.[13]

States were found responsible under this body of law for a variety of kinds of injuries to nationals of other countries — often characterized as "denials of justice"[14] — ranging from what would be viewed today as human rights violations[15] to harm of a strictly economic character.[16] Not all countries followed these norms, however. While they were generally accepted in Europe and North America, they were rejected by the Soviet Union and Latin American countries, which generally viewed aliens as being subject only to the local law of the state to which they had voluntarily come or in which they had invested.

The situation came to a head in the 1970s, when Third World countries, many of which had emerged from colonialism in the 1960s, supported the U.N. General Assembly resolution on the Charter of

---

[10] *See generally* chapter 5, above.

[11] *See* Mavromattis Palestine Concessions case (Greece v. U.K.) (Jurisdiction), 1924 P.C.I.J. (ser. A) No. 2, at 12: "It is an elementary principle of international law that a State is entitled to protect its subjects, when injured by acts contrary to international law committed by another State, from whom they have been unable to obtain satisfaction through the ordinary channels. . . . By taking up the case of one of its subjects . . . , a State is in reality asserting its own rights — its right to ensure, in the person of its subjects, respect for the rules of international law."

[12] Even if State A did pursue a claim against State B on Ms. X's behalf and recovered compensation, since it was State A's right that had been violated international law would not require State A to pass that compensation along to Ms. X. This might be required under State A's domestic law, however.

[13] *See* the Interhandel Case (Switzerland v. United States), 1959 I.C.J. 6, 26-27: "The rule that local remedies must be exhausted before international proceedings may be instituted is a well-established rule of customary international law."

[14] *See, e.g.,* RESTATEMENT 3D, *supra* note 7, § 711 cmt. a.

[15] *See generally* RESTATEMENT 3D, *supra* note 7, § 711(a).

[16] *See generally id.,* § 711(b) and (c), and § 712.

Economic Rights and Duties of States (CERDS).[17] The Charter, which received the affirmative votes of most developing countries and negative votes or abstentions from developed countries,[18] provided that the question of expropriation would be governed by the domestic law of the expropriating state. While the Charter served clear notice of the attitudes of developing countries, as a General Assembly resolution it did not have binding effect. Indeed, the approach it reflected was rejected by the United States and other developed countries, and in the well known case of *Texas Overseas Petroleum Co. v. Libyan Arab Republic*[19] the sole arbitrator ruled that international law, not domestic law, governed such questions.[20]

While it is a distinct body of law in the ways that have been discussed — chiefly, that it applies only to aliens and even they enjoy no direct rights under it — state responsibility may be said to have paved the way for the development of international human rights law. Thus, like human rights law it recognized that nationals of other countries were entitled to a certain minimum standard of treatment,[21] and that if a state failed to meet that standard it would be internationally responsible. The basic notion of "denial of justice" which is often associated with claims under the law of state responsibility also describes violations that are protected against by human rights law. More fundamentally, the philosophical underpinnings of both bodies of law "derived from historic conceptions of natural law, as reflected in the conscience of contemporary mankind and the major cultures and legal systems of the world."[22]

While many of the kinds of claims that formerly would have been brought under the law of state responsibility would today be cognizable as

---

[17] 12 Dec. 1974, G.A. Res. 3281 (XXIX), 29 U.N. GAOR, Supp. (No. 31) 50, UN Doc. A/9631 (1975), *reprinted in* 14 I.L.M. 251 (1975). On CERDS, *see, e.g.,* Charles N. Brower & John B. Tepe, Jr., *The Charter of Economic Rights and Duties of States: A Reflection or Rejection of International Law?*, 9 INT'L LAW. 295 (1975); Burns Weston, *The Charter of Economic Rights and Duties of States and the Deprivation of Foreign Owned Wealth*, 75 AM. J. INT'L. L. 437 (1981); and Robin C.A. White, *A New International Economic Order*, 24 INT'L . & COMP. L.Q. 542 (1975).

[18] The Charter was adopted by a vote of 120 to six, with 10 abstentions. Belgium, Denmark, Germany, Luxembourg, the U.K. and the U.S. voted against the resolution, while Austria, Canada, France, Ireland, Israel, Italy, Japan, Netherlands, Norway and Spain abstained. These sixteen states comprised the bulk of the world's capital exporting countries.

[19] Award of 19 Jan. 1977, 17 I.L.M. 1 (1978).

[20] The sole arbitrator relied principally on G.A. Res. 1803, Permanent Sovereignty over Natural Resources, 17 U.N. GAOR, Supp. 17, at 15, which called for an expropriating country to pay appropriate compensation "in accordance with international law." He found that this standard had not been changed by CERDS because developed countries had not accepted it, indicating that they did not accept a change in the traditional rule.

[21] This is often referred to as an "international minimum standard." *See, e.g.,* the ELSI case, 1989 I.C.J. 14. *See also, e.g.,* the Neer Claim (U.S. v. Mexico), U.S.-Mexican General Claims Commission, 4 R.I.A.A. 60 (1926) ("the propriety of governmental acts should be put to the test of international standards").

[22] RESTATEMENT 3D, *supra* note 7, Part VII, Introductory Note, at 146.

human rights violations,[23] this is not true of all such claims. In particular, corporations and other legal persons are protected by the law of state responsibility but not by human rights law; and while the law of state responsibility protects the property, investments and other economic interests of aliens, human rights law is less concerned with business or commercial matters[24] and the extent to which it recognizes a right to property is unsettled.[25] Of course, the law of state responsibility does not cover offenses committed by a state against its own nationals.

In sum, the law of state responsibility for injuries to aliens is still very much alive, but is focused principally on economic harm to aliens from expropriations or other forms of interference with economic interests. Human rights law covers many other forms of injury to individuals under a state's jurisdiction, whether aliens or nationals, as we will see below.

[C]   International Humanitarian Law

Another branch of international law that is related to that of human rights is international humanitarian law. Also considerably older than human rights law, humanitarian law deals with the protection of individuals — not only civilians but also members of the contesting armed forces and prisoners of war — during armed conflict. It falls within the field of *jus in bello* — the law applicable during war — as distinguished from *jus ad bellum* — the law governing the permissibility of going to war.

While certain related customs were observed by armies — including that of George Washington[26] — considerably earlier,[27] it was not until the 19th

---

[23] These would include offenses to the person, such as assault, inhuman treatment, arbitrary detention, and lack of access to tribunals of the kind that would qualify as a denial of justice. *See* the catalogue in RESTATEMENT 3D, *supra* note 7, § 711, Reporters' Note 2.A. It is worth emphasizing that international human rights law applies to the treatment by a state of aliens subject to its authority. *See id.*, cmt. c.

[24] The Covenant on Economic, Social and Cultural Rights, 993 U.N.T.S. 3, is obviously concerned in part with "economic" rights. But these are by and large rights of individuals such as the right to work (art. 6), the right to just and favorable conditions of work (art. 7), the right to form trade unions (art. 8) and the right to social security (art. 9). No right to engage in business or commerce is mentioned.

[25] The Universal Declaration, *supra* note 3, declares in art. 17 that "Everyone has the right to own property . . ." and that "No one shall be arbitrarily deprived of his property." Neither of the human rights Covenants recognize such a right, however. On the unsettled nature of the right in customary international law, *see* RESTATEMENT 3D, *supra* note 7, § 702 cmt. k. *But see id.*, § 711 cmt. d, stating that while "[t]here is lack of agreement on the scope of this right and permissible limitations on it, . . . the right of an individual to own some property and not to be deprived of it arbitrarily is recognized as a human right."

[26] George Washington's policy of humane treatment of British prisoners of war during the Revolutionary War reportedly took his captives by surprise. *See, e.g.,* Thomas L. Friedman, *George W. To George W.*, N.Y. TIMES, 24 Mar. 2005, at A 23.

[27] For a literary reference to these customs, *see* Shakespeare's *Henry V*, portraying the treatment of prisoners at the famous Battle of Agincourt of 25 Oct. 1415 between British and French forces. *See also* Theodor Meron, *Shakespeare's Henry the Fifth and the Law of War*, 86 AM. J. INT'L. L. 1 (1992).

century that Henri Dunant of Switzerland,[28] shocked by the suffering of the wounded he witnessed at the battle of Solferino in 1859, initiated a campaign that led to the founding of the Red Cross,[29] known today as the International Committee of the Red Cross (ICRC), in the 1864 Geneva Convention.[30] Conferences held at The Hague in 1899 and 1907 led to the adoption in those years of treaties on humanitarian law, the latter being Convention (IV) Respecting the Laws and Customs of War on Land.[31]

Far better known today than these instruments are the four 1949 Geneva Conventions on the protection of the wounded and sick members of the armed forces in the field and at sea, prisoners of war and civilians.[32] These treaties were updated and supplemented by two Additional Protocols of 1977 dealing with the protection of victims of international (Protocol I) and non-international (Protocol II) armed conflicts.[33] In the *Nicaragua* case, the International Court of Justice applied what it referred to as "general principles of humanitarian law" on the basis of common Article 3 of the four Geneva Conventions.[34]

There has been considerable controversy of late over the applicability of the Geneva Conventions to the conflicts in Afghanistan and Iraq,[35] and especially to the treatment of individuals held in U.S. detention centers in

---

[28] Dunant was the winner, along with Frédéric Passy of France, of the first Nobel Peace Prize in 1901.

[29] *See* PIERRE BOISSIER, HISTORY OF THE INTERNATIONAL COMMITTEE OF THE RED CROSS: FROM SOLFERINO TO TSUSHIMA (1985).

[30] Geneva Convention for the Amelioration of the Condition of the Wounded in Armies in the Field, 22 Aug. 1864, 22 Stat. 940, T.S. No. 377.

[31] 18 Oct. 1907, 36 Stat. 2277, TS 539. The aim of the 1907 conference was to expand on the treaty adopted in 1899. For states that are parties to it, the 1907 treaty replaces the 1899 convention of the same name.

[32] Convention for the Amelioration of the Condition of the Wounded and Sick in Armed Forces in the Field, 12 Aug. 1949, 6 U.S.T. 3114, T.I.A.S. No. 3362, 75 U.N.T.S. 31; Convention for the Amelioration of the Condition of the Wounded, Sick and Shipwrecked Members of Armed Forces at Sea, 12 Aug. 1949, 6 U.S.T. 3217, T.I.A.S. No. 3363, 75 U.N.T.S. 85; Convention Relative to the Treatment of Prisoners of War, 12 Aug. 1949, 6 U.S.T. 3316, T.I.A.S. No. 3364, 75 U.N.T.S. 135; Convention Relative to the Protection of Civilian Persons in Time of War, 12 Aug. 1949, 6 U.S.T. 3516, T.I.A.S. No. 3365, 75 U.N.T.S. 287.

[33] Protocol Additional to the Geneva Conventions of Aug. 12, 1949, and relating to the Protection of Victims of International Armed Conflicts (Protocol I), and Protocol Additional to the Geneva Conventions of Aug. 12, 1949, and relating to the Protection of Victims of Non-International Armed Conflicts (Protocol II), 8 June 1977, UN Doc. A/32/144, Annexes I and II, 1125 U.N.T.S. 3 (Protocol I) and 1125 U.N.T.S. 609 (Protocol II), *reprinted in* 16 I.L.M. 1391 and 1442, respectively.

[34] Case Concerning Military and Paramilitary Activities In and Against Nicaragua (Nicaragua v. United States) (Merits), 1986 I.C.J. 14, 113-14. The Court was not able to apply the conventions themselves due to the United States' multilateral treaty reservation to its acceptance of the Court's jurisdiction.

[35] The United States has accepted that it is an occupying power in Iraq and is thus subject to the Fourth Geneva Convention Relative to the Protection of Civilian Persons in Time of War, 12 Aug. 1949, 6 U.S.T. 3516, T.I.A.S. No. 3365, 75 U.N.T.S. 287. *See* John R. Crook, ed., Contemporary Practice of the United States, 99 AJIL 265 (2005).

Guantanamo Bay and Iraq (in particular, the Abu Ghraib prison). The U.S. administration has maintained that those held in these facilities are "unlawful combatants," because in the view of the administration they do not qualify as prisoners of war under the 1949 Geneva Convention (III) Relative to the Treatment of Prisoners of War and are thus not entitled to the protections provided by that convention.[36] Others believe that the Geneva Conventions, and in particular the Third Geneva Convention, are fully applicable.[37]

The ICRC for its part has sent representatives to visit the detainees and has reportedly informed the U.S. government that the treatment of those held in the Guantanamo Bay facility not only falls short of Geneva Convention standards but in some instances has been "tantamount to torture."[38]

(The U.S. Department of Justice had earlier stirred up a separate storm of controversy when it issued a memorandum in August 2002[39] construing the term "torture" as used in the Torture Convention[40] and its implementing

---

[36] Convention Relative to the Treatment of Prisoners of War, art. 4, 12 Aug. 1949, 6 U.S.T. 3316, T.I.A.S. No. 3364, 75 U.N.T.S. 135. A presidential adviser went so far as to characterize the Geneva Conventions in a 2002 memo as "obsolete" and "quaint." Specifically, the memo stated that "the war against terrorism is a new kind of war" and that "this new paradigm renders obsolete Geneva's strict limitations on questioning of enemy prisoners and renders quaint some of its provisions." Alberto Gonzales, White House Counsel, memo of 25 January 2002, *available at* http://www.americanprogress.org/-site/pp.asp?c=biJRJ8OVF&b=246536.

[37] *See, e.g.,* Human Rights Watch, Background Paper on Geneva Conventions and Persons Held by U.S. Forces, 29 Jan. 2002, *available at* http://hrw.org/backgrounder/usa/pow-bck.htm (focusing upon the status and treatment of Taliban and al-Qaeda fighters from Afghanistan in U.S. custody); Lawrence Azubuike, *Status of Taliban and Al Qaeda Soldiers: Another Viewpoint,* 19 CONN. J. INT'L L. 127 (2003); and Michael J.D. Sweeney, *Detention at Guantanamo Bay,* HUM. RTS., Winter 2003, at 15.

[38] The ICRC's conclusions, reported by the New York Times, were contained in confidential reports to the U.S. government based on a month-long visit to Guantanamo Bay by an ICRC inspection team in June 2004. *See* Neil A. Lewis, *Red Cross Finds Detainee Abuse in Guantanamo,* N.Y.TIMES, 30 Nov. 2004, at A1. The ICRC team reportedly found that the "American military has intentionally used psychological and sometimes physical coercion 'tantamount to torture' on prisoners at Guantanamo Bay." *Id. See also id., Fresh Details Emerge on Harsh Methods at Guantanamo,* N.Y. TIMES, 1 Jan. 2005, at A11; *Secret Report Questions Guantanamo Tactics,* N.Y. TIMES, 2 Feb. 2005, at A14. Charges were also made in the ICRC reports, as well as in the *New England Journal of Medicine,* that U.S. military medical personnel violated the Geneva Conventions (as well as standards of medical ethics) by assisting in abusive interrogations. *See* M. Gregg Bloche & Jonathan H. Marks, *When Doctors Go to War,* 352 NEW ENG. J. MED. 1497 (2005). These charges were denied by Defense Department spokesmen. Joe Stephens, *Army Doctors Implicated in Abuse,* WASH. POST, 6 Jan. 2005, at A8. *See generally* ICRC, *The ICRC's Work at Guantanamo Bay,* 30 Nov. 2004, available at http://www.icrc.org/Web/eng/siteeng0.nsf/wphist74/C5667B446C9A4DF7C1256F5CBO403967; and John R. Crook, ed., Contemporary Practice of the United States relating to International Law, *Continued Allegations of Abusive Treatment and Interrogations at Guantanamo Bay,* 99 AM. J. INT'L. L. 479, 486 (2005).

[39] Memorandum from Assistant Attorney General Jay S. Bybee to White House Counsel Alberto R. Gonzales Regarding Standards of Conduct for Interrogation Under 18 U.S.C. §§ 2340-2340A (Aug. 1, 2002) (hereinafter Department of Justice memorandum of 1 Aug. 2002).

[40] Convention against Torture and Other Cruel, Inhuman, or Degrading Treatment or Punishment, U.N. Doc. A/39/708, 23 I.L.M. 1027 (1984), *as modified,* 24 I.L.M. 535 (1985).

legislation[41] to mean the infliction of not mere physical pain and suffering, but of "intense pain or suffering of the kind that is equivalent to the pain that would be associated with serious physical injury so severe that death, organ failure, or permanent damage resulting in a loss of significant body function will likely result."[42] The Justice Department later "withdrew" the August 2002 memorandum and issued a new one on December 30, 2004,[43] which "supersede[d] the August 2002 Memorandum in its entirety" and "disagree[d]" with the limitation of "severe" pain under the statute in the way described in the above quotation from the 2002 memorandum.[44])

The U.S. administration's position on the applicability of the Third Geneva Convention and continuing reports of ill-treatment of detainees by U.S. forces[45] has resulted in embarrassment to the United States, whose own forces consistently, and properly, claim the benefit of the protections afforded by the Geneva Conventions. Those maintaining that the Third Geneva Convention is in fact applicable to those held by the United States in these facilities point out that even if it is technically not applicable, minimum standards of protection afforded by international human rights law and, even more fundamentally, natural law principles reflected in the conscience of humankind today, dictate that the prisoners be treated humanely.[46]

[D] This Chapter

The first principal topic we will address in this chapter is the universal human rights system — i.e., the law of human rights that is binding on all states. In this connection we will look at the instruments that comprise what has become known as the "International Bill of Rights" and the manner in which they are implemented. We will next consider the customary international law of human rights that is universally applicable. Finally, we

---

[41] 18 U.S.C. §§ 2340-2340A.

[42] Department of Justice memorandum of 1 Aug. 2002, *supra* note 39, at 13. *See generally* Sean D. Murphy, ed., Contemporary Practice of the United States, *Executive Branch Memoranda on Status and Permissible Treatment of Detainees*, 98 AM. J. INT'L. L. 825 (2004).

[43] Memorandum from Acting Assistant Attorney General Daniel Levin to Deputy Attorney General James B. Comfey, 30 Dec. 2004, *available at* http://www.usdoj.gov/olc/dagmemo.pdf.

[44] *Id.* at 1-2. *See generally* John R. Crook, ed., Contemporary Practice of the United States relating to International Law, *Justice Department Issues New Memorandum on Torture*, 99 AM. J. INT'L. L. 479 (2005).

[45] *See, e.g.,* R. Jeffrey Smith & Dan Eggen, *New Papers Suggest Detainee Abuse Was Widespread*, WASH. POST, 6 Jan. 2005 at A1; Neil A. Lewis, *Detainee Seeking to Bar His Transfer Back to Egypt*, N.Y. TIMES, 6 Jan. 2005, at A18; and Raymond Bonner, *Detainee Says He Was Tortured in U.S. Custody*, N.Y. TIMES, 13 Feb. 2005, at A1. *See generally* John R. Crook, ed., Contemporary Practice of the United States relating to International Law, *Continued Allegations of Abusive Treatment and Interrogations at Guantanamo Bay, supra* note 38, 99 AM. J. INT'L. L. at 486.

[46] *See, e.g.,* U.N. Standard Minimum Rules for the Treatment of Prisoners, 13 July 1957, E.S.C. Res. 663C, U.N. EXCOR, 24th Sess., Supp. (No. 1), at 11, U.N. Doc. E/3048; and Rosa Ehrenreich Brooks, *War Everywhere: Rights, National Security Law, and the Law of Armed Conflict in the Age of Terror*, 153 U. PA. L. REV. 675 n. 10 (2004).

will survey regional systems for the protection of human rights, in particular, those that have been established in the Americas, Europe and Africa. As we will see, these systems have to a large extent gone beyond the universal system in terms of both the protections they afford and, perhaps more importantly, the mechanisms they have developed for enforcement.

§ 9.02   THE UNIVERSAL SYSTEM

To be truly "universal," a set of rules must be binding on all states in the world. While this might be true of the customary international law of human rights, it cannot strictly speaking be said of the treaty-based system since all states are not parties to the relevant treaties.[47] Nevertheless, the term "universal" is used here in reference to both treaty and customary human rights norms because the rules expressed in human rights treaties are intended to be applicable universally, rather than within a given region only.

The U.N. Charter was the first international instrument to refer specifically to "human rights" and to lay down obligations, though of a general character, regarding those rights.[48] It was certainly not the first legal instrument of any kind to do so, however, as is well known. The American Declaration of Independence (1776) and Bill of Rights (1791), the French Declaration of the Rights of Man and the Citizen (1789) and much earlier, the British Magna Carta (1215), were all forerunners of the Charter and paved the way for acceptance of the idea of international protection of human rights.

Of course, international human rights law did not spring into existence fully formed following the Second World War. Tomuschat has spoken of three phases of development of the law of human rights on the international plane: first, achievement of consensus on what the rights are; second, commitment to those rights through codification of them in treaties and other instruments; and third, the development of effective enforcement mechanisms.[49] While states have largely completed the first two phases, there remains considerable work to be done in relation to the third.

In sum, while the notion that international law would have anything to say about the way in which a country treated those subject to its authority may at one time have been controversial, that is not the case today. There is indeed empirical evidence to support this proposition: the acceptance by all 191 U.N. member states of the human rights provisions of the

---

[47] See the numbers of parties to a number of important human rights treaties indicated in notes 51 and 52, *infra*.

[48] The provisions of the Charter relating to human rights are set forth in note 50, *infra*. As Judge Thomas Buergenthal has written, "The human rights provisions which ultimately found their way into the Charter of the United Nations fell far short of the expectations that Roosevelt's vision and the wartime rhetoric had created." THOMAS BUERGENTHAL, INTERNATIONAL HUMAN RIGHTS IN A NUTSHELL 18 (1988).

[49] CHRISTIAN TOMUSCHAT, HUMAN RIGHTS: BETWEEN REALISM AND IDEALISM 3 (2003).

U.N. Charter[50] and the broad participation in the two human rights Covenants[51] as well as the other major treaties in the field.[52] Thus it seems safe to conclude that the concept of internationally protected human rights, and at least a core of fundamental human rights obligations, are generally accepted by states. We will examine this proposition further when we consider customary international human rights law, below. But for now we may proceed on the assumption that all states are bound by norms of international human rights law, the precise rights protected and the degree of detail depending on whether a state is a party to a relevant treaty.

Finally, a word of caution is in order. It should already be clear that to speak of "international human rights law" as a monolithic field is misleading. As Brownlie has observed: "In the real world of practice and procedure, there is no such entity as 'International Human Rights Law' and, when this concept is imposed on students, it can only be a source of confusion."[53] Thus one should be careful to identify the source of a particular human rights norm, whether it is a statute, a treaty, or general international law. This will reveal much about the norm itself, in terms of its content, its specificity and the mechanisms available to enforce it.

[A]   The "International Bill of Human Rights"

The great British international law scholar Hersch Lauterpact was probably the first to develop the idea of an "International Bill of Human Rights," in a 1945 book,[54] even if he did not use that precise term. The International Bill of Human Rights is generally thought to be comprised of the following: the human rights provisions of the U.N. Charter; the

---

[50] *See* the preamble of the U.N. Charter, in which the member states "reaffirm faith in fundamental human rights, in the equal rights of men and women . . . ;" art. 55, providing that the UN "shall promote: . . . (c) universal respect for, and observance of, human rights and fundamental freedoms for all . . . ;" and art. 56, in which "All Members pledge themselves to take joint and separate action in cooperation with the Organization for the achievement of the purposes set forth in Article 55." U.N. Charter, *supra* note 1, pmbl., arts. 55 & 56, 59.

[51] International Covenant on Economic, Social and Cultural Rights, 993 U.N.T.S. 3 (151 parties), and International Covenant on Civil and Political Rights, 999 U.N.T.S. 171 (154 parties). The Covenants are discussed in subsections 9.02 [A][2] and [3], below.

[52] Prominent examples of the many treaties in the field of human rights, other than the two Covenants, include the Convention on the Prevention and Punishment of the Crime of Genocide, 78 U.N.T.S. 277 (137 parties), Convention Relating to the Status of Refugees, 189 U.N.T.S. 137 (142 parties), Supplementary Convention on the Abolition of Slavery, the Slave Trade, and Institutions and Practices Similar to Slavery, 266 U.N.T.S. 3 (119 parties), Abolition of Forced Labor Convention, 320 U.N.T.S. 291 (162 parties), International Convention on the Elimination of All Forms of Racial Discrimination, 660 U.N.T.S. 195 (170 parties), Convention on the Elimination of All Forms of Discrimination Against Women, A/Res./34/180, 1249 U.N.T.S. 13, 19 I.L.M. 33 (1980) (180 parties), Convention against Torture and Other Cruel, Inhuman, or Degrading Treatment or Punishment, 23 I.L.M. 1027 (1984), as modified, 1465 U.N.T.S. 85, 24 I.L.M. 535 (1985) (139 parties), and Convention on the Rights of the Child, 1577 U.N.T.S. 3, 28 I.L.M. 1448 (192 parties).

[53] BROWNLIE, *supra* note 7, at 530.

[54] HERSCH LAUTERPACHT, AN INTERNATIONAL BILL OF THE RIGHTS OF MAN (1945).

Universal Declaration of Human Rights of 1948;[55] the two human rights treaties of 1966 that grew out of the Universal Declaration, the International Covenants on Civil and Political Rights (CP Covenant), and on Economic, Social and Cultural Rights (ESC Covenant);[56] and the First Optional Protocol to the Covenant on Civil and Political Rights.[57] In the following subsections we will focus on the Universal Declaration and the two Covenants.

[1]   The Universal Declaration

The Universal Declaration of Human Rights was adopted by the U.N. General Assembly on December 10, 1948.[58] The text of the Declaration had been prepared by the U.N. Commission on Human Rights[59] which was chaired by Eleanor Roosevelt.[60] The Universal Declaration laid groundwork for the two human rights Covenants that were concluded almost twenty years later. Indeed, the Human Rights Commission had initially been charged with drawing up an "international bill of human rights"[61] but the states represented on the Commission soon realized that it would be difficult to come to agreement on a binding treaty and therefore contented themselves with a non-binding declaration.[62] While indeed technically non-binding, as a U.N. General Assembly resolution,[63] and despite the statements to this effect of most of the states that supported it,[64] two arguments have been made for giving legal effect to the Declaration.

---

[55] G.A. Res. 217, U.N. Doc. A/64 (1948).

[56] International Covenant on Economic, Social and Cultural Rights, G.A. Res. 2200, 21 U.N. GAOR Supp. 49, U.N. Doc. A/6316 (1967), *reprinted in* 6 I.L.M. 360 (1967) (hereinafter ESC Covenant); International Covenant on Civil and Political Rights, G.A. Res. 2200, 21 U.N. GAOR Supp. 52, U.N. Doc. A/6316 (1967), S. Exec. Doc. E, 95-2 (1978), *reprinted in* 6 I.L.M. 368 (1967) (hereinafter CP Covenant).

[57] 19 Dec. 1966, G.A. Res. 2200 (XXI), 21 U.N. GAOR, Supp. (No. 16) 59, U.N. Doc. A/6316 (1967), *reprinted in* 6 I.L.M. 383 (1967). In 1989 a Second Optional Protocol to the Civil and Political Covenant was adopted, dealing with the abolition of the death penalty. G.A. Res. 44/128, *reprinted in* 29 I.L.M. 1465 (1990).

[58] G.A. Res. 217 A (III), U.N. Doc. A/810, at 71 (10 Dec. 1948). There were no negative votes on the Declaration but eight states abstained.

[59] The Commission on Human Rights had been established by the U.N. Economic and Social Council (ECOSOC) in 1946, pursuant to art. 68 of the U.N. Charter. The principal drafter of the Declaration was René Cassin, a French jurist and Nobel laureate.

[60] Eleanor Roosevelt was by then the widow of United States President Franklin D. Roosevelt, who died in 1945.

[61] *See generally* JOHANNES MORSINK, THE UNIVERSAL DECLARATION OF HUMAN RIGHTS: ORIGINS, DRAFTING, AND INTENT (2000).

[62] NEHEMIAH ROBINSON, THE UNIVERSAL DECLARATION OF HUMAN RIGHTS: ITS ORIGIN, SIGNIFICANCE, AND INTERPRETATION (1958).

[63] As we have seen, except for the power to approve the budget of the U.N. under art. 17 of the Charter, the powers of the General Assembly are confined to discussion, study and recommendation; it is not authorized to adopt binding decisions. U.N. Charter, *supra* note 1, arts. 10-13, inter alia.

[64] *See* 2 OPPENHEIM, *supra* note 7, at 1001, and sources cited in n. 2.

The first argument is that the Declaration is an authoritative interpretation of the provisions of the Charter on human rights, and that states acting inconsistently with the Declaration may be in violation of the Charter.[65] The second argument for legal effect of the Declaration is that in the years since its adoption it has become accepted through state practice as a reflection, in large part at least, of the customary international law of human rights.[66] There is still some debate about these propositions but they at least reflect the significance attributed by many to the Universal Declaration. It may also be observed that many of the rights recognized in the Declaration are in fact guaranteed in binding agreements that have gained widespread acceptance.

The Universal Declaration provides that "everyone" has the right to the following:

- life, liberty and security of person;

- not to be held in slavery or servitude;

- not to be subjected to torture or to cruel, inhuman or degrading treatment or punishment;

- recognition as a person before the law;

- equality before the law and equal protection;

- an effective remedy by the competent tribunals for violations of fundamental rights;

- not to be subjected to arbitrary arrest, detention or exile;

- a fair and public hearing by an independent and impartial tribunal;

- a presumption of innocence until proved guilty in a public trial with all guarantees necessary for a defense;

- not to be convicted on the basis of an ex post facto law or to be punished more severely than permitted when the crime was committed;

- not to be subjected to arbitrary interference with privacy, family, home or correspondence, or to attacks upon honor or reputation;

- freedom of movement and residence within each state and the right to leave any country and to return to one's own country;

- to seek and enjoy asylum from persecution;

- a nationality;

- to marry and found a family, with men and women having equal rights as to marriage, during marriage and at its dissolution;

---

[65] RESTATEMENT 3D, *supra* note 7, § 701, Reporters' Note 4.

[66] *See, e.g., id.*, and sources there cited.

- to own property and not to be arbitrarily deprived of property;

- freedom of thought, conscience and religion;

- freedom of opinion and expression;

- peaceful assembly and association;

- to participate in government, directly or through freely chosen representatives;

- social security;

- to work, including free choice of employment, just and favorable conditions of work, protection against unemployment, just and favorable remuneration and the right to form and join trade unions;

- rest and leisure, including periodic holidays with pay;

- a standard of living adequate for the health and well-being of oneself and one's family, including

  - food,

  - clothing,

  - housing, and

  - medical care and necessary social services;

- education, which is to be free and compulsory at the elementary level;

- participation in the cultural life of the community;

- protection of moral and material interests resulting from any scientific, literary or artistic production of which one is the author; and

- a social and international order in which the foregoing rights can be fully realized.

It will be immediately evident on a reading of this summary[67] of the rights contained in the Universal Declaration that some of them are of a more fundamental character than others, and that certain of the "rights" enumerated are more aspirational, or in the nature of goals, than actual rights that presently exist in all countries. Notwithstanding this unevenness, the Declaration "has been of considerable value as supplying a standard of action and of moral obligation."[68]

The two human rights Covenants, which will be discussed in the following subsections, grew out of the Universal Declaration. Most of the provisions of the Declaration have counterparts in one or the other of the

---

[67] The list is not all-inclusive but represents an attempt to highlight the principal rights enumerated in the Universal Declaration.

[68] 2 OPPENHEIM, *supra* note 7, at 1002.

Covenants. However, there are provisions of the Declaration, such as the right to own property, that are not reflected in the Covenants, and vice-versa.[69]

[2]　The Civil and Political Covenant

The International Covenant on Civil and Political Rights was adopted on December 19, 1966 by the United Nations General Assembly, along with the Economic and Social Covenant.[70] As we have already seen, the two agreements grew out of the Universal Declaration of Human Rights and put into obligatory form most of the rights expressed in that non-binding instrument.

The Civil and Political Covenant is similar in many respects to the Bill of Rights under the United States Constitution. It addresses the most fundamental of human rights, including the right to life (Article 6), the right not to be subjected to torture or to cruel, inhuman or degrading treatment or punishment (Article 7), the right not to be held in slavery (Article 8), the right not to be subjected to arbitrary arrest or detention (Article 9), and other rights of the highest order. It also recognizes basic procedural rights, such as equality before the law, the right to a fair and public hearing, the presumption of innocence, the right to a speedy trial, the right to counsel (Article 14), and the like.

In keeping with the fundamental character of the rights contained in the Civil and Political Covenant, states are obligated under Article 2 to implement them immediately.[71] As we will see, this contrasts with the Economic, Social and Cultural Covenant, which states may implement progressively, over time. Immediate implementation of Civil and Political rights should not be impracticable for most states since the rights to a large extent require abstention by the government from conduct harmful to individuals. However some obligations, such as those relating to conditions of imprisonment under Article 9, would clearly require the expenditure of funds for their implementation.

A critical issue, particularly in a world threatened by terrorism, is to what extent a state may excuse itself from observing the obligations under

---

[69] Both Covenants recognize the right of all "peoples" to self-determination in common art. 1, a right not contained in the Universal Declaration. Further, the Civil and Political Covenant, unlike the Declaration, recognizes a right not to be imprisoned for inability to fulfill a contractual obligation (art. 11).

[70] G.A. Res. 2200 (XXI), 21 U.N. GAOR, Supp. (No. 16) 49 (Economic and Social Covenant) and 52 (Civil and Political Covenant), U.N. Doc. A/6316 (1967), *reprinted in* 6 I.L.M. 360 (Economic and Social Covenant) and 368 (Civil and Political Covenant) (1967).

[71] The precise language of art. 2 is: "Each State Party to the present Covenant undertakes to respect and to ensure to all individuals within its territory and subject to its jurisdiction the rights recognized in the present Covenant. . . ." Civil and Political Covenant, art. 2(1). This constitutes an immediate obligation to "respect and to ensure" the rights contained in the Covenant. *See* Thomas Buergenthal, *To Respect and to Ensure: State Obligations and Permissible Derogations*, in LOUIS HENKIN, ED., THE INTERNATIONAL BILL OF HUMAN RIGHTS: THE COVENANT ON CIVIL AND POLITICAL RIGHTS 72, 72-78 (1981).

the Civil and Political Covenant under exigent circumstances. The Covenant addresses this question early on, providing in Article 4 that parties may "take measures derogating from their obligations under the present Covenant to the extent strictly required by the exigencies of the situation" in the event of a "public emergency which threatens the life of the nation".[72] The emergency must be officially proclaimed and the measures taken may not be discriminatory.[73] However, no derogation is permitted in relation to seven of the most fundamental rights: the right to life (Article 6); the right not to be subjected to torture or to cruel, inhuman or degrading treatment or punishment (Article 7); the right not be held in slavery or servitude (Article 8(1) and (2)); the right not to be imprisoned for inability to fulfill a contractual obligation (Article 11); the right not to be convicted of a criminal offense on the basis of an ex post facto law (Article 15); the right to be recognized as a person before the law (Article 16); and the right to freedom of thought, conscience and religion (Article 18). A state derogating from its obligations as permitted by Article 4 must immediately inform other parties to the Covenant of the provisions from which it has derogated and the reasons for the derogation.[74] The Covenant also allows states to limit the exercise of a number of rights under specified conditions.[75] Unfortunately, governments have invoked provisions allowing derogations and limitations all too often to justify conduct that, *prima facie*, violates the Covenant.[76]

The Civil and Political Covenant provides for the establishment of a Human Rights Committee, consisting of eighteen members elected by the parties on the basis of their expertise in the field of human rights and who serve in their personal capacities rather than as representatives of governments.[77] The Human Rights Committee receives periodic reports from parties to the Covenant on measures they have taken to implement the Covenant's obligations and on the human rights situation in their countries. Committee members may, and usually do, question states on their reports, often relying on additional information of which they, as experts, are aware or that is submitted to them by non-governmental organizations or other sources. The Committee then informs the party of any concerns or recommendations it may have in the form of "concluding

---

[72] Civil and Political Covenant, *supra* note 51, art. 4(1). *See generally* Buergenthal, *supra* note 71, at 78-86; Rosalyn Higgins, *Derogations under Human Rights Treaties*, 48 Brit. Y.B. Int'l L. 281 (1975-76); and Theodore Meron, Human Rights Law-Making in the United Nations 86-92 (1986).

[73] Civil and Political Covenant, *supra* note 51, art. 4(1).

[74] *Id.*, art. 4(3).

[75] *See, e.g., id.*, arts. 12(3), 18(3), 19(3), 21, and 22(2). For example, art. 21 (right of peaceful assembly) provides: "No restrictions may be placed on the exercise of this right other than those imposed in conformity with the law and which are necessary in a democratic society in the interests of national security or public safety, public order (*ordre public*), the protection of public health or morals or the protection of the rights and freedoms of others."

[76] Buergenthal states that this is true in particular of states that do not have a strong and independent judiciary. Buergenthal, *supra* note 48, at 37.

[77] Civil and Political Covenant, *supra* note 51, art. 28.

observations."[78] As discussed further below, this is a principal means by which compliance with the Covenant is monitored and encouraged.[79] The Committee is also authorized to adopt "general comments" dealing with the manner in which it believes the Covenant is to be interpreted, to assist the parties in fulfilling their reporting obligations.[80]

[3] The Economic, Social and Cultural Covenant

As we have seen, the International Covenant on Economic, Social and Cultural Rights was adopted by the U.N. General Assembly together with the Civil and Political Covenant, on December 19, 1966,[81] and like the latter was based on the relevant provisions of the Universal Declaration of Human Rights. Unlike the Civil and Political Covenant, which may be compared broadly to the U.S. Bill of Rights, the Economic, Social and Cultural Covenant has no close counterpart in American law. The rights it recognizes, some of which go beyond those contained in the Universal Declaration, have more to do with an individual's standard and circumstances of living as well as working conditions than with guarantees against state deprivations. They include the right to work in favorable conditions (Articles 6 and 7), to form and join trade unions (Article 8), to social security (Article 9), to the protection of the family (Article 10), to an adequate standard of living (Article 11), to the highest attainable standard of physical and mental health (Article 12), to education (Article 13) and to participate in cultural life (Article 15). These rights are elaborated in great detail, in terms of both their content and the measures that must be taken for their implementation.

Since implementation of these kinds of rights would require many states to undertake comprehensive new programs, necessitating the marshaling and expenditure of significant economic and other forms of resources, it is not surprising that governments are not required to give the rights under the Economic, Social and Cultural Covenant immediate effect. Article 2 of the Covenant provides that each party "undertakes to *take steps*, individually and through international assistance and cooperation, . . . to the maximum of its available resources, with a view to *achieving progressively* the full realization of the rights recognized in the present Covenant. . . ."[82] Thus, unlike the rights under the Civil and Political Covenant which must be implemented immediately, states are required only to give effect to the rights under the Economic, Social and Cultural Covenant progressively. While this is a realistic approach, in view of states' different circumstances,

---

[78] *See* the Committee's website, http://www.ohchr.org/english/bodies/hrc/index.htm.

[79] *See* subsection [4], below.

[80] *See* the Committee's website, http://www.ohchr.org/english/bodies/hrc/comments.htm, which also contains a list of the 31 general comments the Committee has issued (as of August 2, 2005).

[81] G.A. Res. 2200 (XXI), 21 U.N. GAOR, Supp. (No. 16) 49, U.N. Doc. A/6316 (1967), *reprinted in* 6 I.L.M. 360 (1967).

[82] Economic, Social and Cultural Covenant, *supra* note 24, art. 2(1) (emphasis added).

it means that "there can be no uniform standards by which to measure compliance"[83] with the obligations under the Covenant.

The contrast between the importance of the rights under the two Covenants is further underscored by a provision allowing developing countries to determine to what extent they would guarantee the economic rights of non-nationals under the Economic, Social and Cultural Covenant.[84] With this exception, states do have an immediate obligation under the Covenant, namely, not to discriminate in any way in the implementation of the rights it recognizes.[85]

The Economic, Social and Cultural Covenant, like the Civil and Political Covenant, recognizes that states may have to limit the rights it recognizes. But it does so in a general clause providing that those rights may be subjected "only to such limitations as are determined by law only in so far as this may be compatible with the nature of these rights and solely for the purpose of promoting the general welfare in a democratic society."[86] The Economic, Social and Cultural Covenant contains no provision on derogation from the rights it recognizes, presumably because states need implement them only progressively and because they may in any event be subjected to limitations.

Unlike the Civil and Political Covenant, which as we have seen establishes the Human Rights Committee, the Economic, Social and Cultural Covenant does not establish a monitoring body. However, a Committee on Economic, Social and Cultural Rights (ESC Committee) was established by a 1985 resolution of the Economic and Social Council (ECOSOC)[87] and began functioning in 1987.[88] It replaced a Working Group composed of government representatives which, due to its very representative character, had not enjoyed success in monitoring government implementation. The eighteen members of the Committee are elected by ECOSOC, on nomination of states parties to the Covenant, for four year terms and serve in their individual, expert capacities, not as government representatives. As in the case of the Human Rights Committee, and like the Working Group, the ESC Committee's main function is to monitor the implementation of the ESC Covenant by the states that are parties. It performs this function chiefly through receiving reports from the parties, posing questions to them on the reports and, like the Human Rights Committee, issuing "concluding observations," stating the Committee's opinion concerning the status of the parties' implementation of the Covenant. ECOSOC authorized

---

[83] BUERGENTHAL, *supra* note 48, at 45.

[84] Economic, Social and Cultural Covenant, *supra* note 24, art. 2(3). This provision reflects the controversial nature, especially in countries that had emerged from colonialism earlier in the 1960s, of the law of state responsibility for injuries to aliens. *See* §9.01[B], above.

[85] *Id.*, art. 2(2).

[86] *Id.*, art. 4.

[87] ECOSOC Res. 1985/17.

[88] *See generally* Philip Alston and Bruno Simma, *The First Session of the UN Committee on Economic, Social and Cultural Rights*, 81 AM. J. INT'L. L. 747 (1987).

the ESC Committee to adopt general comments on the Economic, Social and Cultural Covenant — as the Human Rights Committee may do in relation to the Civil and Political Covenant — with a view to assisting the parties in the fulfillment of their obligations and to indicate its interpretation of particular provisions.[89]

[4] Compliance Mechanisms

Mechanisms to promote compliance with, or to allow enforcement of, international human rights norms are perhaps more necessary than in other fields of international law. This is so because unlike other norms of international law the typical violation of a human rights obligation does not directly affect other states. They would thus have less incentive to enforce human rights obligations than they would have with regard to other obligations under international law, which are normally characterized by mutuality. This also means there may be less incentive to comply with human rights obligations in the first place, since other states are less likely to respond to violations than if their interests were directly affected. Thus compliance mechanisms are particularly important in the field of human rights because the logic of the normal decentralized system of enforcement does not apply, and without such mechanisms violations may pass without response.

Yet states are notoriously uncomfortable with the notion that their human rights record could be subjected to outside examination and evaluation, especially by other states. (The states participating in the European system, discussed in § 9.03 below, represent an equally well-known exception to this proposition.) This discomfort, coupled with the obvious need for some form of compliance mechanism, probably accounts for the rather weak system that has been established on the universal level. Indeed, "system" is probably too strong a term since there are in fact different systems, and different levels of implementation, for different human rights regimes. This subsection first considers the compliance mechanisms related to the two human rights covenants discussed above, then takes a brief look at the enforcement of human rights law through domestic and international tribunals.

[a] United Nations and Treaty-Based Systems

All human rights obligations are implemented in the first instance on the domestic level, chiefly through legislation or constitutional provisions and their enforcement but also through judicial decisions. The question is,

---

[89] ECOSOC Res. 1987/5; Rule 65, CESCR, Rules of procedure of the committee, 1 Sept. 1993, UN Doc. E/C.12/1990/4/Rev.1, *available at* http://66.36.242.93/general/rules_cescr.php. Rule 65 reads: "The Committee may prepare general comments based on the various articles and provisions of the Covenant with a view to assisting States parties in fulfilling their reporting obligations." *Id.* According to the Committee's website, "The Committee decided in 1988 to begin preparing 'general comments' on the rights and provisions contained in the Covenant with a view to assisting States parties in fulfilling their reporting obligations and to provide greater interpretative clarity as to the intent, meaning and content of the Covenant." http://www.unhchr.ch/html/menu6/2/fs16.htm.

what if anything happens when they are not? Are there procedures or mechanisms by which the affected individual, another state or an international body can call the transgressing state to account?

The answer to this question is "yes," although the exact form of redress will depend in part on whether the state in question is a party to an applicable treaty. However, as in many other areas of international law, the procedures and mechanisms for promoting compliance with human rights obligations do not begin to approach those available domestically in most states, in terms of their lack of capacity for the kind of compulsory and coercive enforcement that may be applied — at least against non-governmental offenders — on the national level.

As we have already seen, monitoring bodies have been set up under both human rights Covenants: for the Civil and Political Covenant, the Human Rights Committee, and for the Covenant on Economic, Social and Cultural Rights, the Committee of that name. The requirement that parties report on the implementation of their obligations under the Covenants serves to spotlight the human rights records of these states and thus to encourage them to comply with the relevant obligations. The publicity that results from the reports, as well as the committees' questions on them and concluding observations, while not qualifying as "enforcement" in the ordinary sense of the term, help to deter flagrant or systematic violations and provide an incentive to comply.

The Civil and Political Covenant also provides for an interstate enforcement procedure in Article 41. A party to the Covenant may make a declaration accepting the competence of the Human Rights Committee to receive and consider claims by another party that the former is not fulfilling its obligations under the Covenant.[90] This system has been characterized as being "extremely weak" because "it provides neither for adjudication or quasi-adjudication, and establishes little more than a formal conciliation machinery."[91]

A more direct avenue of recourse for individual claimants is provided by the First Optional Protocol to the Covenant on Civil and Political Rights.[92] As its name implies, this is a separate agreement that states who are parties to the Civil and Political Covenant may opt to participate in. It allows individuals subject to the jurisdiction of a party to the Protocol to file communications with the Human Rights Committee claiming to be victims of a violation by that state of any of the rights recognized in the Covenant.[93] If

---

[90] A list of the 48 states that have made a declaration accepting the Committee's competence under Article 41 is available at http://www.unhcr.ch/html/menu3/b/treaty5_asp.htm.

[91] BUERGENTHAL, *supra* note 48, at 39.

[92] 19 Dec. 1966, G.A. Res. 2200 (XXI), 21 U.N. GAOR, Supp. (No. 16) 59, U.N. Doc. A/6316 (1967), *reprinted in* 6 I.L.M. 383 (1967).

[93] *Id.*, art. 1. The complaint procedure is described in plain terms in the OHCHR Fact Sheet, *available at* http://www.ohchr.org/english/about/publications/docs/fs7.htm. *See generally* Dinah Shelton, *Individual Complaint Machinery under the United Nations 1503 Procedure and the Optional Protocol to the International Covenant on Civil and Political*

the Committee decides that the complaint is admissible, it informs the state concerned, which has six months in which to respond. If the Committee decides that the state has indeed violated the rights of the petitioner under the Covenant, it forwards its findings, or "views," to the state, including any recommendations on an appropriate remedy,[94] and invites the state to provide information, within three months, on the steps it has taken to give effect to the Committee's views. The Committee's decisions are posted on the website of the U.N. Office of High Commissioner for Human Rights (OHCHR). There is no appeal against Committee decisions.

Beyond the Optional Protocol, there are a number of avenues for individuals to raise human rights violations with the United Nations.[95] The website of the OHCHR states: "Anyone may bring a human rights problem to the attention of the United Nations and thousands of people around the world do so every year."[96] Complaint procedures may be divided into those under individual human rights treaties[97] and those under U.N. political bodies composed of state representatives. The latter are the Commission on Human Rights and the Commission on the Status of Women. While the treaty-based procedures are designed to provide redress in individual cases through quasi-judicial procedures, those under the two Commissions deal on the political level with systematic patterns and trends of human rights violations rather than individual cases.[98]

Rights, in Hurst Hannum, ed., GUIDE TO INTERNATIONAL HUMAN RIGHTS PRACTICE 59, 67-73 (1984); Markus G. Schmidt, *Individual Human Rights Complaints Procedures Based on United Nations Treaties and the Need for Reform*, 41 INT'L & COMP. L.Q. 645 (1992); Natalia Schiffrin, *Jamaica Withdraws the Right of Individual Petition under the International Covenant on Civil and Political Rights*, 92 AM. J. INT'L L. 563 (1998); and Alfred de Zayas, *The Examination of Individual Complaints by the United Nations Human Rights Committee Under the Optional Protocol to the International Covenant on Civil and Political Rights*, in INTERNATIONAL HUMAN RIGHTS MONITORING MECHANISMS 67 (Gudmunder Alfredsson et al. eds., 2001).

[94] E.g., payment of compensation or release from detention.

[95] The website of the U.N. High Commissioner for Human Rights refers to complaint procedures under five human rights treaties (including the First Optional Protocol), the 1503 Procedure, discussed below, and the procedure of the Commission on the Status of Women. *See* http://www.ohchr.org/english/about/publications/docs/fs7.htm.

[96] http://www.ohchr.org/english/bodies/petitions/individual.htm.

[97] Treaties under which individuals may make complaints, assuming the state concerned is a party, are: the First Optional Protocol to the CP Covenant, *supra* note 92; the Optional Protocol to the Convention on the Elimination of All Forms of Discrimination against Women, G.A. Res. 54/4, U.N. Doc. A/RES/54/4 (15 Oct. 1999), reprinted in 39 I.L.M. 281; the Convention against Torture and Other Cruel, Inhuman or Degrading Treatment or Punishment, U.N. Doc. A/39/708, 23 I.L.M. 1027 (1984), as modified, 24 I.L.M. 535 (1985); the International Convention on the Elimination of All Forms of Racial Discrimination, 660 U.N.T.S. 195, reprinted in 5 I.L.M. 352 (1966); and the International Convention on the Protection of the Rights of All Migrant Workers and Members of Their Families, G.A. Res. 45/158, annex, 45 U.N. GAOR Supp. (No. 49A) at 262, U.N. Doc. A/45/49 (1990) (when ten parties have made the necessary declaration). *See generally* http://www.ohchr.org/english/bodies/petitions/. For some of these agreements, e.g., the Convention against Torture, the Convention on the Elimination of Racial Discrimination and the Migrant Worker Convention, the state concerned must have made a special declaration accepting the procedure in question.

[98] *See generally* http://www.ohchr.org/english/bodies/petitions/individual.htm.

The U.N. Commission on Human Rights concluded as early as 1947 that it had no power to act on individual complaints of human rights violations.[99] But ECOSOC has since established procedures for receiving and investigating complaints of human rights violations. In 1967 ECOSOC adopted Resolution 1235,[100] generally authorizing the Commission and Sub-Commission to examine information relating to gross violations of human rights and fundamental freedoms. Then in 1970 it adopted resolution 1503, providing specific procedures for dealing with communications regarding human rights violations received by the United Nations. This complaint procedure relies on the Human Rights Commission's Sub-Commission on the Promotion and Protection of Human Rights (originally established in 1947 as the Sub-Commission on Prevention of Discrimination and Protection of Minorities) to review information and communications regarding human rights violations and decide whether to refer them to the Commission, which may then determine whether to conduct a "thorough study" of the situation concerned.[101]

Looking more closely at the 1503 Procedure, the Economic and Social Council established this mechanism[102] as a result of a request by the U.N. General Assembly in 1966 that it consider urgently how the capacity of the United Nations to combat human rights violations could be improved.[103] The procedure was revised substantially in 2000 to make it more efficient and to facilitate dialogue with the states concerned.[104] Under the procedure, the Sub-Commission receives and reviews "communications, together with replies of Governments, if any, which appear to reveal a consistent pattern of gross and reliably attested violations of human rights and fundamental freedoms. . . ."[105] The communications may be submitted by individuals or non-governmental organizations, whether or not they have been directly affected. In fact, since the communications must allege a "pattern" of violations the procedure is not one of individual petition for redress of particular injuries. It is not restricted to communications involving racial discrimination and the protection of minorities, but applies to all gross violations of human rights.[106] The list

---

[99] ECOSOC Res. 75(V) (1947). *See also* ECOSOC Res. 728 F (XXVIII) (1959), which reaffirms the earlier resolution.

[100] ECOSOC Resolution 1235 (XLII) (1967).

[101] *Id.*, para. 3.

[102] ECOSOC Res. 1503 (XLVIII) (1970), "Procedure for dealing with communications relating to violations of human rights and fundamental freedoms." For text of the procedure as revised in ECOSOC Res. 2000/3 of 16 June 2000, *see* http://www.unhchr.ch/-html/menu2/8/1503.htm. It continues to be referred to as the "1503 procedure."

[103] G.A. Res. 2144 (XXI).

[104] ECOSOC Res. 2000/3 of 16 June 2000.

[105] ECOSOC Res. 1503, para. 1.

[106] *See* Commission on Human Rights, Report on the Forty-Second Session, U.N. Doc. E/1986/22, E/CN.4/1986/65, at 229-30 (1986); and Shelton, *supra* note 93, at 61. This is true more generally of the procedure under ECOSOC Res. 1235, discussed below.

of states whose conduct has been examined under this procedure is a long one, and includes both developed and developing countries.[107]

[b] Enforcement of Human Rights Law in Domestic and International Tribunals

Domestic law has been used and international tribunals have been established to enforce human rights and humanitarian law. This subsection will note experience under a United States statute then look briefly at the international criminal tribunals that have recently been established.

In the Judiciary Act of 1789, the First Congress enacted what is now 28 U.S.C. § 1350, the Alien Tort Statute. That law provides in its entirety as follows:

> "The district courts shall have original jurisdiction of any civil action by an alien for a tort only, committed in violation of the law of nations or a treaty of the United States."

The law lay effectively dormant for almost two centuries, until two Paraguayans used it as the basis of federal court jurisdiction in a suit against a third Paraguayan. This case, *Filartiga v. Pena-Irala*,[108] not only brought the Alien Tort Statute to life but also spawned an entire generation of human rights and similar suits in U.S. courts.

In *Filartiga*, the sister and father of Joelito Filartiga brought suit under § 1350 against Pena-Irala, the former Inspector General of Police of Asuncion, Paraguay, seeking compensatory and punitive damages of $10,000,000 for the torturing and killing of Joelito. The Alien Tort Statute establishes federal subject matter jurisdiction, so in order to get into federal court it was necessary for the Filartigas to make out the statute's elements, in particular, that the "tort" alleged was "committed in violation of the law of nations," or international law. Writing for the Second Circuit Court of Appeals, Judge Kaufman found that it indeed had been. Specifically, the court held that "an act of torture committed by a state official against one held in detention violates established norms of the international law of human rights, and hence the law of nations."[109] Judge Kaufman relied for this conclusion on a variety of kinds of evidence of customary international law, including U.S. case law, the United Nations Charter, the Universal Declaration of Human Rights, resolutions of the United Nations General Assembly, and the American and European Conventions on Human Rights, among other sources.[110]

---

[107] For a list of the 84 states examined by the Human Rights Commission under the 1503 procedure up to 2003, *see* http://www.unhchr.ch/.

[108] 630 F.2d 876 (2d Cir. 1980).

[109] *Id.* at 880.

[110] *Id.* at 880-884.

Since *Filartiga*, the Alien Tort Statute has been used as the basis of federal subject matter jurisdiction in numerous suits, often alleging violations of the human rights of indigenous groups by corporations and foreign state officials.[111] These suits have met with varying success, but they demonstrate the power of international human rights law when it can be asserted before domestic tribunals.

However, a recent decision by the United States Supreme Court will make it more challenging to bring human rights suits under § 1350. In its 2004 decision in *Sosa v. Alvarez-Machain*,[112] the Court clarified the kinds of violations of customary international law that could be used as a basis of a suit under §1350. Writing for a unanimous Court, Justice Souter delcared that "courts should require any claim based on the present-day law of nations to rest on a norm of international character accepted by the civilized world and defined with a specificity comparable to the features of the 18th-century paradigms we have recognized."[113] Those "18th-century paradigms" were identified by the Court as "violation of safe conducts, infringement of the rights of ambassadors, and piracy."[114] The Court also said, however, that "no development in the two centuries from the enactment of § 1350 to the birth of the modern line of cases beginning with *Filartiga* . . . has categorically precluded federal courts from recognizing a claim under the law of nations as an element of common law;. . . . Still, there are good reasons for a restrained conception of the discretion a federal court should exercise in considering a new cause of action of this kind."[115] Only time will tell whether and to what extent this decision will

---

[111] For a few illustrations of the many § 1350 cases, *see, e.g.*, Presbyterian Church of Sudan v. Talisman Energy, Inc., 374 F. Supp. 2d 331 (S.D.N.Y 2005) (company's motion for judgment on the pleadings denied because 2003 opinion demonstrated that corporations could be held liable under international law for violations of jus cogens norms, and no subsequent decision indicated that the opinion's conclusions regarding corporate liability in international law were erroneous); Tachiona v. Mugabe, 216 F. Supp. 2d 262 (S.D.N.Y. 2002) (court had jurisdiction over action by individuals who alleged torture and extrajudicial killing by the defendant foreign government, and awarded damages under federal law which protected torture victims); Flores v. S. Peru Copper Corp., 406 F.3d 65 (2d Cir. 2003) (dismissal of Alien Tort Claims Act suit affirmed on ground that "right to life" and "right to health" were insufficiently definite to constitute rules of customary international law, and treaties cited by plaintiffs were not adequate evidence of such law); and Doe v. Unocal Corp., 110 F. Supp. 2d 1294 (C.D. Cal. 2000), *reversed in part*, John Doe I v. Unocal Corp., 395 F.3d 932 (9th Cir. Cal., 2002), vacated, Doe I v. Unocal Corp., 403 F.3d 708 (9th Cir. Cal., 2005) (Defendants' motion for summary judgment granted; plaintiffs failed to prove that a violation of the law of nations occurred, as required under the Alien Tort Claims Act, alleging that defendants were liable for international human rights violations perpetrated by the Burmese military in furtherance and for the benefit of the pipeline portion of a joint venture project). *See generally* Michael Ratner & Beth Stephens (the lawyers who brought the *Filartiga* lawsuit), *The Center for Constitutional Rights: Using Law and the* Filartiga *Principle in the Fight for Human Rights*, in AMERICAN CIVIL LIBERTIES UNION, INT'L CIVIL LIBERTIES REPORT, Dec. 1993, at 29.

[112] 124 S.Ct. 2739 (2004).

[113] *Id.* at 2761-62.

[114] *Id* at 2761.

[115] *Id.*

stem the tide of suits in U.S. courts to recover for human rights violations abroad.

As discussed in Chapter 6,[116] a number of cases have been brought against foreign officials during the past decade on the basis of universal jurisdiction or similar grounds available under national law for torture, genocide, war crimes and crimes against humanity. As noted there, Spain and Belgium have been particularly active in bringing such cases, but France, Germany and the United States have also been involved.

Despite these instances of human rights suits before domestic courts, enforcement of international human rights law in this way is bound to be difficult and sporadic. In order to ensure that the most serious offences do not go unpunished, the international community has in the past decade and a half finally mustered the resolve to establish one standing and two *ad hoc* international criminal tribunals: the International Criminal Court,[117] and the *ad hoc* International Criminal Tribunals for the Former Yugoslavia[118] and Rwanda.[119] All three courts are functioning, with facilities in The Hague and, in the case of the Rwanda Tribunal, also in Arusha, Tanzania. The theory behind holding individuals, rather than states, responsible for serious human rights offenses was well stated by the Nuremberg Tribunal in 1946: "Crimes against international law are committed by men, not by abstract entities, and only by punishing individuals who commit such crimes can the provisions of international law be enforced."[120] The purpose of these international tribunals is to try and punish those committing crimes of great concern to the international community, such as war crimes, genocide and crimes against humanity. They would thus not have jurisdiction over violations of economic, social and cultural rights or even of many civil and political rights. But the mere exis-

---

[116] *See* § 6.03[E].

[117] Rome Statute of the International Criminal Court, 17 July 1998, art. 25(1), U.N. Doc. A/CONF.183/9. *See generally* WILLIAM A. SCHABAS, AN INTRODUCTION TO THE INTERNATIONAL CRIMINAL COURT (2001); and ANTONIO CASSESE, INTERNATIONAL CRIMINAL LAW (2003). For an update on the Court and its activities, *see generally* the section entitled *Developments at the International Criminal Court*, 99 AM. J. INT'L L. 370-431 (2005), containing four articles on the ICC.

[118] Statute of the International Tribunal for the Prosecution of Persons Responsible for Serious Violations of International Humanitarian Law Committed in the Territory of the Former Yugoslavia since 1991, 25 May 1993, UN Doc. S/25704 and Add.1, Annex, S.C. Res. 827 (1993), as amended by Res. 1166 (1998) of 13 May 1998 and Res. 1329 of 30 Nov. 2000 (2000). *See generally* VIRGINIA MORRIS & MICHAEL P. SCHARF, AN INSIDER'S GUIDE TO THE INTERNATIONAL CRIMINAL TRIBUNAL FOR THE FORMER YUGOSLAVIA (2 vols.) (1995).

[119] Statute of the International Tribunal for the Prosecution of Persons Responsible for Serious Violations of International Humanitarian Law Committed in the Territory of Rwanda and Rwandan Citizens Responsible for such Violations Committed in the Territory of Neighboring States, 8 Nov. 1994, approved by the U.N. Security Council in Res. 955 (1994). *See generally* VIRGINIA MORRIS & MICHAEL P. SCHARF, THE INTERNATIONAL CRIMINAL TRIBUNAL FOR RWANDA (2 vols.) (1998).

[120] International Military Tribunal for the Trial of the Major War Criminals, judgment of 1 Oct. 1946, *reprinted in* 41 AM. J. INT'L L. 172, 221 (1947).

tence of the International Criminal Court should at least deter state officials from committing serious human rights abuses.

[B] Customary International Human Rights Law[121]

The Universal Declaration and human rights treaties discussed above constitute an impressive and dynamic body of law, especially considering the field was only born at the end of World War II. However, there are inevitably gaps in treaties and other international instruments and not all states are parties to all human rights treaties. The question therefore arises, to what extent is there a body of customary international human rights law that fills these gaps and binds states that are not parties to relevant treaties?

There is probably general agreement among states today that there is a body of customary human rights law. Exactly what it consists of is something that there would be somewhat less agreement upon, however. It will be recalled that customary international law consists of two elements: (1) a general practice, that is (2) accepted as law (*opinio juris*). State practice in this field, while to some extent different from that in other areas of international law because it relates to treatment of a state's own inhabitants rather than relations with other states, is in fact quite rich. States generally observe basic human rights obligations and, when they do not, almost never defend their conduct on the basis that there is no applicable norm of human rights law. The fact that human rights law sometimes, and in some countries, seems to be honored as much in the breach as in the observance does not prevent it from being law; breaches are just that, and give rise to international responsibility. The Restatement cites a number of instances of state practice as "being accepted as building customary human rights law," mostly having to do with adherence to, or acceptance of, treaties (including the United Nations Charter) and other instruments (including the Universal Declaration) containing human rights provisions.[122] In addition, the very high number of parties to the basic human rights treaties[123] could be taken as reflecting an *opinio juris* suggesting that there is indeed agreement on both the concept of international human rights law and, to a significant extent, its content.

In the *Barcelona Traction* case, decided in 1970,[124] the International Court of Justice had occasion to discuss obligations *erga omnes* — that is, obligations owed to the international community as a whole. The Court stated that these obligations "derive, for example, in contemporary

---

[121] *See generally* THEODOR MERON, HUMAN RIGHTS AND HUMANITARIAN NORMS AS CUSTOMARY LAW (1989).

[122] RESTATEMENT 3D, *supra* note 7, §701, Reporters' Note 2. These instances might better be viewed as evidence of an *opinio juris* relating to customary international human rights law.

[123] *See* notes 51 and 52, *supra*.

[124] Case concerning the Barcelona Traction, Light and Power Co., Limited, Second Phase (Belgium v. Spain), 1970 I.C.J. 3.

international law, from the outlawing of . . . genocide, as also from the principles and rules concerning the basic rights of the human person, including
protection from slavery and racial discrimination. Some of the corresponding rights of protection have entered into the body of general international
law (*Reservations to the Convention on the Prevention and Punishment of
the Crime of Genocide, Advisory Opinion, I.C.J. Reports 1951* p. 23); . . ."[125]
It will be recalled that the expression "general international law" is another
way of referring to customary international law. This passage is important
because it indicates that even as of 1970 the Court was able to conclude
that at least some of the "basic rights of the human person" had become
part of the corpus of customary international law.

The Restatement, for its part, took a similar approach in 1987, identifying
a somewhat longer list of serious violations of basic rights as being protected
by customary international law: "(a) genocide, (b) slavery or slave trade, (c)
the murder or causing the disappearance of individuals, (d) torture or other
cruel, inhuman, or degrading treatment or punishment, (e) prolonged arbitrary detention, (f) systematic racial discrimination, or (g) a consistent pattern of gross violations of internationally recognized human rights."[126] The
Restatement states that these are rights "whose status as customary law is
generally accepted (as of 1987) and whose scope and content are generally
agreed."[127] Notable for their absence from this list, as well as that given by
the ICJ in *Barcelona Traction*, are certain of the rights reflected in the Civil
and Political Covenant (e.g., the procedural due process rights) and virtually
all of those contained in the Economic, Social and Cultural Covenant.

On the other hand, as noted earlier in connection with the discussion of
the Universal Declaration of Human Rights,[128] respected authorities have
argued that the Declaration may be said to have passed into customary
international law.[129] Further, a number of resolutions and other instruments adopted under United Nations auspices refer to "the duty of states
to fully and faithfully observe the provisions of the Universal
Declaration."[130] If the Declaration does indeed largely reflect customary
international law the rights protected by custom are far wider than the
lists of the ICJ or the Restatement suggest. As a practical matter, if the
rights expressed in the Declaration are to be regarded as being part of customary international law, it would probably be prudent to understand
them in light of the obligations accepted by states in the two Covenants in

---

[125] *Id.* at 32.

[126] RESTATEMENT 3D, *supra* note 7, § 702.

[127] *Id.* cmt. a.

[128] *See* subsection [1], above.

[129] *See, e.g.,* MYRES MCDOUGAL, HAROLD LASSWELL AND LUNG-CHU CHEN, HUMAN RIGHTS
AND WORLD PUBLIC ORDER 273-74, 325-27 (1980); Humphrey Waldock, *Human Rights in
Contemporary International Law and the Significance of the European Convention,* in THE
EUROPEAN CONVENTION ON HUMAN RIGHTS 15 (1963).

[130] *See, e.g.,* G.A. Res. 1904, 18 U.N. GAOR Supp. No. 15, at 35 (stating that every state
shall "fully and faithfully observe the provisions of the . . . Universal Declaration of Human
Rights. . . .").

relation to how they are to be given effect. That is, the rights reflected in the Declaration that are civil and political in nature should be immediately applicable, whereas those of an economic, social or cultural nature would have to be implemented only progressively by states, according to their available resources. This is akin to saying that state obligations in relation to civil and political rights are more of a "strict" nature, while those relating to economic, social and cultural rights are due diligence obligations, requiring states to exercise their best efforts — taking into account their capabilities and available resources — to fulfill them.

It may be concluded that there is indeed a customary international law of human rights but that its content begins to move progressively out of focus as one moves from the most basic protections (e.g., against genocide, slavery, systematic racial discrimination and torture) to those concerning such things as standard of living, work, rest and leisure. Yet states have clearly accepted that there is a minimum standard of protection below which their treatment of individuals is not permitted to fall. Despite the fact that its precise contours are somewhat indeterminate, customary international human rights law is quite real and binds states from America (e.g., in relation to its treatment of detainees in Guantanamo Bay) to Zimbabwe (e.g., in relation to its forced relocation of thousands of its citizens formerly living in Harare[131]), whether or not they are parties to a relevant treaty and despite their interpretation of a treaty's provisions.[132]

§ 9.03   REGIONAL SYSTEMS

Different regions of the world have somewhat different conceptions of, and attitudes toward, human rights. It thus seems fitting that regional human rights systems have developed that are separate from the universal system discussed in § 9.02 above. Thus far there have not been significant problems with inconsistencies between the universal and regional regimes.[133] This section will review briefly the three major regional systems, namely, those of the Americas, Europe and Africa.

The inter-American human rights system may be said to be the most venerable of the three under consideration, by a slim margin, having originated in the American Declaration of the Rights and Duties of Man, adopted in

---

[131] See Warren Hoge, U.N. Condemns Zimbabwe For Bulldozing Urban Slums, N.Y. TIMES, 23 July 2005, at A 5. See also the Human Rights Watch Press Release on the subject, available at http://hrw.org/english/docs/2005/07/06/zimbab11278.htm.

[132] See, e.g., the discussion of the United States' interpretation of the term "torture" in text accompanying notes 42-44, supra.

[133] Any inconsistencies between universal and regional treaty regimes would be resolved according to the rules on successive treaties relating to the same subject matter, set forth in art. 30 of the Vienna Convention on the Law of Treaties, 8 I.L.M. 679 (1969): except for the UN Charter, which would always take precedence under its art. 103, "the earlier treaty applies only to the extent that its provisions are compatible with those of the latter treaty." Id., art. 30(3). In the case of customary law-based human rights rules, given the fundamental nature of the universal customary norms, as discussed in the preceding section, it is highly unlikely that regional regimes would be inconsistent with them.

1948.[134] The way in which it has developed parallels the evolution of the United Nations human rights system in many respects, having begun with a non-binding declaration, followed later by the establishment of a commission — the Inter-American Commission on Human Rights (IACHR), founded in 1959[135] — and the adoption of a binding human rights agreement — the American Convention on Human Rights, concluded in 1969.[136] In addition, both systems have developed under a parent organization, that for the Americas being the Organization of American States.[137] A feature of the American system that does not have a counterpart on the universal level is the Inter-American Court of Human Rights, which was established by the American Convention[138] and whose Statute was adopted in 1979.[139] The Court has both contentious and advisory jurisdiction. Contentious jurisdiction, applicable in suits between state parties over alleged violations of the Convention, may be exercised only on the basis of the general or specific consent of the states involved.[140]

Also like the United Nations human rights experience, procedures for individual petition were slow to develop in the American system. But beginning in 1965, the Commission began receiving and examining complaints from individuals alleging violations of basic rights contained in the American Declaration, requesting information from governments and making appropriate recommendations to them.[141] As of the entry into

---

[134] O.A.S. Res. XXX, adopted by the Ninth Int'l Conf. of American States, 30 Mar.-2 May 1948, Bogot·, O.A.S. Off. Rec. OEA/Ser. L/V/I.4 Rev. (1965), available on the OAS website, http://www.cidh.oas.org/Basicos/basic2.htm. The European Convention, discussed below, was adopted two years later, in 1950, hence the "slim margin."

[135] A meeting of American foreign ministers in 1959 called for the establishment of the Commission; its Statute was adopted by the Council of the Organization of American States in 1960, when it held its first session. See the Commission's website, http://www.cidh.oas. org/DefaultE.htm.

[136] 22 Nov. 1969, OAS Treaty Series No. 36, at 1, OAS Off. Rec. OEA/Ser. L/V/II.23 doc. 21 rev. 6 (1979), reprinted in 9 I.L.M. 673 (1970). The Convention focuses upon civil and political rights, devoting only one article to economic, social and cultural rights. Id., art. 26 (entitled "Progressive Development").

[137] The predecessor of the OAS was the Pan-American Union, which was established at the First International Conference of American States on April 14, 1890, to promote peace, friendship, and commerce among the member states. First known as the Commercial Bureau of the American Republics, the organization was renamed as the Pan-American Union in 1910 by a resolution of the Fourth Inter-American Conference. The OAS was established in 1948. Charter of the Organization of American States, 1948, 2 U.S.T. 2394, T.I.A.S. No. 2361, 119 U.N.T.S. 3, as amended by the Protocol of Amendment, 1967, 21 U.S.T. 607, T.I.A.S. No.6847. For information on the OAS, see its website, http://www.oas.org/.

[138] American Convention on Human Rights, supra note 136, arts. 33, 52-69.

[139] 19 I.L.M. 634 (1980). See Thomas Buergenthal, The Inter-American Court of Human Rights, 76 Am. J. Int'l L. 231 (1982).

[140] The provisions of the Convention on acceptance of the Court's jurisdiction parallel to a significant extent those of the ICJ Statute. See American Convention on Human Rights, supra note 136, art. 62; compare ICJ Statute, 59 Stat. 1055, T.S. No. 993, 1976 U.N.Y.B. 1052, art. 36.

[141] See Official Document of the Second Special Inter-American Conference, Rio de Janeiro, Brazil, 17-30 Nov. 1965, General Assembly Resolution 447, reprinted in 60 Am. J. Int'l L. 445, 459 (1966).

force of the American Convention on Human Rights in 1978, individuals have been specifically authorized "to lodge petitions with the Commission containing denunciations or complaints of violation of [the] Convention by a State Party."[142] The Commission may also refer cases to the Inter-American Court if the state involved has accepted the Court's jurisdiction. More generally, the Commission conducts investigations of the human rights situation in various American countries and issues reports setting forth its findings.[143]

The European human rights system is the most highly developed of any, whether universal or regional. It was launched in 1950 with the signature of the European Convention on Human Rights[144] by the members of the Council of Europe. Like its American counterpart,[145] the European Convention focuses upon the protection of civil and political rights. It originally established two compliance mechanisms, a European Commission of Human Rights and a European Court of Human Rights.[146] This structure changed in 1998 with the entry into force of Protocol No. 11 to the Convention.[147] Protocol No. 11 converted the part-time Court into a full-time ("permanent"[148]) tribunal and eliminated the Commission, whose functions were assumed by the Court.

Any party may refer to the Court an alleged breach of the Convention by another party.[148a] The Court may also receive applications from "any person, non-governmental organization or group of individuals claiming to be the victim of a violation" of one of the rights under the Convention or its protocols.[149]

The Court, which is located in Strassbourg, thus has jurisdiction over complaints by state parties and individuals. While the Court's jurisdiction over individual petitions originally had to be accepted by the states against which they were brought, Protocol No. 11 to the Convention, which entered into force on November 1, 1998, made acceptance of the right of individual application by parties compulsory. The Court's caseload of individual complaints has mushroomed of late, due in particular to the accession of new contracting states to the Convention.[150] Execution of judgments against

---

[142] American Convention on Human Rights, *supra* note 136, art. 44.

[143] *See* American Convention on Human Rights, *id.*, art. 41.

[144] European Convention for the Protection of Human Rights and Fundamental Freedoms, 4 Nov. 1950, 213 U.N.T.S. 221, Eur. T.S. No. 5.

[145] *See* note 136, *supra*.

[146] European Convention, *supra* note 144, art. 19 (prior to entry into force of Protocol No. 11, discussed below).

[147] 11 May 199 Dur. T.S. No. 15.

[148] European Convention, *supra*, note 144, art. 1.

[148a] *Id.*, art. 33.

[149] *Id.*, art. 34. The petitioner must have exhausted domestic remedies. *Id.*, art. 35(1).

[150] The Court's website states that "[t]he number of applications registered rose from 5,979 in 1998 to 13,858 in 2001, an increase of approximately 130%." *See* http://www.echr.coe.int/ ECHR/EN/Header/The+Court/The+Court/History+of+the+Court/.

state parties to the European Convention is supervised by the Council of Europe's Committee of Ministers.[151]

The African human rights system is based on the African Charter on Human and Peoples' Rights (the Banjul Charter) of 1981.[152] The African Charter provides for the protection of a number of human rights, primarily[153] of a civil or political character.[154] As its title suggests, it also provides for "peoples'" rights.[155] In this respect the Charter is unique among human rights instruments.

Like the other principal human rights agreements, the Charter sets up a body that is responsible for the Charter's implementation: the African Commission on Human and People's Rights, established within the Organization of African Unity (now the African Union).[156] The Commission has jurisdiction over both interstate[157] and individual[158] complaints. In the latter case, the petition must "reveal the existence of a series of serious or massive violations of human and peoples' rights."[159] The Commission's competence in this respect thus resembles the 1503 Procedure under the United Nations human rights system, discussed above,[160] more than the individual complaint mechanisms available under the American and European Conventions.[161]

---

[151] European Convention, *supra* note 144, art. 46(2). The parties to the Convention undertake to comply with the Court's decisions. *Id.*, art. 46(1).

[152] 27 June 1981, 21 I.L.M. 59 (1981).

[153] The Charter, *id.*, does protect the right to work (art. 15), the right to physical and mental health (art. 16), the right to education (art. 17), and the family (art. 18).

[154] *See id.*, arts. 2-14.

[155] *Id.*, arts. 19-24. These include equality of peoples, their right to existence, their freedom to dispose of their wealth and natural resources, their right to economic, social and cultural development, their right to national and international peace and security, and their right to a generally satisfactory environment.

[156] *Id.*, art. 30. The Commission's composition and functions are provided for in arts. 31-45.

[157] *Id.*, arts. 47 and 48.

[158] *Id.* art. 55.

[159] *Id.*, art. 58(1).

[160] *See* § 9.02[A][4], above.

[161] *See* BUERGENTHAL, *supra* note 48, at 186-87.

Chapter 10
THE SETTLEMENT OF DISPUTES BETWEEN STATES

Synopsis

§ 10.01   INTRODUCTION

There being no courts with compulsory jurisdiction and recourse to force except in self-defense being unlawful, dispute settlement in the international system is consensual in character. If they cannot settle their disputes by themselves through negotiation, States must voluntarily accept the authority of a third party to do so for them or at least to assist them in the effort.

This chapter will review the basic means of dispute resolution available to states, dwelling in particular upon the principal judicial organ of the United Nations, the International Court of Justice. The chapter will not consider measures taken by states to try to encourage other states to modify their behavior so that they return to compliance with their international obligations, as seen by the state taking the measures. These forms of action, usually referred to today as countermeasures and often of an economic nature, are covered in Chapter 7, Remedies: International Responsibility.

Before considering the way in which international law regulates the settlement of disputes, we should first clarify the meaning of the term "dispute" in the international context. The World Court — either the International Court of Justice or its predecessor — has had occasion to define the term "dispute" in several of its decisions, beginning with the judgment of the Permanent Court of International Justice in the *Mavrommatis* case.[1] The Court there stated that, for the purposes of establishing its jurisdiction under Article 26 of the Mandate for Palestine,

---

[1] Mavrommatis Palestine Concessions (Gr. v. G.B.) (Jurisdiction), Judgment of 30 Aug. 1924 P.C.I.J (ser. A) No. 2, at 6. *See also, e.g.*, Applicability of Obligation to Arbitrate Under Section 21 of United Nations Headquarters Agreement of June 26, 1947, 1988 I.C.J. 12 (quoting the *Mavrommatis* definition); Electricity Company of Sofia and Bulgaria, 1939 P.C.I.J.

the term "dispute" meant "a disagreement on a point of law or fact, a conflict of legal views or of interests between two persons."[2] For our purposes, we will take the term "persons" to refer to legal persons under international law, specifically, states.

In addition to this Introduction, the chapter is organized in three sections: The Basic Obligation: Peaceful Settlement; Forms of Dispute Settlement; and The International Court of Justice.

§ 10.02   THE BASIC OBLIGATION: PEACEFUL SETTLEMENT

The United Nations Charter lays down the fundamental obligation regarding the settlement of disputes between states in Article 2, paragraph 3, which provides as follows: "All Members shall settle their international disputes by peaceful means in such a manner that international peace and security, and justice, are not endangered."[3] The words "and justice" were inserted in the original draft at the San Francisco Conference on the proposal of Bolivia. According to a commentary on the Charter: "The purpose of the change was to prevent appeasement at the expense of smaller states."[4] The United Nations General Assembly has reaffirmed the principle of peaceful settlement in a number of resolutions[5] and the Secretariat has provided helpful compilations directed toward assisting states in the selection and application of appropriate dispute settlement procedures.[6]

In 1970 the General Assembly adopted the Declaration on Principles of International Law concerning Friendly Relations and Cooperation among States in accordance with the Charter of the United Nations (the Friendly Relations Declaration).[7] This resolution is generally considered

---

(ser. A/B) No. 77, at 64, 83; Northern Cameroons Case, 1963 I.C.J. 33-34; and the Nuclear Tests Cases, 1974 I.C.J. 260, 270-271.

[2] 1924 P.C.I.J. (ser. A) No. 2, at 11.

[3] Charter of the United Nations, 26 June 1945, art. 2(3), 59 Stat. 1031, T.S. No. 993, 3 Bevans 1153, 1976 U.N.Y.B. 1043 (hereinafter U.N. Charter).

[4] LELAND M. GOODRICH, ET AL., CHARTER OF THE UNITED NATIONS: COMMENTARY AND DOCUMENTS 41(3d ed. 1969). "Appeasement" refers in particular to the Munich Pact of 29 Sept. 1938 between Germany, Italy, France, and Britain, by which Britain and France accepted Adolf Hitler's demand that the German-speaking Sudetenland, a region of Czechoslovakia bordering Germany, be ceded to Germany. After the devastation they had suffered in World War I, Britain and France accepted Hitler's demands in return for his promise not to claim any other European territory.

[5] The most prominent and important of these is the Declaration on Principles of International Law concerning Friendly Relations and Cooperation among States in Accordance with the Charter of the United Nations, 24 Oct. 1970, G.A. Res. 2625 (XXV), 25 U.N. GAOR Supp. (No. 28) 121, UN Doc. A/8028 (1971), reprinted in 9 I.L.M. 1292 (1970) (hereinafter Friendly Relations Declaration). See also, e.g., G.A. Resolutions 2627 (XXV) of 24 Oct. 1970, 2734 (XXV) of 16 Dec. 1970 and 40/9 of 8 Nov. 1985.

[6] See especially UNITED NATIONS, HANDBOOK ON THE PEACEFUL SETTLEMENT OF DISPUTES BETWEEN STATES (1992).

[7] Friendly Relations Declaration, supra note 5.

an authoritative interpretation of the provisions of the Charter on the use of force and peaceful settlement of disputes. In the *Nicaragua* case, the International Court of Justice concluded with regard to the Friendly Relations Declaration that:

> "The effect of consent to the text of such resolutions cannot be understood as merely that of a 'reiteration or elucidation' of the treaty commitment undertaken in the Charter. On the contrary, it may be understood as an acceptance of the validity of the rule or set of rules declared by the resolution by themselves. The principle of non-use of force, for example, may thus be regarded as a principle of customary international law. . . ."[8]

By this logic, states would also have accepted the principle of peaceful settlement as one of customary international law.

Means of peaceful settlement are indicated in Article 33, paragraph 1, of the Charter, which provides as follows:

> "The parties to any dispute, the continuance of which is likely to endanger the maintenance of international peace and security, shall, first of all, seek a solution by negotiation, enquiry, mediation, conciliation, arbitration, judicial settlement, resort to regional agencies or arrangements, or other peaceful means of their own choice."[9]

While technically this obligation only applies where the continuance of a particular dispute is "likely to endanger the maintenance of international peace and security," the catalogue of means of dispute settlement has been applied more broadly. The individual forms will be considered in § 10.03 below.

The Friendly Relations Declaration includes a "principle that States shall settle their international disputes by peaceful means in such a manner that international peace and security and justice are not endangered."[10] After repeating Article 2(3) of the Charter and the means of dispute settlement set forth in Article 33, the Declaration provides additional detail as to the meaning of the principle of peaceful settlement, including the following paragraphs:

> "States parties to an international dispute, as well as other States, shall refrain from any action which may aggravate the situation so as to endanger the maintenance of international peace and security, and shall act in accordance with the purposes and principles of the United Nations.
>
> "International disputes shall be settled on the basis of the sovereign equality of States and in accordance with the principle

---

[8] Case Concerning Military and Paramilitary Activities in and Against Nicaragua (Nicaragua v. United States), Merits, 1986 I.C.J. 14, 100.

[9] Charter of the United Nations, 26 June 1945, art. 33(1), 59 Stat. 1031, T.S. No. 993, 3 Bevans 1153, 1976 U.N.Y.B. 1043 (hereinafter U.N. Charter).

[10] Friendly Relations Declaration, *supra* note 5.

of free choice of means. Recourse to, or acceptance of, a settlement procedure freely agreed to by States with regard to existing or future disputes to which they are parties shall not be regarded as incompatible with sovereign equality."[11]

As authoritative interpretations of the provisions of the Charter on international peace and security, these statements, although contained in a General Assembly resolution, probably reflect binding obligations.[12]

§ 10.03   FORMS OF DISPUTE SETTLEMENT

In this section we will review briefly the various means of dispute settlement listed in Article 33 of the Charter. Perhaps appropriately, the first one mentioned is negotiation. This is no doubt the simplest way for states to resolve disputes and by far the one most often resorted to. Negotiation does not always, by any means, take the form of sitting down at a table with the other state and discussing the matter under dispute. States frequently exchange views through diplomatic notes, communications through their ambassadors, or in other ways involving diplomatic channels. Why is negotiation used so often? The late Judge Manfred Lachs has written that "States resort to negotiations very frequently, probably owing to the fact that they are rather anxious to retain control to the very end over the decisions arising out of differences which divide them. There are of course many international disputes and problems which cannot be solved otherwise. . . ."[13] The Manila Declaration on the Peaceful Settlement of International Disputes describes negotiation as "a flexible and effective means" of dispute settlement.[14]

In certain international regimes, particularly those involving maritime boundaries, states may actually be under an obligation to negotiate. The International Court of Justice explained the meaning of this obligation in the following way in the *North Sea Continental Shelf Cases*: "the parties are under an obligation to enter into negotiations with a view to arriving at an agreement . . . ; they are under an obligation so to conduct themselves that the negotiations are meaningful, which will not be the case when either of the parties insists upon its own position without contemplating any modification of it."[15] Judge Lachs further clarified the meaning of the

---

[11] *Id.*

[12] *See* the passage from the *Nicaragua* case, quoted above in text at note 8.

[13] Manfred Lachs, *The Law and the Settlement of International Disputes*, in DISPUTE SETTLEMENT THROUGH THE UNITED NATIONS 283, 288 (K.V. Raman ed. 1977).

[14] G.A. Res. 37/10 of 15 Nov. 1982, annex, sect. I, para. 10.

[15] Federal Republic of Germany v. Denmark, and Federal Republic of Germany v. Netherlands, Judgment of 20 Feb. 1969, 1969 I.C.J., 3, 47, para. 85 (a). *See also* the case of Railway Traffic between Lithuania and Poland, 1931 P.C.I.J. (series A/B) No. 42, at 116, cited by the Court in the North Sea Continental Shelf cases, *id.*, at pp. 47-48. The Manila Declaration, *supra* note 14, is to the same effect: "When they choose to resort to direct negotiations, States should negotiate meaningfully, in order to arrive at an early settlement acceptable to the parties." *Id.*, Sect. I, para. 10.

obligation when he observed that "the obligation to negotiate . . . does not imply an obligation actually to reach agreement. The obligation is only to try one's best."[16]

The second form of dispute resolution mentioned in Article 33 is "enquiry." According to the 1907 Hague Convention (I) for the Pacific Settlement of International Disputes, enquiry is a process for settling "disputes arising from a difference of opinion on points of fact, . . . elucidating the facts by means of an impartial and conscientious investigation."[17] The Convention called for the parties to such a dispute to form a Commission of Inquiry, whose task it would be to investigate and report on the facts. The commission's "report was not to have the character of an award, and the parties were free to decide what effect, if any, they would give it."[18] In other words, the commission would investigate the facts and prepare an impartial, non-binding report that the parties could make use of in attempting to resolve the dispute.

The next means of dispute settlement referred to in Article 33 are mediation and conciliation. According to Brierly, in the case of good offices, mediation and conciliation,

> "the intervention of a third party aims, not at *deciding* the quarrel *for* the disputing parties, but at inducing them to decide it for themselves. The difference between [good offices and mediation] is not important; strictly a state is said to offer 'good offices' when it tries to induce the parties to negotiate between themselves, and to 'mediate' when it takes a part in the negotiations itself, but clearly the one process merges into the other."[19]

Conciliation is similar to the process of enquiry, except that the commission has the task not only of finding the facts but of preparing a report containing non-binding recommendations for a settlement.[20] The procedure had its genesis in a series of "treaties for the advancement of peace which

---

[16] Lachs, *supra* note 13, at 289.

[17] 2 Malloy, Treaties, 2220, art. 9 (hereinafter 1907 Hague Convention (I)).

[18] *Id.* art. 35. *See also* J. BRIERLY, THE LAW OF NATIONS 374 (6th ed., Waldock, 1963). For an instance in which such a commission was used effectively *see* the Dogger Bank case between Great Britain and Russia of 1904, J.B. Scott, ed., Hague Court Reports 403 (1916). On fact-finding as a form of "investigation" by the Security Council under article 34 of the Charter, see Raman, *The Ways of the Peacemaker*, in DISPUTE SETTLEMENT THROUGH THE UNITED NATIONS, *supra* note 13, at 410. "If broadly conceived, investigatory functions can facilitate the establishment of disputed questions of fact (fact-finding in a narrow sense), and also enable the parties to establish an objective basis for their future relationships." *Id. See also* Report of the Secretary-General on methods of fact-finding, UN Doc. A/5694 (1 May 1964), examining "international inquiry as a peaceful means of settling disputes or adjusting situations". *Id.* at 10.

[19] BRIERLY, *supra* note 18, at 373 (emphasis in original).

[20] According to Bishop, conciliation "involves the reference of a dispute to a commission of persons whose task is to find the facts and make a report containing recommendations for a settlement, which each party to the dispute remains free to accept or reject as it chooses, without legal obligation and without obloquy for failure to comply with the recommendations." WILLIAM W. BISHOP, JR., INTERNATIONAL LAW 59 (2d ed. 1962).

embodied the so-called 'Bryan peace plan,'" concluded by the United States in 1913 and 1914.[21] These "Bryan treaties," forty-eight of which were eventually concluded, called for the establishment of International Commissions of Inquiry and Permanent Commissions.[22] Brierly explains that the "method of the 'Bryan treaties' was extensively adopted in later developments of international organization, and as it is essentially different from the method of arbitration on the one hand, and not precisely the same as that of mediation on the other, it is convenient to refer to it as 'conciliation.'"[23]

Arbitration, the next means of dispute settlement identified in Article 33, contrasts with the foregoing methods in that it involves the application of rules of international law to the facts of the case and leads to a binding settlement of a dispute. Article 37 of the 1907 Hague Convention (I) provides that "International arbitration has for its object the settlement of disputes between States by Judges of their own choice and on the basis of respect for law. Recourse to arbitration implies an engagement to submit in good faith to the award."[24] International arbitration has a long history, which "can be traced as far back as ancient Greece, and its use as a means of peaceful settlement was frequent even during the Middle Ages."[25] It differs from judicial settlement,[26] or adjudication, the next means mentioned, chiefly in that the parties to an arbitration "must agree upon the constitution of the tribunal and the procedure which it will employ," while adjudication entails bringing a dispute "before an existing tribunal operating under an established procedure."[27] Adjudication will be addressed through the consideration of the International Court of Justice in § 10.04, below.

States may agree in advance to submit any dispute arising out of a treaty to arbitration through a so-called "compromissory clause" in the agreement. On the other hand, they may agree to submit a dispute to arbitration after it has arisen. As already indicated, the parties usually choose the arbitrators and agree on the procedures to be used. The choice may be made from a pre-established list in the case of arbitration through a standing institution. The principal institution in the field of

---

[21] 6 G. HACKWORTH, DIGEST OF INTERNATIONAL LAW 5 (1943). *See also* the discussion of the Bryan treaties in the 1964 Report of the Secretary-General, *supra* note 18, paras. 62-78.

[22] *See* BRIERLY, *supra* note 18, at 374-376; and BISHOP, *supra* note 20, at 59.

[23] BRIERLY, *supra* note 18, at 374-375. The numerous agreements concluded between the two World Wars that provided for conciliation are reviewed in UNITED NATIONS, SYSTEMATIC SURVEY OF TREATIES FOR THE PACIFIC SETTLEMENT OF INTERNATIONAL DISPUTES, 1928-1948 (1948); and HABICHT, POST-WAR TREATIES FOR THE PACIFIC SETTLEMENT OF INTERNATIONAL DISPUTES (1931). *See also* the 1964 Report of the Secretary-General on Methods of Factfinding, *supra* note 18, at 29-33.

[24] 1907 Hague Convention (I), *supra* note 17, art. 37.

[25] L. HENKIN, ET AL., INTERNATIONAL LAW 788 (3d ed. 1993).

[26] Brownlie characterizes the work of many *ad hoc* arbitral tribunals as "judicial settlement." *See* IAN BROWNLIE, PRINCIPLES OF PUBLIC INTERNATIONAL LAW 675 (6th ed. 2003).

[27] BISHOP, *supra* note 20, at 60-61.

international arbitration between states is the Permanent Court of Arbitration, established in 1899.[28] It is not a court per se, but an institution that sets up tribunals to arbitrate individual cases. The parties each select two arbitrators from a panel and that group selects an umpire, or president. There have been a number of well-known international arbitrations during the past two centuries, beginning with the 1872 *Alabama Claims* arbitration between Britain and the United States.[29]

Finally, Article 33 provides that the parties are to "resort to regional agencies or arrangements" to resolve their dispute. Regional organizations such as the African Union (AU), the Arab League, the Organization of American States (OAU), the Organization of Eastern Caribbean States (OECS), and the Organization for Security and Cooperation in Europe (OSCE) may provide good offices or mediation services to assist member states in resolving their disputes. States may also have established dispute resolution mechanisms through sectoral treaties, for example, in the fields of trade or shared water resources.

§ 10.04 THE INTERNATIONAL COURT OF JUSTICE

[A] General

The International Court of Justice,[30] or World Court, was established at the same time as the United Nations, in 1945. The Court's "Statute,"[31] or constitution, is based on that of its predecessor, the Permanent Court of International Justice, and "forms an integral part of the [U.N.] Charter."[32] Members of the United Nations are automatically parties to the Court's Statute,[33] and the few states that are non-members of the U.N. can also become parties since the Statute is a distinct treaty.[34] The Court is located in The Hague, Netherlands, in the Peace Palace which was built in the early twentieth century with a gift from Andrew Carnegie.[35]

---

[28] The PCA was established by the 1899 Hague Convention for the Pacific Settlement of International Disputes, *available at* http://www.yale.edu/lawweb/avalon/lawofwar/hague02.htm. For information on the PCA, *see* its website, http://www.pca-cpa.org/.

[29] 1 MOORE, ARBITRATIONS 653. The *Alabama* was a vessel that had been constructed in London and preyed on Union shipping during the Civil War. Other well-known international arbitrations include the Beagle Channel Arbitration (1977), 52 I.L.R. 93 (award of 18 Feb. 1977); Delimitation of the Continental Shelf (UK/France), decisions of 30 June 1977 and 14 Mar. 1978, 54 I.L.R. 6 and 39; and Case concerning the Air Services Agreement of 27 March 1946 (US v. France), 54 I.L.R. 304.

[30] For information on the Court, see the I.C.J. website, http://www.icj-cij.org/.

[31] Statute of the International Court of Justice, 26 June 1945, art. 1, 59 Stat. 1055, T.S. No. 993, 3 Bevans 1153, 1976 U.N.Y.B. 1052.

[32] U.N. Charter, *supra* note 9, art. 92.

[33] *Id.*, art. 93(1) ("All members of the United Nations are *ipso facto* parties to the Statute of the International Court of Justice").

[34] *Id.*, art. 93(2).

[35] *See generally* ARTHUR EYFFINGER, THE PEACE PALACE (1988).

The International Court of Justice is established by the U.N. Charter as the "principal judicial organ of the United Nations."[36] Its fifteen judges are elected concurrently by the Security Council and the General Assembly[37] which are to "bear in mind . . . that in the body as a whole the representation of the main forms of civilization and of the principal legal systems of the world should be assured."[38] The judges serve staggered terms of nine years, the terms of five expiring every three years.[39] States parties to a case who do not have a judge of their nationality on the Court are entitled to appoint a judge *ad hoc*.[40]

[B] Jurisdiction

"Only states may be parties in cases before the Court."[41] That bald statement reflects the traditional view that only states are subjects of international law. International organizations,[42] and even individuals[43] and corporations,[44] may be affected by judgments or advisory opinions of the Court, but they may not be parties to the cases, as such.

As already indicated, the Court's *in personam* jurisdiction is consensual: states must agree to appear in a case before the Court. They can do this in a variety of ways, which are provided for in Article 36 of the Court's Statute. First, states may include an "ICJ clause" in a treaty to which they are parties.[45] Such clauses typically provide that any dispute concerning the interpretation or application of the treaty in question may be submitted by any party to the ICJ for resolution. Many treaties, both bilateral and multilateral, contain such provisions, and this is a common source of ICJ jurisdiction. Second, states may enter into a "special agreement" by which they submit a particular dispute to the Court for resolution.[46] This,

---

[36] U.N. Charter, *supra* note 9, art. 92. The same phrase is repeated in art. 1 of the Court's Statute.

[37] Judges are elected from a "list of persons nominated by the national groups in the Permanent Court of Arbitration. . . ." ICJ Statute, *supra* note 31, art. 4(1). To be elected, a candidate must receive an absolute majority of votes in both the Security Council and General Assembly. *Id.*, art. 10(1).

[38] *Id.*, art. 9.

[39] *Id.*, art. 13.

[40] *Id.*, art. 31.

[41] *Id.*, art. 34.

[42] *See, e.g.*, Certain Expenses of the United Nations (Article 17, Paragraph 2 of the Charter), Advisory Opinion of 20 July 1962, 1962 I.C.J. 151.

[43] *See, e.g.*, Mavrommatis Palestine Concessions (Gr. v. G.B.) (Jurisdiction), Judgment of 30 Aug. 1924, 1924 P.C.I.J. (ser. A) No. 2, at 6.

[44] *See, e.g.*, Case concerning the Barcelona Traction, Light and Power Co., Limited, Second Phase (Belgium v. Spain), 1970 I.C.J. 3; and Case concerning Elettronica Sicula S.P.A. (ELSI) (U.S. v. Italy), 1989 I.C.J. 15.

[45] ICJ Statute, *supra* note 31, art. 36(1).

[46] *Id.* States may submit specific questions to the Court in a special agreement, thereby in effect restricting its jurisdiction. *See, e.g.*, the *Gabčíkovo-Nagymaros* case, 1997 ICJ 7.

too, is not an infrequent basis of the Court's jurisdiction. Finally, states may declare that they accept the Court's compulsory jurisdiction in relation to any other state accepting the same obligation.[47] As of mid-2004, sixty-five states had made such declarations, many with reservations.[48] Because of the requirement that the other state have accepted the same obligation, only a state that has accepted the Court's compulsory jurisdiction under this so-called "optional clause" may sue another state that has accepted it. Moreover, pursuant to the principle of reciprocity, a state accepts the Court's jurisdiction only insofar as the declarations of the parties match up; states may take advantage of each other's reservations, meaning that the Court's jurisdiction is determined by what both states have accepted.[49]

If there is a dispute over whether the Court has jurisdiction, it has competence to make that decision.[50] But even before it decides whether it has jurisdiction (assuming this is contested, and unless it is clear that consent to its jurisdiction is lacking), the Court may indicate "provisional measures" under Article 41 of its Statute to preserve the status quo pending its adjudication of the case. As discussed in the following subsection, the Court held in the *LaGrand* case[51] that interim measures of this kind are binding on the parties.

The Court has both contentious and advisory[52] jurisdiction. That is, it may hear adversarial cases between states or give advisory opinions at the request of a properly authorized organ or agency of the United Nations. The U.N. Charter allows the Security Council and General Assembly to request advisory opinions,[53] and permits the General Assembly to authorize other U.N. organs and specialized agencies to do so with regard to "legal questions arising within the scope of their activities."[54] It has

---

[47] *Id.*, art. 36(2).

[48] Report of the International Court of Justice, 1 Aug. 2003-31 July 2004 17, *available at* http://www.icj-cij.org/icjwww/igeneralinformation/igeninf_Annual_Reports/iicj_annual _report_2003 2004.pdf.

[49] *See, e.g.,* Electricity Company of Sofia and Bulgaria, 1939 P.C.I.J. (ser. A/B) No. 77, at 80-82; Anglo-Iranian Oil Company, 1952 I.C.J. 93, 103; and Certain Norwegian Loans, 1957 I.C.J. 9, 23-24.

[50] I.C.J. Statute, *supra* note 31, art. 36(6), setting forth the principle of *compétence de la compétence*.

[51] LaGrand (Germany v. United States), order of 3 Mar. 1999; judgment on the merits, 27 June 2001, paras. 98-109, 2001 I.C.J. 466, *available at* http://www.icj-cij.org, 40 I.L.M. 1069 (2001).

[52] The Court's advisory jurisdiction is provided for in ch. IV of its Statute, *supra* note 31, arts. 65-68.

[53] U.N. Charter, *supra* note 9, art. 96(1).

[54] *Id.*, art. 96(2). For a case in which the Court found that the legal question did not arise within the scope of the activities of the agency in question (the World Health Organization), *see* Legality of the Use by a State of Nuclear Weapons in Armed Conflict, Advisory Opinion, 8 July 1996, *available at* http://www.icj-cij.org/icjwww/icases/ianw/ianw frame.htm.

occasionally been charged that the Court's advisory jurisdiction has been used to bring a case before the Court that could not otherwise be brought for lack of jurisdiction over the state in question.[55] It is up to the Court in such cases to decide whether the process is being misused or it would otherwise be inappropriate to render an advisory opinion and, if so, to decline to do so.[56]

[C]   The Effect of the Court's Judgments and Orders

The Court's judgments are binding on the parties.[57] Article 94 of the U.N. Charter provides that: "Each Member of the United Nations undertakes to comply with the decision of the International Court of Justice in any case to which it is a party."[58] In case a state fails to do so, "the other party may have recourse to the Security Council, which may, if it deems necessary, make recommendations or decide upon measures to be taken to give effect to the judgment."[59] I.C.J. judgments are "final and without appeal."[60] This does not prevent the parties, or one of them, from requesting an additional judgment

---

[55] For example, it was argued that it was not appropriate for the Court to give an opinion in Legal Consequences of the Construction of a Wall in the Occupied Palestinian Territory, Advisory Opinion of 9 July 2004, *available at* http://www.icj-cij.org/icjwww/idocket/imwp/ imwpframe.htm. *See id.*, paras. 43-64. *See also, e.g.,* the Separate Opinion of Judge Higgins, and Declaration of Judge Buergenthal, both available at *id.*

[56] In its advisory opinion in the *Legal Consequences of the Construction of a Wall* case, *id.*, the Court addressed its discretion to decline to give an advisory opinion: "In accordance with its consistent jurisprudence, only 'compelling reasons' should lead the Court to refuse its opinion (*Certain Expenses of the United Nations (Article 17, paragraph 2, of the Charter), Advisory Opinion, I.C.J. Reports 1962,* p. 155; see also, for example, *Difference Relating to Immunity from Legal Process of a Special Rapporteur of the Commission of Human Rights, Advisory Opinion, I.C.J. Reports 1999 (I),* pp. 78-79, para. 29.)." *Id.*, para. 44. The Court observed that it had never exercised its discretionary power to decline to give an advisory opinion, and that its predecessor, the PCIJ, had done so on only one occasion, in Status of Eastern Carelia, Advisory Opinion, 1923 P.C.I.J. (ser. B) No. 5. But the Court explained that this decision "was due to the very particular circumstances of the case, among which were that the question directly concerned an already existing dispute, one of the States parties to which was neither a party to the Statute of the Permanent Court nor a Member of the League of Nations, objected to the proceedings, and refused to take part in any way (*Legality of the Threat or Use of Nuclear Weapons, I.C.J. Reports 1996 (I),* pp. 235-236, para. 14)." *Id.*

[57] I.C.J. Statute, *supra* note 31, art. 59, states this in a negative way: "The decision of the Court has no binding force except between the parties. . . ."

[58] U.N. Charter, *supra* note 9, art. 94(1).

[59] *Id.*, art. 94(2). This possibility is, of course, of limited utility where the judgment debtor is a permanent member of the Security Council, as in the *Nicaragua* case. *See* United Nations Security Council: Excerpts from Verbatim Records Discussing I.C.J. Judgment in *Nicaragua v. United States*, 25 I.L.M. 1337, 1352, 1363 (1986).

[60] I.C.J. Statute, *supra* note 31, art. 60. It is, however, theoretically possible to apply for "revision" of a judgment based on "the discovery of some fact of such a nature as to be a decisive factor," provided that the fact was not known to the Court or the party requesting revision. *Id.*, art. 61. The party's lack of knowledge of the fact may not be due to its negligence. *Id.*

from the Court, however, as was done in a recent case.[61] The Court's Statute also permits a party to request that the Court "construe" a judgment.[62]

As we have seen in Chapter 3,[63] Article 59 of the Court's Statute provides that judgments of the Court have "no binding force except between the parties and in respect of that particular case."[64] Thus, formally, ICJ decisions have no value as precedent in other cases. The Court's judgments are widely accepted as authoritative statements of the law, however, and thus in fact have influence well beyond the case at hand.

With regard to the Court's orders, the principal issue that has arisen concerns the effect of its orders of provisional measures under Article 41 of its Statute. As already noted, in the *La Grand* case, the Court held for the first time in its history that such orders were binding.[65] The conundrum with regard to whether such orders have binding effect is that they are issued before the Court rules on any questions of jurisdiction or admissibility. It could therefore, in theory, grant provisional measures under Article 41 and later find it had no jurisdiction. Perhaps for this reason, Article 41 provides that the Court has the power to "indicate" provisional measures, not to "order" them.[66] But in the *dispositif* stating its rulings in the *La Grand* case, the Court stated that it: "finds by thirteen votes to two that, by failing to take all measures at its disposal to ensure that Walter LaGrand was not executed pending the final decision of the International Court of Justice in the case, the United States breached the obligation incumbent upon it under the Order indicating provisional

---

[61] *See* the *Gabčíkovo-Nagymaros Project* case (Hungary/Slovakia), 1997 I.C.J. 7, and I.C.J. Press Release 98/28, *available at* http://www.icj-cij.org/icjwww/idocket/ihs/ihsframe.htm. The possibility of requesting an additional judgment was provided for in the Special Agreement by which the two states submitted the case to the Court.

[62] I.C.J. Statute, *supra* note 31, art. 60. *See, e.g.,* Request for Interpretation of the Judgment of 11 June 1998 in the Case concerning the Land and Maritime Boundary between Cameroon and Nigeria (Cameroon v. Nigeria), Preliminary Objections (Nigeria v. Cameroon) (1998-1999), information available at the Court's website, http://www.icj-cij.org.

[63] *See* § 3.03 [D].

[64] I.C.J. Statute, *supra* note 31, art. 59.

[65] LaGrand (Germany v. United States), order of 3 Mar. 1999; judgment on the merits, 27 June 2001, 2001 I.C.J. 466, paras. 96-109, *available at* http://www.icj cij.org/icjwww/idocket/igus/igusframe.htm.

[66] Interestingly, the French text of art. 41, while using the French word for "indicate," employs more mandatory language thereafter, as the Court notes: "In this text, the terms "indiquer" and "l'indication" may be deemed to be neutral as to the mandatory character of the measure concerned; by contrast the words "doiventêtre prises" have an imperative character." *Id.*, para. 100. The English text, on the other hand, uses the words "ought to be taken" for "doiventêtre prises." The Court applied arts. 31 and 33 of the Vienna Convention on the Law of Treaties to interpret these provisions, finding that both reflect customary international law. *Id.*, paras. 99 and 101. According to art. 33(4), the Court had regard to the object and purpose of the treaty — its Statute — to resolve the difference, with the result described below.

measures issued by the Court on 3 March 1999."[67] The Court reasoned in part that:

> "It follows from the object and purpose of the Statute, as well as from the terms of Article 41 when read in their context, that the power to indicate provisional measures entails that such measures should be binding, inasmuch as the power in question is based on the necessity, when the circumstances call for it, to safeguard, and to avoid prejudice to, the rights of the parties as determined by the final judgment of the Court. The contention that provisional measures indicated under Article 41 might not be binding would be contrary to the object and purpose of that Article."[68]

The Court therefore ruled against the United States' contention that the Court's orders of provisional measures cannot have binding legal effect.

---

[67] *Id.*, para. 128(5).

[68] *Id.*, para. 102.

TABLE OF CASES

[References are to page numbers and footnotes]

[References are to page numbers and footnotes]

[References are to page numbers and footnotes]

INDEX

[References are to pages.]

[References are to pages.]

[References are to pages.]

[References are to pages.]

[References are to pages.]